FORTNIGHT OF INFAMY

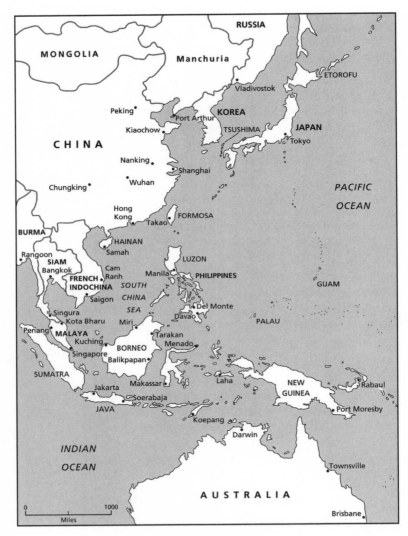

Map of the Far East.

FORTNIGHT OF INFAMY

The Collapse of Allied Airpower
West of Pearl Harbor

JOHN BURTON

NAVAL INSTITUTE PRESS
Annapolis, Maryland

Naval Institute Press
291 Wood Road
Annapolis, MD 21402

Library of Congress Cataloging-in-Publication Data

Burton, John, 1963-
    Fortnight of infamy : the collapse of Allied airpower west of Pearl
    Harbor, December 1941/John Burton.
      p. cm.
    Includes bibliographical references and index.
    ISBN 1-59114-096-X (alk. paper)
    1. World War, 1939–1945—Campaigns—Pacific Area. 2. World
    War, 1939–1945—Aerial operations.   I. Title.
    D767.B87 2006
    940.54'259—dc22

                                                      2006015542

Printed in the United States of America on acid-free paper ♾

12 11 10 09 08 07 06   8 7 6 5 4 3 2
First printing

All of the maps in this book were created by Christopher Robinson.

CONTENTS

INTRODUCTION

Paul PUTNAM WAS NOT INCLINED TO CONTEMPLATE his own misfortune. Like most frontline unit commanders in the U.S. armed forces of 1941, the thirty-six-year-old major was too young to have participated in the Great War. Still, he was one of those few officers who gained experience in the forgotten conflicts of the interwar period. His first assignment as a lieutenant had been to a combat role during the difficult campaign in the jungles of Nicaragua. Putnam was a career soldier. He lived to fight wherever his country needed him, seldom complaining. Those under his command were of the same nature. They were United States Marines.

Despite their stoic resolve, Major Putnam and his aviators would have been forgiven for cursing their current situation. They were literally a thousand miles from nowhere, completely surrounded by a windswept sea and closer to their enemy than to the nearest friendly base. An incessant crashing of waves on the nearby reef left their ears constantly ringing. Even the booming voice of a drill sergeant was difficult to hear beyond the distance of a few yards. Outside the shadows cast by briskly drifting puffy clouds, the sun was harshly bright, more brilliant than in any desert. The blowing sand was relentless; fine white coral dust and seashell fragments penetrated every corner of a tent or barracks and lodged in the crevices of each piece of equipment. Contrary to the typical tourist image of a Pacific island, there were no palm trees to be seen. Shade and natural shelter were nonexistent. Across the three small islets that formed the tiny atoll, hardly any scrub trees rose more than a dozen feet. A single fifty-foot water tower was the tallest feature on the islands.

The largest of the sandy dots in the ocean was the namesake for the atoll: Wake. It housed the new airstrip where Putnam had just assigned four of his pilots to man their planes. Ultimately intended to have three runways in a triangular configuration, the station was unfinished; only a single strip was usable. Though nearly five thousand feet long and surfaced with crushed coral, barely a hundred feet of its width had been completed; there was not even a place to safely taxi aircraft outside the vicinity of that narrow, hard-packed surface.[1] Although more than a thousand civilian construction workers labored around Wake, the air station had taken a back seat to other activities—one of many problems the major desperately wanted to address. As he watched his men climb onto the wings of their planes, he realized he no longer had the time.

Word that Japan had attacked Hawaii—two thousand miles to the rear of their position—came as a complete shock. The Marines could not help but feel exposed. They expected treachery from the Japanese but had been certain that news of the first hostile actions would emanate from Manila, not Honolulu. Now, it seemed a sure bet that their remote little island would be attacked sometime during the already infamous day of December 1941—Sunday the seventh on Pearl Harbor's side of the international date line, Monday the eighth at Wake's longitude.

Paul Putnam was hard-pressed to prepare for the inevitable Japanese air assault. Every U.S. military unit west of Pearl Harbor was lacking in equipment and manpower. Marine Fighting Squadron 211 (VMF-211), which had just arrived at Wake on December 4, was no exception. The squadron was short of everything. In fact, due to the limitations of facilities on Wake, Putnam had to leave more than half of his organization and most of its equipment in Hawaii when the detachment departed from the air station at Ewa. He had only ten other officers and forty-nine enlisted men remaining under his command—just a fraction of the resource normally allocated to a fighter squadron. They had very few tools and hardly any spare parts; even maintenance manuals for the airplanes had been left behind.[2]

The Marines had traditionally been the "poor stepchildren" of the navy. Marine aviators had mastered the art of making do with substandard weapons and other gear. Major Putnam was used to receiving cast-off, secondhand equipment, but, for once, he could take pride in the twelve brand-new Grumman F4F-3 Wildcats he now possessed. The blue-gray planes that sat next to Wake's runway were the best the navy could provide. In many respects, they were the best fighters in the United States' inventory during December 1941. Powered by a 1,200-horsepower, fourteen-cylinder Pratt & Whitney "Twin-Wasp" radial engine mated to a two-stage supercharger, these early Wildcats could fly at altitudes of up to thirty-three thousand feet. More important, peak performance was achieved at twenty thousand feet, where an F4F-3 had a maximum airspeed of 338 miles per hour—just slightly faster than Japan's best fighters. Contemporary U.S. Army fighters may have looked sleeker, or have been faster at sea level, but they literally gasped for air by the time they reached that height. If one had to combat Japanese air forces above the realm of fifteen thousand feet, Putnam's Grummans were the most suitable weapon to use.[3]

In spite of their usual difficulties obtaining up-to-date equipment, the Marines did not often covet anything issued by the army. That morning, however, the one thing that Major Paul Putnam wanted more than anything else belonged to the army: a radar set earmarked for installation at his airfield. Unfortunately, this important item had been stored in a warehouse on Oahu. Shipping capacity was critically low, and it still awaited transport to Wake.

Without air-search radar, VMF-211 was at a distinct disadvantage. Lookouts on the water tower could not possibly spot incoming planes that were more than a few miles away—too close for the squadron to successfully muster a fighter scramble. Even continuous patrols by all twelve fighters could not ensure detection of approaching enemy forces; there was too much ocean to cover, with too few planes. In any case, the difficulty of maintaining the aircraft in the face of insufficient replacement parts precluded such an idea. As a compromise, Major Putnam intended to follow a routine of keeping four Grummans in the air from dawn to dusk. Four more would always be on alert. The others would be held in reserve, or set aside for servicing.

The protection of an early warning system would have been best, but any protection for the valuable aircraft was welcome. It was some consolation to Major Putnam that the atoll's senior officer, Commander Winfield Cunningham, agreed to authorize the Morrison-Knudsen Company contractors to bulldoze revetments for VMF-211's planes. It would be an all-out, top-priority effort, but the task could not possibly be completed before late afternoon. Until then, planes parked on the ground would have to remain in the open. Putnam fretted whether the Japanese would strike at Wake before the bunkerlike shields were finished. Fueled and armed, the grounded fighters were impotent and vulnerable.

The loud wheeze of starters engaging, followed by the sharp cough of exhaust belching from igniting cylinders, was a welcome sound. Paul Putnam watched with relief as slowly turning propellers transformed into roaring, disklike blurs. He was thankful that at least four Grummans would be off the ground within a few minutes. Two other F4Fs were scheduled to join them shortly. That pair of Wildcats would follow the Pan American Airways flying boat *Philippine Clipper* away from Wake's lagoon and fly with it as far as possible in the direction of Midway. Putnam fervently hoped all six assigned fighters would be off the field when the Japanese arrived.

While Captain Henry "Hank" Elrod, 2nd Lieutenant Carl Davidson and Lieutenant John Kinney, and Technical Sergeant William Hamilton revved up their engines to fly away on patrol, Major Putnam wondered if his men would actually be capable of spotting Japanese raiders among the numerous clouds that dotted the horizon. With 360 degrees to cover, the Marines would have to be lucky. It was difficult to guess from which direction the enemy would come. Would they be in flying boats or land-based bombers coming from the Marshall Islands to the south? Could a carrier-based assault come from the east, west, or north? Japan possessed enough resources to pull off either operation, or both. Only one thing was certain: the Japanese held the initiative. If enemy planes avoided the patrolling Grummans and struck during the next few hours, the squadron would take a beating. Putnam crossed his fingers and hoped for the best.

After takeoff, the first flight of Wildcats immediately split into two sections of two planes each. One pair headed away from the island to the east, the other to the west. Unknown to the Americans, thirty-four bombers of the *Chitose Kokutai* had already descended to the low altitude of fifteen hundred feet for a speedy approach from the south, beneath the clouds.[4] Flying high above, at twelve thousand feet, the VMF-211 pilots did not have a chance of tagging the intruders. On a direct course from the island of Roi—at the northern point of the Kwajalein atoll—the Japanese bombers would arrive over Wake at high noon.

Paul Putnam was actually one of the first men to notice the growing specks on the horizon. As he looked at them across the line formed by the eight shiny new fighters still on the ground, he had a sinking feeling in the pit of his stomach. Putnam yelled for his men to take cover and then sprinted across the open space toward the nearest ditch he could dive into, which happened to be the latrine. As he splashed down in the stinking muck, two dozen twin-engine bombers screamed overhead. Metal fragments whizzed everywhere as a hail of bullets and dozens of 60-kilogram fragmentation bombs impacted across the airfield. The entire atoll shook when two aviation fuel tanks and six hundred drums of gasoline ignited in three massive explosions. Rolls of black smoke boiled up past the scattered clouds.

By the time Major Putnam was able to raise his head, the damage had been done. The returning Wildcat flights, beckoned by the smoke, could not get there in time to catch the bombers. In fact, the Japanese had come and gone so quickly that antiaircraft fire could not touch them. In a single pass over the airfield, the attacking planes inflicted serious losses on VMF-211. Machine-gun bullets cut down Lieutenant Frank Holden and Lieutenant Henry "Spider" Webb before they could reach their planes. Holden was killed instantly. Seriously injured, Webb lay motionless in a crimson pool that slowly stained the white coral beneath him. Lieutenant Robert Conderman made it to his aircraft, only to be mortally wounded by shrapnel from a nearby bomb blast. Conderman sealed his own fate by selflessly directing rescuers to other men who desperately needed medical attention. The squadron engineering officer, Lieutenant George Graves, successfully strapped himself into his cockpit, but he died while attempting to start the engine. His Wildcat took a direct bomb hit, its flaming wreckage adding yet another black plume to the sky.

In just a few tragic minutes, seven Grumman fighters were reduced to scrap for the salvage yard; an eighth was heavily damaged. All the mechanics had been either killed or seriously injured as they ran for shelter or hid under the wings of the planes. Thirty-two men from the squadron were on the casualty list; nineteen of them perished.[5] VMF-211 had sustained more than 50-percent losses in less than five minutes of combat!

To add insult to injury, after the four patrolling F4Fs finally landed on the hastily cleared runway, Captain Elrod's plane struck debris on the ground—destroying its propeller and damaging the engine.[6]

In spite of receiving several hours' advance warning, the Marines on Wake's airfield were as stunned by the enemy as had been those unprepared sailors, soldiers, and airmen at Pearl Harbor. When the men finally picked themselves up from the sand, they did so with a new respect for the capabilities of the Japanese war machine.

The strike boldly declared Japan's intent to eliminate U.S. air defenses at Wake. The primary target of this first raid was the military airfield, of course, but the Japanese also struck civilian seaplane facilities across the lagoon on Peale Island. Nine of the marauding bombers attacked the Pan-Am buildings, including the hotel, causing serious damage and killing ten airline employees. Gunfire from the Japanese planes hit the *Philippine Clipper* and wounded two members of its crew.[7] Luckily, the large four-engine airliner was not destroyed. Overloaded with passengers grateful to be leaving the atoll, it would depart for Midway a few hours later without an escort.

PRESIDENT FRANKLIN ROOSEVELT characterized the United States' first day of war in the Pacific as "a date which will live in infamy."[8] Most people readily associate his statement with the surprise attack on Hawaii. Nearly everyone seems to know something about that catastrophe. Hollywood films have imparted a good portion of the public's general knowledge, and dozens of well-researched volumes have been written about virtually every aspect of the raid. Events at Pearl Harbor received most of the attention at the time—and since—but the really important military actions in December 1941 actually took place on the other side of the international date line, in Malaya, Singapore, Shanghai, Hong Kong, Guam, the Philippines, and Wake Island.

To set a proper historical perspective for the story that follows, one should consider that the epic struggle called World War II was actually two distinctly separate wars that occurred in the same time frame, with a common set of participants. The 1941–45 Pacific War was the product of an escalation in conflict between U.S., British, and Japanese economic interests in the Far East. Before the inevitable showdown began, war clouds had loomed on the horizon for more than four decades. The die was cast when the United States acquired the Philippines from Spain during the Spanish-American War of 1898. The gradual march toward battle quickly gained momentum after Japan moved to militarily occupy China in 1937.

Although it would come as a great shock to the American public, the loss of the Philippines—including those desperate stands at Bataan and Corregidor—and other Allied losses in Southeast Asia unfolded exactly as predicted by several generations of U.S. military planners. The long, costly drive to return across the islands of the Central Pacific toward Japan also materialized as foreseen for more than twenty years. For that matter, strategic planning officers always anticipated that Oahu would be attacked at some point during a war with Japan; they just did not expect that a Pearl Harbor raid would be the opening act. One key aspect of the Pacific War not expected in Washington, was the degree to which airpower would play a role in the outcome.

For the first time in a war, attacks by aircraft would both begin and end the battle. From the moment Japan initiated hostilities, Allied and Japanese air forces became entangled in a continuous fight for control of the skies above the Pacific Ocean and Asia. Knights of this aerial realm would clash in daily jousts from December 1941 until August 1945, when Emperor Hirohito finally declared a cease-fire.

Sudden dependence on airpower in the Far East presented a serious problem for the United States. In the fall of 1941, apart from the respected capabilities of the U.S. Navy, the country's armed forces could hardly be considered even second-rate. Ironically, though the United States had given birth to aviation, its air forces were practically at the bottom of the barrel when war broke out in Europe in 1939. In spite of a conscious preparation for eventual involvement in that European war, the Army Air Forces (AAF) was still appallingly understaffed and underequipped by December 1941. It would take time to undo the impact of years of financial neglect of the military by Congress and the American people. As Lieutenant General Lewis Brereton, who would command U.S. air units in the Far East for the first four months of the Pacific War, said: "I fully understood the inadequacy of the Air Forces. We were definitely a third-rate air power. . . . Fighter aircraft and training were conspicuously lacking. . . . In the entire Air Force combat commands on 1 October we had only 64 first pilots and 90 co-pilots qualified for four-engine bombers; 97 first pilots and 108 co-pilots qualified for two-engine mediums, and 171 Pursuit pilots; and not one qualified dive bomber pilot."[9]

In contrast, Japanese air force units—both army and navy—were well prepared, well equipped, and numerous. Almost all of the squadrons were staffed by men with substantial combat experience gained during four years of warfare in China and Mongolia. Since 1937 Japan had been training nearly two thousand navy and 750 army pilots each year. By the autumn of 1941, most of these aviators had accumulated more than five hundred hours of flight time, more than half of which had been flown under combat conditions.[10]

In the opening two weeks of the Pacific War, Japan provided an incredible demonstration of the employment of airpower. Just one fortnight after the first shots were fired, Japan's aircraft-driven invasion of colonial possessions throughout the Far East demolished the entire Western imperialist legacy of the nineteenth century. The unexpected collapse of U.S., British, and Australian air forces in the Far East raised many questions: How was it that Japan rushed out of the shadows to assert its dominance over China and the rest of East Asia? What made Japanese leaders so certain of their ability to win a quick victory over the sea powers of Great Britain and the United States? Why did President Roosevelt completely reverse a forty-year-old military strategy for the defense of U.S. possessions in the Pacific? Where did the British plan to shield Singapore and Malaya fall apart? When did Australia become obliged to shoulder the major burden of protecting the interests of the entire British Empire in the Far East? To understand the answers, the reader needs a background on the political, economic, and technical factors affecting Japan, the United States, and Australia prior to the outbreak of the Pacific War. The first three chapters of this volume reveal the objectives, strategy, and capabilities of these participant nations as each readied itself for combat in the Far East.

Most people do not know that the first hostile acts of the Pacific War took place in the Far East, well before Japanese planes descended on Oahu at dawn on December 7, 1941. Chapter 4 integrates the busy activities of one last week of "peace," with days marked by full alerts, probing reconnaissance missions, small skirmishes, and last-minute military preparations before war commenced in earnest.

Chapters 5 and 6 take the reader into the cockpits of Australian and American fliers for an intimate account of their traumatic first engagements against an unknown and vastly superior foe. The first twenty-four hours of battle unfold in a story of infamy easily rivaling that of the morning at Pearl Harbor. Japanese aviation abilities, heavily downplayed by the United States and Great Britain before the war, were suddenly accorded almost mystical reverence.

Chapters 7 through 11 relate a gripping day-by-day tale of the complete disintegration of Allied airpower in Malaya and the Philippines in the face of an unrelenting Japanese onslaught. Within a mere two weeks, Allied air units in the Pacific were eviscerated, while Japan's air forces had barely been scratched. The tragedy that befell Major Putnam on Wake Island was repeated time and again in the experiences of his peers throughout the Far East.

During the fortnight of disaster, failures in aerial combat led to a far greater debacle for U.S. and British military leaders than the Japanese raid on Hawaii. Chapter 12 analyzes the impact of Japan's assault on the Far East, highlighted by comments from Allied commanders on the scene as they viewed deficiencies in their strategy, their equipment, and the performance of their men and, in some cases, themselves.

CHAPTER 1

Path of the Rising Sun

Japan's Plan for Conquest in East Asia

FOR CENTURIES JAPAN REMAINED IN VIRTUAL ISOLATION from the rest of civilization, secure behind its aquatic fortresses: the Pacific Ocean and the Sea of Japan. In 1853 the United States drew aside the curtain between Japan and the outside world, forever changing the balance of power in Asia. During eighty years of unbridled growth that followed Commodore Matthew Perry's groundbreaking visit, the island nation completely cast aside its age-old isolationist mantle. In that short period of time, Japan developed into the primary economic force of the Far East.

Craving more resources for its burgeoning population, and following in the footsteps of Western imperialists—especially Great Britain—Japan sought a toehold on the Asian continent. With the self-righteous unification of purpose inherent in a society guided by its god-king, and a government dominated by those with a reverence for the martial methodologies embodied in the Samurai *bushido* code, Japan orchestrated dramatic expansions of influence in Asia through a deliberate combination of diplomacy, economic leverage, and, often, military force. Early success in bending foreign countries to their will eventually infected Japanese leaders with a strong feeling of invincibility, ultimately propelling the country along a path of conquest more expansive than any other in history.

By the early 1890s, Japan had developed a powerful army, along with one of the most modern navies in the world. It was more than willing to utilize these forces to expand the imperial realm. During an 1894–95 war with China, Japan demonstrated its military prowess by annexing the island of Formosa (Taiwan), seizing the Korean peninsula, and occupying much of Manchuria. Although Japan returned the prized Manchurian territory to Chinese control after the war—under diplomatic pressure from an uneasy Russia—the pattern for aggressive acquisition was cast. The Imperial Japanese Army (IJA) had proven itself.

Japan was hardly alone in its desire to obtain more control over territory in the Far East. Improvements in ship design and communications encouraged British, Russian, German, and French expansionism in Asia. By the close of the nineteenth century, colonization was increasing at a feverish pace. After the Chinese-nationalist "Boxer Rebellion" of 1900 was quashed by an international coalition of Europeans, Americans, and Japanese, the western European nations made a grab for additional territories within China.

The United States, expanding its own interest in the western Pacific, responded to European division of Chinese provinces by declaring an international "Open Door" policy for free trade with China. U.S. leaders hoped this bit of diplomacy would put an end to foreign annexation of Chinese territory, but the United States, militarily, was in no position to enforce such far-reaching policies.

Wary of Western intentions regarding the governance of China, Southeast Asia, and possibly even Japan itself, Japan's military leaders vowed to build an army second to none and a navy equal to the Pacific fleets of any two of the European powers. With these strong forces, Japan could also play the game of conquest.

While Japan maintained friendly relations with the United States, Great Britain, and other European countries, its dialogue with Russia steadily deteriorated. At issue was Russia's continuing effort to fortify its possessions and expand its influence in Manchuria and on the Korean Peninsula. The Japanese government had never given up its aspiration to control these resource-rich territories. Resentment continued to build for several years while Russia exploited this area that Japan had conquered and then peacefully relinquished after the victory over China.

On the night of February 8, 1904, in a surprise attack made two days prior to Japan's official declaration of war on Russia, Japanese naval forces under the command of Vice Admiral Heihachiro Togo bombarded the Russian Pacific Fleet while it lay quietly at anchor in Port Arthur (Lushun). Japan's subsequent blockade of the harbor prompted the rest of the Russian navy into making a desperate voyage halfway around the world to meet Japan's challenge. While besieged defenders awaited their relief, the Japanese army recaptured much of Manchuria.

On May 27, 1905, the Imperial Japanese Navy (IJN), ably led by Admiral Togo, gained worldwide respect in the Battle of Tsushima. Off the island of Tsushima, Togo's ships almost completely annihilated the Russian fleet as it finally arrived in the Korean Straits. This gunnery duel, which ushered in the age of the battleship, was the most spectacular and decisive naval engagement since Nelson's victory at Trafalgar.

At the time of czarist Russia's defeat, public opinion about the Japanese victory was generally positive in the United States. In retrospect, the event silently signaled Japan's transition from friend to potential foe. With China remaining a weak and divided entity, the Japanese would inevitably assert military, economic, and political control over Asia, an outcome at odds with the U.S. concept of protecting free trade. While the Open Door doctrine formed the keystone of U.S. policy toward China, it was actually up to Japan—specifically the Imperial Japanese Navy—to determine whether the "door" to the Far East would remain open.

Strangely, the first major step on a march toward all-out war in the Pacific was taken in California. In the aftermath of the massively destructive 1906 earthquake in San Francisco, racial tensions between the white settlers of California and the rapidly growing Asian population were whipped into a frenzy by the press—the same press that had instigated the unfortunate disaster on the USS *Maine* into an unnecessary war with Spain. After a number of heavily publicized, racially motivated riots, California passed laws that segregated Asians, barred them from property ownership rights, and limited their immigration, especially from Japan. This was an unforgivable affront to the proud Japanese. Journalists in Japan published accounts of California's treatment of their countrymen as second-class citizens and heralded it as a popular reason for all Asians to distrust and dislike Americans and U.S. policy. Such rhetoric served those seeking to justify Japan's self-ordainment as the protector of oppressed East Asians and their interests.

Japan did not have to wait long for a new opportunity to demonstrate its martial capability. The outbreak of World War I brought another Japanese expansion into China. In support of its alliance with Great Britain, Japan moved quickly to seize the German port city of Kiaochow (Tsingtao). In this little-known campaign, Japan exhibited astonishing foresight in the use of naval airpower. Accompanying the landing-force battle line, the new seaplane carrier *Wakamiya Maru* deployed four Maurice Farman floatplanes to provide gunnery reconnaissance. Desiring to take a more active role in the bombardment, the aviation contingent modified the French planes to carry droppable artillery shells. On September 5, 1914, Lieutenants Hideo Wada and Masaro Fujise carried out a two-plane bombing mission against the main German gun batteries in the city. Although unsuccessful because of a combination of poor aim and failed detonations, the raid attained several historic milestones: it is recorded as the first aerial bombardment operation by any participant in World War I and the very first time naval aircraft attacked an enemy target in any war. The precedent setting continued as the crew of *Wakamiya Maru* regularly conducted raids on German positions throughout the two-month battle that secured Germany's defeat in China.

Deprived of its only viable base in Asia, the German navy was on the run, leaving the rest of the German colonies in the Pacific undefended. Australia—at the urging of Great Britain—was the first to capitalize on this situation and invaded German holdings in the Solomons, the Admiralties, and New Guinea. Japan swiftly seized the remaining German possessions in Micronesia. In a League of Nations resolution at the close of World War I, both Japan and the British Commonwealth were allowed to retain these acquisitions as "mandated territories." This gentleman's agreement between Britain and Japan presented a significant strategic challenge to the architects of the United States' defense for the Pacific. Even though the ministers in Tokyo pledged under the Treaty of Versailles not to fortify the occupied islands, the mere presence of replenishment bases in the Marianas, the Carolines, and the Marshalls was enough to provide Japan with a new defensive shield. In one stroke of the pen, intervention by the U.S. Navy in Japanese home waters was effectively rendered impossible.

Although militarily important to Japan, the Micronesian islands were of little consequence economically, having almost nothing in the way of natural resources and even less in the way of free space for expansion of the Japanese population. To achieve a national objective of reducing its material dependence on the Western powers, Japan surely would have to look elsewhere. Paramount in any plan for future expansion would be unrestricted access to raw materials. Japan needed oil, rubber, timber, and metals to build manufacturing and trade capabilities, and agricultural products to feed a rapidly growing populace. It covetously eyed China and the European colonies of the

Far East, all rich with the fuel for industrial progress and economic dominance. The most tempting targets were the unimaginably vast oil fields of Borneo and the Netherlands East Indies, the mineral-rich and timber-covered expanses of Manchuria and Malaya, and the fertile fields of China, Indochina, and the Philippines.

In September 1931, Japan took a major step toward open conflict with the West. A rapid occupation and annexation of Manchuria—renamed Manchukuo by the Japanese—shocked the world, drawing condemnation from the League of Nations and the United States. However, the West could offer little resistance. Most European economies were in dire straits, and the United States was still headed toward the depths of its own Great Depression. Even the Russians—with the greatest vested interest in Manchuria—chose not to intervene in force. They opted to cautiously station additional troops along their southern borders.

By February of the following year, an emboldened Japan moved to occupy the Chinese port city of Shanghai. Again, there was much international uproar, but no tangible deterrent to further aggression materialized. Censure of Japan by the League of Nations resulted only in Japan's withdrawal from the League. In conjunction with this, Japan renounced any further participation in naval limitation treaties, paving the way for its development and fortification of the Marshall-Caroline-Mariana Mandates.

In Europe during the mid-1930s, Adolf Hitler's Nazi Party came to power in Germany. In 1936 Japan negotiated the Anti-Comintern Pact—a mutual nonaggression agreement—with Germany. This was the first of several diplomatic steps designed to ensure that Germany recognized Japanese interests, which were limited to the Pacific arena, and that Japan supported German ambitions, which would be primarily European in scope. Naturally, these actions on the part of Japan further strained the growing rift in Japanese-U.S. relations.

On July 7, 1937, Japan ignited the spark that flared to a full-scale, though undeclared, war with China. Ultimately, this conflagration would spread across the Pacific and throughout the Far East. Japan used the brief skirmish that followed a bloody confrontation between Japanese and Chinese troops on the Marco Polo Bridge outside Peking (Beijing)—referred to as the "China Incident" by the Japanese—as an excuse to unleash its full fury against the nascent Chinese Nationalist government. Already in a state of extreme turmoil—with internal fighting between Nationalists led by "Generalissimo" Chiang Kai-shek and the growing Communist countermovement of Mao Tse-tung, and between both of these forces and private armies belonging to independent warlords of various cities and provinces—China was ill prepared to defend against a Japanese onslaught.

Japan's first military campaign in China commenced in Shanghai and moved to the west, along the coast, and up the Yangtze River toward the Chinese "Central Capital" at Nanking (Nanjing). To support this campaign, the Japanese delivered one of the most brutal aerial sieges the world has ever known. Japan's air forces deliberately pounded Chinese cities to rubble, indiscriminately killing hundreds of thousands of civilians with incendiary bombardment. Following the bombers, the IJA moved steadily forward, leaving its own trail of carnage as it passed from village to village. If the rest of the world had been more attentive to the plight of the Chinese during 1937, it would have borne witness to a horror even greater than the hellish inferno about to engulf Europe under the German blitzkrieg.

United States Army Air Corps planners seemed unwilling to study the Sino-Japanese War. If they had chosen to listen to their observers in China, they could have learned a great deal about the nature of the impending war in the Pacific. Just a little attention in Washington might have saved the lives of many American and Allied airmen during the first six months of the Pacific War. Chiang Kai-shek's strategic adviser to the Chinese Air Force, former U.S. Army flier Captain Claire Lee Chennault, forwarded to the War Department numerous reviews concerning Japanese tactics and aircraft capabilities. Because Chennault held only a modest rank before his departure to China, and had been an outspoken proponent of fighter-plane development in a bureaucracy dominated by bomber advocates, his views were frequently dismissed.[1] Most of the valuable knowledge in his reports fell on the deaf ears of an army leadership preoccupied with the situation developing in Europe. As a consequence, U.S. fliers knew very little about the Japanese air forces.

The Imperial Japanese naval air service was at the forefront of Japan's offensive. Operating from aircraft carriers off the coast of Shanghai, the IJN provided bombers and fighters to support the advancing army in its initial operations. Land-based attack units—the strategic backbone of Japan's airpower—quickly assumed the primary role in the air campaign, flying from bases on the homeland and Formosa. The men on board these twin-engine bombers were trained in mass-formation, high-altitude precision-bombing techniques. They were also trained to deliver low-level torpedo attacks against warships. The original concept for their use was to execute long-range antishipping strikes against any navy threatening the homeland. For the war in China, these land-based attack units conducted long-range bombardment operations.

As an organization, the IJN air service was structured into autonomous air flotillas known as *koku-sentai*. For shipboard operations, each koku-sentai was associated with one or more aircraft carriers. This carrier division air group was usually composed of three *hikotai*, one for each type of aircraft flown: attack, dive-bomber, and fighter. Each individual carrier in the division was allocated a subset of the flying echelon defined as a *hikokitai*. The hikokitai was typically given the name of the ship to which it was assigned. Land-based koku-sentai were organized similarly but were referred to by a numerical designation commonly associated with a naval district number and their air echelons were known as *kokutai* rather than hikokitai. This was a confusing structure during wartime, so land units were eventually consolidated at the kokutai level: an air group entity that regularly transferred in and out of the various naval districts to participate in combat. Kokutai often operated under the name of their home base.

Reflecting the influence of the British Royal Air Force (RAF), Japanese air formations were based on the grouping of a "vee" flight of three aircraft of the same type working together. In Japan, this core three-plane unit was known as a *shotai*. In most cases, combat was conducted using divisions built from three shotai. That nine-plane unit was defined as a *chutai*. In a rare example of consistency, these flight elements were also used by the Japanese Army Air Force (JAAF).

JAAF combat units were unavailable for use in central China because they were based in Manchuria and Korea to guard against a possible attack by the Russians from the north. In any case, the JAAF was considerably smaller than the aviation branch of the navy, and not as well equipped. Its attack doctrine was tactical in nature, structured solely to provide close support for troops in the field. Each unit was operationally controlled by an air brigade, or *hikodan*. More meaningful, at the deployable unit level, was the *hikosentai*—usually truncated to just *sentai*. The sentai was a group of three to six chutai of a common type of aircraft. As the Pacific War progressed, the IJN kokutai would come to resemble the structure of the JAAF sentai. On the Allied side, sentai and kokutai would be analogous to the U.S. "group" or British "wing" designations.

IJN had been the first service to benefit from an extensive aircraft modernization effort begun in 1934. Planes developed during this period formed the core of Japanese offensive capability throughout the war in China and during the first year of war in the Pacific. Unequivocally, all of them would prove to be fine combatants. Extensive testing in the field during the Sino-Japanese War refined the capabilities of both aircraft and crews. Although their performance in China left no doubt as to their combat effectiveness, Japanese aircraft and aircrews of the period were universally derided outside Japan as being poor copies of those from the West. Such technical bigotry and underestimation would cost the United States and Britain dearly during the first year of the Pacific War.

Japanese fighter pilots—both army and navy—traditionally emphasized the need for outstanding maneuverability in their aircraft. In most cases, they were willing to sacrifice almost everything else to attain superior maneuverability. As a result, Japanese aircraft were often lighter and more simply equipped than those of other nations. Fighter planes often wielded only two rifle-caliber machine guns. This was not perceived as a handicap. Japanese pilots believed they could almost always maneuver into a position where they could strike their enemy accurately and at close range. Hitting power was consciously traded for length of firing time. Armor plate was never added.

That fact should not be cited as evidence of a lack of concern for aircrews, as some historians have stated. It is true that Japanese soldiers were considered as pawns, destined to fall wherever their commanders decreed. However, air unit leaders recognized that aircrew experience was a valuable asset, not something to be squandered needlessly. The lack of pilot protection in Japan's fighters actually represented an odd vote of confidence. Given the higher relative skill of Japanese pilots, and the extra maneuverability advantage afforded by their lightweight planes, air organization leaders thought that an enemy would almost never be able to bring its guns to bear.

Although Japanese aircraft design philosophies initially proved successful, ultimately, by 1943, the emphasis on light construction would be a drawback when Allied aircraft became more powerful, more heavily armed, and more numerous. As Allied pilots learned to apply the type of combat tactics advocated by Claire Chennault—which stressed teamwork and shunned the practice of "dogfighting"—the issue of superior maneuverability would finally be rendered moot. In the meantime, Japan would field the best dogfighters in the world.

When Japan went to war in China, no fighter aircraft better exemplified the performance traits prized by a Japanese naval pilot than the Mitsubishi A5M "Claude", or Type 96 Carrier Fighter. It was Japan's first all-metal, flush-riveted, monocoque airframe design with a fully cantilevered wing and the first modern aircraft to achieve operational status in the Japanese military. Delivered under the 1934 design program, the A5M saw its initial service from Japanese aircraft carriers in early 1936.

Roughly a contemporary of the United States' Boeing P-26A Peashooter army fighter, the A5M shared a similar physical size and description, though the Boeing still utilized a wire-braced wing. Both were monoplanes with fixed, spat-covered landing gear, open cockpits (to afford better pilot visibility), and an equal armament of two 7.7-mm (.30-caliber) machine guns.[2] They were approximately the same weight (about twenty-four hundred pounds), but the A5M, with its nine-cylinder Nakajima Kotobuki radial, enjoyed as much as a 150-horsepower advantage over the P-26, with its Pratt & Whitney Wasp. The A5M's elliptical wing also had about 30 percent greater area than that of the P-26, suggesting significantly better maneuverability than one would expect from the U.S. fighter. In the most important of comparisons, the A5M was some 40 miles per hour faster in top speed, could operate at an altitude more than ten thousand feet higher, and—with a range of 750 miles—could fly twice as far as the P-26. These important facts were not acknowledged at the time by U.S. aviation authorities, who still considered Japanese aviation technology vastly inferior.

Excellence in Japanese aircraft design was not confined to fighters. The Nakajima B5N "Kate", or Type 97 carrier-based attack plane, set a new standard for planes operating from aircraft carriers. This low-wing monoplane, with retractable landing gear and a fully enclosed "greenhouse" cockpit (both novelties for Japanese aircraft), was the world's best torpedol-bomber when introduced in 1937. It would remain so until mid-1942. Placed in service at the same time as the Douglas TBD Devastator, the B5N was more than 30 miles per hour faster than its U.S. Navy counterpart and could carry an additional six hundred pounds of bombs 500 miles farther! Its only weakness—shared by the TBD—was a lack of armor and armament. The B5N only fielded one 7.7-mm machine gun in the aft cockpit. The Douglas mounted a similar gun in its rear crew position, plus an additional .30-caliber weapon in its nose cowling. The versatile Nakajima design would anchor the airborne offensive during the first stage of the Sino-Japanese War and continue on the front lines through most of the Pacific War.

Nakajima B5Ns were Japan's primary carrier-based attack planes during the war in China and the initial battles of the Pacific War. The type could carry large bombs, as pictured, or a single torpedo. B5Ns from Ryujo were used in the December 8, 1941, attacks on USS Preston *and Davao City, Mindanao.* (Courtesy of Rod Larson)

Mitsubishi G3Ms were a mainstay of Japan's bombing campaign in China, and the farthest-ranging bomber used in the early phases of the Pacific War. They were employed against Wake Island, the Philippines, Singapore and the British Royal Navy. This pair of bomb-laden G3Ms from Mihoro Kokutai is engaged in the battle for Malaya. (Courtesy of Rod Larson)

As the war in China moved inland, Japan's new land-based attack plane, the Mitsubishi G3M "Nell", or Type 96 medium bomber, made its record-breaking combat debut. On August 14, 1937—in an unprecedented long-range mission of more than 1,250 miles—Japanese navy fliers departed from their base at Taipei, Formosa, and delivered bomb loads on targets outside Shanghai. This was an amazing feat for its time, but it didn't even approach the limits of this new plane. The G3M was another long-serving aircraft that would continue in Japanese naval service well into the Pacific War. It was a stressed-skin, mid-wing monoplane with twin Mitsubishi Kinsei fourteen-cylinder radials and two vertical stabilizers.

Although the G3M featured retractable landing gear, it still retained external bomb racks along the center of its fuselage. Early G3Ms were somewhat lightly defended, with just four 7.7-mm machine guns and—in the Japanese tradition—no protective armor. Pacific War–vintage G3M3s would have the additional defensive punch of a 20-mm cannon, housed in a dorsal turret—a weapon devastating to fighters carelessly attacking it from above or behind. G3Ms could carry a single torpedo, or an 800-kilogram (1,764-pound) load of bombs, at more than 250 miles per hour, to a ceiling of 33,725 feet. Its ordnance-carrying capacity was just average for the period, but the craft, and its crew of seven, could deliver a 200-kilogram (440-pound) payload as far away as 1,500 miles from its base.

This was a performance no contemporary aircraft could begin to match. To put that in perspective, the G3M's almost unbelievable 3,900-mile range was superior to that of the giant U.S. four-engine bombers that would gain much fame for their long missions into enemy territory: Boeing's B-17 Flying Fortress and Consolidated's B-24 Liberator. Both of those designs were still on the drawing board when G3Ms went to war. Even by the close of the Pacific War, the next generation of U.S. bombers—the Boeing B-29 Superfortress and Consolidated B-32 Dominator—could exceed the range of a G3M only when not carrying a payload.

In spite of their technological merit, the new G3M Mitsubishi bombers pounded away at the Shanghai area and the city of Nanking for only about a month before being withdrawn from combat. Chinese fighter pilots, following carefully laid interception plans, were able to attack unescorted bombers on many of the raids. Without the benefit of fighter cover, and flying at medium altitudes of ten thousand feet or less, the Japanese bombers were vulnerable to the diving, slashing attacks of the Chinese fighters. In a tremendous blow to Japan, as many as half of the new G3Ms failed to return to their bases after each mission.

Japan had learned a valuable lesson in aerial warfare in the most difficult way. Unless they were certain they had established air superiority, IJN air unit commanders would never again allow their bombers to go unescorted over enemy territory during daylight hours. The British would learn this same lesson, painfully, in the spring of 1940, in the skies over France. The Germans would follow an equally costly learning curve later that year, during the Battle of Britain. In turn, the Americans would suffer high crew losses in 1942—above the southwestern Pacific and western Europe—only to reach the same conclusion.

By December 1937, the city of Nanking finally fell to the advancing Japanese army. The government of Chiang Kai-shek went on the run, retreating along the Yangtze River to Chungking (Chongqing). In the melee of this evacuation, the gunboat USS *Panay*—carrying U.S. diplomatic and civilian refugees up the Yangtze—was bombed by Japanese aircraft and sank twenty-five miles upriver from Nanking. One sailor was killed. Twenty others, including *Panay's* captain and executive officer, were wounded.[3] The attack inspired front-page headlines that clamored for retribution. Although several other U.S. and British vessels were damaged or sunk in similar "accidental" bombings, Japan's formal apology was deemed an adequate atonement. After this, it seemed clear that the United States and the British Empire would not go to war to save either the Chinese or even their own interests in China.

Well to the north of the primary battleground in central China, the Mongolian border with Japanese-occupied Manchuria was a latent source of contention with the Soviet Union. Since 1931, periodic skirmishes occurred between Russian and Japanese troops at this borderline and the Amur River boundary. In May 1939, one of these clashes erupted into a full-scale campaign on the ground and in the air along the Khalka River and across the desolate Nomonhan Plain of Mongolia.

The JAAF shouldered the battle against the Soviet Air Force. Air-to-air fighting during the "Nomonhan Incident" raged on a monumental scale, with engagements often involving more than one hundred aircraft at a time. This contest afforded another preview of the upcoming war in Europe, but ended abruptly in

September after the Germans launched their first attack on Poland. Of necessity, the Russians—temporarily allied with the Germans in a nonaggression pact signed on August 23, 1939—disengaged to devote their attention toward the west. Japan was content to set aside the Nomonhan issue to focus its efforts in the south. The bitter memory of this stalemated conflict, however, weighed heavily in favor of a subsequent IJA decision to maintain a large concentration of troops in Manchukuo throughout the Pacific War—a strategic policy that ultimately plagued Japan's South Pacific campaign.

Victory claims on both sides of Nomonhan—heavily exaggerated— exceeded 500 aircraft. The extent of actual Russian losses, obscured for many years, is now known to be 207 aircraft. Japan's army airmen suffered an equally resounding blow: 162 aircraft lost, along with as many as 150 trained pilots.[4] These staggering losses caused the JAAF to regroup and formulate new tactics before embarking on its next adventure in the Pacific War.

Intense combat with Russian Polikarpov I-153 and I-16 fighters had given the JAAF an opportunity to fully assess the effectiveness of its newest fighter, the Nakajima Ki-27 "Nate". Like its naval contemporary—the Mitsubishi A5M—the Ki-27 was a low-wing, stressed-skin monoplane with a nine-cylinder radial engine and fixed, spat-covered landing gear. In spite of the fixed gear, the Ki-27 had an even cleaner form than the A5M. It was the first Japanese fighter design to include a covered cockpit, and the first fighter in the world to employ a "bubble" canopy for 360-degree pilot visibility. The Nakajimas, placed in service during 1938, set a new standard for speed and maneuverability in Japanese aircraft. Some commentators say this fighter may have been the most maneuverable aerial combatant of all time. Its 710-horsepower Nakajima Ha-1b powered the featherweight twenty-four hundred pound fighter to a top speed of 292 miles per hour and a maximum altitude ceiling of more than thirty-five thousand feet. The primary drawbacks of the Ki-27 were its short range of 389 miles, light armament of two 7.7-mm machine guns, and the apparent combat vulnerability of extremely lightweight construction. Combat reports indicate that often only a few hits were necessary to cause critical structural damage or a fatal explosion.

By the end of 1939, the Japanese had conquered about as much of China as originally planned. In the east, the Chinese coast was largely occupied. From Manchuria to the southern border with Indochina, all major port cities except British Hong Kong had fallen under Japanese control. To the west, the Japanese army had advanced far inland, up the Yangtze River into the Szechuan province. While fighting on the ground had come to a standstill, aerial bombardment of Chinese cities continued, both day and night.

The new bombing campaign established the need for a long-range, air-superiority fighter to escort far-reaching IJN bombers during day-light raids. This requirement produced one of the finest fighters to be flown in World War II: the Mitsubishi A6M "Zeke", Type 0 Carrier Fighter, or *Rei-sen* (short for *rei shiki sento ki*, which roughly translates to "Zero Fighter").

During July 1940, the first fifteen A6M2 fighters were rushed directly from the factory to Wuhan airfield in China. These planes impressed their pilots as none had before. While the smooth lines of this enclosed-cockpit monoplane were pleasing to the eye, the A6M2's outstanding performance more than matched its appearance. With excellent low-drag aerodynamics and relatively light construction, the Zero was exceptionally maneuverable and possessed an astounding initial rate of climb of up to 4,500 feet per minute. From a sea-level takeoff, the Zero could climb to an altitude of 17,000 feet in less than six minutes. It was at least a generation ahead of Allied fighters in climb performance. Even the fabled North American P-51 Mustang would not be able to keep pace with its ascent. In fact, the only propeller-driven U.S. fighter ever to match its climb rate was the Grumman F8F Bearcat, which was not deployed to frontline Navy fighter squadrons before the autumn of 1945.

Although flight control became more difficult in the thin air above 25,000 feet, the Zero's performance did not drop off appreciably until very close to its 33,790-foot ceiling. Its fighting capabilities are even more impressive when one considers its range of operation. Using a centerline-mounted drop tank, the A6M's maximum flight duration could be extended up to a distance of 1,900 miles—better than three times the range of 1941-vintage U.S. fighters. Its armament also broke new ground for a Japanese fighter. In addition to the typical twin 7.7 mm cowl-mounted machine guns, the Mitsubishi had real punch from a 20-mm cannon in each wing. The early Zero's top speed may have been just average at 331 miles per hour, but its overall perfor-mance envelope was superior to that of any fighter available, from any nation. The design was a model of efficiency. Considering that its fourteen-cylinder Nakajima Sakae engine only developed a modest 950 horsepower, it is amazing that the A6M2's overall combat effec-tiveness would not be surpassed until 1943.

Nakajima Ki-27 fighters of the 64th Sentai lined up on the vast Nomonhon Plain of Mongolia in 1939. Combat with the Soviet Air Force reshaped Japanese Army Air Force policies for fighter operations. Ki-27s, well suited to use from rough fields, were employed extensively during the first few months of the Pacific War in the Philippines and Malaya. (Courtesy of Rod Larson)

Superior performance of the Mitsubishi A6M "Zero" came as a very unpleasant surprise to Allied airmen. Zeros played a central role in the defeat of American air forces in the Philippines, in part because a 20mm cannon in each wing made the Zero a devastatingly effective strafer. This is one of the early model A6M2s used in China. The aircraft in the background is a Mitsubishi A5M. (Courtesy of Rod Larson)

By the time the Zero fighter went into action over China, the Chinese Air Force had become adept at avoiding Japanese fighters. Claire Chennault's primitive, but effective, air raid warning system allowed Chinese air unit commanders to choose their combats wisely. Japanese planes would only be engaged when the Chinese could do so with an advantage of numerical strength and altitude.

On August 19, 1940, Lieutenant Tamotsu Yokoyama of the *12th Kokutai* Fighter Squadron led the first A6M2 combat mission: escorting

G3M bombers on a daytime mission to Chungking. Lieutenant Yoko-yama's pilots were eager to engage Chinese fighters, but none rose to intercept the formation. The following day, Lieutenant Saburo Shindo's flight of Zeros fared no better in getting a chance to prove superiority of the new plane in combat. The third Zero mission, flown on September 12, brought no aerial contest but finally gave the Japanese pilots a chance to fire their guns. They were allowed to disengage from the bomber formation to strafe the Chinese airfield at Shihmachow. Fortu-nately for the Chinese, these gunnery runs only succeeded in destroying a number of decoy aircraft.

The next day, the Chinese were not so lucky. Lieutenant Shindo's flight of Zeros encountered a reported twenty-seven Polikarpov fight-ers above Chungking. Caught by surprise, all the Chinese aircraft were shot down—or run off smoking—without even damaging a sin-gle A6M2. Chinese records acknowledge the destruction of thirteen fighters, and no victory claims were made by the Chinese pilots.[5] This wild melee showcased an outstanding aerial combat debut for the Rei-sen; its capabilities were even more impressive when one con-siders that the dogfight—which lasted over thirty minutes—was undertaken while the Japanese fighters were on a 1,150-mile-long escort mission. It would have been impossible for the Allies to have attempted fighter operations of this duration prior to the service entry of the Lockheed P-38F Lightning in the autumn of 1942.

By December 1941, the Japanese had thoroughly proven their potent air-superiority fighter. During its yearlong service in China, not a single Zero was lost in air-to-air combat. Only three A6Ms were lost to enemy action, and all were brought down at low altitude, by short-range antiaircraft fire. One of those unlucky Zeros, piloted by Petty Officer 1st Class Ei-ichi Kimura of the *12th Kokutai*, was shot down while strafing Taipingssu airfield, near Chengdu, on May 20, 1941. Recovered largely intact, this craft was personally inspected by Claire Chennault. Detailed information gained in the inspection—including photographs—was forwarded to both U.S. and British mili-tary authorities.

Though the British circulated this intelligence to field commands, their briefing information discounted the fact that any useful quanti-ties of the new fighter might be available. The U.S. War Department almost completely ignored the report—as they had several of Chen-nault's earlier reports—adding comments to the intelligence record that performance specifications attributed to the Type 00 were grossly overstated. If anything, the report from China would later prove conservative. After the war, Chennault—by then a legitimate lieutenant general in the Army Air Forces—claimed he had evidence that some records he had provided to Washington had been deliberately destroyed because the specifications were so outstanding that U.S. engineering analysts found them difficult to believe, let alone credit to the Japanese.[6]

Cover-up or no, poor use of the intelligence from China meant that the appearance of a large number of Zeros at the start of the Pacific War would come as a very unpleasant surprise to Allied airmen. Flown by pilots of great skill and boundless confidence, the mysterious Japanese fighter would gain legendary fame as it swept Allied aircraft from the skies by the score, seemingly without effort.

In June 1940, France fell to the Germans, upsetting the balance of power in Europe. Division of sentiment between Vichy French colonies—compliant to the Axis cause—and Free French colonies—sympathetic to Great Britain and the United States—encouraged Japan to take bolder action in the Pacific. During September, Japan occupied the northern part of Vichy French Indochina (Vietnam, Cambodia, and Laos). The United States responded to this occupation with an embargo on steel and scrap iron sales to Japan.

On September 27, 1940, Japan concluded the Tripartite Pact with Germany and Italy. The terms of this agreement specified that the signatories would "assist one another with all political, economic and military means when one of the three Contracting Parties is attacked by a power at present not involved in the European War or in the Sino-Japanese conflict."[7] This threat was pointedly directed at the United States, should it choose to intervene in either arena.

Throughout the first half of 1941, Japanese naval and army squadrons trained at a feverish rate; many were reequipped with brand-new aircraft. A large number of air groups—especially bombardment units—were relocated from China to Formosa and Indochina. From these movements, the Allied intelligence community deduced that Japan's air forces were being readied for use in a new theater of operations. The Pacific would not remain pacific for long.

Ineffective diplomatic efforts by the United States to delay, if not avert, the onset of war proceeded slowly while Japan continued along a path of conquest and occupation. In July 1941, Japanese forces moved to occupy the southern portion of Indochina, focusing on the large port at Cam Ranh Bay and several airfields near Saigon. The United States, along with Great Britain and the Netherlands East Indies, again responded with an embargo. This time, access to petroleum products would be restricted. As an extra measure, Japanese financial assets in those countries were frozen.

This political action did not have the desired impact. If anything, it accelerated the onset of hostilities. Without access to critical oil sources, and deprived of cash resources, Japan would have to play its hand soon, or give up the game. In its Supreme War Council, convened on September 6, 1941, Japan's plan for conquest of the Pacific was laid out. Nevertheless, at Emperor Hirohito's personal request—even though a definitive path toward war had already been clearly charted—Japan's prime minister, Prince Fumimaro Konoye, was asked to delay the start of hostilities in order to continue the peace negotiation process with the United States.

With due regard for the emperor's wishes, but with the intent to move quickly, the Japanese High Command placed a deadline of October 15, 1941, as the last possible day for conclusion of any negotiations. Beyond that date, the High Command felt that Japan's opportunity to conduct its operations under optimal conditions would gradually decline. When negotiations continued to be unsuccessful, Konoye and his entire cabinet resigned on October 16, 1941, forcing one final delay. General Hideki Tojo—formerly Japan's war minister—was chosen as Konoye's successor and obliged to make a last feeble attempt at diplomacy. Short of the United States' complete concession to Japan's political demands, negotiation could never have averted the obvious course of action that Japan would follow.

The plan to defeat the United States and Great Britain in the Far East depended heavily on the IJN. In its original war plans, the IJN assumed that the British would be forced to retain their capital ships in the Atlantic Ocean.

Success in containing the fortress at Singapore would depend on the speed with which the Japanese army could invade Malaya. The idea was to execute that part of the operation so rapidly that the British Admiralty would not have time to muster a suitable reinforcement expedition before the cause was lost. Assistance to Singapore that the less-distant Dutch navy might provide in the Netherlands East Indies was not considered much of a challenge to Japanese plans. The Netherlands possessed no battleships and only a few cruisers. Therefore, Japanese battleships would only provide distant cover for the "Southern Operation" invasions. It was assumed that a decisive defeat of the U.S. Navy could only occur during a deepwater slugfest between dreadnoughts in the western Pacific. If the U.S. Pacific Fleet rushed to aid the

Philippines, the Japanese trap would be set. Recalling the glorious victory at Tsushima, the IJN had supreme confidence in its ability to outgun the United States in any traditional naval engagement.

Elimination of Allied airpower was the greatest concern for Japan's military strategists. The ground offensive could not move quickly enough to ensure success unless Japan controlled the air. IJN land-attack units and escorting Zero fighters would form the core of the strike force charged with neutralizing Allied air defenses in the Philippines and Singapore. In addition, the entire weight of the JAAF bomber commands would be thrown against Malaya, Singapore, and the Philippines. A coordinated strategic bombardment campaign was designed to bring the Allies to their knees.

The bold concept of the Pearl Harbor raid was a late-breaking afterthought. As air-minded as the Japanese navy had become, the concept of "the great naval battle" never evolved into serious consideration as an aircraft carrier–oriented conflict. Because the carriers were not a crucial part of the main battle force, and since it was felt that land-based air units could destroy U.S. and British air forces in the Philippines and Malaya without assistance from the carrier air groups, the Commander in Chief of the Combined Fleet, Admiral Isoroku Yamamoto, was willing to consider the proposal for an initial carrier-based attack on the Hawaiian fortress. If the raid was enough of a success, it would buy time for the Japanese invasion forces to complete their tasks in the Far East before engaging in the main shooting match with the Americans.

Having spent much time in the United States, the Harvard-educated admiral knew that Japan could prevail only in a short-term war. U.S. industrial capacity could compensate for Japan's initial advantage within a few years. Therefore, anything Yamamoto could do to knock out the U.S. Navy quickly, or keep it away from center stage, would increase Japan's odds of ultimate victory. The Pearl Harbor strike plan was daring, even theatrical, in concept. It was certainly a gamble. The lightly escorted carrier force would be placed at great risk if it was detected by U.S. patrols. It is worth mentioning that Yamamoto's two great passions were gambling and theater. For him, it was the perfect plan—a dramatic gesture, well worth the gamble.

In addition to the naval units participating in the preemptive surprise attack on the U.S. fleet at Oahu, the Japanese amassed two major striking forces in the western Pacific: one in southern Formosa, poised to move rapidly south into the Philippines; a second, in French

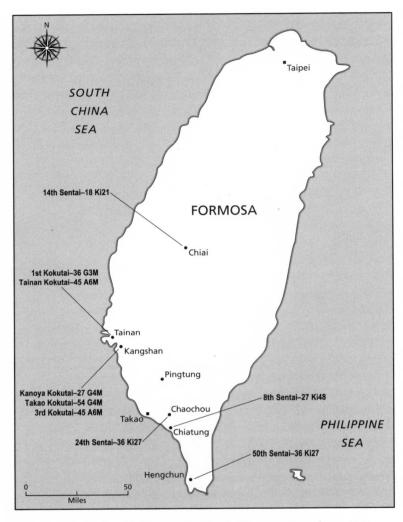

Japanese Combat Air Units on the Island of Formosa; December 7, 1941.

Indochina, ready to launch a vast offensive into Malaya, Burma, and the East Indies. The Japanese were well prepared for this two-pronged attack. Both striking forces and their support units were covered by powerful naval air fleets. To a man, Japan's invasion forces were perhaps the best-trained and certainly the most experienced military units in the world. In the skies especially, their opposite numbers were anything but well drilled or expert.

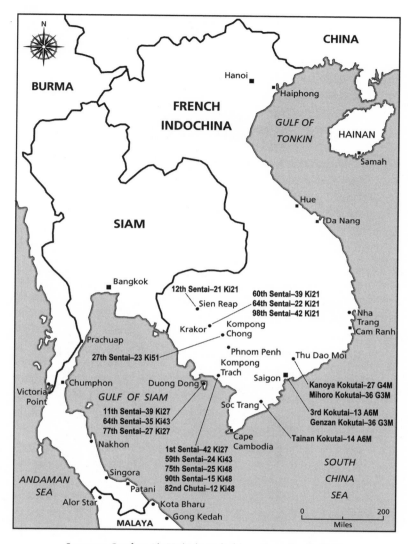

Japanese Combat Air Units in Indochina; December 7, 1941.

CHAPTER 2

Gateway to China

American Fortress in the Philippines

BEFORE 1898 U.S. INFLUENCE IN THE PACIFIC OCEAN stretched only tenuously beyond the West Coast. In fact, no official land acquisition occurred until 1867, when Midway Island was annexed as a useful waypoint for replenishing steamships on the trade route to Shanghai. That desolate coral formation at the northwest tip of the Hawaiian "Leeward Island" chain remained the sole U.S. possession outside the North American continent until the Spanish-American War.

In April 1898, U.S. foreign policy changed significantly when the United States declared war on Spain, after affixing blame on that country for the mysterious explosion of the USS *Maine* in Cuba's Havana Harbor. On May 1, 1898, halfway around the world, the U.S. Navy steamed into Manila Bay. Easily defeating the Spanish fleet moored there, Commodore George Dewey put Marines ashore to occupy the city of Manila. After the Spanish-American War was concluded diplomatically in December, a victorious United States found itself in possession of several Caribbean islands and two new Pacific territories: the Philippine Islands and Guam. In a complementary effort, Washington finally completed a less-than-friendly takeover of the Hawaiian Islands. The following year, the United States annexed Wake Island (about half the distance between Guam and Midway) and the portion of Samoa not already under European control. The United States' Manifest Destiny suddenly extended all the way across the Pacific Ocean to the doorstep of Asia.

Using the Philippines as a gateway to the Far East was a considerable advantage for the United States. Naval forces based in the

Philippines could project power across the South China Sea to protect trade routes and U.S. interests within China. Undoubtedly, the ideal place to base naval units was at Manila Bay, off the island of Luzon. It was the only U.S.-controlled harbor west of Hawaii with a sheltered anchorage sizable enough to accommodate an entire fleet. The key issue was how the location—more than seven thousand miles away from the U.S. West Coast—could be fortified and reinforced in time of war.

The first critical task was protecting Manila Bay from a naval attack, such as the one Commodore Dewey carried out against the Spanish. Shore-based defenses were put in place on Luzon in 1904, when the U.S. Army started to develop the small islands at the mouth of the bay into a line of "unsinkable battleships." Elaborate artillery fortresses sited at Fort Mills (on Corregidor), Fort Drum (on El Fraile Island), Fort Frank (on Carabao Island), and Fort Hughes (on Caballo Island) were in complete command of the seaborne approach to Manila. Centerpiece facilities on Corregidor were designed to sustain these battlements during a siege as long as six months without reinforcement or replenishment. The heaviest guns emplaced in these facilities were more than equal to those in any warship afloat at the time. If artillery was not enough of a deterrent, hundreds of mines were strung across the channels between the islands and Mariveles Harbor, at the southern tip of the Bataan Peninsula. Thus, the entrance to Manila Bay was well secured against both surface ship and submarine intrusion. It would have been suicidal for an enemy fleet to venture close enough to Manila to do damage either to the dockyard facilities at Cavite Naval Station or to any ships anchored in the bay.

Protecting the Manila Bay anchorage from the landward side was another matter entirely. With more than 120 miles of coastline, and thirty-five miles from the entry channel at Corregidor, in the west, to its eastern shore by the city of Manila, the bay dwarfs Pearl Harbor. The island of Luzon—with a coastline as long as that of California, Oregon, and Washington combined—offered many suitable landing spots for invasion. It did not seem practical to consider a defense for the entire island. In fact, it was not even clear that securing Manila was feasible, yet it was politically impossible to concede the Philippines at the first enemy shot. The only reasonable alternative was to fight a delaying action on the ground, gradually retreating away from enemy landing zones toward the Bataan Peninsula, at the north side of the entrance to Manila Bay. Like the gunnery fortresses, the position on Bataan could be held as long as supplies of food and ammunition were sustained. At some point, however, the army in the Philippines would have to be rescued from the invaders, or surrender.

The security challenge for the Philippines was a formidable one. Many refinements of the proposed U.S. response to an invasion of the Philippines were completed prior to 1941. One basic premise remained the same throughout the various iterations of this War Plan Orange: Manila Bay could not possibly be defended from the land-ward side with any size of armed force likely to be available for that purpose.[1] The fortifications around Corregidor could deny use of the bay to an enemy navy for an extended period of time. However, ships based in Manila Bay would have to seek shelter elsewhere once hostile armies and their artillery approached overland from the most likely invasion points. Thus, the U.S. Navy could expect to launch harassing attacks on enemy landing zones and supply lines from the Manila base for just a few weeks. When aerial bombardment became a factor in the planning process, it was clear that Manila Bay could be a haven for U.S. warships only if a very large air force could be deployed to provide air cover. Because requirements for that task always specified a force larger than the entire combined U.S. Army and Navy air strength, strategists had to refine their defense plan for the Philippines to call for the immediate withdrawal of navy surface ships upon commencement of any hostilities.

U.S. military and political leaders clearly saw that even though Japan was an ally, it would pose the greatest security threat to the Philippines and to aspirations for trade development with China. To prevail in a counterattack against Japan in the Far East, the U.S. Navy would have to send a superior armada across the Pacific to deal a crushing blow to the IJN. Once the Japanese capital ships were destroyed, Japan's supply lines could be severed; only then could U.S. troops land to reinforce Bataan and retake Luzon.

The Russian defeat at Tsushima was never far from mind when strategists contemplated deployment of a rescue fleet that could sail across the Pacific to relieve troops on Bataan and Corregidor. Any move across the ocean was planned to be undertaken with caution. Safely advancing the Navy Battle Force and its supply train across Japan's Micronesian barrier would necessarily be a slow and arduous process, requiring the potentially costly capture of several key atolls along the way. The possibility of the navy's accomplishing these tasks before a greatly outnumbered army garrison in the Philippines succumbed to superior Japanese ground forces was always a long shot, at best.

The Washington Naval Arms Limitation Treaty of 1922 embodied a political effort to curb the rapidly escalating costs of a naval arms race. This diplomatic solution placed serious restrictions on naval buildup in the Pacific. Signed by the United States, Great Britain, and Japan, the agreement imposed limitations on the construction of specific types of warships and forbade development of any new, permanent fortifications in the western Pacific. In many respects, the treaty handicapped the United States and Great Britain more than Japan. Because the agreement allowed the U.S. Navy only a five-to-three numerical advantage over the IJN, the United States could no longer provide enough capital ships to guarantee success in a showdown with Japan in the western Pacific and, at the same time, protect a supply line stretching across the entire Pacific. Without additional fortresses in the Philippines or on the island stepping-stones across the Pacific (Guam, Wake, and Midway), planners considered it virtually impossible for defending forces to secure U.S. possessions west of Hawaii in the face of a major attack by the Japanese.

By the mid-1920s, military strategists conceded that the Philippines, along with most of its defending soldiers, would be forfeited if Japan moved to war. As such, it did not seem rational to invest a great deal more in Philippine defenses. The likely outcome of any headlong dash across the Pacific to relieve besieged troops on Luzon would be a naval disaster. In the early 1930s, when these strategists finally considered the damage a mandates-based Japanese air force could inflict on the proposed relief mission, the idea of a quick, decisive sea battle to defeat the IJN effectively dissolved. War planner assessments of a timetable for transpacific progress varied, but most agreed that victory in the Far East would require several years of difficult fighting in the Central Pacific and a fleet the size of which only the boldest admirals dared dream.

In the depth of the Great Depression, the U.S. Congress made a political decision to the effect that protecting the Philippine Archipelago was more difficult and costly than justifiable. After all, the great promise of profitable trade with China had never been fulfilled, and keeping the peace with various insurrectionist groups around the Philippines had seldom been easy. The Tydings-McDuffie Act of 1934 created a plan that would provide for complete Philippine independence by 1946. In effect, this action would release the United States from any direct obligation to engage in battle for interests in the Far East.

During 1935, at the urging of the newly elected president of the Philippine Commonwealth, Manuel Quezon, the United States agreed to guarantee security of the archipelago until an independent Philippine military force could be established, or until 1946. Quezon's plan received a solid boost when General Douglas MacArthur resigned his commission as chief-of-staff of the United States Army, "retiring" into the handsomely paid position of field marshal for the proposed Philippine army. MacArthur held a belief—not shared by many others—that, given proper arms and adequate training, the Filipinos could defend themselves without possessing a major naval force. In his new role, Field Marshal MacArthur planned to develop a rapidly deployable army capable of repulsing any enemy landing attempt at the beaches. Although Douglas MacArthur was never considered "air-minded," he expected his new command to develop a strong air force presence in the islands to defeat enemy carrier-based aircraft and land-based bombers that were likely to support an invasion effort. Until the proposed Philippine Army Air Corps (PAAC) was ready to take on a leading role, the United States Army Air Corps would have to provide an aerial defense for Luzon.

The commander of the U.S. Army's Philippine Department, Major General George Grunert, faced a daunting challenge in building an effective air force. His 4th Composite Group—constituted from the 3rd Pursuit (active in the Philippine Islands since 1919), the 28th Bombardment (originally deployed to Luzon in 1926), and the 2nd Observation squadrons—was hardly adequate for the job.

The primary base for this tiny air force was Clark Field, situated approximately sixty-five miles northwest of Manila, on a vast plain that connects the Lingayen Gulf with Manila Bay. Clark serviced the 28th Squadron's bombers and the assorted aircraft of the 2nd Squadron. Nichols Field, just south of Manila near the dockyards, was home to the fighters of the 3rd Pursuit and the assembly and repair facilities of the Philippine Air Depot. A third, very small airstrip—Nielson Field—was adjacent to Army Headquarters at Fort McKinley, on the northern fringe of Manila. It also served as the city's commercial airport. Nielson was not intended to be a staging point for combat operations. It was basically an "executive airport" for high-ranking officials. As a rule, the 4th Composite only received aircraft that had been deemed no longer useful to first-line units elsewhere

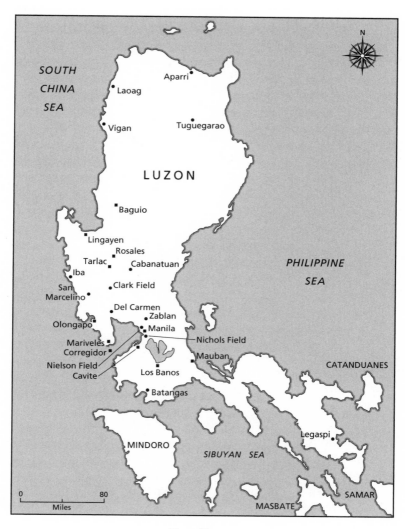

Map of Luzon.

around the globe. The assignment of thirty-odd 1934-vintage, P-26A Peashooters of the 3rd Pursuit Squadron was evidence of how little the United States planned to expend on Philippine security. The well-worn Peashooters represented the sole investment in fighter protection for the islands from 1937 until the close of 1940. Aircraft of the 28th Bombardment were also hand-me-downs. The best planes available to that squadron before 1940 were a dozen or so Martin B-10s. Equipped in this manner, the 4th Composite Group was hardly credible.

On September 1, 1939, Germany invaded Poland. France and Great Britain—demonstrating solidarity with Poland—declared war on Germany by September 3. American public opinion clearly favored the cause of the French, British, and Poles, but the United States desperately wanted to maintain its neutrality and avoid entanglement in another European war. Initially, the United States hoped the combined might of France and Britain would be enough to quickly demolish the forces of Nazi Germany, without the need for U.S. involvement. Unfortunately, the devastating effectiveness of the German blitzkrieg stunned the world and provided proof that containing Nazi expansion would consume far more resources than even the most pessimistic military planners had previously imagined. This new era of mechanized and aerial warfare would require a commitment of staggering numbers of men, ships, planes, and other implements of war.

Of all U.S. services, the Army Air Corps faced the greatest challenge. President Franklin Roosevelt had already secured a number of additional appropriations to prepare the country's military response to events abroad. After his address to Congress on January 12, 1939, Roosevelt obtained $300 million to finance procurement of aircraft for the Army Air Corps. That emergency defense bill funded a plan for twenty-four combat-ready air groups to be deployable by mid-1941. Even though the plan seemed aggressive, once all-out air war was raging in Europe, it was quickly revised upward to a new goal of developing a total of fifty-four tactical combat groups before the end of 1941. In 1940 the Army Air Corps plan would grow again to the more ambitious target of eighty-four air groups (approximately 270 squadrons) scheduled for activation by June 1942.[2] Only at that point would the United States field a competitive air force.

War in Europe presented Japan with a golden opportunity. European colonies in the Far East suddenly received less attention and support from their parent countries. Military commitments in Europe limited the size of British, French, and Dutch forces in the Pacific to mere garrison strength in most locations. Materiel support for China waned. Even the "neutral" United States became distracted as it politically maneuvered to stay out of the European fray. The Japanese planned to take maximum advantage of this situation to consolidate their position in China while regrouping to launch a new offensive against the weakened European holdings in Southeast Asia.

U.S. military leaders understood this new threat in the Pacific. To them, it was only a matter of time before Japan would play its hand to eliminate U.S. presence in the Philippines. To prepare any defense against such an action, the United States had to keep a close eye on the movements of Japanese military and merchant marine units throughout the Far East. Some activities could be monitored through radio traffic analysis or agents on the ground, but there was no substitute for the eyes and cameras of observers in aircraft.

The new maritime reconnaissance mission was assigned to the U.S. Navy's Asiatic Fleet. At the time, that minuscule flotilla existed primarily to "show the flag" in Asia and support operations of a squadron of river gunboats in China. The main body of warships consisted of just a few aging cruisers and a handful of World War I–vintage destroyers based in Shanghai and Manila Bay. Admiral Thomas Hart, commander of the Asiatic Fleet, made it known in Washington that he would need submarines, aircraft, and more surface ships to effectively patrol his area of responsibility. However, the only units immediately available were a patrol squadron of new Consolidated PBY Catalina flying boats and their support ship, USS *Langley* (AV-3).

The new eyes of the Asiatic Fleet were well suited to the role of maritime reconnaissance. The versatile Consolidated PBY Catalina flying boat was an easily recognizable design, having a unique parasol wing structure, with retractable wing-tip floats and large, ovoid Plexiglas gun blisters on its flanks. VP-21's Catalinas were the PBY-4 seaplane version, without the characteristic waist-gun enclosures or the retractable landing gear of later amphibious versions. Two highly reliable fourteen-cylinder Pratt & Whitney Twin-Wasp radials were strong enough to lift its fully laden seventeen tons out of the water to an altitude of 14,700 feet, yet economical enough to give the PBY a range of more than 2,500 miles. For shorter missions, the Catalina could be armed as a bomber with an under-wing load of up to four thousand pounds, consisting of bombs, torpedoes, or depth charges. On paper, its defensive armament of two .50-caliber waist guns, a .30-caliber front turret gun, and a rear-facing .30-caliber tunnel gun appeared adequate. In practice, the poor location and ergonomics of these weapons—along with a tortoiselike 117-mile-per-hour cruising speed—discouraged use of the Catalina as a strike weapon. The PBY-4 model was especially risky to fly in combat because it lacked self-sealing fuel tanks and protective armor.

The planes of Navy Patrol Squadron 21 (VP-21) were the first military aircraft stationed in the Philippines to fly there under their own power. All fourteen PBYs assigned to the unit traversed the

The Consolidated PBY Catalina was the U.S. Navy's primary long-range patrol bomber at the start of the Pacific War. Patrol Wing Ten deployed to Manila with twenty-eight PBY-4 flying-boats in late 1939. This PBY carries the markings of VP-13, which was renamed VP-26 and later became VP-102 after transfer to the Philippines. Catalina crews performed a valuable service tracking Japanese shipping movements prior to the war. A British Catalina was the first Allied plane shot down in the Pacific War—more than a day before the attack on Pearl Harbor. (Courtesy of Emil Buehler Naval Aviation Library)

Pacific, from Hawaii to Manila, using the same transoceanic route employed by the Pan American Airways flying boats since 1936. It was a long journey: 1,150 miles from Pearl Harbor to Midway, 1,050 miles from Midway to Wake, 1,350 miles from Wake to Guam, and almost 1,500 miles from Guam to Manila Bay. In 1939 only long-range sea-planes like the PBY were capable of such a journey. None of the islands had operable airfields.

Upon their arrival in Manila, VP-21 crews had to be serviced by the *Langley* because their base facilities at Sangley Point—just north of the navy yard at Cavite—were not yet ready. As the naval aviators quickly discovered, construction activity in the Philippines tended to proceed at a leisurely pace. Even projects of great importance regularly fell behind schedule. The typical contractor workday usually consisted of a few hours of effort in the morning, followed by a long lunch and siesta during the heat of the day, and a few hours of labor in the later afternoon. Military officers tolerated the relaxed environment. For the most part, duty around Manila was a pleasant diversion, almost a privileged existence. The standard of living for American soldiers on Luzon was generally much higher than in stateside service.

About nine months later, in June 1940, a second navy patrol squadron was assigned to join VP-21 in the Philippines. The chosen unit, VP-26, had also been stationed in Hawaii. Equipped with almost the entire balance of PBY-4 production—in freshly overhauled condition—the squadron eagerly completed its trek across the long Pan American Airways route to Cavite. The base at Sangley Point was finally prepared to accept the planes, but their crews would linger in the Philippines for only a few days. The aircraft belonging to VP-21 had never been overhauled, and two years of heavy use had taken its toll. Unfortunately, the new seaplane facilities at Sangley were not equipped to perform extensive airframe and engine service. The reconditioned Catalinas of VP-26 were transferred to VP-21, and the VP-26 crews were asked to ferry the tired VP-21 planes back to Pearl Harbor for a thorough refitting. Men who already missed Honolulu were elated, but those who longed for the more adventurous setting in Manila were disappointed.

When overhauls on all the PBYs were completed, the crews of VP-26 again traversed the Pacific. Organizational changes took place when they returned to the Philippines: VP-21 was redesignated VP-101, and VP-26 became VP-102.[3] Together with a utility squadron of single-engine floatplanes, the two PBY units were consolidated under the command of Navy Captain Frank Wagner. His organization—which also included Langley, Heron (AVP-2), and two other tenders, Childs (AVP-14) and William B. Preston (AVP-20)—would be known as Patrol Wing Ten (PatWing-10).

The planes of PatWing-10 could maintain surveillance of shipping movements but offered only a rudimentary defense against Japanese invasion fleets. The flying boats would be unable to attack if enemy ships were covered by carrier-based fighters. For this reason, it was incumbent upon the army's Philippine Department to respond to any Japanese attack, if and when it came. Admiral Hart had requested assignment of a dive-bomber contingent, but navy and Marine land-based units were too few in number to be considered for deployment in the Philippines. Stationing aircraft carrier task forces west of Wake Island was far too risky; the flattops would have been vulnerable to surprise attack by superior Japanese forces at any time. In addition to that possibility, U.S. leaders feared that any buildup of capital ships in the western Pacific would be viewed in Tokyo as an aggressive move by the United States, provoking Japan into an immediate strike at the Philippines. There was precedent for that line of thinking: the presidential order relocating the majority of the U.S. Fleet to Pearl Harbor upon completion of its spring training exercise had already increased diplomatic tensions with the Japanese. Franklin Roosevelt was not anxious to prod the Japanese further, for the moment.

Even though an armed forces buildup was in progress throughout 1940, the United States still lacked virtually every military asset. Very few of the aircraft ordered for Army Air Corps expansion programs had actually been delivered to operational units. In fact, only about a dozen understrength army air groups—including the poorly equipped 4th Composite—were considered combat ready at the end of the year.

To consider the 4th Composite Group ready for battle was practically laughable. Just a trickle of Air Corps resources had made their way as far as the Philippine Islands since 1937. Most of those additions were liaison aircraft for the 2nd Observation Squadron. During all of 1940, only three well-worn Douglas B-18 Bolo bombers had been shipped to the 28th Squadron.[4] This was not much of an upgrade.

The B-18 was the standard first-line bombardment aircraft in U.S. Army service from 1936 through 1941. Its design was developed from the fabulously successful twin-engine DC-2 airliner introduced in 1933. Although the Douglas was supposed to deliver significantly improved performance over the B-10, the only category in which it really bested the Martin bomber was in its bomb-load capacity of up to sixty-five hundred pounds. Using essentially the same Wright Cyclone engines as in the B-10, though up-rated to 1,000 horsepower each, the B-18's top speed of 215 miles per hour was only 2 miles per hour faster than its predecessor. With its range of 1,200 miles and service ceiling of 23,900 feet, the B-18 actually had inferior capabilities compared to the older Martin.

The promise of renovation for the Philippine fighter defense got some traction in November 1940. Personnel of the 17th Pursuit from Selfridge Field, Michigan, and the 20th Pursuit from Hamilton Field, California, made the long sea voyage from San Francisco to Luzon. Aircraft to equip these units began to arrive at Manila near Christmastime from an unlikely source in the direction of the North Pole.

The air force of neutral Sweden had purchased 120 Republic EP-1-106 fighters in two blocks of 60 aircraft each. Due to a critical need for fighter aircraft, the Army Air Corps commandeered the second batch of planes from the assembly line in Farmingdale, New York. Almost all of these were shipped directly to Luzon, still equipped with Swedish instrumentation and national insignia. Ultimately, 57 of the repossessed fighters arrived in the Philippines.[5]

The EP-1-106 was an export version of the Seversky P-35 used by the Army Air Corps, specially tailored to Sweden's requirements. Its configuration was reclassified for U.S. service as a Seversky P-35A, though the manufacturer had already been renamed Republic Aircraft when Alexander de Seversky was ousted from the company board in 1939. P-35As were better-equipped fighters than the P-35s that the 17th Pursuit had flown at Selfridge Field. In fact, the P-35As were superior to the Curtiss P-36 fighters on duty with most squadrons on the mainland and Hawaii. The "A" had a 100-horsepower advantage over a standard P-35. Its top speed of 310 miles per hour was almost 10 percent faster than previous U.S. Army versions, and slightly better than that of the Curtiss. The Swedish model was also more heavily armed, with two .30-caliber machine guns in the nose and one .50-caliber in each wing. It is interesting to note that both the P-35A and Mitsubishi A6M2 had almost identical wing area and power loading. However, given the P-35A's poor aerodynamic drag characteristics and eight hundred pounds of additional weight, the Zero maintained significant advantages in terms of climb, turn rate, and maximum speed.

Uncompetitive designs and an inadequate inventory of fighter aircraft reflected the general military unpreparedness of the United States. Outside the realm of commercial aviation, U.S. airframe manufacturers were in a sorry state. By the end of December 1940, the Army Air Corps possessed only 210 radial-engine P-36 fighters and 200 inline-engine P-40s.[6] These Curtiss planes—which shared the same basic fuselage and wing—constituted the United States' total first-line army fighter strength. Newer, more advanced fighter designs—the Lockheed P-38 Lightning, Bell P-39 Airacobra, and Republic P-43 Lancer—were still undergoing service acceptance testing. Until the latter half of 1941, only the P-40 would be manufactured in quantity. Great Britain's pressing demand for fighters in its battle for Europe and the Mediterranean dictated that the vast majority of P-40 production output would be scheduled for purchase by the

America's Far East Air Force began a build-up of fighter planes on Luzon with fifty-seven Seversky P-35As repossessed from a Swedish order. The export Seversky was a significant improvement over P-35s in U.S. Army stateside service, but still no match for a Zero. Constant use without spare parts caused the fighters to wear out before the war began. This unarmed example is one of only three P-35As not sent to the Philippines. (Courtesy of Jaques Trempe, *1000aircraftphotos.com*)

RAF. The needs of the United States would have to take a back seat for the moment.

The combat readiness of U.S. Army fighter forces was appalling, but the situation with regard to bombers was nothing short of frightening. The primary U.S. bomber in use during 1940 was still the antiquated B-18, of which the Army Air Corps had procured 350 since 1936.[7] The Air Corps had only thirty-nine B-17B and eighteen B-17C four-engine bombers in operation—barely enough for one heavy bombardment group, but divided between two.[8] Only two medium bomber groups existed, and they were actively service-testing brand-new aircraft types. Similarly, there were only two light bombardment groups, also testing new equipment.[9]

Containing the threat posed by Japan would require creativity, boldness, bluff, and a little solid leverage. With this in mind, keeping China successfully engaged in battle with the Japanese was a very important agenda item for President Roosevelt. The 1940 decision to bolster defenses in the Philippines was, in part, linked to the idea of providing support for the Chinese. Maintaining a transpacific supply line to Asia was crucial.

On December 19, 1940, Roosevelt convened a meeting in the Oval Office with Secretary of State Cordell Hull, Secretary of the Treasury Henry Morgenthau, Secretary of War Henry Stimson, and Secretary of the Navy Frank Knox. This core group of advisers had been assembled to discuss an air support proposal delivered to Morgenthau by Claire Chennault. At the heart of their debate was a request from Chiang Kai-shek for five hundred aircraft to use in the direct bombardment of the Japanese homeland. Roosevelt was very keen on the idea, but the United States just did not have the resources in bombardment aircraft to comply.[10] Still, a pivotal seed had been planted. As a direct result of this dialogue, Chennault would be charged with creating the American Volunteer Group—eventually to become famous as the Flying Tigers. Indirectly, it would spawn the creation of a transworld route for delivery of bomber aircraft and would lead other air corps officers to focus on a new role for the Philippine Department.

In spite of obvious trouble brewing in the Pacific, the U.S. military establishment was primarily focused on the situation in Europe. Leaders in Washington hoped that supplying weapons of war to U.S. allies would be enough to sustain them in the battle with Germany, without the need to commit U.S. forces to the European front. If the United States ultimately could not avoid direct entry into the war, then an investment in equipment now might at least diminish any future efforts U.S. troops would have to expend in defeating the Axis. This was the theory behind the 1939 Cash and Carry Act and would be the guiding principle for the 1941 Lend-Lease Act, which affirmed the role of the United States as the "Arsenal of Democracy." It was a fine political line to walk. Finding a means to supply arms to a belligerent nation, while maintaining official neutrality, was no easy task. Fortunately, President Roosevelt's methods worked. Large aircraft purchases by France and the British Commonwealth did much to prod U.S. aircraft manufacturers to establish the production capacity necessary for wartime demand. Without the benefit of these orders, it is highly unlikely that the United States could have deployed any aircraft reinforcements to the Far East during 1941 or 1942.

Even with dramatically increased manufacturing activity, the flow of aviation supplies to the Philippines during the first few months of 1941 was hardly noticeable. Taking advantage of the fact that Manila was a waypoint for all military cargo in transit from the United States to the Far East, Admiral Hart expeditiously commandeered a shipment of ten North American A-27 light-attack bombers destined for Siam

(Thailand). The A-27 was a combat-equipped variant of the North American AT-6 advanced trainer, with a more powerful engine, three-bladed propeller, bomb racks, and five .30-caliber machine guns. The army air organization was unsure what to do with its windfall. Siamese-language instrumentation and other foreign-market equipment diminished the usefulness of these A-27s as combat aircraft, so they were parceled out as advanced trainers for flying skills practice.[11] The March 1941 shipment of eighteen more weary B-18s to the 28th Squadron was of greater significance than the "dive-bomber" seizure. These secondhand Douglas bombers, cast aside by the Hawaiian Department, were all the combat aircraft that could be spared.[12]

In the background, big plans were being drawn up. Cooperative U.S. and British strategizing on a hypothetical basis began behind the scenes almost as soon as the war in Europe commenced. However, it was not until March 27, 1941, that the first official, joint strategic doctrine was released to U.S. and British senior staffs. Generally known as ABC-I, it set forth guidelines for conduct of the war that would be followed quite closely when the United States became a combatant.

The Douglas B-18 Bolo was the most common bomber in U.S. Army squadrons at the end of 1941. The 28th Squadron in the Philippines retired its B-18s just before the outbreak of war; they were not utilized in combat roles, but performed valuable missions evacuating equipment and personnel from Luzon and Mindanao. (Courtesy of AFHRA)

Two of ten North American A-27 attack bombers at Nichols Field, Manila. Seized by the U.S. Navy from a shipment in transit to Siam (Thailand), these aircraft were assigned as "transition trainers" for instruction of fledgling Army fighter pilots. The type was very similar in configuration to the Commonwealth Wirraway, the Douglas A-24, and Japan's Mitsubishi Ki-51. (Courtesy of the National Museum of the U.S. Air Force)

The basic premise of ABC-I was a resolution to use all combined effort necessary to defeat Germany as a first priority. It specified collaboration in a massive bombardment offensive against German territory to destroy Axis fighting capacity and morale in advance of an actual Allied invasion of Europe. Under the plan, the British would command the campaign against Germany in the Mediterranean and North Africa. The Royal Navy would guarantee security of the eastern portion of the North Atlantic supply route and the vital link from the Middle East to Australia and Singapore. The U.S. Navy would be responsible for protecting the Western Hemisphere, including the Atlantic convoy route, as far as Iceland. Of course, the U.S. Navy would have to provide the primary defense against Japanese aggression in the Philippines, Hawaii, and the Pacific island stepping-stones to the Far East and Australia. U.S. sailors might also be called on to assist the Royal Navy at Singapore. ABC-I anticipated the United States' entry into the war with Germany sometime in 1942, and it assumed achievement of the First Aviation Objective—the fifty-four-group plan—by spring of that year.[13] ABC-I conveniently postulated that Japan would not commence hostilities against the Philippines, Malaya, or the East Indies until mid-1942, after the necessary Allied resources had been put in place.

The United States' participation in ABC-I drove some changes within the War Plans Division of the General Staff. A decision was made to formally adopt the RAINBOW No. 5 plan for U.S. mobilization and action. This most closely resembled the alliance situation outlined in the ABC-I accord. It would supersede the long-considered War Plan Orange as soon as hostilities commenced. RAINBOW Five specified a concentration of offensive power for use in the European theater and a strategic defense of the Pacific. In naval terms, this plan instructed Admiral Hart's Asiatic Fleet to fall back immediately to aid the British and Dutch navies in protection of the "Malay barrier" in the East Indies. The Pacific Fleet, under Admiral Husband Kimmel at Pearl Harbor, was instructed to protect the West Coast and Hawaii. Kimmel was also ordered to plan and execute hit-and-run attacks on Japanese Central Pacific bases, as practicable. An effort would be made to hold Wake Island as a base to facilitate these raids.

The planners predicted that a major offensive in the Pacific would not be possible for more than two years after war began, due to a critical lack of shipping capacity and a shortage of escort escorts. Under RAINBOW Five, it was absolutely clear that there would be no reinforcement of the Philippines by sea once the Japanese attacked. In contrast with the overly optimistic ABC-I calendar, the new strategy realistically acknowledged that U.S. mobilization for war with Germany or Japan could occur as soon as September 1941.

In readying the Philippines for the anticipated battle, a shortage of modern aircraft was only one of many critical deficiencies. Virtually no development of operational airfields for the 4th Composite Group had taken place since the start of the war in Europe. Any large influx of aircraft—fighters or bombers—would exacerbate a serious problem created by a lack of proper airfields, dispersal areas, service facilities, and trained personnel.

The only new air base was at Iba Field, located on Luzon's western coast between Manila Bay and the Lingayen Gulf. Because of its remote location, Iba was used primarily for gunnery training. It was an idyllic, tropical beachfront location, with gently swaying palms and a beautiful stretch of sandy shoreline. As a military base, however, it was hardly a paradise. Iba had almost nothing in the way of facilities. The most prominent feature was a large two-story wooden barracks next to the beach, associated with Iba's previous service as a training ground for the Philippine Constabulary. The pitching of tents provided accommodation for support activities. These canvas structures were stiflingly hot when the sun shone, or miserably damp and musty when it rained. Apart from the discomfort, conducting regular flight operations from Iba in wet weather could be hazardous. The small turf field had a tendency to pond during frequent heavy rains, and the only place to park aircraft was directly alongside the runway. Poor field conditions contributed to landing accidents. As pilot trainees continued to cycle through their instruction, Iba's bone-yard of broken planes grew. Once an aircraft was wrecked there, poor roads, a shortage of heavy truck transport, and minimal major maintenance capabilities at other bases guaranteed its carcass would remain at the remote field.

Dispersal would become a major headache for air force commanders as the number of aircraft increased. To store airplanes, commanders had little choice except to use Clark and Nichols Fields. Even the Philippine Air Depot at Nichols was of limited value. It had the only hard-surfaced runways in the Philippines but was located on landfill overlaying swampy ground that had once been a rice paddy. Nichols had little suitable space for spreading out dispersal areas. Naturally, the three bases belonging to the fledgling PAAC were also available to the 4th Composite Group: Zablan Field, to the immediate northeast of Manila; Cabanatuan, on the opposite side of Mount Arayat from Clark Field; and Batangas, fifty miles due south of Manila, on a large bay facing the Verde Island Passage. These PAAC airfields would not be of much use to the Americans because they were even less developed than the other bases and suffered from their own dispersal problems. There were civilian airstrips throughout the islands, but all shared a common trait of short, dirt or grass runways; they could be used for emergency landings and fuel service, but not much else.

In short, the Philippine air facilities were quite incapable of supporting any sizable air force, especially under combat conditions. None of the airfields had been properly equipped for major overhaul work, nor were any of them defensively prepared for wartime operations; there were no fixed antiaircraft guns and no air-raid shelters.

The 4th Composite Group was further handicapped by the inexperience of its pilots. A lack of proficiency in combat flying was pervasive, particularly within the ranks of the fighter squadrons. Many young pursuit pilots had been drawn directly from advanced flight classes and had little or no transition training in high-performance aircraft. Most had never even fired aircraft guns, let alone become skilled in air-to-air gunnery.

Because the rosters of the three pursuit squadrons were filled with new pilots, available flying time was dedicated to pilot checkouts in A-27s and P-26s. Once the new pilots amassed about twenty hours in local flying experience, their qualification exercises were expanded to include combat maneuvers and gunnery training in P-35s. Only .30-caliber nose guns were used for live firing because supplies of .50-caliber ammunition were critically low. The piloting skills improved, but this intensive regimen—conducted from primitive airfields under harsh, tropical weather conditions—quickly wore out the new aircraft. Because few replacement parts were available for any army planes in the Philippines, the combat readiness of the fighter units actually deteriorated within a very short period of time.

On Sunday, May 4, 1941, passengers on board Pan American's China Clipper were welcomed to Philippine airspace in an unusual manner. The large silver flying boat was swarmed by a flight of eighteen brightly painted, blue and yellow P-26As. The airliner was arriving at Manila with a new commander for the army air units in the Philippines, Brigadier General Henry Clagett. Tall, portly, and graying, regal in manner but for the constant presence of a cigar in his mouth, Clagett was an old-line army officer with a reputation for operating by the book. His chief of staff, Colonel Harold "Hal" George, was short, trim, dark-haired, intense, and direct, and as different from Clagett in outlook as he was in appearance. Older members of the 17th Pursuit Squadron would remember both men from Selfridge Field and the 1st Pursuit Group. These two pioneers of pursuit aviation would work vigorously to reshape the old 4th Composite Group into a larger Philippine Department Air Force that could finally provide adequate defense for Luzon. Together, they would face great challenges in getting a sleepy, backwater, peacetime organization prepared for round-the-clock wartime operations.

Before General Clagett could even settle into his new office, he was instructed to pay an immediate visit to Chiang Kai-shek in Chungking to negotiate for U.S. use of air bases on the Chinese mainland. Colonel George accompanied him. The trip was especially enlightening for the young colonel, who learned a great deal about the Chinese air defense system. He also had the opportunity to witness the employment of Japanese airpower on a firsthand basis. His "prizes" from the visit were a highly detailed five-by-twelve-foot map of all the airfields in the combat zone in China and an agreement from Chiang's government to construct several new bomber bases on the Chinese mainland.[14] Another seed had been planted.

The recently arrived Philippine Department Air Force commander and his chief of staff were not immediately missed. In fact, the pursuit squadrons were quite distracted. On the same day Clagett and George had left for China—May 17—a welcome cargo was off-loaded at the docks in Manila. Thirty-one brand-new, crated Curtiss P-40B fighters were delivered to the Philippine Air Depot.[15]

The P-40 was the United States' current first-line fighter aircraft, which most army pilots believed was superior to any plane the Japanese could field. With its twelve-cylinder, liquid-cooled Allison engine tucked into a streamlined, sharklike nose, the Tomahawk certainly appeared formidable. The "B" variant was armed with two .50-caliber machine guns in the fuselage and two .30-caliber guns in each wing. The P-40 had a better roll rate than the Mitsubishi Zero and could also outdive the Zero, and probably every other fighter in service at the time. In a dogfighting comparison, however, the high wing-loading of the almost two-thousand-pound heavier Curtiss seriously handicapped its turn radius and climb rate. The critical climb characteristic was only slightly better than two thousand feet per minute—less than half that of a Zero.

A P-40B had an impressive top speed of 360 miles per hour—noticeably faster than an A6M2 in level flight at low altitudes—but its pace dropped off dramatically at heights greater than fifteen thousand feet. Poor high-altitude performance was a direct result of the absence of either two-stage or turbo supercharging. To illustrate the P-40B's capabilities in a more useful context, an A6M2 could take off and climb to twenty thousand feet in less than seven and a half minutes, while the cortiss required almost thirteen minutes.[16]

The new Tomahawks inspired a great deal of excitement in the eager pursuit pilots of the Philippine Department Air Force, who were completely unaware of their handicap. Twenty-five of the P-40Bs were assigned to fully equip the 20th Squadron. The remaining aircraft were split equally between the 3rd and the 17th squadrons for familiarization flights.[17]

Initial enthusiasm about the new fighters dampened when pilots discovered that no Prestone coolant had been shipped with the planes. In a bureaucratic blunder, the supply organization had not seen fit to send any antifreeze to a tropical location, or it had been erroneously shipped to Panama. In either case, none of the P-40s could be flown until an expedited shipment of the critical fluid finally arrived in Manila two months later.[18]

Back in Washington, in conjunction with the tremendous growth planned for U.S. airpower, a new organization was formed to unify the training and materiel command of the Army Air Corps with the combat operations organization of GHQ Air Force. On June 20, 1941, the Army Air Forces was officially created under the leadership of Lieutenant General Henry "Hap" Arnold as Chief of the Army Air Forces, a position reporting directly to General George Marshall, the U.S. Army Chief of Staff.

Two days later, Nazi Germany turned eastward to attack its former ally, the Soviet Union. Following that action, the diplomatic process for dealing with Japan essentially derailed. The Japanese would no longer abide prolonged negotiations regarding their demands in the Far East. The opportunity to move south without fear that the Red Army would take advantage of a weakened position in Manchuria was too tempting. The only remaining obstacles standing in the way of Japan's master plan for Greater East Asia were the U.S. Navy at Pearl Harbor and the Allied air forces in the Philippines and Malaya.

Japan wasted little time. Eager to exploit the situation, the Japanese boldly occupied the southern half of pro-Axis, Vichy-French Indochina on July 25, 1941. Most knowledgeable observers anticipated Japan's next move would be a military occupation of neighboring Siam (Thailand). The Thai government tended to be pro-Japanese, so it was plausible that the country might easily submit to Japanese pressure. Japanese forces roaming freely in Siam would, of course, present a grave threat to Malaya. In addition to the immediate imposition of a refined oil product embargo against Japan, and the freezing of Japanese assets by Allied countries, Japan's sudden occupation of Indochina spawned many other changes in the Allied military posture for the Far East.

Expecting Japan to strike at any time, U.S., British, and Dutch armed forces stepped up to an alert status. In Manila, Douglas MacArthur was immediately recalled to active duty as a lieutenant general and placed in command of the United States Army Forces in the Far East (USAFFE). General Clagett's organization officially became the Air Force, USAFFE.

Halfway around the world, on board the HMS *Prince of Wales* and the USS *Augusta* in Placentia Bay near Argentia, Newfoundland, Franklin Roosevelt and Winston Churchill quietly engaged in a series of secret meetings between August 9 and August 11. For public consumption at the time, the primary product of these discussions was the Atlantic Charter agreement denouncing Nazism and pledging political cooperation in the destruction of Hitler's Germany. In spite of the Eurocentric window dressing, the first major conference topic was the matter of how to deal with Japan. Before the two leaders parted, the British agreed to defer delivery of a large number of heavy bombers allotted to them under Lend-Lease. The intent was to station all of these aircraft in the Philippines under General MacArthur's command to support a political deterrence strategy based on aerial bombardment capability.[19] This ploy represented a significant departure from the widely publicized "Germany first" philosophy.

The idea of a bombardment campaign conducted from air bases on Luzon was first formally suggested in a 1939 strategy brief that Lieutenant Colonel Carl Spaatz presented to General Arnold.[20] The report was released on September 1, the day Nazi Germany invaded Poland, and apparently was shelved until shortly before the Argentia Conference. The December 1940 proposal for a China-based bombardment campaign instigated by Chiang Kai-shek and Claire Chennault reawakened the Air Corps to the possibility of large-scale attacks on the infrastructure of the Japanese war machine. Most important was that President Roosevelt regarded the proposal favorably. Though Major General George Brett in communications to General Marshall endorsed the basic premise of that concept in February 1941, the timing was still poor.[21]

General Clagett's mission to China was the next pivotal step toward developing the concept of strategic deterrence through the use of bomber aircraft. Sometime between mid-June (when he received the report from Colonel George and General Clagett) and July 16, 1941, General Marshall came to the conclusion that the Philippines was defensible using an air force and that the island of Luzon could serve as the springboard for a strategic bombing campaign aimed directly at the Japanese homeland. Undoubtedly, Germany's sudden betrayal of Russia—embodied in the Operation Barbarossa campaign that began on June 22—was a factor in Marshall's decision.

The capabilities of U.S. four-engine bomber aircraft in 1941 dictated the need for staging bases in China or in Soviet territory near

Vladivostok.[22] Given that the Russians were now allies of the United States, such usage was finally plausible. If Premier Stalin would cooperate, the Allies could credibly threaten Japan with destruction from the air as retaliation to any future hostile movements. Perhaps Japan's militarists might actually be brought to heel without the need for a costly war in the Pacific. Of course, any viable alternative to the defeat preordained under War Plan Orange was worth a try.

General MacArthur learned of the basic concept on July 31.[23] Because General Clagett was away from Manila on a liaison mission to Singapore, MacArthur summoned Colonel George to USAFFE Headquarters to discuss air defense plans for the Philippines. The general wanted to submit his own requirements to Washington. Hal George had been ruminating over ideas since his trip to China, so it did not take him long to craft an ambitious plan analogous to similar activities taking place in the War Department.[24] George's proposal was the boldest yet. Although the plan unnerved General Clagett in its demands for resource, Douglas MacArthur endorsed it enthusiastically.

From the outset, the AAF had high expectations regarding the capability of its heavy bombardment aircraft. Bombardment's most vocal advocate, Brigadier General William "Billy" Mitchell, left an indelible impression on many air officers during the 1920s. By the late 1930s, his disciples were the men leading the army air services. In line with Mitchell's theories, the U.S. Army's emphasis on developing strategic bomber aircraft was pervasive, almost to the exclusion of all other aerial warfare tactics and equipment.

U.S. fighter aircraft of the period may have been second-rate, but the Boeing B-17 Flying Fortress epitomized the AAF's first-class concept of a strategic bomber. Boeing's Model 299 was a truly revolutionary leader in aviation technology. In all respects, the 299 greatly exceeded the army's specifications for a heavy bomber. At its rollout ceremony in Seattle, a local news reporter, Richard Williams, described it as resembling a "flying fortress" with "gun blisters everywhere you looked."[25] The description was so appropriate that the moniker stuck. Unfortunately, development of the Flying Fortress design was significantly delayed. The prototype B-17 crashed during testing at Wright Field, Ohio, in October 1935, killing the flight crew and, temporarily, Boeing's lucrative contract for sixty-five more planes.

Although the U.S. Army purchased a large quantity of the competing Douglas bombers, it never gave up on the Flying Fortress. New contracts were eventually let, and Boeing's design became the cornerstone of AAF bombardment operations. Persistence paid off. The B-17D models of 1941 were outstanding aircraft for their time. In size alone the plane was impressive by 1941 standards. Four nine-cylinder Wright Cyclone radial engines—each equipped with a turbo supercharger and capable of producing 1,000 horsepower at up to twenty-five thousand feet—could lift the giant Fortress, its crew of eight, and up to forty-eight hundred pounds of bombs to a height of thirty-seven thousand feet. At the same time, the B-17 was capable of missions in excess of a 1,000-mile radius—more than double the range for a Douglas B-18. Lighter and slimmer in the tail section than its successor models, the B-17D was actually the fastest version, with a maximum speed rating of 323 miles per hour at twenty-five thousand feet. At this altitude, it was nearly twice as fast as a Douglas bomber. In fact, this velocity was just slightly off the pace of a Mitsubishi Zero flying at the same altitude. It was fortunate that the B-17s were hard for a Zero to catch, because high-altitude fighter escort was out of the question. The newest model of Curtiss fighter, the P-40E, was not even rated for operation at twenty-five thousand feet and could barely manage 250 miles per hour at that height.[26]

Consistent with its name, the B-17D Flying Fortress was the most heavily armed aircraft in the AAF's prewar inventory. For beam defense, two .50-caliber machine guns were flexibly mounted in waist hatches on each side of the fuselage. Two more "fifties" were twin-mounted in a hatch above the radio compartment, aft of the wing, providing protection from above and rearward. The final two .50-caliber weapons were dual-mounted in a tub underneath the waist positions. These had a somewhat limited field of fire below and aft of the plane. Still, the Fortress had two defensive shortcomings: there was no tail gun for coverage directly behind the bomber, and the front of the aircraft was largely unguarded. In the nose, a single hand-held .30-caliber gun could be mounted in any one of six "pivot-ball" fittings in the Plexiglas panels. This forward gun had a good field of fire but could not provide much hitting power.

High-altitude, heavy bombardment was unquestionably the driving factor in the AAF's strategy. Dive-bombing was barely an afterthought. Although "attack aviation" had been a part of the air services since World War I, and the dive-bomber had been included in the navy arsenal since its inception, the army never gave this type of aircraft much consideration. Not until the Germans, using the Junkers Ju-87 Stuka during the sweeping blitzkrieg of 1939–40, provided an awesome demonstration of its value did the U.S. Army awaken to the possibilities of dive-bombing. If anyone had paid equal attention to the air war in China, Japan's compelling example of dive-bomber employment might have convinced U.S. generals to seriously evaluate the type two years earlier. By the time General Marshall finally encouraged General Arnold to add dive-bombers to the AAF's inventory, there was no time left for the army to develop an aircraft of its own specification.

Initially, the Army Air Forces wanted to procure the new Curtiss SB2C Helldiver, but found that its development had slipped well behind schedule. Desperate to gain experience with dive-bombing, General Arnold persuaded the navy to divert seventy-eight Douglas SBD-3 Dauntless bombers from its production backlog. This model was powered by a nine-cylinder, 1,000-horsepower Wright Cyclone. Capable of a top speed of 250 miles per hour while carrying a thousand-pound bomb, the Dauntless normally cruised at a more leisurely 150 miles per hour, which allowed for a maximum mission range of nearly 1,200 miles. With its distinctive perforated dive flaps split open, the two-seat bomber could plunge at a frighteningly steep 70-degree angle. The rugged plane could place its load with pinpoint accuracy, even on a moving target, a characteristic that would eventually earn SBDs the nickname of "Slow But Deadly." Though slow, it was highly maneuverable. In the hands of a skilled pilot, the Dauntless and its two .50-caliber cowl-mounted machine guns could prove fatal to enemy fighters that attacked carelessly. The single, flexibly mounted .30-caliber machine gun in the rear cockpit was considerably less useful but occasionally found its mark.

Given the army's lack of focus on the type, it is more than a little ironic that dive-bombing equipment was the one category in which a comparable aircraft in the U.S. lineup actually exceeded the performance of its Japanese counterpart.

Designated as A-24 Banshees, the first army Dauntless dive-bombers were allotted to the 27th Bombardment Group (Light) at Hunter Field, Georgia. Colonel George had the foresight to recognize the value of these potential ship-killers in General MacArthur's plan to defend the Philippines at the beaches. Fifty-two dive-bombers promised under the new presidential commitment to a Philippine defense were to be used to equip the 27th Group when it reached Luzon.

Adoption of the plan to defend the Philippines using a large bomber force meant that Colonel George would have to address the inherent vulnerability of existing Philippine bases. With the help of his engineering officer, Captain Harold Eads, Colonel George immediately set out to expand the number of runways available for regular operations. The two officers established an accelerated development plan for airfields throughout the island chain. Unfortunately, they were hamstrung by a painfully slow land-acquisition process and the availability of only one underresourced Aviation Engineer battalion. By midsummer, just two new projects had been started: one, a turf field at Rosales, fifty miles north of Clark Field; the other, a dirt strip fifteen miles south of Clark, at Del Carmen. In spite of George's persistence, only Del Carmen would be in active use before the Japanese attacked.

After the Argentia Conference, War Department planners elevated USAFFE priority for aircraft to the highest possible level. In fact, the new Philippine defense plan was allotted almost the entire production output of four-engine bombers to be manufactured in the United States through March 1942. The resources committed were impressive: four heavy bombardment groups to form the striking force, one light bombardment group to provide defense against an invasion of the Philippines, and at least six more pursuit squadrons for base protection. This amounted to a transpacific deployment of 165 B-17 bombers, 52 dive-bombers, and 130 additional first-line fighters. All of these planes were to be delivered to Manila before the spring of 1942.[27] This was a large quantity of aircraft, but still far less than either the War Department or Colonel George had specified as being necessary for the task.

Anticipating the receipt of large shipments of aircraft and pilots, General Clagett made a number of staff changes to build the resources of his air force headquarters and the "Interceptor Command." Senior leaders from existing squadrons were reassigned to staff duties in the new air organization, eventually leaving all three pursuit units under the command of first lieutenants instead of majors—the customary squadron commander rank.

Dive-bombers and fighters could be easily crated, shipped across the Pacific, and reassembled. Heavy bombers would have to cover the great ocean distance under their own power. Highly experienced aviators had flown unarmed B-17s from San Francisco to Honolulu successfully in May 1941, but flying large numbers of combat-ready four-engine bombers from Hawaii to Luzon using green aircrews was an unprecedented challenge. If this could be done without significant aircraft attrition, the strategic deterrence scheme for the Air Force, USAFFE, would receive its final blessing from General Arnold.

To test the concept of overseas delivery, nine B-17C and D models of the 14th Bombardment Squadron (Heavy) departed from Hawaii on September 5. Led by Major Emmett "Rosie" O'Donnell Jr., the Fortresses crossed the Central Pacific along a 7,100-mile route to Manila from Honolulu. Using hastily constructed navy airstrips at Midway and Wake Island, and Royal Australian Air Force (RAAF) bases at Port Moresby, in Papua New Guinea, and at Darwin, in Australia's Northern Territory, this record-breaking flight was conducted in strict secrecy. The longest stretch of the journey—2,078 miles from Wake to Port Moresby—overflew the Japanese island base on Ponape, in the Carolines. Two planes had difficulty on this leg of the flight to the Far East: Captain William Fisher suffered an oil line rupture shortly after his takeoff from Wake Island and had to return for repairs, and Lieutenant Edward "Ed" Teats had engine trouble but continued to his destination. While the other eight planes crossed above the Carolines in darkness, as planned, Fisher's craft was forced to fly over Japanese territory in broad daylight. All nine B-17s landed safely at Clark Field on September 12, but only eight remained in serviceable condition. Landing during a severe rainstorm, one of the planes had its tail section severely damaged in a ground-based accident.[28]

In spite of the small mishap on Luzon, Major O'Donnell and his men successfully demonstrated that bomber forces in the Philippines could be quickly reinforced across the long ferry route to Manila. The War Department was now ready to bet heavily on General MacArthur and the plan to restrain Japan using bombers as a strategic deterrent. MacArthur would receive the rest of his bombers as quickly as the factories could build them and the Army Air Forces could man them. Strategic deterrence was a gamble—a long shot at that—but it was really the only hand the United States could play against Japan in the fall of 1941.

Unfortunately, without properly camouflaged dispersal areas, the gleaming silver flagships of the Army Air Forces seemed more like inviting targets than a strong arm supporting political strategy. The natural metal finish reflected the bright tropical sunlight, making the B-17s visible from miles away.[29] Observed from the skies, the parked bombers were like beacons pinpointing the location of Clark Field. Though these shiny planes added to Colonel George's dispersal problems, the very presence of such powerful weapons was a great morale

A Boeing B-17D Flying Fortress of the 14th Bomb Squadron on the RAAF airstrip at Darwin, Australia. This was one of the first nine B-17s to fly from Hawaii to Clark Field during September of 1941. American four-engine bombers in the Philippines were expected to act as a strategic deterrent to Japanese aggression in the Far East. (Charles Eaton Collection, courtesy of Aviation Heritage Museum, Western Australia)

booster to soldiers in the Philippines. Everyone had high hopes for what the Flying Fortresses might accomplish if the Japanese decided to start a war.

Protecting the precious B-17s would require more than a coat of camouflage paint and parking shelters. Fighter cover for the airfields was the primary problem to address. On September 16, General MacArthur issued an order activating the 24th Pursuit Group, which would be constituted from the existing 3rd, 17th, and 20th squadrons. General Clagett selected Major Orrin Grover—originally transferred to the Philippines as leader of the 20th Squadron—to be the group commander. This new group was intended to anchor a completely new fighter force that would soon include the 35th Pursuit Group from Hamilton Field, California. Henry Clagett, whose entire career was in pursuit aviation, would preside over this Interceptor Command. A higher-ranking officer, with broader management capabilities, would be needed to run MacArthur's expanded air force, but Clagett's organization would be the hub of activity for several months.

On September 29, the Philippine Air Depot received its first shipment of fifty Curtiss P-40E Warhawk fighters.[30] This new version of the P-40 incorporated many changes. Range could be increased through attachment of a fifty-two-gallon droppable fuel tank. The cockpit canopy was revised for better pilot visibility, and more armor protection was provided. In addition, the engine was more powerful. The change in engines was noticeable externally: the radiator and oil coolers were enlarged, giving the traditional "shark" nose a pronounced chin. Firepower was greatly increased, with six .50-caliber machine guns located in the wings. Any aircraft that crossed the cone of bullets from those heavy guns would be shredded in short order. The drawbacks of the "E" were less obvious. Much to the dismay of 24th Group pilots, the nine-hundred-pound weight gain from the new equipment offset any performance improvement over a P-40B. Gross weight was now more than one and a half times that of the feather-weight A6M2. With the extra mass of heavy guns and ammunition in the wings, the roll rate of the "E" also suffered considerably, further reducing the P-40's already lackluster turning performance. One on one, it was no match for a Mitsubishi Zero. However, additional weight allowed the Curtiss to dive even faster than its older siblings.

If a P-40 pilot was smart—choosing a steep dive as his evasive maneuver—he could almost guarantee his survival in an escape from a Japanese fighter. Following an aggressive dogfighter's instinctive choice of turning or climbing would likely prove fatal. Proper tactical use of the aircraft was a lesson the United States would have to learn the hard way.

With some rejoicing, the arrival of the new Curtiss fighters allowed the 24th Pursuit Group to retire its overworked Severskys to second-line use. The 3rd and 17th squadrons would split the quantity of new "Es." The 20th Squadron would retain its P-40Bs and absorb the rest of the "Bs" that the other squadrons had used for aircraft familiarization—or pilot recreation.

The influx of new fighter and bomber aircraft from the United States allowed the army to pare some of its long-serving, obsolete planes from the inventory. In a windfall of sorts, the PAAC gratefully accepted these aircraft. It did not matter so much to the Filipino pilots that the cast-off Peashooters or Martins had seen better days; the men were happy enough to finally be flying monoplanes. Their newly formed air force was largely engaged in basic training using a variety of biplanes, so some combat capability was better than none. Most remaining P-26s were handed over to the fledgling 6th Pursuit Squadron of the PAAC, while the 28th Bombardment gifted its last airworthy B-10s to the 10th Bombing Squadron. The only modern

The Curtiss P-40E Warhawk was United States' first-line fighter at the end of 1941. It had limited combat capabilities at high altitude and could not compete in dogfights with Mitsubishi Zeros. Young Army pilots in the Far East had to learn by trial-and-error how to use the P-40 effectively. Planes in this picture reached Australia after the air battle for the Philippines was over, but are identical to those flown by the 24th Pursuit Group. (Courtesy of Australian War Memorial)

aircraft belonging to the PAAC—the only aircraft independently acquired—were two Beechcraft Model 18s that high-ranking staff officers used as executive transports.[31]

On October 16, 1941, the first of twenty-six additional B-17s from the 30th and 93rd Bombardment Squadrons of the 19th Bomb Group (Heavy) took wing at Hamilton Field and headed west toward Hawaii. This flight was not flown in a mass formation. Each Fortress was to proceed separately toward Manila at its own best-possible rate. In part, this was because the airfield at Wake Island could handle only nine of the large Flying Fortresses at a time. The one remaining squadron from the group, the 38th Reconnaissance, stayed in Albuquerque, New Mexico, until its ranks could be filled with new aircraft and crews.

By October 31, all the 19th Group Fortresses in transit to the Philippines had traveled at least as far as Wake Island. At Wake, some of the bomber crews crossed paths with their future leader, Major

General Lewis Brereton. The general was traveling on the Pan-Am route to Manila to assume command of the Air Force, USAFFE, which would become known officially as the Far East Air Force (FEAF). Arriving in the Philippines on November 3, he would actually land on Luzon ahead of most of the army fliers he met at Wake. With no airfield available on Guam, the army planes had to take a different route from that of the Pan-Am seaplane. The B-17s would fly more than triple the distance covered by the civilian clipper before reaching their new home at Clark Field.

Lewis Brereton had been personally selected by General Arnold to command MacArthur's air force in the Philippines. Brereton had an unusual background for an army general. Transferring to the army upon his graduation from the U.S. Naval Academy, he had begun his service in a manner quite different than most officers. Though he served on General Mitchell's aviation staff in France during the Great War, and had been the commander of the Air Service's 12th Aero Squadron and the Corps Observation Wing during their training period at the front, General Brereton was not a traditional combat leader. He was chosen to command the FEAF because he was exceptionally skilled in setting up logistics, maintenance, and training operations.

Preparing Luzon and the other Philippine islands for a large influx of aircraft was a monumental task. Arnold was certain that Brereton was equal to it, if only he had enough time. Lewis Brereton was fairly sure time had run out. He had great personal reservations about placing a large number of valuable bombers under the noses of the Japanese. In fact, Brereton doubted that the concept of strategic deterrence would sway Japan from its course toward war. Having reluctantly left Washington with a revised copy of RAINBOW Five in hand for delivery to General MacArthur, Brereton was acutely aware that the last grains of sand were about to fall through the neck of the hourglass.

The 19th Group's transpacific journey was considerably more difficult than General Brereton's trip on the luxurious Pan-Am flying boat. The long flight through Australian territory was not as trouble-free as the earlier passage by the 14th Squadron. Severe weather over the Caroline Islands may have helped shield the B-17s from Japanese eyes, but it significantly raised fuel consumption. Three of the planes—those piloted by Major Birrell "Mike" Walsh and 1st Lieutenant Walter Ford and 1st Lieutenant Sam Maddux Jr.—ran so low on gas that they were forced to land at Rabaul, New Britain. The

RAAF detachment at Vunakanau airfield had been prepared to refuel the Flying Fortresses, but the runway was not really suitable for use by such heavy aircraft. All three B-17s bogged down in the soggy grass and had to be dug out from the mud before they could depart. These were not the only planes to have trouble. On the flight segment from Port Moresby to Darwin, Captain William McDonald's B-17 developed mechanical difficulties: two engines failed and had to be shut down. McDonald continued to Australia on the remaining two engines without additional drama, but two propellers were destroyed when his heavy aircraft broke through the thin surface of the RAAF field at Darwin.[32] The crew was stranded there for two weeks but finally got their plane to Luzon on the afternoon of November 20, more than a month after leaving California.

Captain McDonald had no way of knowing when he set his Fortress down at Clark Field that it would be the last bomber delivered to the Philippines before the war began. Still, his crew did not quite have the distinction of being the last Army Air Forces personnel to arrive in the Far East. On the same day they landed at Clark, the troop transport *President Coolidge* docked in Manila. This former luxury liner carried most personnel of the 27th Bombardment Group, twenty-eight pilots from an advance echelon of the 35th Pursuit Group's 21st and 34th Pursuit Squadrons, and the 5th Air Base Group.

In the absence of their parent headquarters organization, the fighter pilots were temporarily assigned to the 24th Pursuit Group. The thirteen pilots of the 21st Squadron were to receive brand-new P-40Es from a shipment of twenty-four that would be delivered the following week, but the fifteen pilots of the 34th Pursuit were assigned cast-off P-35As from the other squadrons.[33] The men of that squadron would complain vociferously about this misfortune, but they were still in better shape than their peers in the planeless 27th Bombardment Group.

The men of the FEAF would soon face the grim reality of the United States' ill-preparedness for war. With the buildup of U.S. aircraft in the Philippines barely under way at the time of the Japanese attack, General Brereton's command was equipped with only 116 serviceable fighters (less than half its minimum required pursuit strength), only 34 operational B-17s (about 15 percent of the planned bomber force), and none of the critically needed dive-bombers.[34]

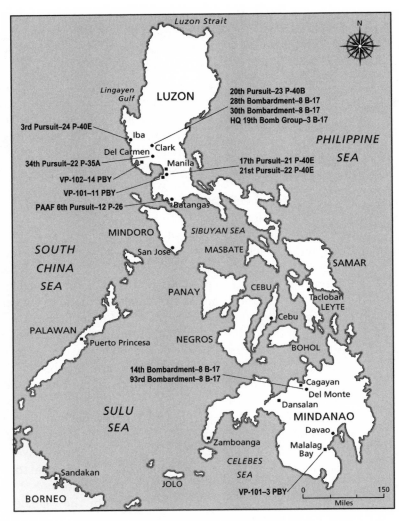

American and Philippine Combat Air Units in the Philippines; December 7, 1941.

CHAPTER 3

Marching to War

Preparations in Australia and Singapore

THE ISLAND CONTINENT OF AUSTRALIA has a shoreline about twenty-three thousand miles long, a total distance almost as great as the circumference of Earth itself. At the same time, Australia has the lowest population density of any country in the world. Even though the majority of Australians reside near the sea, large sections of the coast remain uninhabited. This expansive perimeter, with its many undeveloped areas, is difficult for Australia's relatively small land forces to patrol or defend.

Until World War I, the strategy for securing Australia was straightforward: the first line of defense was necessarily the Royal Australian Navy, charged with intercepting and destroying enemy invasion forces while they were still at sea. In spite of shouldering such a heavy burden, that service was a small entity. Fortunately, as a dominion of the British Commonwealth, Australia could expect some assistance from Great Britain's Royal Navy to counter any potential seaborne threat. With this safety net in place, most Australians believed their continent was reasonably secure. By the close of World War I, the only naval powers capable of seriously threatening Australian territory were those of Japan and the United States, both staunch allies of Great Britain and Australia at the time.

In reparation agreements at the close of the First World War, Australia was delegated custodianship of former German territories in the South Pacific. North Eastern New Guinea, the Admiralty Island Archipelago, and the islands of Bougainville, New Britain, New Ireland, Nauru, and German Samoa all fell under Australian control.

55

As a result, unforeseen military challenges arose for Australia. The Treaty of Versailles forbade fortification of these widely spread possessions, so providing adequate protection for the far-flung islands could easily press the already lean Australian forces beyond their breaking point. Still, Australia could not ignore the defense of these islands. For example, New Guinea, in the hands of a hostile nation, could be used as a springboard for direct attacks on the vital eastern coast of Australia. Enemy bases in the Solomon Islands could be used to disrupt the important trade route to the Americas.

At the same time, if the Royal Australian Navy could develop its ability to sustain maritime reconnaissance operations from the Mandated Territories, Australia would finally have some barrier against a sudden attack from the east. Several protected anchorages in the Mandates were selected for use by the Royal Australian Navy: Simpson Harbor, at Rabaul, on the eastern tip of New Britain; Kavieng, on the northern point of New Ireland; Buin, at the southern end of Bougainville, in the northern Solomons; Tulagi, in the southern Solomons; Lae, on the Huon Gulf of North Eastern New Guinea; and Manus, in the Admiralty Islands, to the north of New Britain. Of these sites, Rabaul was the most valuable, but also one of the most difficult to defend. Consequently, maintaining Simpson Harbor became a significant consideration in the war-planning process for Australia and Great Britain. U.S. and Japanese military strategists also recognized the importance of this port location. Both the United States and Japan developed operational plans to capture and use Rabaul in the event of a war in the Pacific. This represented the investment of an incredible amount of attention in such a remote portion of the southwestern Pacific, but harbors were the necessary focus of a battle between sea powers.

Within the Australian government there was an early and healthy appreciation for the importance of aviation in its defense strategy. Although the Australian Flying Corps participated in the Great War, it did so only as an expeditionary force of four squadrons that were disbanded soon after the armistice. In January 1920, the Australian Cabinet formed an Air Board to provide recommendations for creation of a permanent air service.

Prophetically, the new Air Plan assumptions included the following prediction: "Japan might consider that, if opportunity offered, and particularly if the attention of the British was occupied in other parts, she could obtain her wishes without too great a commitment other than that of her naval forces."[1]

The prime minister, William Hughes, in declaring his support for the establishment of an air force during a September 1920 speech to the Australian House of Representatives, stated: "It is on the sea that our destiny lies and it is on the sea that we must uphold our freedom. The air, that new element which man has now conquered, is but the sea in another form and it is on the sea and in the air that we shall have to look for our defence. We believe that in the air we may hope to create a force which will be of incomparable service in defending us against an enemy."[2]

Although commerce with Japan was important to Australia, the Australian government did not underestimate the ambitions of the Japanese, or their willingness to use force to achieve political and economic objectives. Unlike the British and the Americans, the Australians seem to have had few illusions regarding Japan's military aviation capability and the quality of Japanese aviators. Such understanding is evident in the following excerpt from a June 1923 speech in the Australian House of Representatives by Mr. W. M. Marks, a former officer in the Royal Navy, and recent guest of the IJN:

> If Japan should be considered the potential enemy of Australia, as certain sections of our Press would have us believe, then there is nothing to prevent her . . . from sending the *Akagi* or the *Hosho*, or both, accompanied by her battle-flagship *Nagato*, to Australia, and if she does, who is going to stop her from hauling down our flag? These aeroplanes could fly over Sydney Heads from 100 miles away and Australia would be taken. . . . The Naval Air Force of Japan has been organised by the Master of Sempill, the great British airman, and a number of aviators who distinguished themselves during the war. I find that there is no foundation whatever for the opinion expressed . . . that the Japanese have no "air" or "engine" sense. The Japanese are not inferior to Australians or British—they can fly all right.[3]

Unfortunately, awareness alone could not prepare Australia for the eventuality of war with Japan. Australia's ability to implement any adequate air force plan was highly constrained, both by a lack of local funds and through political commitments dictated by the Commonwealth government structure. For more than a dozen years, the Australian government engaged in rigorous debate with British officials in London regarding the extent and nature of Australia's participation in both local defense and defense of the British Empire as a whole. During this period, Britain's strategy for the Far East came to revolve around a single linchpin: an impregnable fortress base at Singapore. The British asserted that Singapore was their most critical position in the Far East. They stubbornly maintained that this island city-state at the southern tip of the Malay Peninsula was absolutely vital in supporting any projection of military force in the Far East. As such, Singapore came to have a significance similar to that of the fortress at Gibraltar in the Mediterranean.

The idea of a "Gibraltar of the East" was alluring. Unlike Luzon, the island of Singapore was small enough to defend successfully against a seaborne invasion, without the need for a large army. At the same time, the Johore Strait, between Singapore and Malaya itself, could harbor as many naval units as desired. Singapore's location allowed for the immediate protection of Malaya and was close enough to provide relief support for Hong Kong, the British gateway to China. It was also about midway along the critical shipping route between Australia and India. Lastly, Singapore had been exempted from the treaty bans on fortification that affected all other desirable locations in the Pacific and Far East. In treaty discussions, it had been agreed that a fortress base at Singapore was too far away from Japan and the key ports of China to pose a military threat to the Japanese. On this pretext, Great Britain embarked on the type of stronghold-based strategic plan for Singapore that the United States had just abandoned for Manila Bay.

In spite of Great Britain's numerous pledges of security assistance, many Australians had less than full confidence in the concept of defending their country using British forces based in Singapore. As an example, John Curtin—the leading member of the Australian House of Representatives who would later become prime minister— made the following comment summarizing this view: "How can Singapore be so far away from the Yellow Sea as not to be able to hurt it and be a thousand miles farther away from Sydney and yet be able to protect it?"[4]

Inevitably, Australia's defense would have to be contained within the umbrella of the British forces at Singapore. Under this plan, the RAAF would be forced to operate under the shadow of RAF units stationed on Singapore Island. In the event of armed conflict in the Far East, it was generally accepted that Britain would provide aircraft and operating organizations for any forces stationed outside the Australian continent, although it was likely that Australia would be compelled to provide aircrews to augment the strength of these RAF units.

In preparation for the anticipated war in Europe, the RAF was absorbing all the aircraft that Great Britain's industrial base could manufacture. To alleviate expected shortfalls in British production, it was agreed in early 1936 that Australia should develop its own aircraft industry to support the local needs of the RAAF and the growing Australian civil transport services. On October 17, 1936, a consortium of Australian businesses founded Commonwealth Aircraft Corporation (CAC) in Melbourne, with the intent that the new company would license-build aircraft already developed in either Great Britain or the United States. Optimistically, CAC's backers expected that the firm could soon provide additional fabrication capacity to augment British airframe production.

The first design chosen for assembly by CAC was a variant of the North American NA-33. This was a tandem-cockpit, single-engine, low-wing monoplane derived from the U.S. Army Air Corps BC-1 (a predecessor of the well-known AT-6 trainer family). As an airframe on which to base an important general-purpose combat aircraft for the RAAF, the choice was necessarily a compromise. CAC wanted to cut its teeth on a relatively simple airframe, and the NA-33 design was very straightforward in terms of manufacturability. It also utilized the proven Pratt & Whitney Wasp radial engine, which was readily available for license manufacture in Australia. The Australian-modified version, called the Wirraway—an aboriginal word meaning "challenge"—was officially designated as a CA-1. It included the unique features of a three-bladed, variable-pitch propeller, two .303-caliber fixed machine guns in the upper fuselage cowling, a flexibly mounted .303-caliber machine gun in the rear cockpit, and bomb racks. It was similar in concept to the A-27, but less powerful.

Whatever shortcomings the Wirraway may have had in its role as a tactical combat aircraft, they were slight in comparison to the RAAF's deficiency in maritime reconnaissance aircraft. During 1938 the standard Australian land-based reconnaissance bomber was the Avro Anson Mk I. This twin-engine craft was designed as a light-transport navigation and gunnery trainer, but it was pressed into service as a reconnaissance bomber for both the RAAF and the RAF Coastal Command. The Anson's range of 790 miles was only slightly better than that of the Wirraway, and its maximum speed was only 188 miles per hour. On the positive side, it did offer the added reliability of two engines, but it is doubtful that any airman would have preferred taking an Anson into combat. As a crew trainer, the Anson performed admirably. As a protector of the vast Australian coastline, it was woefully inadequate.

Following the lead of the British Purchasing Commission, the RAAF decided to base its new patrol bomber specification on the twin-engine Lockheed Hudson. The Hudson—a rapidly developed evolution of the popular civilian Electra airliner and transport—was a vast improvement over the Anson. In fact, it epitomized the original RAAF concept for an airframe that could take on dual roles of civilian and military service. The Australian Mk I and Mk IV versions, which were ordered with fourteen-cylinder Pratt & Whitney Twin-Wasp engines—rather than the original nine-cylinder Wright Cyclones—provided strong performance. Top speed was in excess of 260 miles per hour, service ceiling was almost twenty-five thousand feet, and range was an impressive 2,160 miles, even with one thousand pounds of bombs or depth charges. Armament was adequate, with up to seven .303-caliber machine-gun mounts available; however, most unmodified RAAF Hudsons would field only four: two in the dorsal turret and two fixed in the nose. In November 1938, Australia placed fifty Hudsons on order directly from Lockheed's drawing board. The RAAF would procure these U.S. planes until the Bristol Beaufort bomber—specifically designed for maritime reconnaissance and torpedo attack—was fully developed and could be produced in Australia.

For longer-range reconnaissance, the RAAF planned to equip its No. 10 Squadron with new, four-engine Short Sunderland flying boats. The Sunderland was a militarized development of the Short Empire flying boats in service with Britain's Imperial Airways and Australia's Qantas Empire Airways. With up to a 3,300-mile range, these would be excellent aircraft for patrolling the vast ocean distances between the Mandated Territories.

In spite of all its extensive planning, when war finally began in Europe on September 1, 1939, the RAAF had yet to realize much actual expansion. None of the Sunderlands had been transferred from the British Isles to Australia, and only half the roster of No. 10 Squadron crews had been sent to England for training with the new flying boats.

War in Europe disrupted fulfillment of most foreign orders for military aircraft that had been placed with U.S. manufacturers. Getting around the limitations of a long-standing series of neutrality acts preventing the sale of U.S. arms to belligerent nations would require six months of political maneuvering by the Roosevelt administration. An initial step was taken in November 1939, when the United States suspended some of its isolationist legislation in favor of a "Cash and Carry" plan that allowed sales on a direct-purchase basis for noncritical armaments—that is, those that U.S. forces did not immediately need. Virtually every aircraft that France and the British Commonwealth wanted fell outside this niche, including the desperately needed Hudsons. In March 1940, the plan was modified to allow sales of specified U.S. military aircraft types, including most of those in first-line service. Almost immediately after this new rule was established, Australia received delivery of its original order for fifty Hudsons, as well as a second order for fifty more. In addition to those Lockheeds, seven Consolidated Catalina flying boats were ordered to re-equip No. 11 Squadron for reconnaissance operations in the Southwest Pacific. It was unlikely that any Sunderlands would be forthcoming from England.

Italy's declaration of war on the British Empire on June 10, 1940, and the collapse of France less than two weeks later, placed Great Britain and its Commonwealth in a desperate position. In one stroke, the primary air and shipping route through the Mediterranean and Suez Canal to Australia was severed. Supplies from the United Kingdom destined for the Far East would have to travel more than twice as far, through sea-lanes infested with German U-boats and merchant raiders. Worse yet, the British—having to battle alone against the combined might of Germany and Italy—would be unable to provide adequate materiel or manpower to support their bastion at Singapore. The Royal Navy, so critical to the Far East defensive strategy, could not afford to deploy any capital assets to Singapore. It would be stretched to its limit protecting the vital North Atlantic trade routes to the Americas and West Africa.

Faced with the new reality of limited naval investment, the British Far East Command would have to rely on air forces to shield its Asian holdings. For this, Great Britain had little choice but to enlist the aid of its Commonwealth. Suddenly, Australia not only found itself responsible for its own defense but also was compelled to shoulder much of the burden for protecting Singapore and Malaya. The situation was even worse than the most pessimistic Australian planners and legislators had predicted during the 1920s.

With some reluctance, the Australians followed through on the request to support Singapore. Though they could hardly be spared at home, on June 30, 1940, the first flights of two new RAAF Hudson squadrons, No. 1 and No. 8, began winging their way north from

Darwin, across the Netherlands East Indies, and toward Sembawang airfield on the island of Singapore. While the new Hudsons were just being broken in, their crews were among Australia's most experienced military fliers.

When Japan moved forces into Vichy French–controlled Indochina and concluded the Tripartite Pact in September 1940, it became clear that Great Britain would have to prepare a response to counter Japan's southward movement. Japanese activity and several bold antishipping strikes by German merchant raiders convinced the RAAF to make its first deployment to Papua New Guinea on September 25, 1940. Two Qantas Empire flying boats, the *Centaurus* and *Calypso*, were impressed into reconnaissance service with No. 11 Squadron. Under the command of Flight Lieutenant James Alexander, this pair of former airliners would operate from Port Moresby, on the

American-built Lockheed Hudsons were used extensively in British and Australian service as maritime reconnaissance bombers. Hudsons from RAAF No.1 Squadron are seen flying over Singapore Island in the company of a No. 21 Squadron Wirraway (GA-B) in the fall of 1941. These planes staged the only successful aerial repulse of a Japanese invasion fleet, forcing Japanese army transports away from the beachhead at Kota Bharu, Malaya, before the ships could complete the assigned landing operation. (Courtesy of Australian War Memorial)

southern coast of the island. They would be the only patrol and air-transport force in the Mandated Territories for more than a year.

On October 22 in Singapore, a conference of British and Commonwealth armed forces leaders set out to develop an honest appraisal of their readiness to defend against a full-scale Japanese attack in the Far East. After ten days of deliberation, the delegates to the Singapore Conference came to the same conclusion that the Australian government had made years earlier: without Royal Navy protection, the fortress at Singapore was useless. The delegation's assessment was, at the very least, sobering.

The political posture of Siam (Thailand), though officially neutral, could readily be swayed to favor Japan—especially if the Japanese threatened occupation, as they had with French Indochina. Without the physical barrier of a neutral Siam, Japanese troops might easily sweep into northern Malaya. Once entrenched in Malaya with local air support, the Japanese army would be almost impossible to contain, particularly if the Royal Navy was not available to interdict their supply routes from Indochina across the Gulf of Siam. Should the entire Malay Peninsula be lost, then Singapore itself would be virtually defenseless, except by air. Ironically, as a political gesture of respect to the sultan of Johore, Singapore's heavy gun batteries were emplaced so that they could not be fired across the Johore Strait against Malaya. Without adequate naval forces to defend the straits, Singapore would be open to an invasion of its northern shore. In addition, Japanese aircraft carriers could roam freely in the South China Sea, exposing Singapore to the constant threat of air attack. Unless a strong air force could be deployed there, Singapore could hold out against invasion for only a very short time. Once the British fortress was lost, the IJN could steam through the East Indies at will, flooding the area with Japanese troops up to the shores of Australia itself.

Aside from the fact that the loss of Singapore would open the entire Southwest Pacific and East Indies area to Japanese aggression, it could have potentially disastrous consequences for Chiang Kai-shek and the Chinese. Because the Japanese had finally occupied the key southern Chinese port of Canton, the last lifeline to China was the Burma Road, which connected the docks at Rangoon with the Chinese army depots in Kunming. If the Japanese occupied Malaya, there would be nothing to stop them from moving northward into Burma, where this vital transportation link could be cut with relative ease. Using this strategy, Japan could probably starve China into submission.

If China was forced to capitulate, the Japanese might redeploy and entrench so many soldiers in the western Pacific, the East Indies, and Southeast Asia that the Far East region would never be recaptured.

The Singapore conferees recommended that at least 582 first-line combat aircraft would be needed to adequately defend Malaya and Singapore, and Burma and China by proxy. The forces available amounted to a pitifully small fraction of the quantities specified. To summarize the problem, there were no fighters of any kind, and the overall deficiency in aircraft was almost five hundred planes. If that was not enough to discourage the commanders, the conference delegates postulated that the RAAF would need to provide another 320 aircraft to ensure security of the northern Australia–New Guinea–Solomons perimeter to prevent a Japanese flanking maneuver from the east. It was an incredibly tall order.[5]

On November 14, 1940, Air Chief Marshal Sir Robert Brooke-Popham was recalled from retirement and received in Singapore as the new British Commander in Chief, Far East. His résumé was impressive. The long list of his accomplishments included service with both the army and the RAF, management of the RAF staff college, overall military command in Iraq, and a retirement posting as governor of Kenya. With the Singapore Conference proceedings in hand, Brooke-Popham was well briefed regarding the vulnerabilities of Malaya and Singapore, the desperate state of his air force, and some serious shortcomings in the organization charged with processing his intelligence and reconnaissance information.

Brooke-Popham knew that changes were necessary and wasted no time preparing for a large air force presence. On his orders, the Far East Command began constructing sixteen new advance airfields on the Malay Peninsula. Even though it was unclear when a supply of aircraft might arrive, work on the air stations progressed at a furious pace. Most of the fields would be temporary deployment bases with only fuel-service facilities, but they would greatly supplement capacity of the four regular aerodromes the RAF had established on Singapore Island: Seletar, Sembawang, Tengah, and Kallang. In a parallel effort to secure Rangoon and the Burma Road, Brooke-Popham dispatched Group Captain E. R. Manning—an Australian RAF officer—to Burma to create an air force command and a network of new airfields in that country.

Brooke-Popham's actions were promptly rewarded by the welcome news that his Far East Command would receive additional Blenheim bombers and 167 Brewster fighter planes in early 1941.

These would not solve his problems, but they represented a big first step toward outfitting an air force for Singapore.

The "E" model Buffalo was an English export version of the U.S. Navy Brewster F2A fighter. Visually, it was about the most corpulent fighter aircraft design one can imagine. Looks and grace are fortunately not everything; the sixty-two hundred pound Buffalo was much more agile than its shape would suggest, if not quite agile enough to dogfight with lightweight Japanese fighters. Powered by a 1,100-horsepower Wright Cyclone radial, its maximum speed was about 321 miles per hour at sixteen thousand feet. Nominally, this was as fast as a Mitsubishi A6M2. Still, performance of the 339E—like that of most U.S. fighters— fell off dramatically above twenty thousand feet. Four .50-caliber machine guns provided adequate firepower, though full loads of the heavy ammunition added to a 339E's weight disadvantage, giving it the worst power-to-weight ratio of all Buffalo variants. Its initial climb rate of twenty-five hundred feet per minute was better than average for the time—it actually climbed faster than a Curtiss P-40 up through twenty thousand feet—but the Buffalo required more than half an hour to reach its service-ceiling altitude of thrity-three thousand feet.

This was a problem. In order to engage Japanese fighters effectively at combat altitude, Brewster pilots would need a very early warning of their enemy's approach. To illustrate the dilemma: if a Mitsubishi Zero and a Buffalo both took off at the same time in a race to ascend from sea level to thirty thousand feet, the Japanese fighter would actually have time to climb to the objective, dive back down, touch its wheels on the runway, and then rise back up again to meet the Brewster before the U.S. plane got to the finish line.[6]

To those unfamiliar with the capabilities of Japanese aircraft, the Buffalo may have appeared up to the task of defending Malaya. As it happened, the British Far East Command had little choice of fighters because the Buffalo was the only type available in sufficient numbers for deployment to Asia. Britain, at the height of its own battle for survival against the German Luftwaffe, could not spare any of its first-line Spitfire or Hurricane fighters. The British Purchasing Commission had already turned to the United States to provide additional fighter aircraft, and even took over all French contracts with U.S. manufacturers after the collapse of France. However, no designs suited for the high-altitude combat over Europe were available from the United States. RAF testing of the first three 339Es and a batch of Belgian-specification 339Bs in the fall of 1940 indicated that the Brewsters had neither the speed nor altitude performance to compete with Axis fighters over Europe or the

Mediterranean. Since the Curtiss P-40 was being manufactured in large numbers and was reasonably capable of countering Italian and French fighters on duty in the Middle East and North Africa, the RAF was anxiously absorbing all Tomahawk production not critical to the U.S. Army. Apart from Curtiss, Brewster was the only U.S. company producing any fighters in quantity at the time.

Brewster was able to fulfill British orders for Buffaloes only because the U.S. Navy was willing to delay its own receipt of backlogged F2A-3s. The U.S. Navy was not being entirely altruistic in this deferral. It had recently decided to accept Grumman's F4F Wildcat as its standard fighter, in place of the Buffalo. This decision in favor of Grumman was not really because of the Wildcat's superior performance, as some have stated. The Buffalo and Wildcat aircraft were remarkably similar in all performance characteristics, though the Grumman F4F-3—equipped with a two-stage supercharger—had a definite climbing advantage above an altitude of twenty thousand feet. The choice of designs was driven primarily by the Navy Department's disenchantment with Brewster's poor management practices and

A Brewster Buffalo of RAAF No. 21 Squadron sits on the sidelines as Bristol Blenheim IF night fighters from RAF 27 Squadron "buzz" the field. The pudgy Brewsters and their Australian pilots anchored the air defense of Malaya—receiving much blame and little credit. British Blenheim fighters and bombers failed to make any impact at all on advancing Japanese air and ground forces. (Courtesy of Australian War Memorial)

dismal contract performance. Those characteristics, more than aircraft capability, led to the termination of future Buffalo orders and the ultimate demise of Brewster as a manufacturer. Despite this unhappy situation, the Royal Navy would have gladly adopted the Buffaloes if the changes required to "navalize" the 339E model would not have delayed their delivery. But because these modifications required too much time, the Fleet Air Arm also chose to purchase Grumman F4Fs. Therefore, the 167 remaining Buffaloes built for the RAF were scheduled for factory shipment to the British Far East Command; thirty-two would be sent to Rangoon, and the rest to Singapore.[7]

In March 1941, the first Buffaloes landed at the docks in Singapore. At the same time, RAF personnel from England began arriving to form two new fighter units: 67 Squadron and 243 Squadron. Unfortunately, all of these fliers, except squadron commanders and flight leaders, were fledgling pilots who had not even completed fighter transition training. Thus, RAAF No. 21 Squadron and its Wirraways were assigned the task of providing advanced operational training to the inexperienced RAF pilots. On completion of this activity, both RAF squadrons were graduated to the new Buffaloes. A third untrained unit, 453 Squadron, arrived in Singapore during August. This squadron was entirely composed of recent, mostly Australian graduates from the Empire Air Training Scheme program. Again, the "old hands" of No. 21 Squadron were called on to provide operational training for the new students. Finally, in September, No. 21 Squadron completed its own conversion to Buffaloes. The following month, RAF 67 Squadron—with the greatest number of combat-experienced pilots from Europe—was abruptly transferred to Burma to fly the Buffaloes received in Rangoon. This unit would gain notoriety fighting alongside Claire Chennault's "Flying Tigers" in defense of the Burma Road.

As was the case with the P-35As in the Philippines, transition training exacted a heavy toll on operational aircraft inventory. During the six-month period preceding Japan's attack, fifteen new Brewsters had been wrecked in accidents and written off to the scrap pile.[8] Most of these losses were a direct result of engine failures, which led to a British investigation of Brewster Company practices.

Brooke-Popham accurately recognized that his intelligence organization was one of the great weaknesses of his command, yet apparently he ignored some of the useful information it did provide. Among the items presented to him were the specifications of the Mitsubishi A6M2 supplied by Chennault and the results of the Buffalo flight trials in England. In spite of the available facts, he demonstrated neither respect for Japanese capabilities nor a great understanding of Japan's successes in the air war over China. In statements to the Australian War Cabinet, he firmly expressed the opinion that he did not regard the Japanese as being "air-minded, particularly against determined fighter opposition."[9] Up to the last moment, Brooke-Popham continued to express his disdain for Japanese air forces: "We can get on all right with Buffaloes out here, but they haven't got the speed for England; let England have the 'super' Spitfires and the 'hyper' Hurricanes. Buffaloes are quite good enough for Malaya."[10]

Back in Australia, the United States' last-minute adoption of the strategic deterrence concept meant additional headaches for RAAF commanders already struggling to cope with the demands coming from Singapore. Support for U.S. equipment in transit to the Far East would require significant commitments in Australia and throughout the East Indies.

When the AAF 14th Bombardment Squadron passed through Australian territory in September, it became evident that existing RAAF airfields would not be well suited for use by heavy bombers. Consequently, the U.S. Army sought a number of improvements to facilities on the air route across Australian territory. The Australian War Cabinet endorsed the U.S. requirements on October 18, 1941, granting approval for upgrades to the RAAF bases at Vunakanau airfield, Seven-Mile aerodrome, Rockhampton (between Townsville and Brisbane), and Batchelor Field (just south of Darwin). These urgent projects would strain the Australian air organization to its absolute limit.

With war rapidly approaching, the workload continued to mount. Major General Lewis Brereton, in his new command of the U.S. Army Far East Air Force, fully comprehended the vulnerabilities of the U.S. locations in the Philippines. He felt that effective use of his new air organization would necessarily depend on large-scale rear-area operations by units stationed outside the immediate battle zone. The only reasonably safe location was Australia. As such, Australian air bases would have to play a key role in hosting training and maintenance operations for Brereton's command. Cooperation with the RAAF was important enough to him that he embarked on a personal inspection tour of airfields in Australia and the Australian Mandated Territory less than two weeks after his arrival at Manila.

Leaving Clark Field at about 0300 on November 16, 1941, Brereton and some of his senior staff officers climbed on board a 19th Group Flying Fortress.[11] With the group commander, Lieutenant Colonel Eugene

Eubank, as their pilot, the party flew first to Darwin and then on to Townsville, Port Moresby, and Rabaul. Spending a day at each location, Brereton met with the RAAF station commanders and developed specific plans for improving each air base he visited. Arriving at Vunakanau airfield on November 19, Eubank's B-17, like the others that landed there before it, broke through the field surface. The plane was not damaged, but the event dramatically illustrated the need for the proposed airfield upgrades. From Rabaul, the FEAF survey mission flew back to Archerfield at Brisbane—the home base for most of the Australian airline industry. At this point, Brereton and his staff were forced to continue on to Melbourne using smaller aircraft; no Australian runway south of Brisbane could support the weight of a loaded B-17.[12]

Once in Melbourne, Brereton conferred with Air Chief Marshal Sir Charles Burnett, overall commander of the RAAF. Brereton and Burnett got along famously. Their very productive meetings fostered a new level of integration between U.S. and Australian air services that would endure throughout the Pacific War. Burnett agreed to develop assembly and repair depots at Brisbane and Townsville so that short-range aircraft delivered from the United States by ship could be unloaded and assembled, and battle-damaged aircraft returned from the northern combat zones could be overhauled. New airfields were to be constructed at Cloncurry and Daly Waters, allowing short-range aircraft built in Brisbane to fly all the way from there to Darwin under their own power. Burnett's enthusiastic support for Brereton's requests enabled the new FEAF commander to consider a completely different strategy for supporting the Philippines. In Brereton's new concept, the AAF would conduct all FEAF operational transition training in Australia, and as much as half of General MacArthur's strategic deterrent force would be regularly based there. Neither Brereton nor Burnett could have guessed just how important the actions initiated under their agreement would prove when war finally reached Australia itself.

Nonetheless, in December 1941 the air defense for Australia, like that for the Philippines, was mostly an unfulfilled promise. Preparation continued as the clock counted down the hours to war. When the alarm finally sounded, Australia would find its most valuable air resources on the British front line in Malaya. Under the best of circumstances, this small force would have been slowly broken down by the massive Japanese assault about to be launched against it. As fate would decree, the very worst was in store.

Australian and British Combat Air Units in Malaya; December 7, 1941.

CHAPTER 4

A Matter of Hours

The Final Week of Peace

ONE CAN HARDLY IMAGINE A MORE REMOTE or inhospitable location during winter than Hitokappu Bay on the island of Etorofu. The eastern side of Etorofu is constantly battered by the high surf of the restless North Pacific Ocean; and the western side, by the forbidding Sea of Okhotsk. This is a place of gray rock, covered by gray volcanic ash, shrouded within the perpetually gray skies of a thick overcast. In November snow and ice often cover what little vegetation graces the rugged landscape. The dark, frigid waters of this lonely outpost on the chain of vulcanian lands known as the Kuriles provided a secret gathering spot for the *Kido Butai*: Japan's 1st Carrier Striking Force, charged with carrying out the surprise attack on Pearl Harbor. At 0600 on November 26, 1941, the sound of clanking iron links reverberated across the bay as the Japanese fleet weighed anchor to begin its long voyage toward Hawaii. By the time these ships returned to Japan, the Allied air forces in the Far East would already be eliminated.

Thousands of miles to the south, the snowy peaks of another volcanic island protruded through a solid layer of clouds. A lone green-and-gray plane flying above this moist blanket gave the visible mountaintops and taller clouds a wide berth. Several of those ice-coated summits reached a height of more than fifteen thousand feet, and some of the towering cumulus clouds undoubtedly contained rocks. To passengers bundled in heavy clothing and peering out the Plexiglas windows, the view was hardly congruent with the fact that the terrain beneath them was located in the Southwest Pacific.

In the nose of a Flying Fortress, abreast of the four droning engines, it was difficult to engage in conversation. Riding immediately behind the pilots, Major General Brereton had plenty to think about, and much to discuss with his staff, but it would all have to wait until they left the New Guinea skies far behind. The general was anxious to expedite the next round of heavy-bomber reinforcements to his FEAF in the Philippines before the Japanese cut the flying route across the Central Pacific. Given the airfield conditions he observed in Australia, it would also be desirable to avoid using the RAAF station at Darwin as a waypoint until improvements could be completed.

To explore the possibility of rerouting the 7th Bomb Group—scheduled to start its transpacific journey on December 6—along a more direct path to Luzon than that previously used by the 19th Bombardment Group, Brereton had asked Colonel Eubank to pilot their B-17 directly from Seven-Mile Field at Port Moresby back to Clark Field. This last flight of the U.S. liaison mission to Australia covered a pioneering 2,700-mile course that had never been flown before. The expert crew completed the journey without incident, but the bomber's fuel tanks were nearly empty. Eubank felt that the margin of safety for this route was even less than for the long overwater hop between San Francisco and Honolulu. In addition to the extra mileage, it was evident that weather above New Guinea could be unpredictable and hazardous. Extreme turbulence in combination with fuel consumption and navigation problems might present too much of a challenge for inexperienced pilots and navigators.

Brereton was disappointed about the potential difficulties with the course from Port Moresby, but his view from the landing pattern near Clark inspired instant wrath. As Eubank circled the plane to line up on the runway, the general had a full view of his fighter planes and bombers neatly lined up alongside the airstrip. On stepping down from the cabin ladder, the tired FEAF commander had the following words for his welcoming committee: "Gentlemen, I have just seen this field from the air. Fortunately for you and for all who depend upon us, I was not leading in a hostile bombing fleet. If I had been, I could have blasted the entire heavy bombardment strength of the Philippines off the map in one smash. Do you call that dispersal? It's wrong. Completely wrong. And wrong practices will have no place in the functioning of this field—or any other field under this command. You will rectify this condition at once. And you'll never permit it to occur again."[1]

Five hundred miles south of Brereton's chagrined audience, Major Raymond "Ray" Elsmore was leading the 5th Air Base Group in its effort to pitch tents before fading evening light gave way to darkness. Such sunsets were spectacular at the Del Monte Company plantation. At nearly two thousand feet above sea level, the vast plain containing the world's largest pineapple plantation often bathes in clear air above low-hanging clouds that frequently cling to the northern coast of Mindanao. Sometimes it seems as if the endless gray-green expanse of grass and pineapple spikes continues right on into the white carpet of moisture. In the distance, darker green mountains ringing the plateau rise to heights of more than nine thousand feet. The location is remote and quiet, with a view unobstructed by any naturally growing trees. A clubhouse and some outbuildings were the only manmade structures in the area. The two major improvements were a golf course and a small airfield. The pineapple fields and this improbable executive retreat were connected by a narrow dirt road that snaked its way some twenty miles down the mountain to the town of Cagayan del Oro and the shipping pier at nearby Bugo, on Macajalar Bay.

In response to Colonel George's suggestion that a good bomber base might be built on Del Monte's plantation, Major Elsmore's unit had volunteered to relocate from Manila to the largest, southernmost island in the Philippine Archipelago. The urgent need for this proposed airfield was confirmed by General Brereton's flight from Port Moresby and by his observations about the state of FEAF aircraft dispersal. The Del Monte location could serve as an intermediate destination for heavy bombardment aircraft flying to Luzon from New Guinea or Australia. At the same time, it could provide a reasonably safe dispersal area for a good portion of the all-important B-17 strike force, well out of range of any Japanese aircraft on Formosa. As an added bonus, Del Monte's remoteness made it difficult for Tokyo's agents to observe, an important consideration given the large Japanese population on Mindanao.

The morning after their arrival, Elsmore and his engineering team were ready to begin the work of clearing a larger runway on the plantation. Thanksgiving Day, November 27, 1941, was no holiday for the 5th Air Base Group at Del Monte. Every man was busy. However, they could be thankful for one stroke of good fortune: the terrain of the pineapple field was hard packed and offered excellent drainage. It was so well suited for airfield development that Major Elsmore's men had to do little more than marking out field boundaries, harvesting some of the delicious fruit, and cutting the grass. By the end of the weekend, they were ready to land large airplanes on the new airstrip.

The following day, General MacArthur received an ominous signal from Washington that General Marshall had sent:

> Negotiations with Japan appear to be terminated to all practical purposes with only the barest possibilities that Japanese government might come back and offer to continue. Japanese future action unpredictable but hostile action possible at any moment. If hostilities cannot, repeat cannot, be avoided the United States desires that Japan commit the first overt act. This policy should not, repeat not, be construed as restricting you to a course of action that might jeopardize the successful defense of the Philippines. Prior to hostile Japanese action you are directed to take such reconnaissance and other measures as you deem necessary. Report measures taken. Should hostilities occur you will carry out the tasks assigned in revised Rainbow Five which was delivered to you by General Brereton. Chief of Naval Operations concurs and requests you notify Hart.[2]

General Brereton promptly ordered all units of his FEAF to a full twenty-four-hour alert status. This was essentially a wartime level of readiness. Admiral Hart scheduled PatWing-10 to conduct a thorough daily surveillance of Japanese maritime activity in the South China Sea and along the east coast of Indochina. Of particular interest were the large ports at Cam Ranh Bay and Samah (Yulin Bay, on the island of Hainan). In consideration of the combat vulnerability of the slow, low-flying navy PBYs, it was decided that Colonel Eubank's 19th Group would assume responsibility for all patrols north of Luzon in the direction of Formosa.

Brereton, in line with General Marshall's instructions, requested permission to conduct high-altitude photo sorties directly over Japanese bases on Formosa. General MacArthur declined—afraid that Japan might misconstrue the presence of Flying Fortresses over Japanese territory as an "overt act of war." He allowed the 19th Group to fly only as far as "two thirds of the distance between Luzon and Formosa." This was not very helpful for assessing Japanese deployment capabilities, but occasionally, due to "piloting error," some Fortresses got close enough to Formosa to observe activity along the southern coast of the island.[3] Lieutenant Frank Kurtz of the 30th Squadron colorfully describes one such event, as he and his crew were conducting a "routine high-altitude test":

> Finally we reached her ceiling—came out on top—and I happened to look down, and my God! we were right over, not the blue sea, but the big Japanese base on the island of Formosa! A big black ugly hunk of something that was forbidden. I couldn't see much, but a camera could have picked out plenty. I didn't try to. I hadn't been ordered on any reconnaissance mission—this was only a high-altitude test. At any minute we might be hit by Jap fighters. I didn't want "Old 99" to become the first international incident, so I got out of there quick.[4]

After several days of constrained patrols by the 19th Bomb Group, orders were amended to allow Fortress crews to approach Formosa's international treaty boundary. Flying at a height of more than five miles and a distance of only three miles from the Formosan shore, the B-17s came close enough to obtain excellent photographs of some Japanese installations. Amazingly, no photos are known to have been taken, and nothing useful was learned about the sizable Japanese air unit concentrations on the island.

IN THE SAME MANNER as General Marshall had notified General MacArthur, the U.S. War Department also informed the British government of the apparent breakdown in negotiations with Japan. In response, Air Chief Marshal Brooke-Popham placed his Far East Command at a heightened state of readiness. Thirteen Lockheed Hudsons of RAAF No. 1 Squadron, based at Kota Bharu (near Malaya's northeastern border with Siam), would share a patrol area with two, four-plane flights from RAAF No. 8 Squadron, due to arrive at Kuantan (near the midpoint of the Malayan east coast) on December 4. Together, these planes would scan the seas from the Kra Isthmus, eastward to Cape Cambodia (at the southern tip of Indochina), southward to Great Natuna Island (halfway to Borneo), and back to Kuantan. RAF 205 Squadron's three Catalinas, and a like number of Dutch Catalinas, all flying from Seletar (on the north shore of Singapore), would patrol up the Malayan coast as far as Kuantan, then east to Great Natuna, and on to Kuching, in Sarawak (on the island of

Borneo).[5] These few aircraft would be responsible for visually scanning more than 200,000 square miles of the South China Sea each day. It was fatiguing work for the crews, who would often spend more than eight hours at a time in the air.

BACK IN WASHINGTON, the military leadership was convinced that when the winds of war eventually blew across the Pacific, they would first touch down in the Philippines. News from the failing diplomatic process between Washington and Tokyo gave ample evidence of an impending threat of violent action by Japan. At the end of November 1941, it seemed only a matter of days before Japan's forces would swarm southward from their Formosan stronghold to envelop Luzon. Japanese aerial reconnaissance operations observed around the island during the first weekend of December pointed strongly in that direction. Reaction to this overt activity overshadowed any perception of immediate threat to Pearl Harbor, even among the select few personnel with access to the ultrasecret "MAGIC" decodes of Japanese diplomatic communications.

The week after Marshall issued his memo, military installations in Hawaii continued to operate at a somewhat relaxed pace, while units of General Douglas MacArthur's USAFFE command were poised on a razor edge of alertness. Regardless of other possibilities, it was absolutely clear that a Japanese attack on the Philippines would come soon. Unfortunately, any possibility of containing Japanese incursions at their beachheads depended completely on an ability to deploy the planned level of airpower. Without local air superiority, a campaign to secure the Philippines was doomed to the fate delineated in the War Plan Orange scenarios—in other words, a guaranteed loss.

Even with the allocated air fleet in place, an initial failure of MacArthur's forces to protect Clark Field would lead to disaster. Once Japanese bombers were allowed to strike the vital base successfully, U.S. offensive operations in the air over the Philippines would surely cease. There was no other suitable location from which to sustain extended operations of the FEAF heavy-bomber force.

To equip the hastily cleared airstrip at the Del Monte plantation with facilities equal to those at Clark would have required at least another six months of intensive effort. In the larger scheme of things, this would not have been done. The island of Mindanao had the smallest of army garrisons. Therefore, it would have been virtually impossible to defend Del Monte against an enemy ground assault. Additionally, Del Monte was too far away for Flying Fortresses to directly attack Japanese installations on Formosa without using an intermediate staging base. Another bomber field was under development at San Marcelino, between Iba and Olongapo, on Luzon's western coast, but Colonel George wanted this new base to serve as a home for the 27th Bombardment Group. It would not be ready for regular operations for several months. Even when functional, San Marcelino would have no fixed service facilities. The remote airstrip could provide only for dispersal, refueling, and rearming of aircraft. Repairs for the bombers would still have to be made at Clark. Without Clark's service facilities, the B-17 squadrons would be forced to send their planes back to Australia for all but the most minor maintenance procedures.

General Brereton knew that his FEAF would have to respond quickly and effectively in meeting any Japanese air strike. To prevail in a defensive strategy, FEAF fighter units would have to successfully break up Japanese bomber formations well before they could get to Clark Field. Brereton was acutely aware that his chance to blunt a Japanese offensive would be fleeting at best and highly dependent on receiving an early warning for any inbound enemy air attack. Even under optimal circumstances, readily available tracking information from the Air Warning Service (AWS) on Luzon could not completely offset the advantage of quantitative superiority possessed by Japanese air units on Formosa.

The cornerstone of the FEAF's AWS was the single SCR-270B radar trailer set up on the fringe of Iba Field. This revolutionary device allowed its operators to use reflected radio waves to track aircraft at distances of slightly more than one hundred miles. From the installation at Iba, this meant that any aircraft traveling southward along the western coast of Luzon could be detected just before it entered the Lingayen Gulf. Once a contact-tracking report was developed, radio or telephone lines were used to connect with the AWS plot room in FEAF Interceptor Command Headquarters at Nielson Field. From Nielson, these reports were relayed via Teletype to 24th Pursuit Group Headquarters at Clark. It was then up to the 24th Pursuit Group commander, or his duty officer, to dispatch fighters to intercept the unknown aircraft. There were several weak links in this process, including one critical shortcoming unique to this early type of radar unit: the inability to determine the altitude of a contact. With just one available radar, only the western coastal approaches to the north of Manila Bay could be monitored. The northern and eastern coasts of Luzon could not be afforded any better warning of approaching aircraft than was possible through the generally unreliable spotter network or from sighting reports by FEAF and navy airborne patrols.

At 24th Pursuit Group Headquarters, Major Orrin Grover was tasked with managing five fighter squadrons: three squadrons of his regular command, plus the 21st and 34th Squadron personnel who had just arrived from the advance echelon of the 35th Pursuit Group. These units were deployed across four flying fields: Clark, Del Carmen, Iba, and Nichols. The difficulty of managing this complex operation was compounded by poor communications with units at the three remote bases. There was only one dedicated and secure land line under army control, which linked Clark with FEAF Headquarters at Nielson. While Grover could count on receiving orders through this line, it was of no use in contacting his own units. All telephone service between the other airfields was handled by the local civilian utility, which all too often was subject to disruption.

Direct radio communications were also less than totally reliable. From Clark to Nichols Field, reception was usually quite good; the terrain provided no natural obstacles between the two locations. Such was not the case with Iba, where the Zambales Mountains, or weather gathered above them, regularly interfered with radio traffic. At Del Carmen Field—just activated in the first week of December as an operational satellite airstrip to Clark—only second-line, portable radio gear was available, and there were no standard phone lines at all. Even though the two airfields were almost within sight of each other, communication between Clark and Del Carmen was actually the worst.

Affected by all of these factors, Grover had great difficulty in issuing timely commands to his squadrons. The situation deteriorated completely once the fighters became airborne: reliable communication with flight leaders was frequently impossible due to the very limited range of the airborne equipment. In typically unfavorable tropical atmospheric conditions, the distance for clear radio reception in fighters could be reduced to a scant twenty-mile radius from Clark Field.

Because the 3rd Pursuit Squadron was colocated with the radar unit at Iba, it could easily be scrambled to investigate contact reports without having to wait for dispatch through the AWS. Fighters flying from Iba were also geographically well positioned to intercept aircraft traveling along the most likely offshore course from Formosa to

Manila. For these reasons, and to avoid any confusion due to aircraft misidentification, Major Grover and Colonel George elected to keep only the 3rd Pursuit on full alert during hours of darkness; all other aircraft would be grounded at night. Unfortunately, the interception capability of this sentinel squadron was seriously limited by the fact that no oxygen supplies were available at Iba.[6] Without oxygen equipment, the pilots themselves could safely sustain operations only up to an altitude of about fifteen thousand feet. Positioned against a higher-flying foe, the planes of the 3rd Pursuit would be of no defensive value at all. At the time, this important fact was not viewed with appropriate concern—no U.S. authorities recognized or acknowledged a qualitative superiority in the high-altitude capabilities of Japanese aircraft.

Offensively, General Brereton planned from the outset to use his B-17s for a strike on the major Japanese port facility at Takao (Kaohsiung). Ideally, he hoped that Takao could be bombed before any Japanese naval transports set sail from Formosa. In spite of the AAF's unbounded faith in the abilities of the Flying Fortress, Brereton, as a Naval Academy graduate, understood that it would be much more difficult to inflict serious damage on the Japanese fleet if individual ships were maneuvering at sea. Although the AAF optimistically claimed that a B-17 and its sophisticated, top-secret Norden bombsight could "hit a pickle barrel from 20,000 feet," a bombardier's task is unquestionably harder when the "barrels" are in motion.

It might seem that, in adhering to the above strategy, General Brereton was ignoring the threat from Japanese air units on Formosa. To the contrary, he was adamant that his bombers should attack Formosan airfields at the earliest possible opportunity. The simple fact was that the FEAF staff had no intelligence data regarding the location of any of those bases, let alone the disposition of any air units stationed on them. The target intelligence that the FEAF possessed— provided by the War Department to support the campaign of strategic deterrence—was limited to the Japanese home islands. Given restrictions on his ability to overfly Formosan territory, Brereton would have to wait until war actually broke out before he could obtain any worthwhile reconnaissance photos of Japanese air installations. FEAF Headquarters did not have any targeting photos of the Takao area either, but there was enough generally available information about this major port city to plan a reasonably effective bombing mission.[7] To supplement those data, Captain Wagner's wily Catalina pilots had visually snooped around Takao in less volatile times. Their flight reports would be of some use.

Another area that represented a significant threat—for which the army and navy had absolutely no intelligence information—was the Caroline Islands, especially the naval and air installations at Jaluit, Truk, Ponape, and Palau. Upon sending out the "war warning" of November 28 (the date it was received in Manila), General Marshall asked General Arnold to dispatch long-range, photo-reconnaissance aircraft on high-altitude surveys of the Japanese strongholds at Truk and Jaluit. Radio intercept information indicated that the Japanese fleet was gradually disappearing from its home ports, perhaps secretly massing at some hidden location. With the recent breakdown of diplomacy, it was of vital importance to know where Japan's navy was hiding, especially if that location was somewhere east of the Philippines. To accomplish this, Arnold needed an aircraft with even greater range than a B-17. The only available planes with such capability were nine unarmed B-24A Liberators of the Ferrying Command at Bolling Field (near Washington, D.C.). Two of these transports were immediately pulled from regular transatlantic diplomatic shuttle duty, and their crews were ordered to fly them to Hamilton Field within forty-eight hours. Once in California, they would be prepared for the urgent, top-secret mission.

UNKNOWN TO THE ALLIES, December 1, 1941, was destined to be the last day of peace in the Far East for quite some time. In the early hours of December 2, the cryptic message *"Niitaka-yama nobore* 1208" was broadcast from Tokyo to all Japanese military commands.[8] This coded phrase, translated as "Climb Mount Niitaka on December 8," was the order to commence the planned attacks on the United States and Great Britain. In the eyes of the Japanese, their country was now at war. Realistically, there would be no turning back, regardless of the diplomatic charade playing out in Washington.

At his Formosa headquarters, Vice Admiral Fushizo Tsukahara, commander of the IJN's 11th Air Fleet, quickly issued his first order of the Pacific War. He directed the units under his command to immediately commence a daily overflight of U.S. airfield installations on Luzon. The first Japanese intrusion over Clark Field occurred within hours. It was tracked by the new radar set at Iba and reported to FEAF Headquarters, but no interception was ordered.

In addition, the JAAF in Indochina conducted daily high-altitude photo-reconnaissance surveys of British airfields in northern Malaya.

The first target for the aerial photographers was the RAF base at Kota Bharu. The intelligence take was not too exciting; only a few Lockheed Hudsons sat alongside the runway.

If Japanese air units had undertaken a similar reconnaissance of Singapore on December 2, they would have noted with keen interest the arrival of one of the Royal Navy's newest battleships, HMS *Prince of Wales*, and its veteran companion, the battle cruiser HMS *Repulse*—the largest Allied naval combatants ever to be stationed in the Far East. The recently commissioned aircraft carrier HMS *Indomitable* was supposed to accompany these two capital ships. Unfortunately, its journey was delayed to repair damage it suffered during a maneuvering accident while docking at Kingston, Jamaica. As a result, Vice Admiral Sir Tom Phillips's Far Eastern Fleet was fated to have no air protection of its own. As an interim measure, it was decided that the Buffalo pilots of the fledgling Australian No. 453 Squadron would assume temporary coverage for the fleet after that squadron's deployment to the Malayan air stations at Kota Bharu and Kuantan—scheduled to happen on the afternoon of December 8.

Ironically, Japanese reconnaissance aircraft were actually the least successful intruders on this first quiet day of undeclared war. A PatWing-10 PBY, piloted by Lieutenant (j.g.) William Robinson of Squadron VP-101, broke through the clouds over Cam Ranh Bay and spotted more than thirty Japanese freighters and transports in the harbor.[9] Several single-engine floatplanes were patrolling the area, but these did not move to intercept the lone Catalina before it disappeared back into the safety of the clouds. Robinson's exciting discovery lent substantial confirmation to suspicions about a Japanese move to the south.

On December 3, another PatWing-10 PBY made the torturous eighteen-hundred-mile, twenty-hour round-trip from Manila to Cam Ranh Bay. The Catalina's crew noted the presence of more than fifty ships in the harbor, including a number of destroyers and cruisers.[10] This observation seemed to guarantee that Japan would make a large military movement into the South China Sea within several days. Radio and telegraph lines buzzed around the globe as transmissions of this information made their way to the highest echelon of Allied military commanders and politicians.

One can imagine how agitated intelligence officers became the next day when the Asiatic Fleet reconnaissance Catalina observed a completely vacant Cam Ranh Bay. All of the Japanese ships had evidently left their harbor in Indochina sometime during the previous night. Undeniably, something was about to happen. Japanese air activity in Philippine airspace also had stepped up a notch or two. Early in the morning of December 4, the Iba radar tracked another bogey over the Lingayen Gulf, and, north of Clark Field, a flight of P-40s from the 20th Pursuit Squadron nearly collided with an unidentified aircraft during a dawn interception exercise. By mid-morning, a PatWing-10 aircraft on a local patrol around Manila encountered a twin-engine Japanese bomber just off the coast of Luzon. This was the most solid evidence yet that Japan might be contemplating near-term action around the Philippines. Similar sightings during the early morning hours of December 5 finally prompted General MacArthur to approve orders authorizing FEAF fighters to intercept and shoot down any unidentified aircraft encountered above Philippine soil.

General Brereton and Colonel Eubank were both anxious to move at least some of their precious striking force out of the range of Japanese bombers as soon as possible. With approval from General MacArthur's office, they issued orders for an immediate transfer of half of the 19th Group to the giant pineapple plantation on Mindanao. Sixteen B-17 bombers of the 14th and 93rd Bomb Squadrons lifted off from Clark Field after dark on December 5 and spent the rest of that night winging southward out of harm's way.[11]

The decision not to send all of the Flying Fortresses to Del Monte would become a subject of lasting and unresolved controversy. One assumes—based on his other actions in the strategy for deployment of the bombardment force—that General Brereton would have preferred to send all of his bombers to Mindanao, especially in light of the Japanese air activity around Luzon. According to Brereton, Brigadier General Richard Sutherland, General MacArthur's chief of staff, expressed that the USAFFE chief did not want to permanently move B-17s to Del Monte because the ground forces available on Mindanao were inadequate to protect the remote airfield. Such a stance was not unreasonable. After all, the whereabouts of the large Japanese naval formation discovered at Cam Ranh Bay had become a matter of great concern. For all the Americans knew, an invasion fleet could have been heading to Mindanao. In any case, Sutherland's resistance to Brereton's request seems to have been the most critical factor in limiting the number of B-17s sent south.

Apparently Colonel Eubank was also against moving more than two 19th Group squadrons because of the congestion that would occur when planes of the 7th Bombardment Group started to arrive at Del Monte at the end of the week. Brereton intended that the entire 7th Group be based on Mindanao until new airfields in southern Luzon and on Cebu could be completed. Eubank's reluctance to move all of the bombers south is even more understandable when one considers that his group needed to continue its reconnaissance operations to the north of Luzon. Running shuttle missions for this purpose from Del Monte would have been very hard on the planes.

Although none of the Japanese ships had been relocated by the Americans, it was generally assumed they were somewhere in the South China Sea, under the cover of storm clouds that blanketed most of the region. A detachment of three PBYs and their tender, the *William B. Preston*, had been relocated to Mindanao in an effort to comb the southern Philippine seas. So far, these PatWing-10 aircraft had not found anything out of the ordinary. Unfortunately, for two days heavy monsoon rains had grounded the Australian and British reconnaissance aircraft in northern Malaya, which were tasked with scouting the cloud-darkened Gulf of Siam. With all the bad weather, it was impossible to tell where the Japanese were headed. In the absence of any actual information, it was deemed most likely that the Japanese were bound for Siam as part of their anticipated move to occupy that country.

Early in the morning of December 6, Admiral Sir Phillips flew from Singapore to Manila for a secret conference with General MacArthur and Admiral Hart. He was in the Philippines to ask for resources. In particular, Phillips asked MacArthur and Hart to lend him some air support and screening destroyers for the British Far Eastern Fleet. Although Hart agreed to send some destroyers to "conduct exercises with the British," MacArthur declined to provide any aircraft, fearing that such an "alliance" might be seen by the Japanese as an "offensive" move on his part. Intimating that "the inability of an enemy to launch his air attacks on these islands [the Philippines]" left him "with a sense of complete security," MacArthur also told Phillips that his own Philippine defenses would be complete in about four months and that he did not expect the Japanese to attack before that time.[12] Given all the information available to MacArthur when he made these comments, one is left to ponder whether he could have been naive enough to truly believe what he said or whether he was simply justifying a position to dodge Phillips's request.

Colonel Harold George, in the new position of chief of staff for the FEAF Interceptor Command, was much less sanguine about the short-term security of the Philippines. After the recent series of mysterious aircraft sightings, Colonel George was convinced that the time for peace had run out. In the mid-morning of December 6, he convened the pilots of the 17th and 21st Pursuit Squadrons at Nichols Field for a candid briefing on strategic and tactical developments. George's speech was anything but encouraging. Characteristic of the young colonel, his opening was blunt and to the point: "Men, you are not a suicide squadron yet, but you're damned close to it. There will be war with Japan in a very few days. It may come in a matter of hours. The Japs have a minimum of three-thousand planes they can send down on us from Formosa and from aircraft carriers. They know the way already. When they come again they will be tossing something."[13] Colonel George went on to inform the group about the Japanese task force that had disappeared somewhere in the South China Sea. The airmen listened to their leader in stunned silence. For many of the fliers, it was the first time they were forced to come to terms with the seriousness of their situation and the overwhelming odds against them.

While the 24th Pursuit Group pilots in the Philippines were recovering from the shock of Colonel George's message, three Hudsons of RAAF No. 1 Squadron rolled down the rain-soaked runway at Kota Bharu and climbed out over the dripping jungle foliage into clearing skies over the Gulf of Siam.

Shortly after noon, Flight Lieutenant John Ramshaw—charged with responsibility for the northernmost patrol sector—was about 215 miles away from Kota Bharu when he and his observer spotted three warships heading north-northwest past Cape Cambodia. Further reinforcing suspicions that Japan was moving against Siam, those three ships were headed precisely in the direction of Bangkok. He radioed this information at 1215, identifying at least two of the ships as minecraft. Continuing eastward, Ramshaw traveled another sixty miles before spotting a large convoy that was heading due west into the Gulf of Siam. His radio transmission at 1230 identified this formation as consisting of one battleship, five cruisers, seven destroyers, and twenty-two transports. When one of the ships catapulted a floatplane, Ramshaw ducked his Hudson into a nearby cloud. He requested permission from Air Headquarters in Singapore to shadow these Japanese ships until relieved by another Hudson crew. Amazingly, the request was denied.[14] Denial would prove to be a significant mistake—the first of many blunders soon to be made by Allied commanders.

Ramshaw's first sighting was almost certainly a detachment of two minecraft, accompanied by a frigate, sailing to a rendezvous point near Phu Quoc Island to meet and escort two transports with JAAF personnel. His second sighting was the main element of General Tomoyuki Yamashita's 25th Army "Malaya Force," composed of two cruisers (*Chokai*, a heavy cruiser that very closely resembled a battleship in size and configuration, and *Sendai*, a light cruiser), twelve destroyers (the larger ones could easily have been misidentified as cruisers), eighteen transports, a hospital ship, and the seaplane tender *Kamikawa Maru* (which indeed launched a plane).[15]

At 1245, only fifteen minutes after Ramshaw's second report, Air Headquarters picked up a transmission from Flight Lieutenant James Emerton's Lockheed. Emerton's crew, covering the central patrol sector, was presumed to be some distance east of Ramshaw. The radio operator on board this Hudson reported a surface force consisting of two cruisers, ten destroyers, and twenty-one transports heading northwest about 415 miles from Kota Bharu.[16] This sighting caused great confusion back in Singapore. Was it possible there were two large Japanese forces headed into the Gulf of Siam? Because the sightings occurred only fifteen minutes apart and allegedly were separated by nearly a hundred miles, and because neither Hudson crew observed another Hudson, it is possible that two different forces were spotted. However, the similarity in the reported force composition was difficult to ignore. Ultimately, the question of identification for the sightings would never be reconciled; Air Headquarters did not allow either Ramshaw or Emerton to maintain contact with the ships sighted.

To the east of Yamashita's large Malaya Force, there were in fact two smaller Japanese formations sailing in fairly close proximity: one was the invasion covering force, consisting of the battleship *Haruna*, with the cruisers *Atago, Kumano, Mikuma, Mogami, Suzuya,* and *Takao* and thirteen destroyers; the other was the Southern Expeditionary Force, embarked on seven transports escorted by the cruiser *Kashii* and a frigate.[17]

The most important question for the British Far East Command was to determine where the IJN was heading. Belatedly, Air Headquarters decided that another Hudson should be dispatched in an effort to regain contact with the Japanese fleet. At 1620 Flight

Lieutenant Ken Smith and his crew took off from Kota Bharu to relocate the ships their squadron-mates had previously seen. It was too late. As evening approached, cloud cover began to build again across the Gulf of Siam, and Smith's crew was unable to spot anything at all.

When word of the Japanese fleet sightings in the South China Sea reached Manila, Admiral Phillips cut short his visit with Admiral Hart and General MacArthur to return to his fleet in Singapore. Phillips assumed that the Japanese were headed toward the Kra Isthmus, or possibly Malaya, rather than northern Siam as many others postulated. He hoped to mobilize *Prince of Wales* and *Repulse* as soon as possible to interdict any invasion attempt along the Malayan east coast. After failing to find the flight crew of his personal Sunderland flying boat—they had journeyed off to a movie theater without telling anyone—an angry Phillips was finally flown back to Singapore in a PBY piloted by Ensign Duke Campbell of VP-101.[18]

To conduct a long-endurance night search for Japanese ships in the Gulf of Siam, Air Headquarters in Singapore ordered one of RAF 205 Squadron's Catalinas to take over the reconnaissance area normally covered by RAAF No. 1 Squadron. This plane, piloted by Flight Lieutenant Atkinson, took off from the ramp at Seletar at 1830.

By midnight, when no transmissions had been received from Atkinson's crew, a decision was made to send out another Catalina to take over the patrol. At 0200 on December 7, Flying Officer Patrick Bedell, an Australian pilot, lifted his RAF Catalina off the waters of the Johore Strait and headed north into the darkness.

Unknown to those in Singapore anxiously awaiting word from the Catalinas, Bedell came nearly within viewing distance of the Japanese fleet and was actually headed directly toward it. After dawn, his aircraft was spotted by a floatplane from *Kamikawa Maru* in the proximity of Phu Quoc Island. Firing the first shots of the Pacific War, more than sixteen hours before the Pearl Harbor attack began, Ensign Eiichi Ogata opened up on Bedell's flying boat from below and astern. Ogata did not observe any resultant damage, but the Catalina did alter its course away from the direction of the Japanese fleet. The Catalina had not answered Ogata's fire, and Ogata did not pursue it. Some forty minutes later, at about 0900, Bedell was again intercepted, this time by five patrolling Ki-27s of the JAAF 1st Sentai. Gunners in the Catalina immediately returned fire as each plane from Lieutenant Toshiru Kubotani's flight made an attacking pass. When the fifth Ki-27 fired, the flying boat exploded. The Catalina's wreckage, along with the bodies of Flying Officer Bedell and his seven crew members, plummeted into the sea.[19]

No radio message from either Atkinson or Bedell was received by daybreak. Air Headquarters assumed that both planes had either experienced radio equipment failure or crashed in the darkness. Atkinson's aircraft eventually returned without having observed anything. As far as the British were concerned, Bedell's Catalina had simply vanished. A loss to hostile action was not out of the question, but nobody in Singapore wanted to sound an alarm without definitive proof.

CHAPTER 5

The Battle for Kota Bharu

December 8, 1941—Malaya

THE WAIT FOR INFORMATION about the Japanese invasion fleet was unsettling. After a full day passed with no reconnaissance reports, tension in the Singapore command center was understandably very high. Air Chief Marshal Brooke-Popham believed the Japanese would not attack Malaya until they occupied Siam to acquire bases closer to Singapore. He thought an occupation would most likely be accomplished by land forces moving across Siam's eastern border from Indochina. For that contingency, the British Far East Command prepared a response plan—code-named MATADOR—that specified a rapid British counterinvasion of southwestern Siam's Kra Isthmus. This action was designed to create a buffer against any subsequent Japanese incursion into Malaya by denying Japan the use of ports and airfields located near the southern Thai border. Underlying the plan was a politically motivated prerequisite that Japanese troops would have to be the first to set foot on Thai soil. With this constraint, MATADOR could only be executed if Japan chose a conservative approach to an occupation of Siam. If Japanese actions were more aggressive, preparation for MATADOR would actually leave the British forces in a position of weakness.

Along the whole eastern coast of Malaya there were only two widely separated strongholds lying in the path of a Japanese advance to the south. The northeastern cornerstone of the British defense was at Kota Bharu. The base was in a region so geographically isolated that it was accessible on the ground only by one railway route winding across a single pass in the mountains to western Malaya. Its airfield,

88

adjacent to the Peng Chepa River, was one of the best in Malaya. The single large runway had even been engineered to support the operation of U.S. heavy bombers in anticipation of joint missions with the United States. However, its seafront location was uncomfortably within range of naval gunfire. Ground defense for the air station was also problematic. The base lay amid a marshy confluence of rivers and lesser tributaries that were spanned by only a few connecting bridges. Near Kota Bharu were two less vulnerable auxiliary airfields at Gong Kedah and Machang. Unfortunately, these air stations were still largely undeveloped. Of the two, only Gong Kedah was occupied by air force support personnel. Machang was usable for emergency landings, but not much else. Its most important feature was a small number of wooden decoy aircraft, placed to distract high-flying reconnaissance planes. The second eastern outpost was at Kuantan, 180 miles south of Kota Bharu, along a sandy stretch of coastline surrounded by swamps and impenetrable jungle. Like Kota Bharu, Kuantan was isolated, connected overland by only one track that snaked westward through densely forested lowlands to a rail junction at Jerantut. The Kuantan air station itself was not nearly as well prepared, nor as well defended, as Kota Bharu. There were no antiaircraft weapons of any type, very few ground troops, and no secondary fields for aircraft dispersal or emergency use.

The western side of the Malayan Peninsula was generally better developed and more populous than the eastern region. There were a number of good roads and railway spurs and several active port facilities. In the extreme northwest, British troops were massed around Jitra, near the Malayan border with Siam, about sixty miles south of the Thai port at Singora. A second rallying point was at Kroh, in the mountains along the road that links the Thai town of Patani with the Malayan city of Taiping. The northernmost RAF station was at Alor Star (Alor Setar), south of Jitra, just twenty-five miles from the Thai border. Thirty miles south of Alor Star was a better-developed airfield at Sungei Patani that served as the primary fighter base in northern Malaya. Several satellite fields were available in the vicinity of Sungei Patani: Butterworth, Lubok Kiap, and Bayan Lebas (on Penang Island). Of these auxiliary fields, only Butterworth had operational facilities; the other two were intended solely for emergency landings, refueling, or temporary dispersal. Further to the south, there were operational bases at Ipoh and Kluang, along with a handful of satellite airstrips.

British airpower was arrayed primarily to expedite the forward movement of army units engaged in MATADOR. Squadrons on the west side of the peninsula had been located near the Thai border to provide tactical ground-attack support for a rapid advance to Singora. The vast majority of fighter aircraft had been retained in Singapore because the Thai air forces were not expected to pose any real threat. The Australian bomber units in eastern Malaya were not intended for use in MATADOR; their role was to conduct maritime reconnaissance in the South China Sea. Unfortunately, these assignments left a large number of RAF and RAAF aircraft outside the perimeter of their own defensive radar network and, unwittingly, within range of Japanese air strikes from Indochina. In spite of all the preparations, MATADOR would be of no use if Japan initiated action with seaborne landings in southern Siam or the northeastern tip of Malaya. In fact, if Japanese landings were simultaneously made farther south at Kuantan, British troops concentrated near the Thai border would be at extreme risk for loss in a double-envelopment action unless they made a hasty retreat down the western side of the Malayan Peninsula to Kuala Lumpur.

GOOD FORTUNE SMILED UPON the Japanese fleet throughout the morning and early afternoon of December 7, 1941, as it churned across the Gulf of Siam, secure beneath a veil of clouds and mist. These were the most critical hours of passage; discovery at this point would have affirmed that the landing force was bound for either Malaya or Siam's Kra Isthmus, giving the British Far East Command time to prepare a better air defense.

Late in the afternoon, at about 1545, an RAF Hudson crew from No. 8 Squadron at Kuantan finally spotted a motor vessel to the north of Kota Bharu. The ship was carrying "a large number of men on deck in khaki" and heading west.[1] It was not heading in the direction of Malaya, but the Japanese were clearly getting too close for comfort. Two No. 1 Squadron Hudsons, piloted by Flight Lieutenants John Lockwood and Jim Douglas, were dispatched from Kota Bharu to investigate this report and to search along the Thai coastline as far north as Singora and Patani—locations that possessed good anchorages with airfields nearby and were considered to be the most likely landing spots for a Japanese invasion of the southern Kra Isthmus. In the early evening, Douglas reported contact with four large, unidentified ships heading south toward Patani from a distance of about sixty miles.

Shortly thereafter, at 1750, Lockwood radioed a report that his crew had seen a motor vessel with an escorting "cruiser" about 120 miles due north of Kota Bharu. It appeared that both ships were headed in the direction of Kota Bharu.[2] The Hudson crew broke off its observation when the ship identified as a "cruiser" suddenly opened fire. Bad weather and nightfall precluded any further search activity.

Even though a definite shooting incident had occurred, the Far East Command and Air Headquarters in Singapore still needed time to assess the situation. To act, they needed concrete information, but all the answers lay beneath a storm front that covered the South China Sea. While the senior officers pondered Japan's intent, the Australian fliers at Kota Bharu convinced one another that the Japanese were headed their way. Still, they could only sit and wait for an attack to come. Standing orders forbade any offensive operation on their part, so the men of No. 1 Squadron were obliged to let the Japanese strike first.

During the hours after it was spotted by Lockwood's Hudson, the Japanese convoy continued along through the darkness toward Kota Bharu. The "cruiser" that had fired on Lockwood was actually a destroyer, *Uranami*, traveling in loose formation with the light cruiser *Sendai* and three other destroyers: *Ayanami*, *Isonami*, and *Shikinami*. The heavy cruiser *Chokai* trailed behind. Warships were escorting Major General Hiroshi Takumi's 56th Infantry Division of fifty-six hundred soldiers embarked on three transports: *Awagisan Maru*, *Ayatosan Maru*, and *Sakura Maru*. Shortly before 2300 on December 7, these ships emerged from the protective cover of the cloudbank into moonlit shallow waters, just four miles from the sandy shore at Sabak Beach.[3]

Although the Japanese transports commenced their unloading operation far enough out to sea to avoid being spotted from the beach, alert sentries noted the presence of several suspicious small boats moving about in the marsh near the mouth of the Kemassin River. Just after midnight this sighting information was relayed to the operations room at the Kota Bharu airfield. The report was hardly necessary. Within minutes, Japanese warships began shelling the beach defenses. The concussion of exploding 5-inch shells was readily heard and felt at the airfield only a mile and a half inland. The first major battle of the Pacific War was under way more than two hours before Japan's carrier planes descended on Hawaii.[4]

Wing Commander Reginald Davis—RAAF No. 1 Squadron's commanding officer—was the senior duty officer for the Kota Bharu station that night. He wasted no time requesting authority from Air

Headquarters at Singapore to conduct an armed reconnaissance of the coastline. Approval to send out a single Hudson to drop flares and assess the strength of the enemy naval force was immediately granted. Although no counterattack was ordered at that time, it was of little consequence; none of the Hudsons was loaded to conduct a bombing mission. Davis quickly returned responsibility for base operations to Kota Bharu's regular station commander, RAF Wing Commander C. H. Noble. Moments after Davis left the operations room to ready No. 1 Squadron for battle, Noble received Air Vice Marshal C.W.H. Pulford's order to dispatch its planes for an all-out attack on Japanese ships in the area.

Of ten Hudsons in commission, seven could be immediately prepared for bombing operations—each loaded with four 250-pound bombs fused for low-altitude bombardment. Because this was a night operation, there would be no coordinated flying formation. The Hudson pilots were briefed to attack individually, focusing on enemy troop transports as their top-priority targets.

The crashing blasts of naval guns had ceased, but the din of battle at the beachhead was easily heard at the airfield. A cacophony of small-arms fire, exploding mines and grenades, and screaming soldiers was soon augmented by the raucous bark of fourteen Twin-Wasp engines running up for a hurried takeoff. First off the field, Flight Lieutenant Lockwood started his Hudson rolling at 0208. When it was certain his bomber had cleared the runway, Lockwood was followed in turn by Flight Lieutenants John Ramshaw, Colin Verco, John Leighton-Jones, John O'Brien, James Emerton, and Oscar Diamond.[5]

By the time Lockwood's plane leveled out at two thousand feet, it had already passed over the twinkling flashes of gunfire on the beach. Flight Lieutenant Lockwood continued several miles out to sea. Three Japanese transports were spotted easily enough where the phosphorescent wakes of their landing craft fanned out from the anchorage toward the shore. The young Australian pilot swung his bomber in a wide path around the ships and then pushed it over into a dive in the direction of one of the transports. Pulling out at no more than fifty feet above the water, he released two bombs. Both missed the target. Drawing light antiaircraft fire from the ships, Lockwood stayed at low altitude and pulled his Hudson around for another pass at the same ship. Ramshaw caught up just in time to see Lockwood's last two bombs exploding directly amidships on the *Awagisan Maru*. Guided by the light of fires on board the ship, Ramshaw dropped his own bombs on that same transport. His salvo was followed immediately by a string of explosives from Verco's plane. In the dramatic contrast between the dark-of-night background and the glow of rising flames, none of the aircrews could observe any new hits on the enemy ship. All three pilots quickly turned back toward the airfield to rearm their planes.

Flight Lieutenant Leighton-Jones's Lockheed became separated from the others after it took off. At some point, Leighton-Jones zoomed low across the beachhead to strafe Japanese soldiers and landing barges. His Hudson was hit, either by ground fire from the beach or by antiaircraft fire from the Japanese landing craft. Suddenly, the Australian bomber veered off course, careening into the water directly on top of a barge loaded with enemy troops. Leighton-Jones, his crew, and some sixty Japanese soldiers and sailors riding in the boat perished instantly.[6]

Emerton piloted his plane past the activity near the transports, heading out to sea in search of other Japanese ships. He encountered what he described as a "large flat ship," which he thought might have been a small aircraft carrier. Emerton attacked this ship, making two passes at it, but apparently inflicted no damage. Although his description of the ship closely matches that of *Ryujo Maru*—a special-purpose landing barge carrier and floating headquarters for General Yamashita's 25th Army—it is not possible to determine the identity of the ship Emerton bombed. In any event, it was certainly not an aircraft carrier; none were assigned to the Japanese invasion fleet.

The other two pilots in the initial wave of Australian bombers, O'Brien and Diamond, had no more luck in their attacks than had Emerton, Ramshaw, or Verco. Each Hudson made low-level bombing runs on the transports, but Diamond's bombs missed their intended target and O'Brien's failed to release from his bomb racks.

As the first Lockheeds returned from their mission, three more commenced a second-wave attack on the Japanese landing force. Flight Lieutenant Douglas led fellow pilots Ken Smith and Gil White into the melee.[7] Only Smith and his crew generated observable results. Rather than attacking the transports, they targeted a group of ten landing barges clustered together near the shore. The combined explosion of two bombs managed to capsize several of the small craft, dumping their occupants and cargo into the sea.

Because of the previous sightings of the large convoy crossing the Gulf of Siam, Air Headquarters decided that a search for other enemy ships should be undertaken. O'Brien's Hudson, with its bombs still loaded from the aborted sortie, was the first plane ready for this mission. He was instructed to confirm the composition of the nearby landing force and then conduct a broader sweep for additional ships. Departing on his second flight of the battle at around 0330, O'Brien flew nearly thirty miles across the water before he observed a cruiser and three destroyers heading to the northwest at high speed. Without sighting any other ships, he turned back toward Kota Bharu.

When O'Brien was still about ten miles out, he came across the shadowy form of another large ship. Already flying at masthead height, he proceeded to execute a bombing run on the ship. As it happened, this was the cruiser *Sendai*, which put up a fierce barrage of antiaircraft fire in the path of the Hudson. Realizing the mistake in attacking such a heavily armed warship from low altitude, O'Brien took immediate evasive action. Dropping his bomber down to the wave-tops, he skidded past the cruiser's bow and roared away in the direction of the coastline, extremely fortunate that his aircraft had not been damaged. Out of range of *Sendai*'s guns, O'Brien picked out the transport nearest the shore, *Awagisan Maru*, as his next target. Continuing in at an altitude of about fifty feet, he released his bombs in a "stick" (all four dropped in a line) across the unlucky ship's bow. This earned him at least one direct hit, and likely damaged or overturned a number of barges lingering close alongside the transport. On the return course to the airfield, O'Brien's gunners shot up a number of landing craft that were moving toward the beach.

While O'Brien was carrying out his solo mission, No. 1 Squadron's third strike got under way. This time, Flight Lieutenant Ramshaw led the bombers off the field. He selected one of the warships as his target. Unlike O'Brien, Ramshaw continued to press his attack in the face of heavy antiaircraft fire. As a result, his Hudson was shot down into the sea before it could even complete one pass at the target. Of Ramshaw's crew, only his observer, Flying Officer Don Dowie, lived to tell of the tragic end to this mission. He lost consciousness during the crash but awakened to find himself floating alone in his life preserver, away from the scene of the battle. In a stroke of good luck, Dowie happened to be near an abandoned native prahu. He was able to climb into the drifting boat, but, without oars, he could not navigate it toward shore against the strong cross-current. For two days, he was adrift as the small craft carried him farther out to sea before it was finally discovered by a Japanese patrol boat. Starving and dehydrated, the young officer was taken on board, the first Australian airman to be captured as a prisoner of war.[8]

The other men from the third-wave attack fared considerably better. Flight Lieutenant Verco's crew believed they scored one or more hits on a transport (probably *Sakura Maru*). Diamond selected the burning *Awagisan Maru* as his target and placed one bomb directly on its deck, just forward of the bridge, causing a large explosion and more fires. Smith, in his second successful bombing run of the battle, attacked the third transport, *Ayatosan Maru*. Dropping a stick of bombs that straddled the ship, Smith noted that the explosions seemed to momentarily lift the vessel out of the water. By the time these sorties were completed, all three transports had taken such a severe beating from the Hudson crews that the naval force commander ordered an immediate withdrawal of the landing convoy and its escorts. While *Ayatosan Maru* and *Sakura Maru* had sustained significant damage, both were capable of making way. Before dawn, they departed. *Awagisan Maru*, heavily damaged and still on fire—with at least 110 of its crew either killed or wounded—was disabled and could not join the retreat as the other ships set a course back out to sea.[9]

The night battle off the shores of Kota Bharu would occupy a unique chapter in the annals of the Pacific War: it was the only time a Japanese naval force engaged in a landing assault was driven away from the beachhead before completing its planned unloading operation. The Australian fliers would also hold the distinction of being the only airmen ever to repel a naval force from the beaches with aircraft alone.

In spite of its success in forcing the Japanese task force to retire ahead of schedule, No. 1 Squadron suffered considerably. At 0500 Wing Commander Davis ordered the squadron to stand down and take stock of its situation. After less than three hours of battle, half of the serviceable Hudsons in No. 1 Squadron had been either destroyed or damaged to the point that they were no longer airworthy. Flight Lieutenant Diamond had been lucky to return for a safe landing at Kota Bharu. His aircraft had taken the brunt of a large antiaircraft shell burst that had knocked out his starboard engine and peppered the wing, fuselage, and tailplane with holes. Miraculously, none of Diamond's crew was injured. With holes in the fuel tanks and severely damaged flight controls, Flight Lieutenant Douglas also had some difficulty making it back to the airfield. His aircraft would be written off upon its return. Flight Lieutenant Verco made it back to the airstrip easily, but an inspection of his Lockheed found enough problems that it was classified as "temporarily unserviceable." Although the damage sustained by Lieutenant Smith's aircraft was minimal, a gunner in the Hudson was not so lucky: Sergeant Robert Hart was wounded in his left leg and arm by flying shrapnel that penetrated the thin fuselage. After the mechanics finished their assessments, only five of the bombers checked out as available to conduct additional missions.

WHILE THE MEN OF NO. 1 SQUADRON had been busy distinguishing themselves in the opening battle of the Pacific War, Singapore experienced its first bombing raid. At 0415 seventeen Mitsubishi G3M bombers of the *Mihoro Kokutai* dropped their loads on the downtown area, the waterfront, and the RAF bases at Seletar and Tengah. The raiders crippled three Blenheims of RAF 34 Squadron at Tengah, but otherwise caused only minor damage. It could have been much worse: fourteen other G3Ms of the *Mihoro Kokutai*, and thirty-four more from the *Genzan Kokutai*, were forced to abort their missions due to bad weather conditions encountered over the South China Sea.[10] Even without the physical impact of a heavier raid, the psychological wound was great enough; the bombing was a stunning blow to the British Far East Command. Ignoring intelligence about Japanese aircraft performance that had been gathered in China, Air Headquarters refused to accept that Japanese air forces were capable of striking directly at Singapore from airfields more than six hundred miles away in Indochina. In the words of Lieutenant General Arthur Percival, commander of the ground forces in Malaya: "It must be admitted that this raid came as rather a surprise, for the nearest Japanese aerodromes were 700 miles from Singapore, which was a considerable distance at that stage of the war, and we hardly expected the Japanese to have any very long-range aircraft."[11]

This first intrusion over Singapore highlighted another key shortcoming in the British defenses. Although inbound planes had been detected by a radar station on the Malayan eastern coast at Mersing almost an hour before they reached the island, Brooke-Popham's command possessed no "night-fighters" with which to intercept them. Three No. 453 Squadron Buffaloes were prepared for a scramble from Sembawang. When the lead pilot, Flight Lieutenant Tim Vigors—a decorated veteran of night battles against the German Luftwaffe—requested permission to send them off, he was flatly denied. Station commanders feared that inexperienced antiaircraft gunners would accidentally fire on the Buffaloes while trying to hit the Japanese planes. Later, this reason was supplemented with the ludicrous excuse that Buffaloes were generally considered suitable for action only during daylight hours and could not be used at night. It seems the only properly classified "night-fighting" aircraft assigned to the Far East Command were a dozen Bristol Blenheim IFs of RAF 27 Squadron. Paradoxically, these had been deployed to Sungei Patani, Malaya, as ground-attack aircraft.

SHORTLY AFTER THE FIRST BOMBS FELL on Singapore, the main Japanese landing force, consisting of 25th Army Headquarters and the 5th Division, flooded into Siam on the beaches near Singora. The 42nd Infantry Regiment was simultaneously put ashore at Patani, midway between Singora and Kota Bharu. Both of these landings met with only token resistance from local Thai army and police units. Securing additional points along the Kra Isthmus, the Southern Expeditionary Force landed elements of the 55th Division in four other places: Prachuap, Chumphon, Bandon, and Nakhon. The landing at Prachuap anchored the Japanese northern flank at a strategic location where the Kra Isthmus reaches its narrowest point—less than ten miles across from the sea to the mountain ranges that frame the Burmese border. Farther south, at Chumphon, the objective was to secure the landing position in Thailand and then thrust inland sixty miles to Victoria Point, at the southern tip of Burma. Seizing the British airstrip there would enable the Japanese to use long-range fighters to disrupt the vital air transport route between Singapore and Rangoon. The occupations of Bandon and Nakhon were not strategic, but they did ensure a uniform distribution of Japanese bases along the Thai coastline in preparation for large-scale movement westward into Burma.

At Singora and Patani, the primary invasion objective was to capture the airfields and, as rapidly as possible, to make them ready to receive more than one hundred fighters of the JAAF 1st, 11th, and 77th Sentai. These units employed the diminutive, fixed-landing-gear Ki-27s, which could cope well with the boggy, undeveloped Thai airfields. Once the fighters arrived, the Japanese army could maintain a nearly constant presence over all British airfields in northern Malaya. Other aircraft types would have to remain at distant bases in Indochina until captured Thai runways could be improved or some of the British airfields could be taken and placed in service.

Japanese planners hoped that the valuable Kota Bharu base could be seized with its runway reasonably intact. With luck, it might be put into operation a week or two after the invasion. For this reason, Kota Bharu airfield was granted exemption from naval bombardment and the initial bombing raids planned for other British air installations.

Japanese commanders expected the appearance of a strong British bomber force after daybreak. Until the JAAF could establish its advance echelon of fighters on the Kra Isthmus, the IJN would provide defensive air cover for the fleet. For the morning of December 8, the Singora landing forces were protected by rotating chutai-strength (nine-plane) formations of Zeros from the temporary fighter group attached to the 22nd Air Flotilla in Saigon. Aircraft and pilots for this duty had been drawn about equally from detachments of the *Tainan Kokutai* and the *3rd Kokutai*—groups normally based at Takao, Formosa. Reconnaissance and second-line fighter support were locally available in the form of twenty-two floatplanes operating with the seaplane tenders *Kamikawa Maru* and *Sagara Maru*.

Japan's air forces began the day by executing heavy bombing strikes. The raids were carefully calculated to knock out all British air operations in northern Malaya outside Kota Bharu. Having the advantage of surprise, the first Japanese bombers launched against these targets would take the risk of flying unescorted. Later in the day, if the Thai airstrips could be used, JAAF bombers conducting strikes on British positions could be shepherded by fighters.

JAAF fighter operations requiring un-refueled round-trips across the Gulf of Siam could only be accomplished using the Nakajima Ki-43 *Hayabusa* (translated as "Peregrine Falcon"), or "Oscar." The Ki-43 had been adopted as the standard army fighter to replace the Ki-27 and was initially deployed to selected units during mid-1941.

About the same size as a navy A6M, and confusingly similar in form, the Ki-43 was powered by an almost identical fourteen-cylinder Nakajima Sakae radial engine. In the early days of combat over Malaya, many British and Commonwealth airmen misidentified Ki-43s and reported engagements with Zeros in areas where none were actually present. Although the Ki-43 had no cannon, and only fielded the same light, twin 7.7-mm machine-gun armament as its predecessors, it weighed six hundred pounds more than a contemporary Zero. With this extra mass—and a much less efficient airfoil pattern than that of the Mitsubishi—the Ki-43 did not possess the same outstanding rate of climb as a Zero, nor did it share the A6M's maximum velocity or endurance. Top speed was a modest 308 miles per hour, and its range was about 750 miles—figures comparable with a Brewster Buffalo. The Ki-43's performance was a great leap forward from that of the Ki-27, and the Ki-43 was endowed with a significant fighting advantage in its unique "combat-maneuver" flaps. This control enhancement boosted roll rates, enabling the otherwise unremarkable fighter to outmaneuver any other contemporary aircraft, including the vaunted A6M.

Often misidentified as a Zero, the Nakajima Ki-43 was the primary JAAF fighter of the Pacific War. It was used successfully by the 59th and 64th Sentai in combat against Australian Brewster Buffaloes above Malaya. These Ki-43-Is are in 50th Sentai markings from the Burma campaign. (Courtesy of via Rod Larson)

Japanese Army Air Force Mitsubishi Ki-21s on a training mission. These bombers were at the forefront of the air campaign in Malaya, but played only a supporting role to Japanese navy planes over the Philippines. (Courtesy of via Rod Larson)

The bombers deployed over Malaya on December 8, 1941, were the mainstays of the IJA bombing campaign in the Far East: the Mitsubishi Ki-21 "Sally" and Kawasaki Ki-48 "Lily." Both of these designs had been combat proven in China and would serve as the standard JAAF twin-engine bombers well into the Pacific War. More Ki-21s would be built during the war than any other JAAF bomber type. The Ki-21—with a bomb capacity of 800 kilograms (1,650 pounds)—was classified as a heavy bomber. It had a crew of seven and was capable of a relatively high maximum speed of 268 miles per hour. This made the Ki-21 somewhat faster than a G3M, though its 1,700-mile range was only half that of its naval service contemporary. The Ki-21 did not rely on speed alone for defense; its complement of six 7.7-mm machine guns afforded the most robust defensive firepower of any Japanese aircraft of the time. Conversely, the Kawasaki Ki-48 was lightly armed, with only three flexibly mounted 7.7-mm machine guns. It was a fast bomber and could usually count on its top speed of more than 300 miles per hour to evade interception. Naturally, ample velocity and a healthy range of almost 1,500 miles were achieved at the expense of a modest 400-kilogram (880-pound) bomb load and the combat vulnerability inherent in lightweight construction.

Japan's timetable for the invasion of Malaya would depend a great deal on the success of these aircraft, but an even greater responsibility would be borne by the newest heavy bomber in the Japanese navy: the Mitsubishi G4M1 "Betty," Type 1 land-based attack bomber. Sometimes nicknamed "the flying cigar"—due to its cylindrical fuselage cross-section and the pronounced taper of its nose and tail sections—the G4M was the intended replacement for the aging G3M. In general specifications, the G4M might not have seemed to offer much improvement over its predecessor. Its absolute range and altitude ceiling were slightly less than those of a G3M; its top speed and ordnance-carrying capacity were only marginally greater. Of course, absolutes seldom tell the entire story. The G4M could actually carry a heavier load farther and faster under more typical combat conditions. With a larger fuselage—ten feet longer than a G3M—the new twin-engine bomber was more adequately armed, with several additional 7.7-mm machine guns and a potently stinging 20-mm cannon in its tail.

In the best tradition of Japanese aircraft design, the G4M was a model of efficiency: two powerful fourteen-cylinder Mitsubishi Kasei

Kawasaki's Ki-48 light bomber was a regular combatant in the Malayan and Philippine campaigns. Operating at low altitude, it relied on speed and fighter protection for safety. Buffalo and P-40 pilots registered numerous "kills" against unescorted Ki-48s during the first fortnight of the Pacific War. (Courtesy of via Rod Larson)

This photo captures a formation of Mitusubishi G4Ms. Above the Philippines, these bombers typically flew in groups of twenty-seven to fifty-four. The accuracy and weight of their high-altitude bombardments was devastating. At wave-top height, their torpedo attacks proved equally deadly in the sinking of Prince of Wales *and* Repulse. (Courtesy of via Rod Larson)

engines endowed it with range, speed, and altitude capabilities superior to the U.S. twin-engine bomber types equipped with Wright Cyclone-14s of similar displacement and output. In spite of its defensive weaponry, without protective armor plating or self-sealing fuel tanks, the Mitsubishi bomber was vulnerable to attacks by heavily armed U.S.-built fighters. Later in the war, in line with the cigar analogy, the Betty would earn the epithet "one-shot lighter." Once hit, it would likely catch fire. Such deficiencies would matter only in the event that Allied interceptors could get at the G4Ms. At this opening stage of the Pacific War, IJN bombers were at risk only when executing low-altitude attacks. In the rarified atmosphere of twenty thousand feet or more, P-40 and Buffalo pilots had little chance of gaining enough height and speed to approach a G4M. At lower altitudes, the Allied pilots usually faced the formidable challenge of breaking through an ever-present shield of escorting Zeros.

Rear Admiral Matsunaga, commander of the 22nd Air Flotilla in Saigon, had every reason to be confident in the capabilities of his bomber forces. From experience in China, the men could be counted on to deliver telling blows to targets on land. In addition to a sizable force of G3Ms, twenty-seven new Mitsubishi G4M1 bombers of the *Kanoya Kokutai* were available. The latter were not assigned to the task of airfield elimination. Instead, the G4Ms were being held in reserve for exactly the type of mission for which they had been designed: long-range antishipping torpedo attack. While the effectiveness of land-based attack bombers against warships at sea was an article of faith, an unanticipated development in the Far East would give Admiral Matsunaga a chance to test the concept.

In spite of its apparent strength in warships, the IJN had a bit of an inferiority complex regarding the capabilities of *Prince of Wales* and *Repulse*; naval experts did not consider *Haruna* an equal to the Royal Navy dreadnoughts. Consequently, Japan was reluctant to risk its battleship in a surface engagement with the British. The planes of the *Kanoya Kokutai* and their top-notch crews provided the only insurance against a potentially devastating intervention by the Royal Navy. Of course, these IJN bombers could only hope to wound or sink the British battleships if Malaya-based fighter support was eliminated. Japanese naval air officers worried whether their massive strikes against British airfields would be heavy enough to prevent successful retaliation by Air Vice Marshal Pulford's air forces. Failure to achieve that objective might lead to severe losses for the Japanese invasion fleet lying off the coast of Siam. As Japanese army aircraft readied for departure from a half-dozen fields in western Indochina, anxiety grew in the IJN command centers—naval officers would never be comfortable consigning their fate to the actions of an army.

In darkness, the first chutai of A6Ms departed from Soc Trang airfield on a course to Singora. These were the only navy planes assigned to the air armada. Before long, waves of Ki-21 and Ki-48 bombers rose above the misty jungles of Southeast Asia and headed toward British bases in northern Malaya.

By first light, Japanese air unit and naval commanders received welcome news from the IJA landing forces. Singora airfield had been secured and was ready to receive aircraft. Within an hour of that communication, Japanese forces already in the air were joined by flocks of Ki-27 fighters staging for Singora through Duong Dong airfield on Phu Quoc Island. Ships at the Singora and Patani anchorages would have constant fighter cover available before noon. Japan's campaign was progressing well, so far.

ON THE SOUTHERN SIDE OF THE GULF OF SIAM, British and Commonwealth bomber squadrons were busy preparing their own flight plans during the final hours of darkness. Air Headquarters decided that all available twin-engine bombers in Malaya and Singapore would fly up to Kota Bharu, attack any Japanese forces they could find in the vicinity, and then land and rearm at designated forward airfields in northern Malaya, where they would receive further instructions. Planning for this mission was anything but thorough, and each squadron would operate independently. There would be no coordination of activity until late afternoon.

Already fatigued by dawn Flight Lieutenant O'Brien glimpsed the first pinkish rays of sunlight filtering across the eastern horizon as he piloted his Hudson on its third combat mission of the morning. This time, in passing over the beach at Kota Bharu, the Australian pilot noted that only one burning transport remained offshore. He continued flying north-northwest out to sea in an effort to locate the fleeing Japanese ships. Although the weather had already begun to deteriorate, O'Brien's crew was able to spot a formation consisting of two cruisers, four destroyers, two transports, and one smaller escort ship steaming in the general direction of Singora. O'Brien believed, correctly, that this was the retreating Kota Bharu landing force and its escort. Directly above these ships, a formation of nine twin-engine aircraft was seen heading south, toward the coast. Upon spotting the enemy planes, O'Brien immediately wheeled his Hudson back around to return to Kota Bharu.

As the shroud of darkness gradually lifted, the Indian troops along Sabak Beach realized their position was weakening. Several key points in the defenses had been captured during the night. The glow of first

light exposed a number of barges full of Japanese soldiers being towed
up the Kelantan River toward the town of Kota Bharu. Worried about
this obvious attempt to outflank another strongpoint, the Dogras
requested tactical air support at 0630. The two Buffaloes of RAF 243
Squadron were immediately dispatched to shoot up any boats they
could find floating on the Kelantan. While these aircraft constituted
the only fighter defense for the area, it made sense to deploy them in a
strafing role. The concentrated fire of four .50-caliber heavy machine
guns in each Buffalo would be much more effective than that of the
light .303-caliber weapons in the Hudsons.

In the process of attacking the boats and troops along the shore,
one Buffalo was hit by return fire and suffered damage to its flight
controls. The pilot, Flying Officer M. H. Holder, nursed his wobbling
fighter back to the airstrip but lost control during the landing run. In
an abrupt departure from the runway, Holder's Buffalo collided with
Flight Lieutenant Diamond's previously damaged Hudson, which sat
disabled on the grass apron. Both aircraft were wrecked beyond
repair, but no one was injured.

Pilot Officer R. S. Shield, in the other Buffalo, continued to patrol
the skies. Before long, the New Zealander spotted a group of nine
large twin-engine bombers cruising along a southeastward track,
toward the auxiliary field at Machang. This was almost certainly the
same formation O'Brien had encountered at sea. Shield increased his
speed and attempted to intercept the bombers. He closed in from
behind and squeezed the trigger. Nothing happened. The guns were
jammed. Feeling that he had missed an incredible opportunity, the
Buffalo pilot glumly returned to Kota Bharu. Unimpeded, the chutai
of 62nd Sentai Ki-21s bombed the Machang airstrip.

Meanwhile, in response to Flight Lieutenant O'Brien's reconnaissance report, seven Vickers Vildebeest torpedo-bombers from the RAF
36 Squadron detachment at Gong Kedah were sent out to attack the
retreating warships. A second Vildebeest-equipped unit, RAF 100
Squadron, was already flying twelve more of the lumbering biplanes up
from Seletar to Kuantan to stage another strike on the Japanese navy.

By the time these ancient fabric-covered biplanes lifted off the
runway, virtually every operational bomber in the British Far East Command was airborne and on its way to attack Japanese forces around the
Kota Bharu beachhead. RAF 34 Squadron sent up nine of its Blenheims
that had not been damaged during the early-morning bombing of
Tengah. Eight of RAF 27 Squadron's Blenheim IF "night-fighters,"

loaded with bombs, had been dispatched across the mountains from Sungei Patani. Another eight Blenheims from RAF 60 Squadron departed from Kuantan in company with twelve Hudsons from RAAF No. 8 Squadron. On the opposite side of Malaya, eighteen Blenheims of RAF 62 Squadron at Alor Star were about to leave their base. The only unassigned British bombers still on the ground after daybreak were four Blenheim IFs of 27 Squadron at Sungei Patani, the few airworthy Hudsons of RAAF No. 1 Squadron being serviced at Kota Bharu, and six RAF 100 Squadron Bristol Beauforts.

The 100 Squadron crews were quite disappointed not to be flying any of their new Beauforts into combat. This twin-engine design—a torpedo-carrying evolution of the Blenheim—had been significantly delayed in production, mostly due to problems with its new sleeve-valve Bristol Taurus engine. More powerful and reliable Pratt & Whitney Twin-Wasps had been chosen to equip the Australian-built planes assigned to 100 Squadron. With this engine, the Beauforts were faster than their British siblings and could operate at a much higher altitude. In most performance characteristics, they were remarkably similar to a Lockheed Hudson. Astonishingly, none of the six examples on hand had been delivered fully equipped or armed, and there were no parts available in Singapore to make up for such a glaring deficiency. Five of the bombers had been retained at Seletar for use in conversion training for aircrews. The sixth, hastily fitted with machine guns and cameras, was on temporary assignment to Kota Bharu for use in photo-reconnaissance operations. Because nothing definite was known about the situation in Siam, this bomber took off from Kota Bharu at about 0700 to make a high-altitude photo survey of the Singora and Patani areas. Flight Lieutenant P. D. F. Mitchell and his crew had no idea that this simple assignment would give them the ride of their lives.

Barely ten minutes after the Beaufort's departure, Flight Lieutenants Lockwood and Smith lifted off again from Kota Bharu. As the sun climbed higher in the sky, offshore fog rapidly developed into storm clouds. Lockwood could not clearly scan seaward because of the weather, but he could verify O'Brien's previous report that only one burnt-out ship remained in the Kota Bharu area. The presence of a large oil slick some distance away from the hulk fooled Lockwood into reporting that a second ship must have already been sunk. Deciding not to waste any bombs on the heavily damaged transport, Lockwood and Smith shot up more landing craft and provided whatever close air support they could for the Indian troops along the beaches. In the process, Lockwood's Hudson was damaged slightly by return fire from the ground. Bullets tore through the bomber's aluminum skin, narrowly missing the gunner, Sergeant Adrian Munday.

On the western side of the Malayan mountains, at Sungei Patani, the dozen Buffaloes of RAAF No. 21 Squadron awaited the call to action. Two of these fighters were manned for immediate takeoff. Two more were on alert, their pilots sitting nearby with helmets, goggles, and parachutes at the ready. The ground crew had the engines warmed up on all four Buffaloes. Across the field in the operations room, tension ran high as men listened to the reports from Singapore and Kota Bharu. At 0700 an urgent message was received. Troops near the Thai border had sighted enemy aircraft flying in the direction of Sungei Patani.

While Flight Lieutenant Fred Williams and Flying Officer Daryl Sproule sat restlessly in their cockpits, No. 21 Squadron's command- ing officer, Squadron Leader William Allshorn, requested permission from the RAF station commander, Squadron Leader F. R. C. Fowle, to scramble their alert fighters. Inexplicably, Fowle would not assent to Allshorn's request, so the order for an interception never came. Within ten minutes, five unescorted Ki-21 bombers of the 98th Sentai droned overhead. Williams and Sproule, admonished not to take off unless specifically instructed to do so, could do nothing. The pair quickly climbed down from their fighters and ran for the shelter of a drainage ditch as falling bombs whistled toward the air station.

The pilots of the two standby aircraft, Flight Lieutenant Robert Kirkman and Flying Officer John Hooper, had not been bound by the same direct orders. This brave duo hopped into their planes and roared off down the strip. They got into the air just as Japanese bombs began bursting around the field. Those first weapons exploded near four Blenheim IFs of 27 Squadron, severely damaging three of the fighter-bombers and mortally wounding the crewmen in one. More explosives fell on the runway and among the parked Buffaloes, com- pletely destroying two of the fighters and damaging five others. The final string of bombs fell on the operations and communications buildings, killing two men as it knocked out the station's primary radio and telephone equipment.[12] Kirkman and Hooper were fortu- nate to have gotten airborne under the shower of ordnance. They climbed as fast as their Brewsters could manage, hoping to make the enemy pay. The two Australians gained a good deal of ground on the retiring bombers before they tested their guns and discovered that none would fire. Greatly disappointed at their inability to strike back at the audacious attackers, the two Buffalo pilots flew back to land at the ravaged airfield.

In cloud-blanketed skies over the sea between Kota Bharu and Patani, the seven Vildebeests from RAF 36 Squadron labored along through drenching rains. Scanning choppy, gray seas for retreating ships was miserably wet and uncomfortable duty in the water-soaked, open-cockpit biplanes. At about 0730, a cruiser was sighted. Four of the fabric-covered torpedo-bombers closed in for an attack. Low visibility precluded any synchronization of torpedo drops that might have effectively boxed their quarry in a corner. The Japanese warship was able to adroitly maneuver out of the paths of the individually launched weapons. This mission was a failure, and not without cost to the British. One attacking Vildebeest was hit in the landing gear by antiaircraft fire from the cruiser and then further damaged as that wheel strut collapsed on landing at Gong Kedah. Another—one of three that never found a target—was wrecked when its pilot caught a wingtip on the ground while making a rough landing of the torpedo-laden aircraft.

Shortly after 0800, Hudsons from RAAF No. 8 Squadron began to arrive over Kota Bharu. Squadron Leader Andrew Henderson's first section of four bombers bored in on the smoking *Awagisan Maru* from an altitude of five hundred feet. Apparently, his flight had not received an urgent signal broadcast from the Kota Bharu operations center to all incoming RAF and RAAF bombers. This communication directed the bombers toward coordinates of Flight Lieutenant O'Brien's last reported contact with the retiring Japanese transports and their escorts. One pilot from Henderson's flight dropped his bomb load on the burning transport, probably scoring at least one hit, but not accomplishing much; the ship had already been abandoned. Henderson and his other two wingmen released their weapons on a number of boats and barges milling about along the shore. These crews recorded the sinking of several landing craft before they headed back toward Kuantan.

A second flight of No. 8 Squadron Hudsons did receive the radio transmission. It was the only formation of bombers to act on these redirection instructions. This section dutifully continued on past Kota Bharu and out to sea in search of the invasion force. The four Lockheeds soon encountered the same turbulent weather that had confounded RAF 36 Squadron. Realizing the clouds were impenetrable even as he skimmed the waves, the flight leader opted to reverse his course back toward Kota Bharu. If his Hudsons could not find enemy shipping, at least they would expend their ordnance on the beachhead.

The third section of Hudsons arrived over the Kota Bharu battle-ground while the four bombers of the second flight were still out searching for Japanese ships. Flight Lieutenant Russell Bell observed some fifty to sixty enemy boats still shuttling around the beaches and the mouth of the Peng Chepa River, near the airfield. Bell and his three wingmen directed their attacks against as many of the small craft as possible. In the process, Bell's aircraft was hit by machine-gun fire from an armored patrol boat. With a seriously damaged hydraulic system that prevented the operation of his landing gear and bomb bay doors, he left the rest of his flight behind and sped directly back toward RAF Headquarters at Seletar. This airfield was the only place where he could hope to make a wheels-up landing and still save his Hudson for future use. No other base in Malaya or Singapore could repair airframe damage resulting from a belly-landing.

Meanwhile, the crew of the lone Beaufort from 100 Squadron had been stealthily observing and photographing the Japanese land-ing force at Singora through broken clouds. Flight Lieutenant Mitchell's cameras recorded at least twenty ships of the invasion force and an armada of landing craft in the bay, as well as more than sixty single-engine aircraft parked on the airfield.[13] The film continued to roll as the Beaufort crew spotted six planes flying well beneath their own altitude of twenty thousand feet. Having only a limited understanding of Japanese aircraft capabilities, the men did not view these as an immediate threat to their high-flying, rapidly moving Beaufort.

What happened next surprised them. Within a precious few min-utes, three A6M Zeros from the 22nd Air Flotilla detachment had climbed more than fifteen thousand feet and were swarming around the British plane. As the first bullets struck his Beaufort, Mitchell hauled the bomber into a steeply banked turn. The turret gunner, Sergeant W. L. Barcroft, frantically drew a bead on one of the attack-ers and fired a long burst at the Japanese fighter as he himself was struck in the leg by one of its 7.7-mm bullets. Continuing through the turn, the Beaufort was hit in its port engine nacelle. A fuel line was severed, causing the engine to quit suddenly. The unbalanced loss of power on one side flipped the damaged bomber over onto its back and sent it spinning crazily downward toward the sea.

Witnessing the spectacle of the inverted Beaufort tumbling out of control into a cloudbank, the Japanese navy pilots believed they had shot it down and claimed destruction of one "Blenheim" bomber. The assumption was actually fortunate for the British crewmen. The Zeros chose not to pursue their "kill." In any case, the Japanese fliers were preoccupied. During the brief exchange of fire with Barcroft, the A6M of the shotai leader, Lieutenant Tadatsune Tokaji, was hit in its engine and damaged enough to force him into an emergency landing at Singora.

In an amazing feat of piloting, Mitchell was able to regain control of the plunging aircraft. Under the cover of thick clouds, his attackers never noticed. While the Zero pilots did not know that the Beaufort had escaped, the Beaufort crew was equally unaware that Sergeant Barcroft's aim had in fact been true, downing one A6M.[14]

The second flight from RAAF No. 8 Squadron had not flown far enough west to run afoul of Zeros before aborting its search for Japanese ships. Returning from the weather-foiled hunt, all four Hudsons roared back across the shore above the enemy landing site at Sabak Beach. Flight Lieutenant Charles "Spud" Spurgeon broke away to conduct yet another bombing run on the derelict *Awagisan Maru*. He gained one hit on the doomed ship, but the resultant explosions riddled his low-flying Hudson with shrapnel from its own bombs. None of the crew was injured, but Spurgeon was obliged to execute an emergency wheels-up landing in the grassy apron of the Kota Bharu airfield.

Flight Lieutenant Emerton of RAAF No. 1 Squadron had gotten his Hudson back in the air at 0900, just before Spud Spurgeon's crash. Emerton radioed that the single Japanese transport was apparently abandoned. No more barges were moving around near it. As he joined the few remaining planes of No. 8 Squadron in attacking enemy ground positions and landing craft, Japanese fighters made their initial appearance in the skies above Kota Bharu.

Flight Lieutenant Geoffrey Hitchcock of No. 8 Squadron was flying the first Hudson to be bounced by enemy planes. Hitchcock's gunners reported that they were being pursued by a "Japanese Navy Zero fighter," which quickly registered a number of small-caliber hits on the Hudson. Sergeant Richard Jansen returned fire, striking the nearest Japanese plane. Trailing smoke, the "Zero" broke off and ditched in the sea.[15]

Emerton's Hudson was also pursued by a fighter that his crew described as a "Navy Zero." Like Hitchcock, Emerton quickly received some bullets from this attacker before his gunners could respond. He was able to avoid more damage by abruptly turning his bomber into the path of his opponent, forcing the Japanese pilot to overshoot. After a couple of similarly unsuccessful passes, the Japanese pilot diverted his attention to another Hudson. Emerton seized the initiative and turned to chase the enemy fighter. Firing with his two nose guns, the aggressive bomber pilot startled his former pursuer into breaking off the attack on the other Hudson. With holes in one fuel tank and a wounded observer, Emerton was soon compelled to disengage from the fight and return to the airfield.

The hulk of the Japanese transport was still the most tempting target for several Blenheims from RAF 60 Squadron that arrived as the Hudsons were completing their attacks on the Japanese beach positions. It was a bomb from these aircraft that actually sank *Awagisan Maru*.[16] The badly battered ship slipped beneath the waves around 0930, the first Japanese surface ship to be sunk during the Pacific War.

In spite of this success, the RAF paid a heavy price for sinking the transport and numerous smaller craft around the enemy beachhead. Two of eight Blenheims were shot down by antiaircraft fire: one ditching in the sea, the other crashing among the coconut palms just across the Thai border. A third Blenheim was severely damaged but managed a safe return flight to Kuantan.

Amid all of this activity, nine Blenheim IV bombers of RAF 34 Squadron arrived at Kota Bharu after their long flight from Singapore. By this time, no obvious targets were left to bomb at sea. The 34 Squadron planes did not have enough fuel to loiter. They dropped their ordnance along the beaches and turned inland to climb across the mountains in the direction of the air station at Butterworth. Some Blenheims managed a clean getaway, but a few were intercepted by 64th Sentai Ki-43 fighters that had been strafing the Kota Bharu airstrip. Major Tateo Kato's wingman, Lieutenant Yohei Hinoki, claimed a shared victory over one of the British bombers. A single Blenheim was in fact hit by the fighters. This damaged bomber circled around to make an emergency landing at Machang, although it was not actually destroyed in the action.[17]

During a brief lull in the air battle over Kota Bharu, Flight Lieutenant Mitchell brought his damaged Beaufort in for a safe return from its harrowing reconnaissance. Naturally, the commanders in Singapore were anxious to get their hands on the photos of Singora. Air Headquarters requested that the Beaufort be immediately refueled and sent back to Singapore. Unfortunately, several flights of Japanese army fighters were subjecting the Kota Bharu airfield to a furious strafing. The Beaufort was hit multiple times by gunfire. The crew was lucky enough to retrieve the cameras from the plane, but the strafers eventually succeeded in setting fire to the bomber. When the enemy fighter attacks finally subsided, the films were delivered to Brooke-Popham's staff in Singapore by Flying Officer Holder, who flew them back to Seletar in his wingman's undamaged Buffalo.

Eleven Blenheim IVs from RAF 62 Squadron were the last British planes to attempt a bombing of the Japanese landing zone at Kota Bharu on December 8. Under the command of Squadron Leader C. H. Boxall, these bombers had taken off from Alor Star just after 0900. By the time they arrived over Kota Bharu, no obvious targets remained. On his own initiative, Boxall led the flight northwestward up the coastline to Patani, where he observed a number of transport ships in the process of unloading troops and supplies. Bombing the enemy from eight thousand feet, through scattered clouds, the RAF crews observed no definite results. The Blenheim formation returned to its base at Alor Star, unmolested by either antiaircraft fire or several Japanese fighters that had been in the vicinity of Patani. Boxall's impromptu raiders would have the distinction of being the only aircraft to manage an attack on the Japanese landing armada at its Kra Isthmus anchorage during the first day of war.

In the aftermath of the Japanese raid on Sungei Patani, the western side of Malaya returned to tranquillity for several hours. RAAF No. 21 Squadron commenced an airborne patrol around its airfield. Flying Officer Hooper was engaged in this duty at 0900, when he spotted another formation of seven Mitsubishi Ki-21 bombers heading toward his base. After unsuccessfully attempting to radio the new, makeshift Sungei Patani control center for instructions, he rose to intercept the bombers. As Hooper's Buffalo slowly climbed after the enemy, six Nakajima Ki-43 fighters—which he incorrectly thought were "Navy Zeroes"—dove to meet him. Significantly outnumbered, and realizing he would have little chance of inflicting damage on the rapidly escaping Japanese bomber formation, Hooper rolled his Brewster onto its back, pulled hard on the control stick, and dove as fast as he could down to treetop level. To his relief, the Japanese fighters ignored him. They continued south with the bombers, passing over Sungei Patani without attacking.

By mid-morning, Air Headquarters still had no solid information about Japanese activity in Siam. Mitchell's photographs would not reach the Air Staff officers before noon. Without data, Air Vice Marshal Pulford could not decide where to target additional counterattacks beyond those already directed at the vicinity of Kota Bharu. In an attempt to fill the gap in knowledge regarding Japanese troop movements in the north, a pair of No. 21 Squadron Buffaloes was expeditiously prepared for a visual reconnaissance of the harbors at Singora and Patani. The fighter pilots flying the mission were also asked to scout along the roads leading from those towns back to the Malayan border. The two Australians would have no cameras, but a thorough debriefing could provide some actionable information.

Flight Lieutenant Jack Kinninmont and Sergeant Norm Chapman took off from Sungei Patani around 0930. The duo headed north to Singora, flying at a comfortable altitude of ten thousand feet. When they were about two miles away from Singora, they were intercepted by twelve Ki-27s of the 11th Sentai. The fixed-gear Japanese planes—mistakenly identified by the Australian pilots as "Navy Type 96 fighters"—literally swarmed over the two Buffaloes. Twisting and turning, Kinninmont and Chapman had too many targets to track. They fired wildly in the direction of any plane that crossed their paths. The Buffalo pilots were quickly outmaneuvered. Within minutes, each had several of the nimble Ki-27s stuck to his tail. As tracers from the pursuers whipped past the hapless fighters, the Australians dove for the deck.

While passing through three thousand feet, Kinninmont glimpsed the outline of a four-engine Kawanishi flying boat. After taking an opportunistic shot at this large aircraft, he dropped on down to treetop level. One of the Ki-27s managed to stay with Kinninmont in the dive. It continued to fire on the Buffalo, splattering the Australian plane with rifle-caliber bullets. Going to full power, and staying dangerously close to the dark-green jungle canopy, Kinninmont was able to shake the aim of the Japanese pilot by violently turning his fighter each time he saw muzzle flashes from the Ki-27's nose guns in his rearview mirror. Near the Malayan border, the enemy fighter broke off the engagement—probably after expending all of its ammunition. Kinninmont, unsure what had become of Chapman's Buffalo—which he had last seen diving with three Japanese fighters glued to its tail—landed back at Sungei

Patani, where he was greatly relieved to discover that Chapman had also made a safe return.

No sooner had Kinninmont's and Chapman's bullet-scarred fighters been serviced than another group of Japanese bombers was seen approaching Sungei Patani. No. 21 Squadron had only five Buffaloes ready to scramble, but the pilots were eager to climb into battle. Frustration gnawed at the anxious fliers once again. For the second time that morning, Squadron Leader Fowle refused to authorize them to take off for an interception. The senior Australian, Squadron Leader Allshorn, was furious, but he obeyed the order after a heated discussion with Fowle.

At 1045 fifteen Mitsubishi Ki-21s of the 12th Sentai cast dark shadows over the airfield as they dropped their sticks of bombs from an altitude of six thousand feet. This attack was even more devastating than the first. Though only one of the Buffaloes was seriously damaged, five of nine operable RAF 27 Squadron Blenheims were either destroyed or damaged beyond repair; the main fuel dump containing more than 200,000 gallons of gasoline was ignited; most of the permanent buildings on the field were damaged to some significant degree; and the runway was severely cratered.[18] As a British base, Sungei Patani was finished.

To the north, a formation of twenty-seven Ki-21s from the 60th Sentai appeared in the skies above Alor Star just before 1100. On that airstrip, the recently returned Blenheims of RAF 62 Squadron were being refueled and rearmed. As crews and service personnel scattered to seek cover around the wide, grassy field, more than a hundred bombs rained down on them. Four Blenheims were completely destroyed. All but two of the others received significant shrapnel damage. Miraculously, only a handful of men were killed.[19]

While Japanese bombers concentrated on the northernmost of the Malayan airfields, their fighter umbrella was extended as far south as Penang Island and Butterworth. In the final minutes of a long mission, Blenheims from RAF 34 Squadron again fell prey to Ki-43 fighters. To the tired British fliers making their landing approach at Butterworth it must have seemed that the Japanese were everywhere over northern Malaya. This time, the attacking Nakajimas came from the 59th Sentai. One of the Blenheims was thoroughly shot up and made a crash landing on the Butterworth airstrip, with minor injuries to its crew. Another Blenheim was chased away at treetop height and filled with holes, but returned to make a safe landing after the Japanese fighters departed. The Australian turret gunner in that Blenheim, Sergeant Keith Burrill—though wounded in the jaw by a Japanese bullet—continued to man his position and claimed the destruction of his pursuer. During a final exchange of gunfire with Burrill, the Ki-43 suddenly tumbled away into the jungle.[20]

Excitement over this victory was short-lived. The Blenheims had barely started to refuel when another formation of Hayabusas swooped down on them. Major Kato, the 64th Sentai commanding officer, and his 1st Chutai trailed the unsuspecting British bombers from Kota Bharu to Butterworth. The Ki-43s had no opportunity to shoot down any planes, but they worked over the Butterworth station thoroughly. Though armed only with rifle-caliber machine guns, Kato's pilots severely damaged four refueling Blenheims.[21]

On the eastern side of Malaya, the day continued to get worse. By noon, small groups of Japanese soldiers skirted defending troops at Kota Bharu airfield and commenced with sporadic small-arms fire in the direction of the RAF facilities. During the confusion and panic caused by this threatening activity, the Operations Room received a new report that enemy transports had been spotted in the Kelantan River estuary. Four No. 1 Squadron Hudsons from Kota Bharu and three RAF 36 Squadron Vildebeests from Gong Kedah were promptly sent out for an antishipping strike. This hastily mustered mission was an unnecessary waste of resource; the report was soon found to be based on information from much earlier in the day. With no ships to attack, the Hudsons and Vildebeests worked over some landing craft. Strafing armed boats along the shore proved costly: two of the Lockheeds were damaged by return fire. Flight Lieutenant Verco's plane had a tire shot out, forcing him to make a one-wheel landing. The ensuing ground-loop crash took his Hudson out of the fight permanently.

STATISTICS WERE FAR FROM COMPILED, but it was obvious to Air Vice Marshal Pulford that his air force had failed. Realizing that it was no longer possible to initiate productive bombing sorties against the Japanese invasion fleet, Air Headquarters shifted its focus to the protection of surviving aircraft. Given the significant losses already absorbed, it would be important to conserve as many planes as possible. As a defensive precaution, orders were issued to relocate flyable aircraft from Kota Bharu to Kuantan, and from Alor Star and Sungei Patani to Butterworth. It was an uncomfortable command decision to suggest evacuating the air forces after just one day of battle, but additional severe bombings could be expected at any time. Clearly, the range in Japanese air operations enabled by the occupation of the Singora air-field made all British air stations in Malaya vulnerable to sudden attack.

As the bomber crews prepared for their migration southward, Flight Lieutenant Kinninmont volunteered to conduct one more reconnaissance along the road from Alor Star to Singora. In the heat of mid-afternoon, his green and tan camouflaged Buffalo flew low over a ribbon of highway that cut through the dense jungle. Crossing into Siam, the Australian flier noted that Japanese motor columns had progressed well on their way south toward the Malayan border. As Kinninmont neared the coast of Singora, he was intercepted again, this time by "Zero-type" fighters. Before fleeing the area, he was able to spot about forty ships in the harbor, numerous single-engine air-craft parked on the Singora airfield, and a number of large flying boats floating on Lake Singora.[22] As the Japanese fighters closed in, the young Buffalo pilot raced his plane flat-out at treetop level toward Sungei Patani, only turning when fired upon. In a repetition of his previous experience, Kinninmont's pursuers gave up the chase when their ammunition was expended.

By mid-afternoon, the men at Kota Bharu found themselves under nearly constant Japanese fighter attack. This aerial harassment, plus sustained ground fire from enemy snipers, made some locations around the airfield so hazardous that repair crews were unable to service two Hudsons dispersed at the south end of the field. In fact, the Japanese presence at the southern edge of the air station became cause for alarm. To jittery air force personnel, it seemed that their base was surrounded. The airmen would be only too happy to leave when the opportunity presented itself.

At around 1600, during an ebb in Japanese strafing attacks, the last five airworthy Hudsons of RAAF No. 1 Squadron, carrying as many supplies and personnel as possible, were dispatched southward to join No. 8 Squadron at Kuantan.[23] The definition of airworthiness was applied a bit loosely: the plane piloted by Flight Lieutenant Douglas was already damaged to the extent that its landing gear would not retract, and its inoperable wing flaps had been tied in the "up" position with baling wire. Douglas's flight was challenging, though perhaps less nerve-wracking than the experience of Flight Lieutenant O'Brien and his seventeen passengers, who were on the last plane to depart. As O'Brien's heavily overloaded Hudson flew low over the trees after takeoff, enemy troops immediately fired at it. The situation became even more perilous when O'Brien spotted several patrolling Japanese fighters nearby. Fortunately, he saw these planes before their pilots observed the slow-moving Lockheed. By diving down so close to the water that his propellers churned a wake on its surface, he avoided detection. The men in his Hudson had to look up to see the tops of palm trees rushing past during most of their journey along the coast to Kuantan. They got there safely, but it was an episode none of them wished to repeat.

After the Hudsons departed, Air Headquarters authorized the closure and demolition of the air station at Kota Bharu. Though the Japanese assault on Badang and Sabak beaches suffered a large number of casualties during the early hours of battle, the final outcome was essentially predetermined. Enough troops had been put ashore to overpower the thin line of defenders and move inland one short mile to the airfield. It was apparent to the local British army commander, Brigadier B. W. Key, that his ground forces could not secure the area around Kota Bharu or its satellite locations.

There was a preestablished plan to conduct airfield abandonment operations in an orderly manner that would conserve equipment and, at the same time, destroy materiel in order to prevent the enemy from readily using the runway or base facilities. To the detriment of the British Far East Command, Air Vice Marshal Pulford's order to execute this plan was received and improperly acted on at a time when Wing Commander Noble was out of the Operations Room and Wing Commander Davis was preoccupied with air operations. As a result, the situation at the Kota Bharu air station devolved to a state of near-panic before Noble and Davis could reorganize the evacuation of air force personnel and Brigadier Key could put the reins on a retreat of the Indian soldiers.

The three senior officers reacted promptly to quell the chaos started by their junior officers, but they ultimately failed to delay the withdrawal long enough ensure proper demolition of the valuable runway and substantial stores of munitions and fuel cached around the station. A premature departure of air station ground staff and the 8th Indian Brigade allowed Japan to seize this critical foothold in Malaya with relatively modest effort. Associated lapses in procedure regarding the destruction of useful materiel conceded an enormous and immediate tactical advantage to the enemy air offensive. With great surprise, Japanese officers marveled at their good fortune in capturing the best runway in Malaya completely intact—with the undreamed-of bonus of vast stores of aviation gasoline, weapons, and food in perfectly usable condition.

CHAPTER 6

Disaster on Luzon

December 8, 1941—Philippines

Most evenings, the tranquil sounds of rustling palm fronds and the rhythmic drumming of the surf were all that could be heard at Iba. On the night of December 7, 1941, a steady breeze was blowing in from the South China Sea under a broken layer of low clouds that gently filtered the bright tropical moonlight. The location would have maintained its resortlike ambience if not for the periodic disturbance caused by crew chiefs of the 3rd Pursuit Squadron. Readiness for piston-engine fighter planes meant warm engines. Every few hours, Iba's peaceful beachfront was awakened by the unnatural growling and snorting of Allison V-12s being started and revved up. Acting on Colonel George's order from the previous day, the mechanics had been keeping all six P-40Es of the alert flight at the ready for an immediate departure.

Near the flight line, in one of the tents, the 3rd Pursuit's commanding officer, 1st Lieutenant Henry "Hank" Thorne and the other five pilots of his "A-Flight" sat restlessly in the near-darkness of the canvas enclosure. Awaiting the call to scramble at a moment's notice seemed more fatiguing than actually flying a mission. Some discussion was directed at Thorne's decision to test a new method of guiding nighttime interceptions. The numerous Japanese intrusions over Luzon during the past week had given Thorne good reason to think about the process. Because of the poor quality of voice transmissions between ground and aircraft, his P-40s would not be able to receive voice information from the base radio during much of their flight. Realizing Morse transmissions might be intelligible at a somewhat greater range, Thorne requested the radar and radio teams to develop and transmit concise intercept vectors in code. By posting a pilot with Signal Corps training to his flight—to act as an interpreter—Thorne could be guided to an intercepting course when the flying signalman decoded each vector message. Fortunately, the 3rd Pursuit possessed just the pilot needed in the form of 1st Lieutenant Gerry Keenan—a radioman who had found his way into flight training.

Not far away, in another dimly lit temporary structure, the radar crew scanned their oscilloscope for any "blip" that might indicate the presence of incoming aircraft. The wait was not in vain. Shortly after midnight, on December 8, the signal officer in charge of the radar unit lifted the tent flap and handed Thorne some initial information regarding a multiplane contact that had just been tracked. The "blip" indicated a formation of aircraft about 115 miles northwest of Iba, apparently on a southeastward course toward Corregidor.[1]

Within five minutes, Thorne and the other pilots had strapped themselves into their cockpits. The ground crew already had the engines running. Moments later, Thorne's left hand moved steadily forward on the throttle. Twelve little flames licking at the exhaust stacks of his engine suddenly became blinding blue tails, streaming back toward the canopy as the Warhawk roared forward into the darkness, clawing its way into the sky. One after another, the shadowy forms of the olive-drab fighters surged ahead, lifting off the ground as they crossed the white sand of the beach. Banking sharply to the left, they headed out over the black surface of the sea. As the flight climbed through four thousand feet, it emerged into an area of clear skies. Thorne took his fighters up to almost nine thousand feet, just under a wispy, thin layer of clouds that spread in a ghostlike, translucent veil across the horizon. Keenan continued to receive vector information nearly to the point where the radar track of the P-40s intersected the plotted course of the Japanese aircraft—about four miles west of the island of Corregidor. Although visibility below them was fairly good, none of Thorne's pilots could spot the intruders.

Unfortunately for Thorne, the enemy planes—a flight of four G3M bombers from the IJN's *1st Kokutai*—were flying a "pathfinding" weather reconnaissance at considerably greater altitude. They were hidden by the high clouds and dark sky. Back at Iba, radar operators noted that the Japanese executed a 180-degree turn and headed back toward Formosa very shortly after passing Thorne's flight path. From the ground, it appeared as if an interception had been made.

The real story was revealed after the disappointed pilots returned to talk with the radar team. The experiment had actually worked very well, considering that no altitude information was available through the radar equipment. It was milestone enough that the 3rd Pursuit had been efficiently directed to an intercepting course. If not for the stratified cloud layers, the P-40 pilots might have been able to see the bombers, though that may have proved even more frustrating. Thorne and his men would not have been happy to discover that their Warhawks could not climb far enough to catch the Japanese. At least they could take satisfaction in having managed to complete their first night landings at Iba. Lining up their approaches with the aid of headlights on vehicles parked along the edges of the airstrip, all six fighters set down without incident. Night landing was the one skill in which the American fliers were better trained than their Japanese counterparts.

As word of the radar contact and 3rd Pursuit's failed interception percolated through the AWS, 1st Lieutenant Joseph "Joe" Moore—commanding officer of the 20th Pursuit Squadron at Clark Field—was awakened and ordered to prepare his unit for a "standby alert" at 0130. Moore sent runners to round up the eighteen pilots of his "1st Section." With no further information forthcoming, the tired pilots were sent back to their barracks at Fort Stotsenberg after an hour of waiting at the flight line. Another eighteen pilots of 1st Lieutenant Charley Sneed's "2nd Section" were summoned to stay with the planes until further notice. From his post at 24th Pursuit Group Headquarters, Major Grover took the added precaution of placing 1st Lieutenant William "Ed" Dyess's 21st Pursuit Squadron on standby alert at Nichols Field. Dyess and his men were roused just long enough to disturb their sleep. A scant fifteen minutes after receiving Grover's orders, the pilots of the 21st Pursuit were allowed to go back to bed. It seemed the danger had passed. Of course, none of the men had an inkling of news from Malaya about the Japanese attacks under way at Kota Bharu.

If any of the fliers actually managed to doze off, they would not get to sleep for long. The hammer blow from the IJN was just then falling on Pearl Harbor. A few miles across the bay from Manila, the U.S. Navy radio station at Cavite began picking up signals from Hawaii at 0228, local time (0758 on Sunday, December 7, Honolulu time). That first message, of course, was the now famous "Air Raid, Pearl Harbor—This is not drill" broadcast by Lieutenant Commander

Logan Ramsey of Patrol Wing Two on Ford Island.[2] As shocking as the transmission may have been, it was of little actionable value without authentication of its source.

By 0240 the Asiatic Fleet had received official confirmation of the attack, and messengers were on their way to wake Admiral Hart. The admiral hurriedly scrawled out the following note for broadcast to all units under his command: "Japan started hostilities. Govern yourselves accordingly."[3]

Hart's brief instruction established the fact that the United States was at war with Japan but neglected to mention that Pearl Harbor was the location attacked. This lack of information caused some consternation at PatWing-10 Headquarters, where the message was received at 0315. It was not exactly clear to PatWing-10's commander, Captain Wagner, where to meet the Japanese threat. Wagner was not a man to sit on the sidelines, so he ordered the two PBY squadrons to execute a previously discussed deployment for wartime dispersal. This first operation was nothing more than a dispatch of seven PBYs from VP-102 at Olongapo to join their tender USS *Childs* on Manila Bay. Four Catalinas from VP-101 at Sangley Point were sent to a temporary anchorage near Los Baños, on the southern shore of a very large lake to the southeast of Manila known as Laguna de Bay. Five operational VP-101 PBYs still at Sangley taxied the short distance across the Cavite turning basin to join the VP-102 detachment near the main naval station. Relocating the patrol planes to provide better support for navy battle plans seemed better than doing nothing at all. Seven of VP-102's aircraft stayed at Olongapo. Two VP-101 planes were still confined to the new hangar at Sangley Point for routine repair and maintenance service, and three others remained with the tender USS *William B. Preston* at Malalag Bay in the Davao Gulf of southeastern Mindanao.[4]

Navy aircrews were already busily arming the PatWing-10 Catalinas with bombs and machine-gun ammunition at 0355 when General MacArthur's staff finally awakened him with a confirmed report of the attack on Hawaii. MacArthur immediately summoned the most senior officers for a conference in his Fort Santiago headquarters at 0500.

General Brereton received this notification from the USAFFE chief of staff, General Sutherland, just after 0400.[5] Before departing from Fort McKinley for the meeting with MacArthur, Brereton ordered his own FEAF Headquarters staff to spread the news about Pearl Harbor within the air units. He asked Colonel George to alert the fighter squadrons for action.

By 0430 both the 17th and the 21st Pursuit Squadrons had pilots in their planes, ready to scramble from Nichols Field. The 20th Pursuit at Clark was also contacted. Joe Moore and the pilots of his "1st Section" were again mobilized to the flight line. There, they joined the "2nd Section" men who were still with the planes after the earlier alert. As it happened—probably due to radio problems—neither the 3rd Pursuit at Iba nor the 34th Pursuit at Del Carmen received any communication regarding Pearl Harbor or the new alert status.

Colonel Eubank of the 19th Bomb Group was at Clark Field when he first spoke with General Brereton at about 0415. The general had telephoned to fill him in on news of the Pearl Harbor attack and the bombing of Hickam Field. Some of Eubank's new planes had been caught in the raid on Oahu. At that time, Brereton told Eubank to start loading his Clark-based B-17s for the anticipated mission to Takao. He also instructed Eubank to fly down to Nielson Field to attend the FEAF staff meeting at 0600. Before Eubank departed for FEAF Headquarters at 0530, he met with his own 19th Group staff officers and command pilots from both the 28th and 30th Squadrons. Three Flying Fortress crews had already been scheduled to patrol over Luzon at dawn. In deference to the new situation and the expected bombing mission, two of those sorties were canceled. Lieutenant Hewitt "Shorty" Wheless and his crew were allowed to take off as planned—with modified instructions to patrol to the north as far as Formosa. Wheless's B-17 was not equipped with any cameras, but his single-plane mission would allow the FEAF to spot southbound Japanese attack forces. Wheless could also provide a timely weather report for the 19th Group's upcoming mission to Takao.

When General Brereton arrived at the Fort Santiago office, he found that General MacArthur was already behind closed doors—presumably in conference with the president of the Philippines, Manuel Quezon. Meeting with General Sutherland, Brereton requested authorization for an immediate raid on Takao by the Flying Fortresses of the 28th and 30th Squadrons based at Clark. Sutherland said that this seemed appropriate but insisted that MacArthur must approve the mission before any action could be taken by the 19th Bomb Group.[6] Even though verification of the Japanese attack on Hawaii had been obtained, USAFFE had not yet received notification from Washington to the effect that the United States was "officially" at war with Japan. In the absence of such confirmation, and with no reported direct assault on the Commonwealth of the Philippines, Douglas MacArthur could not seem to bring himself to initiate offensive action from Philippine soil.

One can only speculate why MacArthur delayed his response that morning. When considering his actions, or inaction, one must recall that the general occupied a unique and unusual multirole office as the ranking commander of USAFFE, the leader of the Philippine army, and a senior adviser to the Philippine government. That he served several masters did nothing to simplify his decision-making process. Polished personal relationship skills did not often subdue his ego, but MacArthur was more politically sensitive than most generals. Though he reported to General Marshall in December 1941, he had once been the highest-ranking general officer in the army—and Marshall's boss. That experience as U.S. Army chief of staff undoubtedly instilled in him a sense of caution in making any decision to take his forces to war without express permission from Washington. As an employee of the Philippine Commonwealth, he definitely felt compelled to honor President Quezon's desire that U.S. forces not launch attacks from Philippine bases until the Philippines itself was attacked. Given the latent issues to be resolved with Philippine governance after independence, neither man would have wanted to initiate any action that would have made Filipinos believe that the United States was inviting a Japanese counterattack on their homeland. Still, the rationale behind MacArthur's hesitation is anything but clear. Whatever the reason, he chose not to issue any immediate orders to his command.

As the sun began to rise, Lewis Brereton became more anxious for the well-being of his air force. He eventually left for Nielson Field to host his own FEAF senior staff meeting. General Sutherland promised to notify Brereton by telephone once the decision had been made to authorize a bombing of Formosa.

Meanwhile, Lieutenant Colonel Eubank and Major Mike Walsh arrived at Brereton's conference room only to find that Brereton had not yet returned from USAFFE Headquarters. The rest of the FEAF staff was assembled and actively reviewing plans for the proposed raid on Takao. When Brereton finally walked into the meeting—nearly two hours late—he stunned the assembled officers with his recounting of Sutherland's instructions. Until notice was received from General MacArthur, no offensive operations were to be conducted, period. Everyone in the room was incredulous that the USAFFE commander and Sutherland were apparently not considering the attack on Pearl Harbor as Japan's commission of the "first overt action" and, thus, a legitimate reason for retaliation in force. Brereton's staff fumed at MacArthur's apparent lack of decisiveness. Had these men known that Japan's first attack on the Philippines was already under way, they probably would have been downright furious.

UNEXPECTEDLY, THE FIRST ENEMY STRIKE came not from the feared direction of Formosa, but from the southern seas near Mindanao. Before daybreak, thirteen Nakajima B5N bombers with an escort of nine Mitsubishi A5M fighters were launched from *Ryujo*.[7] This small aircraft carrier—the only one to be assigned to the Southern Operation—had steamed unnoticed from the Japanese base in the Palau Islands to within one hundred miles due east of Mindanao. Just after 0600, *Ryujo's* aircraft swept in over Davao City. Finding nothing that seemed worthy of much attention, the Japanese planes continued flying south over the waters of Davao Gulf toward Malalag Bay—a known location for U.S. seaplane operations.

In response to the alert issued by Captain Wagner from PatWing-10 Headquarters, one of *Preston's* PBYs, flown by Ensign Ira Brown, had been sent south at 0515 on a mission to patrol the entrance of Davao Gulf. Of course, this plane had no chance of stumbling upon *Ryujo* or its small task force. Brown and his crew would eventually spot three destroyers that had been detached to hunt down any seaplane tenders, naval auxiliaries, or oil tankers they could find in the gulf. The other two PatWing-10 Catalinas at Malalag Bay remained tethered on their anchor buoys between *Preston* and the beach. Each aircraft had only its minimal "plane guard" crews on board. The other airmen had been bunked on the ship. *Preston* was still at anchor, but its prudent skipper, Lieutenant Commander Etheridge Grant, had his boilers lit and kept half of the tender's antiaircraft guns manned for action. The crew of this converted World War I "four-piper" destroyer was one of a very few U.S. units ready for a fight.

At Del Monte Field, Major O'Donnell—ranking officer of the 19th Bomb Group contingent on Mindanao—received word of the Pearl Harbor attack at 0630. Accompanying this news was an order to muster a search of the Mindanao coastline. He quickly dispatched two of his B-17s for the long patrols. The Fortresses of 1st Lieutenant Henry Godman of the 14th Bomb Squadron and 1st Lieutenant Edward "ED" Teats of the 93rd Squadron took off to circle the large island in opposite directions. Each plane would have a great distance to cover, and they could not reach *Ryujo's* location before the carrier retired to the east.

At 0710 lookouts on *Preston* sounded the "general quarters" alarm when six Japanese fighters appeared from the overcast and zoomed in low across the water. The barrels of the enemy machine guns began blinking with deadly fire, dispensing a hail of bullets that ripped into the two moored PBYs. The unarmored fuel tanks in both flying boats instantly ignited. In moments, the sitting ducks were flaming wrecks. Survivors from the plane-guard crews were left to fend for themselves for the moment.[8] The men, some of them wounded, had no choice but to swim for the nearby beach as their support ship quickly got moving to avoid any enemy bombers that might join in the attack.

Word of the raid was hurriedly flashed from *Preston* to PatWing-10 and Asiatic Fleet Headquarters within five minutes of the first shots. The light machine guns of the fighters could not do any harm to the ship, but *Preston's* captain was wise to get under way. Almost as soon as the marauding fighters disappeared, at least seven single-engine bombers descended on his ship. It was fortunate that *Preston* had once been a destroyer and still possessed the assets of speed and maneuverability. For the next half-hour, the ship adroitly dodged falling bombs.

Apart from the loss of the two Catalinas, and the casualties from their aircrews, no damage was done at Malalag Bay. In exchange, two of the A5Ms and one B5N were riddled by machine-gun and cannon fire from *Preston*. The B5N was hit badly enough to prevent its recovery on board *Ryujo*. The disabled bomber was forced to ditch near one of the carrier's escorting destroyers.[9]

These first Japanese raiders were followed several hours later by two more B5Ns in the company of three A5Ms. That tiny formation had been assigned to attack the small airfield and fuel storage tanks at Davao City. Though Davao was only lightly defended, ground fire scored hits on one of the strafing fighters, bringing it down near the outskirts of the city. The A5M pilot—Petty Officer 2nd Class Hiroshi Kawanishi—survived the crash, dutifully burned the aircraft, and then committed suicide rather than allowing himself to be captured and interrogated.[10] It was the United States' first experience with the strict principles of Japanese warrior philosophy.

WHEN JAPANESE BOMBERS FAILED to materialize over Luzon after dawn, FEAF Headquarters was confounded. Brereton's staff could not believe the Japanese would miss such an opportunity. Had they been able to obtain a report from Lieutenant Wheless—who was at that very moment bouncing around in the stormy weather that blanketed the Luzon Strait and the southern half of Formosa—the reason would have been clear enough.

The Japanese fully expected to rain destruction upon Luzon at first light; however, their primary strike units were grounded by a heavy fog that closed all airfields near Takao for almost six hours. In a stroke of good luck for Japan, the first warplanes to depart from Formosa were actually from the secondary, tactical bombing groups of the JAAF. Eighteen Ki-21s from the 14th Sentai took off from Chiai and were soon followed by twenty-five Ki-48s from the 8th Sentai at Chiatung.[11] The actions of these aircraft were destined to thoroughly disrupt U.S. air defenses. That was not their intended objective, but no planned operation could have achieved any greater success.

Since General MacArthur's office still refused to authorize the proposed bombing mission to Takao—even after reviewing news of the attack on the *Preston*—Brereton decided around 0800 to modify his orders to Colonel Eubank. In an attempt to accomplish at least some useful task, General Brereton ordered three of the Flying Fortresses to be equipped with cameras and sent immediately to Formosa to photograph any air bases they could find. This added greatly to the confusion at 19th Bomb Group Headquarters, as expressed by Lieutenant Kurtz of the 30th Squadron:

> As we left, Gibbs [Major David Gibbs, 30th Squadron commanding officer; in charge of the group during Colonel Eubank's and Major Walsh's absence] said: "You're on the stand-by. Orders will be coming through fast all morning." Then I went back to Old 99. She was one of the few which hadn't been loaded with bombs, as she had been scheduled for camouflaging that morning. Only the orders that now came seemed conflicting as those final hours slipped away.
>
> First came one countermanding the camouflaging. Seemed something was afoot, and they couldn't wait for it. Instead we were to load bombs, so we taxied over toward the ammunition dump. Then Bill Cocke [30th Squadron engineering officer], who was to be running back and forth all morning with conflicting orders, came screaming down the field. "Take her back to the hangar; they want the camouflaging finished by all means!"

Presently came another order for me and two other planes of the 30th Squadron to unload our bombs and insert cameras. Nothing more than that, but it was clear they were preparing us now for reconnaissance over Formosa.[12]

The two B-17 crews scheduled to undertake the reconnaissance with Lieutenant Kurtz were those of Captain Edwin Broadhurst and 1st Lieutenant Sig Young. Major Walsh was to have led the mission, flying in Kurtz's plane. However, the departure of this photographic mission was significantly delayed. First of all, it was discovered that there were not enough cameras available at Clark to equip all three planes. Someone would have to make a trip down to the Air Depot at Nichols Field for the missing items. On a more urgent note, the radar crew at Iba had just picked up a large group of inbound bogeys headed south toward the Lingayen Gulf. Once alerted, the AWS duly notified the 19th Bomb Group and 24th Pursuit Group commands at Clark. To avoid the possibility that his bombers would be caught on the ground by a raid, Major Gibbs ordered all fifteen flyable Fortresses off the field in an emergency scramble.

Major Grover must have been aware that the B-17s were choking up the field in their attempt to get airborne. Before he alerted the 20th Squadron to take to the air, he ordered 1st Lieutenant Boyd "Buzz" Wagner's 17th Pursuit Squadron at Nichols Field to take off immediately and set up an interception screen between the latitude of Tarlac and Rosales, about fifty miles north of Clark. Grover instructed the 20th Squadron to proceed to Tarlac to join the 17th Pursuit. While the last few Flying Fortresses were clearing Clark's runways, the P-40Bs of the 20th Pursuit began racing to take off beside them. By 0830 all thirty-six P-40s were headed north toward an incoming enemy formation. The fourteen B-17s that managed to get off the field milled around to the northeast of Mount Arayat. Lieutenant John Carpenter's bomber, which had frequently been plagued with generator trouble, failed to start and was left behind. To provide proximate cover for Clark Field, Major Grover radioed 1st Lieutenant Sam Marett's 34th Pursuit Squadron to send its eighteen P-35As up from Del Carmen for cover directly above the vital air base.

The phone in General Brereton's office rang at 0850. It was General Sutherland. USAFFE Headquarters still did not want to approve an "offensive" strike on Takao.[13] It was, by that time, a moot point: the U.S. bomber force was scattering all across the skies above Luzon. Even if

Sutherland had been calling to approve the mission, it would have been several hours before the planes and crews could be made ready, rendering it impossible for the 19th Group to bomb Formosa before late afternoon. At least the fighters were in place. Colonel George, on behalf of FEAF Interceptor Command, reported to General Brereton that he had "54 planes in the air and 36 in reserve" by 0910.[14]

At roughly the same time Buzz Wagner's 17th Pursuit Squadron appeared to the west of Tarlac at about twelve thousand feet, Charley Sneed's formation from the 20th Pursuit arrived from the east, at about seventeen thousand feet. The airmen of both squadrons were already quite fatigued; Wagner's pilots had been in their cockpits since 0415, and Sneed's fliers had been on alert with their aircraft since about 0200. Nevertheless, with adrenaline pumping in anticipation of combat, the men of both squadrons anxiously scanned the skies for other aircraft. As their watches ticked on past 0900, the pilots began to wonder what had happened to the Japanese; they all knew the enemy planes should have crossed their paths by that time.

Lieutenant Wagner was first to spot incoming bombers. Signaling the rest of his six-plane flight to follow, he dived to intercept two large aircraft flying beneath him. The P-40Es screamed downward, but as each approached within firing range, the pilots realized that their targets were actually two of the 19th Group's Flying Fortresses. Fortunately, no shots were fired.

At Tuguegarao, more than two hundred miles north-northeast of Clark Field, the twenty-five 8th Sentai Ki-48 bombers devastated a small auxiliary airstrip and army encampment. The Japanese planes participating in that raid remained beyond range of the radar set at Iba. By 0925 the FEAF staff learned where the contacts tracked on the Iba radar had gone when reports of large-scale bombing attacks came in from Baguio. The planes sought by the 17th and 20th Squadrons had abruptly turned inland, across the mountains, to the Philippine "Summer Capital." In doing so, the formation vanished from the radar screen. Just minutes after 0900, less than half an hour after their disappearance, the eighteen Mitsubishi Ki-21s of the 14th Sentai bombarded Camp John Hay military barracks and landing field.[15]

Shortly thereafter, Interceptor Command decided that the immediate threat to Clark Field had passed. The 34th Pursuit was relieved of its close cover duty and returned to Del Carmen. The 17th and 20th Squadrons continued with their patrols around Tarlac. They would return to Clark when their fuel ran low.

General Brereton, on learning of the Baguio and Tuguegarao raids, telephoned General Sutherland to renew the request for approval of a mission to Takao. Sutherland again demurred. Brereton was overheard responding with a warning to Sutherland, "If Clark Field is attacked we won't be able to operate on it."[16] Because reports about Baguio and Tuguegarao were mingled in with those of a number of other sightings—most erroneous and exaggerated—it was not until about 0950 that USAFFE received adequate confirmation of their authenticity. There would be no further questioning the fact that the Commonwealth of the Philippines was indeed at war with Japan. Why this was still an issue more than two hours after the attack at Davao Gulf remains a mystery.

At 1014 General MacArthur personally telephoned General Brereton and authorized him to take offensive action as he saw fit; unfortunately, the initiative had already been lost.[17] Evidently, at some point in the interval between his last call with General Sutherland and this first discussion with General MacArthur, General Brereton changed his own opinion of the efficacy of the planned strike at Takao. Rather than blindly launching two squadrons of B-17s at the Formosan port, he would shift the focus of the 19th Bomb Group to reduction of the Japanese airfields. To accomplish this, Fortress crews would need to be briefed using photographic reconnaissance information.[18] Adopting this course of action meant awaiting results of the photo mission already tasked to the three crews from the 30th Squadron. Since those planes were still airborne because of the earlier warning, photo missions could not be launched for several hours. No bombing raids would be launched from Clark until late afternoon.

It is not clear why General Brereton changed the operational plan when he did. It was a pivotal decision, yet one for which a satisfactory explanation has never surfaced. Did his FEAF staff feel that the Baguio and Tuguegarao raids were as bold an action as the Japanese would attempt that day? Could the fact that those raids were not escorted by fighters have given Brereton the impression that the Japanese would not attack a strongly defended area until their aircraft carriers approached Luzon? It was, of course, much later in the day than he expected the Japanese air forces to attack his airfields, so his sense of danger may have been diminished. Possibly Brereton felt that his chance to hit Japanese warships and transports before they left Takao had passed, so he had no choice but to shift targets. The only definitive observation is that Lewis Brereton suddenly felt he had some extra time on his side.[19]

When Lieutenant Colonel Eubank and Major Walsh returned to Clark from Nielson Field at about 1030, the first B-17s were just reappearing over the base. Major Gibbs had recalled the Group some ten minutes previously. Ironically, Lieutenant Carpenter's plane was the only Fortress ready to take to the air. A decision was quickly made to send Carpenter up the east coast of Luzon for a reconnaissance of the sea approaches not covered by the radar set at Iba.

Soon after Carpenter's plane departed, and the other B-17s touched down, P-40s of the 17th and 20th Squadrons roared across the field into an approach pattern. The planes had been on patrol for more than two hours, and their fuel was nearly depleted. Except for the B-17s of Lieutenants Carpenter and Wheless, all of the army combat aircraft based on Luzon were on the ground by 1100. For another half-hour, the skies above Luzon remained clear and serene. Civilians going about their regular business must have had a hard time believing their country was at war.

At 1127 the radar scope at Iba lit up in warning for the third time that day. A large formation of aircraft was approaching Luzon from about 129 miles northwest of Iba, on a track toward the south.[20] This group was following a course nearly identical to the one recorded for the flight Hank Thorne attempted to intercept in the middle of the night. Given that coincidence, it was logical to suppose that the designated target would be either Manila or Cavite. Making just such an assumption when he received this information from the AWS Teletype at 1140, Major Grover immediately radioed the 3rd Pursuit. He told Lieutenant Thorne to position his squadron at fifteen thousand feet to intercept the incoming flight as it passed Point Iba.

By the time the P-40 pilots at Iba were strapping themselves into their fighters, 24th Pursuit Group Headquarters was receiving another message from the AWS. This was a new contact report from the Iba radar. It indicated that another large formation, farther to the east, was about to enter the Lingayen Gulf.[21] Unquestionably, this represented a direct threat to Clark Field. Orrin Grover faced a dilemma: neither the 17th nor the 20th Squadron was ready for action. Though the duty roster of the 20th Pursuit had been rotated back to Joe Moore's "1st Section" when Charley Sneed's tired pilots climbed out of their planes after the Tarlac patrol, the planes of that squadron were still being gassed up and having their oxygen tanks replaced. The hungry pilots of the 17th Squadron—who had eaten nothing all day—were finishing the lunch they had started on while having their planes refueled. Their planes were ready, but the men had not returned to the flight line. Therefore, Major Grover radioed for both the 34th and 21st Squadrons to scramble and cover Clark Field. The 21st Pursuit was tasked with high cover and designated to patrol at twenty-four thousand feet—roughly the operating ceiling of their brand-new P-40Es. The 34th Pursuit would only be able to fly low cover, because no oxygen was available for their "Swedish" P-35As.

The electrons did not cooperate with the 24th Pursuit Group. At this particular point in time, radio communications to Del Carmen Field failed, again. For that reason, Sam Marett and his squadron never received Grover's order. At Nichols Field, Ed Dyess received the radioed instruction in his operations tent without difficulty. Outside, his pilots had just left their planes to grab some sandwiches and Cokes—their first meal of the day. Within minutes, they were back in their cockpits and roaring down the asphalt strip into the blinding midday sun. As Dyess's "A Flight" and 2nd Lieutenant Ben Irvin's "B Flight" climbed out toward Manila Bay, they received another call from Major Grover. This message redirected the 21st Pursuit to patrol over Manila Bay, between Cavite and Corregidor. With that change and the miscue of the 34th Pursuit, there was no immediate fighter protection for Clark Field.

The 21st Pursuit's "C Flight" never received the change in orders. Its pilots were probably still on the ground at noon and, therefore, incapable of receiving the transmission when the direction to relocate the patrol was broadcast. It seemed that gremlins were on the loose around Nichols Field. A couple of the brand-new P-40Es had trouble starting, which delayed the departure of "C Flight" for about ten minutes. Most of the 21st Pursuit Squadron's aircraft had been assembled by the Philippine Air Depot during the previous week; many had never even been "slow-timed"—flown gently for several hours to break in their engines. Almost as soon as the flight left the ground, it was plagued by more engine troubles. The Allisons of the flight leader and his wingman immediately began throwing oil. Visibility quickly diminished as the sticky substance streamed back over their windscreens. Unable to continue, these two planes broke away to return to the airfield.

The remaining four planes—now led by 2nd Lieutenant Sam Grashio—turned eastward to swing out over Laguna de Bay. Once they were above the large lake, Grashio and the other pilots tested their .50-caliber machine guns. This was the first time the guns in these planes had been used. Never having fired this type of armament before, the inexperienced pilots were startled by the tremendous noise and vibration the weapons generated. After its brief gunnery pass across the lake, Grashio's flight climbed to the northwest, in the direction of Clark Field. These four rookies and their fresh-from-the-crate P-40s were destined to be the only U.S. fighters capable of providing high cover for the all-important air base.

It is hard to understand why Major Grover suddenly shifted the designated patrol area for the 21st Pursuit Squadron. Perhaps he was overcome by the realization that the 3rd Pursuit would be unable to cover the approach to Manila at high enough altitude. It is impossible to know. Grover's next round of decisions would prove both bewildering and fatal.

The pilots of the 3rd Pursuit Squadron had been experiencing difficulties departing from Iba. The problems had nothing to do with engines. Lieutenant Hank Thorne's flight, positioned at the south end of the airfield, was the first to sortie. These six P-40Es lifted off in the customary direction for Iba: northward, into the prevailing wind. Because of the dry winter weather, each takeoff produced enormous clouds of dust. To avoid some of that dust, the leader of the second flight, 1st Lieutenant Ed Woolery, made a last-minute decision to take off downwind, to the south. With the six planes of his flight initially positioned at the northern edge of the field, this also saved time that would have been required for them to taxi to the other end of the airstrip. Dust billowed in both directions around the third flight waiting at midfield. The flight leader, 1st Lieutenant Herb Ellis, followed the regular process, taxiing to the south and taking off to the north, just moments before the rest of his confused flight began their takeoff rolls in the opposite direction. Only good fortune prevented a disastrous collision within the giant dust cloud.

As Woolery's flight climbed away to the south, followed by four errant pilots from Ellis's flight, a radio message was received from 24th Pursuit Group Headquarters. New orders, transmitted by Major Grover, instructed the 3rd Pursuit to fly cover above the entrance to Manila Bay. Responding, the ten P-40s being led by Woolery continued along their initial course in that direction. Thorne's flight, along with Ellis and 2nd Lieutenant George Ellstrom—who had become completely separated from the third flight after takeoff—did not receive Grover's message. This loosely gathered congregation of fighters continued to spiral upward to the north of Iba Field.

Still on the ground at Clark Field, Buzz Wagner and the other two flight leaders of his 17th Squadron, 1st Lieutenant William "Willie" Feallock and 1st Lieutenant John Brownewell, stepped into the 24th Pursuit Group Operations Room shortly after 1200. The three young men stood by as Grover modified the orders for the 3rd and 21st Squadrons. Their eighteen fighters, parked in a neat line outside the hangar, had just been refueled. Wagner was anxious to get them off the ground. Grover seemed to be having difficulty deciding what to tell his impromptu audience. He appeared certain that the intended Japanese target was going to be Manila, and he was committed to placing all available aircraft in position to defend the city.

At 1215 Grover finally told Wagner and his two companions to man their aircraft and fly south to patrol near Corregidor at eighteen thousand feet.[22] This would give the 24th Pursuit Group three stacks of fighters screening Manila Bay at different altitudes. For that task, the deployment made sense. Given the overall situation, however, his orders are difficult to rationalize. Inexplicably, Major Grover completely ignored the direct threat to Clark Field posed by the large enemy formation moving down from Lingayen Gulf. Of course, he did not know that the 34th Pursuit had missed its invitation to cover Clark. But even if the Severskys showed up, Grover must have understood that he was leaving the most critical airfield in the Philippines without any high cover until the 20th Pursuit could complete its refueling and climb to altitude. In effect, his allocation of the 17th Pursuit to cover Manila meant that Clark Field would have no air cover at all for a period of at least twenty minutes—well after the Japanese formation tracked at Iba would have passed overhead. Grover's action was in flagrant disregard of prior directives issued by Colonel George and General Brereton.

Back at Nielson Field, in the Interceptor Command headquarters, Colonel George was beside himself, pacing back and forth around the room. He was tracking Major Grover's deployments on the plotting board. Had he known that the B-17s were all neatly parked on the grass at Clark, the normally cool and collected colonel would have become apoplectic. Angry enough about Grover's fighter direction, George had his operations officer—Captain Charles "Bud" Sprague— issue a direct order to Grover at 1220, via the Teletype link, to defend Clark Field. Grover did not acknowledge the communication. Nor did he take immediate action. However, the message, "Tally-ho, Clark Field; all pursuit to Clark," was somehow sent out on the command frequency shortly thereafter, with, or without, Grover's approval. This was the last transmission to emanate from Clark.[23]

Scrambling to get airborne for their assigned patrol, the pilots of the 17th Pursuit did not hear the overriding "Tally-ho" call. This was a most unfortunate twist of fate. Had Wagner's men heard the call, they possibly could have intercepted the incoming Japanese. Seventeen planes from the squadron headed south toward Manila, trailed by Willie Feallock, who had flooded his engine in a hasty attempt to restart the aircraft.

The 3rd Pursuit pilots following Lieutenant Woolery received the urgent radio message. They were just approaching Cavite from the west at a relatively low six thousand feet. Woolery wasted no time responding. He immediately banked his fighter to the north, heading in the direction of Clark at full throttle. In executing this quick maneuver, two straggling pilots—2nd Lieutenants Don Steele and John "Ship" Daniel—became completely separated from the rest of the flight. In only ten minutes, Woolery and his remaining companions covered the distance from the middle of Manila Bay to Clark Field. When they arrived and began to circle the airfield, just before 1230, the situation seemed normal.

Woolery's wingman, 1st Lieutenant Andy Krieger, noted two single-engine aircraft flying slightly above their altitude. Krieger hand-signaled to Woolery, and the two pilots chandelled upward to chase the unidentified aircraft. They quickly realized these were Warhawks. Without approaching close enough to determine the squadron to which the two strays belonged, Woolery and Krieger broke away to rejoin the rest of their flight. When the pair pulled back into formation, only six planes remained. First Lieutenant Fred Roberts and 2nd Lieutenant William Powell had split from Woolery's flight just before the eight P-40s arrived at Clark.[24] A check of fuel gauges showed that gas reserves were dwindling after the high-speed run from Manila. Assuming the radio call must have been another false alarm, Woolery led the five pilots still with him back in the direction of Iba.

Sam Grashio and the other three pilots of 21st Pursuit's depleted "C Flight" reached Clark at nearly the same time Woolery's planes began orbiting the field. Lieutenant Grashio, flying more than ten thousand feet above Woolery, did not spot the planes from the 3rd Pursuit until they began to head west toward Mount Pinatubo. Grashio led his comrades in a power dive to give chase. As Grashio's flight quickly closed in on the six planes, he was able to identify them as friendly P-40s. He continued to overtake these other fighters, hoping that they were part of his own squadron. Before Grashio could find out, his earphones blasted with the anxious call, "All pursuit to Clark Field! All pursuit to Clark Field! Enemy bombers overhead!"[25]

On the ground at Clark, Major Grover still had not decided what to do with the 20th Pursuit Squadron. The fighters were fueled and ready. Joe Moore was in his squadron operations shack discontentedly waiting on word from Grover when one of the enlisted men outside yelled, "Good God Almighty—yonder they come!"[26] Droning toward the field, at an altitude of more than twenty thousand feet, was a giant "double V of Vs" formation composed of fifty-three large planes. Moore rushed from the shack and sprinted toward his airplane as he ordered that the red "scramble" flag be run up the pole outside. Masked by the rumble of more than one hundred Japanese engines, eighteen Allisons snorted to life in the P-40s. Moore and the others knew it was far too late to save Clark Field, but at least they would try to pursue the enemy bombers and make them pay.

As the air-raid siren blared a belated warning, Moore gunned his engine. Turning abruptly onto the runway, he thrust the throttle in his left hand forward to its stop. Right behind him, four 2nd Lieutenants— Randall Keator, Ed Gilmore, Dan Blass, and Max Louk—began to roll into position. As soon as Moore's wheels left the turf, his main gear twisted backward, lifting into place under the wings. Building speed, the Tomahawk raced low across the field. The images of men scurrying for shelter became a blur.

Behind Moore, screaming off the ground in close succession, Keator and Gilmore sped to the east as a rain of bombs consumed the field and the rest of the planes behind them. Lieutenant Blass did not make it off the ground, but was extremely lucky, nonetheless: just before his P-40 could get airborne, shrapnel from a fragmentation bomb ripped its tires to shreds. Blass skidded his plane to a halt, jumped out of its cockpit, and ran headlong for shelter in one of the trenches alongside the field—without being injured. Behind Blass, Max Louk's fighter was caught squarely by an incendiary bomb, which nosed the craft over and turned it into a raging inferno. Louk, unable to extricate himself from under the jammed canopy of his cockpit, was incinerated. Two other pilots from the 20th Pursuit, 2nd Lieutenant Jesse Luker and 2nd Lieutenant Lowell "Tod" Mulcahy, were also killed instantly by direct bomb hits on their planes while they tried to taxi onto the runway. The rest of Moore's "1st Section" pilots were fortunate to escape from their cockpits, cheating death as bombs burst over nearly every square yard of the airfield.

In the last few minutes before these explosions engulfed Clark Field—while they themselves were frantically hailing for pursuit aircraft—the radio operators in the SCR-197 van outside 24th Pursuit Group Headquarters were still receiving a coded status report from the 3rd Pursuit when the Iba operator suddenly broke into voice transmission, hurriedly announcing that many bombers were also above his location. The transmission from Iba ceased abruptly, seconds before those first bombs impacted at Clark.[27]

If it had not been more important to take shelter and keep their heads down, the men around the airfield would have noticed that the twenty-seven Mitsubishi G4Ms of the *Takao Kokutai* and twenty-six G3Ms of the *1st Kokutai* had executed a perfect raid on their base. The accuracy of the Japanese bombardiers was astounding. Of more than six hundred bombs released from an altitude above four miles, not a single one fell more than two hundred feet outside the perimeter of Clark's fences. And—if the IJN performance over Clark had not provided dramatic enough evidence of precision planning and execution—twenty-six G4M bombers of the *Kanoya Kokutai*, in formation with another twenty-seven from the *Takao Kokutai*, released more than five hundred bombs above the fighter base at Iba at almost exactly the same moment.[28]

Given the late hour of the day, and the advance warning provided by news of the Pearl Harbor attack, Japanese aircrews anticipated a furious response from U.S. fighters based at the small airfield. Aircrews in the bombers, and pilots of the fifty-one escorting A6M Zeros from the *Tainan Kokutai* and *3rd Kokutai*, were amazed when no opposing aircraft rose to meet them.

Only a handful of P-40s remained in the vicinity of Iba when the Japanese bombers got there. Just before the enemy appeared, Lieutenant Thorne, hearing the frantic last-minute call from Clark, turned east and flew at high speed in that direction. He was trailed by four other planes from his regular flight. Thorne's departure made little difference. Even if those Warhawks had still been above Iba, the pilots would have found themselves almost ten thousand feet below the enemy formation. For lack of oxygen, the men would not have been able to climb high enough to intercept the bombers, which were flying at an altitude above twenty-three thousand feet.

Japanese photograph taken during the bombardment of Clark Field on December 8, 1941. Fort Stotsenberg is at the top of the photo. Clark's hangars are obscured by the upper row of bomb blasts progressing from west (right) to east (left) across the American base. Almost all of the protective dispersal revetments for B-17s are clearly vacant (IJN Photo Courtesy of O. Tagaya)

When Thorne's flight departed, Gerry Keenan, still loitering in the area, spotted an aircraft he erroneously identified as a "Messerschmitt Me-109" flying just off the coast at about fifteen thousand feet. Keenan swung his Warhawk around and charged directly at the

mysterious target, guns blazing. Actually, the other plane was the
P-40E of his friend Herb Ellis. A shocked Ellis quickly spotted the
stream of tracers arcing in his direction. To avoid this friendly fire, Ellis
rolled his plane over onto its back and dived for the ground. Hitting an
indicated five hundred miles per hour in this dive, he blacked out
while pulling the craft from its screaming descent. Ellis regained consciousness just above the palm trees near the airstrip. Though Keenan
followed him down, the abrupt maneuver was enough to ensure a safe
separation of the two P-40s, both of which headed off to the south
moments before the bombs fell.

Barely avoiding the scuffle between their squadron-mates, the six
P-40s led by Lieutenant Woolery descended on Iba from the east. Woolery and his second element, Lieutentant Ray Gehrig and Lieutenant
Richard Root, lowered their gear and dropped their flaps to make a
landing approach. Andy Krieger flew a covering circle at five thousand
feet. Lieutenants Frank Neri and Dana Allen—originally from Lieutenant Ellis's flight—split off from the other four to investigate a boat
they saw speeding along the coast a few miles offshore. Coming in from
the south, Woolery touched down on the runway in a perfect three-
point landing. Before he could complete his landing roll, the north end
of the field erupted with geysers of earth and smoke, punctuated by the
bright red-orange flashes of exploding bombs marching down the field
toward him. In one thunderous concussion, the tail section was ripped
from the fuselage of Woolery's coasting fighter. Unbelievably, Woolery
emerged from the cockpit unscathed and dashed to safety in one of the
few machine-gun pits alongside the field.

Ray Gehrig, witnessing the plight of his flight leader, rammed his
throttle forward, past its stop, to "full military power." Shooting
ahead, Gehrig raised his gear and flaps as the Warhawk roared
upward past the north boundary of the field. He would try to pursue
the bombers with what little fuel he had left.

Richard Root, using the same emergency procedure, attempted to
follow Gehrig away from the holocaust. He was just a little too
far behind his section leader and met with misfortune when the
second salvo of bombs exploded close beside him. The turbulent blast
wave knocked the tail of Root's plane upward, vaulting his P-40 into
the ground just as it cleared the end of the runway. Root was killed
in the crash.

Lieutenants Neri and Allen, coming back to the field after inspect-
ing what turned out to be a PT boat, watched in shock as their base
was smothered in a cloud of dust and smoke. Confused and horrified,

the two pilots separated. Neri began to climb alone after the departing Japanese. Allen was unsure what to do.

Ellis, finally turning around toward Iba after his encounter with Keenan, saw falling bombs and looked up to see the bombers high above. Like Neri, Gehrig, and Krieger, Ellis instinctively started to climb in a slow circle intended to position him behind the enemy.

Lieutenant Gehrig, shaken by his brush with death, low on fuel, and realizing the Japanese were too high and too fast to follow, gave up the chase before his squadron-mates caught up with him. Turning east, Gehrig leveled out and decided to head over the mountains to Clark Field.

Lieutenant Krieger stopped pursuing the bombers when his engine overheated. Forced to quit his climb as he passed through twelve thousand feet, he turned back toward Iba. Looking down on the scene of destruction below him, he noted some mysterious gray planes diving at the field. They somewhat resembled P-35s. Krieger did not recall them from his aircraft recognition guide, but he easily saw the unmistakable round, red *hinomarus* on their wings. He called out on his radio, "All 3rd Pursuit to Iba," then sped down into the middle of the Japanese formation that was strafing the airfield.[29] Getting behind one of the enemy fighters, Krieger registered some hits on it with his heavy machine guns. Mesmerized as his bullets knocked pieces off the aircraft, he didn't immediately realize what was happening when tracers suddenly appeared from behind his own plane. Startled, he looked over his shoulder. Three of the gray intruders were on his tail, firing at him. Pushing the throttle forward, and yanking back on the joystick, Krieger sailed up into the cloud of smoke that blanketed Iba. The Japanese chose not to pursue him, so Krieger decided it was a good time to leave the area.

Shortly after Krieger made his pass at the enemy, Frank Neri and Herb Ellis—flying separately—turned back toward their field. Each had climbed above eighteen thousand feet, venturing well out to sea before they realized the impossibility of intercepting the retreating bombers. The altitude was beginning to affect both the pilots and their planes. Neri let down to a more comfortable ten thousand feet and headed east across the Zambales Range. When he reached Mount Pinatubo, he circled while attempting to contact other pilots of the 3rd Pursuit on his radio.

Ellis decided to investigate conditions back at Iba more closely, gradually descending back toward the smoke-darkened coast. Looking down, he spotted some light-gray planes flying in what seemed to be a clockwise landing pattern, the opposite direction to that used by the Americans. Ellis realized that these must be Japanese strafers working over his airfield, so he let down toward the south so he could approach the enemy from the sea and astern. After switching on his guns, he lined up one of the strange-looking fighters and dived through the flight pattern behind it. Holding his fire to the last moment, Ellis bored in on the unsuspecting Japanese. He pressed the trigger and felt his P-40 jolt from the recoil of its six .50-caliber guns. He was so close to the other plane that his tracers struck the wings on both sides of its cockpit. Even though he was only at an altitude of five hundred feet, and closing rapidly on the tail of his target, he ducked his P-40 under the plane he had just shot up. Ellis then banked out to sea in order to climb a thousand feet for another run. Without being seen, he made a second run that was almost as successful as the first, but several of his guns jammed in the process. On his third pass, only two guns would fire. In a fourth run at the strafers, none of his guns functioned, so he broke off the attack and climbed away from Iba toward Clark Field.

The young flight leader could not claim any sure victories, but he probably damaged a few of the Zeros.[30] When Ellis departed, Japanese planes from the *3rd Kokutai* continued to methodically shoot to pieces any aircraft sitting on the airfield. Their companions from the *Tainan Kokutai* headed east toward Clark.

The 3rd Pursuiters who thought of seeking refuge at Clark Field would be sorely disappointed. The situation there was even worse than at Iba. As the P-40s of the 20th Pursuit scrambled to get off the ground ahead of the falling bombs, a lone plane approached Clark from the south. In spite of its large size, the aircraft went virtually unnoticed. This was a Flying Fortress piloted by 1st Lieutenant Earl Tash of the 14th Squadron. Major O'Donnell had ordered Tash to take this B-17 up to Luzon for repairs to its fuel tanks. The trip would also give Tash a chance to meet with officers of the 19th Group staff who might have more information for O'Donnell. Along for the ride was a ground crewman who needed minor eye surgery at Fort Stotsenberg Hospital.

The Fortress had departed from Del Monte at 0830. It was just coming in for its landing at Clark when the bombs fell. As crewmen peered out to check that the landing gear was properly lowered from the inboard engine nacelles, they were stunned to see the runway in front of them going up in smoke. Moving his throttles ahead to full power, Tash raised the gear back up and gently banked away from the base to the northeast. Not sure what to do, he opted to head for nearby Mount Arayat, where he could circle and wait for instructions, or a better opportunity to set the plane down at Clark. The crew quickly calculated that they had at least a half-hour of fuel to burn before they would need to decide whether to head back to Mindanao or try another landing.

While Tash's Fortress continued along its eastward course, the three 20th Pursuit fighters that barely escaped from Clark Field climbed back over their smoldering air base. Joe Moore led the other two P-40Bs in a steady climb to the west, hoping they could gain enough altitude to position themselves for an interception of the enemy bombers that had veered off to the southwest but would almost certainly head north on their return to Formosa.

Behind Moore's planes, two P-40Es appeared about eight thousand feet above the southeast corner of Clark Field. These were the mounts of Lieutenants Steele and Daniel, who had been lagging behind Lieutenant Woolery's formation and lingered above Manila after Woolery departed. The pair finally headed north when they received the desperate final radio messages from Clark. Speeding onto the scene after the bombing, they were appalled at the condition of the airfield. All of the buildings and most of the aircraft visible below were on fire. Even the cogon grass turf of the runways was burning. Raging flames from the fuel depot spewed a sinister pillar of black smoke up to almost twenty thousand feet.

Down on the deck, several small gray planes were darting back and forth above one of the old B-18s. Steele decided to dive after these strafers. As Steele and Daniel descended, six more gray planes swung into a head-on pass from above. Steele pulled up to face the diving fighters and pressed his trigger. Only one of his machine guns fired as Japanese bullets and cannon shells tore at his left wing and the side of his P-40's fuselage. Still, Steele's fire was on the mark. The enemy fighter streaked past, only a few feet from his wingtip, belching smoke. Steele turned to follow it as the other Japanese planes zoomed overhead. The smoking Zero trailed off to the west, slowly downward to about three thousand feet, where it stalled and then plunged in a fatal spin to the foothills near Mount Pinatubo.[31] With fuel running low, and most of their guns malfunctioning, the American duo decided to head back to Iba.

While Steele and Daniel battled their way from east to west, Lieutenant Sam Grashio's fragmented flight from the 21st Pursuit approached Clark Field on an opposing course. Gus Williams was still flying with Grashio, but the two-ship element of Lieutenant Joe Cole and Lieutenant Johnny McCown drifted away from them on reaching the outskirts of Clark. Grashio circled above the burning airfield, noting the strafers far below and building up the courage to dive on them.

In a few moments a single gray plane dashed upward out of the smoke. Grashio decided to pounce on the loner, zooming up behind it and blasting away with all six guns until it began smoking and dropped off to one side. Williams, holding tightly on Grashio's wing, saw nine more gray single-seaters pulling up from below, in the opposite direction. When the two young pilots banked hard to follow this new formation, they were surprised that the enemy planes were easily able to out-turn their P-40Es, even while climbing. As tracers from the Japanese fighters flashed by their canopies, both pilots tried unsuccessfully to turn away. Grashio's plane was hit in mid-turn by 20-mm cannon rounds that exploded squarely in the ammunition canisters of his left wing, blowing a hole in the outer panel large enough to "throw a hat through."[32] Williams rolled his aircraft onto its back and then yanked it into a steep dive for the deck. The heavy P-40E dropped like a rock, quickly pulling away from the lighter Zeros. In a similar maneuver, Grashio was able to elude his pursuers, eventually leveling off at treetop height. Independently, Grashio and Williams headed flat out for Nichols Field, "hedge-hopping" most of the way.

Lieutenants Cole and McCown elected to dive on the low-flying strafers but failed to inflict any damage in their first high-speed pass. As they began to climb back out, the pair became entangled in a swirling dogfight that got the better of Cole's new engine—which began leaking prodigious amounts of oil. With his vision obscured by an oil-drenched windscreen, Cole was lucky to escape. He quickly departed to the south, heading toward Nichols. Not wanting to fight alone, McCown exited the melee to the east, choosing to circle around Mount Arayat in the hope of finding friendly fighters to join for a new counterattack.

Two more P-40Es returned to Clark Field at nearly the same time as Lieutenant Grashio's flight, but at a lower altitude. These were the 3rd Pursuit planes flown by 1st Lieutenant Roberts and his ad hoc wingman, 2nd Lieutenant Powell. They had not heard any of the radio messages. However, while prudently checking his tail, Roberts spotted plumes of smoke rising from the vicinity of the air base and decided to investigate. The two P-40s were well positioned for a surprise attack on five enemy fighters below them. As Roberts charged into the group of Japanese planes, he discovered that only one of his machine guns was firing. Powell was even more disturbed to find that none of his guns was working. What began as an easy victory setup quickly became a defensive life-or-death struggle. Powell dived immediately away from the fracas without taking any damage. His escape was made easier because several of the Zeros were already chasing Roberts, rapidly filling his aircraft with holes. Wounded in the lower legs, and desperate to shake the fighters off his tail, Roberts rolled his P-40E to an inverted position and pulled into a vertical dive. Turning out toward Iba at the bottom of his steep descent, the bleeding pilot gratefully found himself to be alone.

The largest single grouping of U.S. fighters to appear over Clark Field during the battle was Lieutenant Thorne's flight of five P-40Es coming in from Iba at about twelve thousand feet. Thorne led his planes in a wide arc along the west edge of the airfield. Drifting smoke obscured his vision of the ground. Remaining on the down-wind side of Clark, he did not notice the gray enemy strafers or any of the green P-40s flying around beneath him. Significantly, he also failed to notice three enemy fighters climbing rapidly behind his flight. As Thorne began to descend for a better look at the devastated base, he heard Lieutenant Krieger's call for pursuit coverage at Iba. The young squadron commander pulled up immediately in a climbing turn just as the Japanese closed in from below. Lieutenant Bob Hanson and Lieutenant Howard Hardegree managed to stay with Thorne. Second Lieutenant Gordon Benson—Thorne's wingman—became separated from the others in the smoke. Lieutenant Vern Ireland—the flight's "tail-end Charlie"—was the last to pull up. Ireland may have attempted to make a tighter turn outside the smoke by executing a chandelle and half-Immelman, as described by Japanese shotai leader Saburo Sakai:

> The fifth plane spiraled to the left—a mistake. Had he remained with his own group he could have escaped within the thick smoke. Immediately, I swung up and approached the P-40 from below; the American half-rolled and began a high loop. At 200 yards the plane's belly moved into my sights. I rammed the throttle forward and

closed the distance to fifty yards as the P-40 tried desperately to turn away. He was as good as finished, and a short burst of my guns and cannon walked into the cockpit, blowing the canopy off the plane. The fighter seemed to stagger in the air, then fell off and dove into the ground.[33]

At about this time, Lieutenant Tash chose to leave the refuge of Mount Arayat and make his second attempt to land at Clark. The Japanese bombers had disappeared over the western horizon, but Tash noted some pursuit activity low over the field. Thinking the aircraft were probably friendly fighters, he continued to follow his landing procedure and lowered his wheels again. After all, it didn't seem logical to Tash that Japanese fighters would be around if no aircraft carriers were in the vicinity. Moments later, a fighter plummeted out of the smoke straight into the ground, exploding in front of the B-17.[34] At the same time, he realized that Clark Field's excited antiaircraft gunners had begun to fire indiscriminately at his Flying Fortress. Worse yet, Tash's flight engineer, Staff Sergeant John Sowa, looking up through the flight-deck observation dome, spotted a vee of three gray fighters diving on them from several thousand feet above.

Aborting the landing, Tash wisely descended to treetop height. Even with full power on all four engines, the bomber rapidly lost ground to the enemy fighters, which trailed behind it in a "line-astern" formation. Closing in on the B-17's tail, the lead fighter fired with its nose guns, striking the rear fuselage and hitting Staff Sergeant Michael Bibin in the chest as he manned one of the guns in the waist position. Fortunately, the explosive cannon fire from the Zero mostly passed ahead of the Fortress. Breaking from its attack, the nimble fighter pulled up sharply above the bomber's tail, preventing the B-17 gunners from taking a shot. The second A6M followed the same attack procedure, causing more damage but no injuries. The third Japanese fighter did not pull up as abruptly as the others, giving the radioman, Private First Class Arthur Norgaard, a brief but clear glimpse of its belly. Norgaard's twin .50-calibers chattered noisily; brass cartridges and steel links ejected from their breeches bounced wildly around the radio compartment. The Zero screamed overhead and "wobbled away" without going down, though Norgaard probably stitched a line of large holes down the entire length of its fuselage.[35] Tash had no idea when he left Del Monte that he would be flying right into the middle of a war. He was thankful that the enemy fighters chose not to make a second pass as he continued south toward Manila, back to Del Monte.

At Del Carmen Field, eighteen pilots of the 34th Pursuit had been standing at the ready, waiting for the orders their unit never received. Being less than twenty miles away from Clark Field, everyone on the small dirt airstrip heard the dull thumping and felt the quaking concussion of bombs exploding. When no orders came, but black smoke rose on the horizon from the direction of Clark, Lieutenant Sam Marett took the initiative and instructed his pilots to take off. They would hightail it for the main base to offer whatever support they could.

While his third flight was still emerging from the clouds of red dust kicked up by the takeoffs of the leading Severskys, Sam Marett's first flight was bounced by several unidentified gray planes sporting bright red circular markings. They fired on Marett's wingman, 2nd Lieutenant Frankie Bryant. Though Bryant's plane was hit, he crisply rolled the small fighter into a reversing dive, avoiding major damage. He recovered from his descent and quickly climbed back into the dogfight, only to discover his guns were inoperative. Coming up from under Bryant, 2nd Lieutenant Don Crosland turned hard and fired into the Japanese plane. His own plane stalled before he could critically damage the Zero.

Lieutenant Marett realized his guns were not firing. He had no choice but to turn south and return to the primitive base. First Lieutenant Ben Brown assumed command of the remaining planes of the 34th Pursuit, but the squadron did not get much farther in the direction of Clark before they were attacked by another flight of Zeros. Brown himself claimed destruction of one of these Mitsubishis. Firing at the shotai leader in a difficult 90-degree deflection shot, Brown missed. By sheer luck, his stream of bullets brought down one of the wingmen following behind the intended target.[36]

Apart from Brown's good fortune, it was a lopsided encounter that weighed heavily in favor of the Japanese. Second Lieutenant Stewart Robb—leading the third flight of P-35As—was so focused on trying to target a Japanese fighter in front of him that he neglected to notice one that was on his own tail—at least until his windscreen was blown apart in front of his gunsight. By instinct, Robb rolled right, pulling into a vertical turn that forced his opponent to overshoot. In an incredible display of maneuverability, the pursuing Zero roared past into a tight half-Immelman and dove back down on Robb's slower plane before his P-35 could even complete the turn. In a long burst of cannon and machine-gun fire, the Seversky was nearly blown to pieces. Escaping complete destruction by virtue of a spin induced when his engine was shot out, the scared young lieutenant was able to recover and glide back to a dead-stick emergency landing at Del Carmen. His P-35A—riddled by more than thirty bullets and cannon rounds—was a total wreck.

Chasing Japanese fighters around at low altitude with worn-out P-35s had proved to be a nearly futile effort. Amazingly, none of the Seversky pilots had been killed. They picked up many a bullet hole for their trouble, and they were very fortunate to escape with their lives.

On the other side of Clark Field, Lieutenant Joe Moore was still climbing westward through an altitude of twenty-one thousand feet. Keator and Gilmore followed, below and behind him. At 1310 Moore spotted a flight of single-engine airplanes coming east from the direction of Iba. Figuring these must be fighters from the 3rd Pursuit, he waggled his wings as a signal for them to join with his own flight. Moore was surprised when the nine planes passed underneath him, until he saw they were painted gray with big red balls on their wings. With the enemy planes behind him, Lieutenant Moore fell off on his right wing into a steep turn. Randy Keator, likewise, turned hard to the right to chase the Japanese.

Gilmore, flying almost three thousand feet below his companions, suddenly found himself the object of much unwelcome attention when the Japanese turned back to face the P-40s. In the midst of a barrage of tracers, Gilmore reversed course in a steep dive to the left and then skidded his fighter to the right. The sudden turn and sideslip bought him enough distance. Alone, and feeling vulnerable, he raced away from the battle toward Del Carmen.

Initially, Moore screamed in from behind Gilmore, firing as he dived through the Japanese formation. The Japanese flight appeared to break apart in all directions as the unbelievably maneuverable Zeros banked, twisted, and even looped to turn and meet Moore and Keator head-on.

Keator engaged himself like a knight jousting in contest as his P-40B sped to meet one onrushing opponent. Closing rapidly, he pressed the trigger on his joystick. The noise in his cockpit was deafening as the twin .50-caliber guns on either side of his instrument panel banged away. Spellbound, he watched the flaming balls of their tracers strike the engine and canopy of the Japanese plane. The two fighters were on a collision course. Seconds before impact, the Zero exploded in a blinding flash.[37] Pieces of the destroyed aircraft ricocheted off Keator's fighter, scarring his wings and fuselage as he flew through the blast.

Looking over his shoulder, Keator noticed that another of the agile fighters had already latched onto his tail. Reacting quickly, he shoved his stick forward. The P-40 instantly dropped out of the Zero's firing line. When he leveled out a few thousand feet below, Keator saw Moore diving behind one Japanese fighter while being trailed by another enemy closing in from astern. Slipping into another dive, Keator fell into position behind the Zero on Moore's tail. The alert Japanese pilot quickly pulled up to the right in a chandelle. Keator followed its turn, firing all the way, until his plane buffeted at the brink of a stall. The enemy fighter continued in a tightly banked curve that the American could not hope to match. Keator fell off and dived to gain speed for a zooming climb back to altitude. By the time Lieutenant Keator got back up to nineteen thousand feet, he was alone in the sky. He climbed a bit higher, to twenty-two thousand feet, before deciding to head back to Clark. As he flew east, he saw a lone fighter heading across his path, perhaps fifteen thousand feet below him. It was a perfect setup, if the plane was an enemy. Keator screamed down toward the aircraft. It was indeed Japanese, and its pilot had not noticed the American diving from behind. Keator let loose with his two .50-caliber and four .30-caliber guns right on the Zero's tail. The enemy fighter continued on its path, trailing smoke until it lazily rolled over and plunged earthward.[38]

The final combat over Clark Field that day occurred when Herb Ellis arrived in the vicinity after his tense action over Iba. Hoping to land at Clark, but hardly able to see the runways through all the smoke, Ellis flew north in order to get upwind for better visibility. As he emerged into clear air, Clark's antiaircraft batteries opened up in his direction. Finding himself surrounded by black puffs from exploding 3-inch shells, Lieutenant Ellis dived rapidly past the east side of the airfield toward Mount Arayat. Turning in a slow arc to his right at five thousand feet, he scanned above the field for enemy fighters. Without functioning guns, Ellis had no intention of tangling with the Japanese. As he briefly glanced to the left, he was jolted by the sight of tracers coming directly at his face. Diving away, he realized he was in trouble when he smelled smoke. Opening his canopy for a better look, Ellis saw that his P-40 was trailing flames more than a hundred yards long.

It was time to bail out. With some difficulty, he managed to get loose of his stricken fighter. Dropping backward through the fiery plume, he was painfully struck in the back by his plane's stabilizer. Temporarily disoriented, Ellis barely recovered his senses in time to pull the ripcord on his parachute.

As Lieutenant Ellis swung helplessly in the harness, he spotted a Japanese fighter heading directly for him. Fearing that he might be strafed while hanging in his chute, he was relieved to hear the unmistakable—if deafening—roar of a P-40E racing by at close quarters. Its guns were blasting at the enemy. As it happened, this was Johnny McCown of the 21st Pursuit. He had seen Ellis's plight while circling Mount Arayat and came to the rescue just as Ellis bailed out.

In the distance, another parachute fell earthward. Dangling from the shroud lines was Ellis's squadron-mate, Lieutenant Ellstrom. Bounced by a shotai of Zeros from the *Tainan Kokutai* as he loafed along alone above the northeastern ridges of the Zambales Mountains, Ellstrom was unable to elude the experienced Japanese pilots as each made firing passes at his P-40E. Like Ellis, Ellstrom was forced to jump from his stricken fighter at high speed. While Ellis had been lucky to manage a safe landing without sustaining serious injuries, it appears that George Ellstrom must have suffered a serious abdominal blow—perhaps through striking the tail assembly of his plane. Though he survived the landing and managed to identify himself to an officer from an army unit that witnessed the brief air combat, Ellstrom later died from internal injuries.[39]

When the last of the Mitsubishi fighters withdrew from Clark Field at 1330, army personnel began to venture forth from their slit trenches to survey the extensive damage all around them. The cannon-wielding strafers had kept heads down in the dirt almost as effectively as the falling bombs. Japanese Zeros were so efficient in their destruction of aircraft parked on the field that many Americans and Filipinos huddled in their earthen refuge presumed they were being attacked by dive-bombers. Of course, the relatively long "greenhouse" canopy of the A6M provided an image consistent with that erroneous observation—to those brave enough to gaze skyward. In the air above Clark Field, however, there was no question as to the nature of the "mysterious gray planes"; they were fighters all right—and damned good ones. It would not be long before the legend of the Japanese navy Zero's performance was born in tales told by the stunned pilots of the 24th Pursuit Group.

CHAPTER 7

The Morning After

December 9, 1941

THE TIMING OF THE INITIAL JAPANESE ASSAULT in the Pacific could hardly have been better for Japan; the United States and Great Britain were both caught flat-footed. Within the span of fourteen hours, Japan's series of carefully prepared and well-timed attacks delivered decisive blows against the Allies across an unprecedented six-thousand-mile front. From Southeast Asia to the Hawaiian Islands, every Allied foothold in the Pacific was in turmoil. The raid on Pearl Harbor galvanized the American public to a common cause—unity in the resolve to defeat Japan—but events on the other side of the Pacific suggested that many setbacks would occur before the pendulum swung in the other direction.

As the sun rose on Tuesday, December 9, 1941, U.S. and British air force personnel reeled in disbelief at the nearly fatal blow just dealt them by the Empire of Japan. It was like awakening from a nightmare only to find out that the memory was real. Allied offensive airpower in both the Philippines and Malaya had been crippled. To the east, the vital supply line from the United States was in shambles: Guam was surrounded by the enemy; the critical air-transit point at Wake Island was threatened; Midway lay isolated and defenseless; and the men at Pearl Harbor struggled to contain the damage caused by Admiral Chuichi Nagumo's fliers.

The initial Japanese bombing missions in the Far East had been incredibly effective in disabling Allied air force assets. Two bomber squadrons and four fighter units were literally blasted out of existence: the 28th and 30th Bombardment and the 20th Pursuit Squadrons of the AAF would not fly again. VMF-211 was left with only three fully functional Wildcats. RAF 27 Squadron was reduced to just one plane. None of RAAF No. 21 Squadron's four flyable Buffaloes could be considered combat ready. Four key airfields had been taken out of operation entirely, and a fifth was marginally usable. The sheer magnitude and unexpected accuracy of Japanese bombardments left many witnesses on the ground in a state of shock. From the fighter base at Iba Field, frantic airmen chaotically abandoned their posts, literally taking to the hills in the aftermath of the heavy strike. Iba was so heavily cratered by the blasts that it was no longer used as an airfield. As at Iba, the devastation of Sungei Patani and Alor Star was complete; neither would be used again—at least not by British air forces.

From the frontline location at Kota Bharu, RAAF personnel evacuated the airfield in near panic when Japanese troops encroached on its borders just before sunset. Word of this Japanese occupation quickly spread to other frontline locations in Malaya. At the heavily bombarded Alor Star field, knowledge that enemy troops were motoring down the road in their direction motivated dazed RAF crews to feverishly patch up whatever aircraft they could in preparation to flee southward at dawn. The squadrons would be gone before a single gunshot had been fired.

Clark Field was still operational, but just barely. Only a portion of one runway was usable, and most of the critical structures had been gutted by fire. To make matters worse, U.S. Army leadership demonstrated a nearly complete—and quite embarrassing—inability to cope with the carnage around the base. On the night of December 8, the living and the dead mingled together at Clark amid the wreckage of aircraft, trucks, and buildings in a macabre moonlit silence. Airplanes had to be serviced, but "the brass" could not agree who was responsible for collecting corpses and handling death records and burial services. That bizarre argument would persist for more than a week as bodies of the deceased Americans lay bloated and rotting on the runways and parking areas—a grotesque reminder that the United States was as mentally unprepared for war as it was militarily ill equipped.

Malaya's defenders had taken unrecoverable losses. Given the extent of damage to British and Australian bomber units, it would be impossible to mount immediate counterstrikes against Japanese positions in Siam. The RAF squadrons had been very nearly wiped out by supernaturally timed bombing and strafing attacks on airfields in northern Malaya. Of fifty Blenheims available at the commencement of hostilities, only fourteen remained in somewhat airworthy condition by the close of December 8. Though not suffering as severely as the British units, Australian bomber squadrons experienced a combined loss of two Hudsons in combat and eight more permanently stricken due to battle damage or enemy strafing. Almost every one of the fourteen flyable Hudsons still in Malaya had been struck by bullets or shrapnel as a result of defensive air action near Kota Bharu.

In the Philippines the fight was not over, but one hand had been quickly tied behind the Americans' back. On the island of Luzon, ten fighters either were shot down by Zeros or crashed during the brief air battle; twenty-six indispensable P-40s, a dozen precious B-17 bombers, and numerous second-line and utility aircraft had been completely destroyed on the ground by fire or enemy munitions. Future interception efforts were hamstrung by the unfortunate collateral loss of the radar equipment at Iba Field. In a near knockout punch to the AAF's heavy bombardment plans, Clark Field was all but lost as a hub for bomber operations. Exiled from its only real base, the 19th Bombardment Group would be greatly inhibited by its dearth of support facilities. In desperation, Flying Fortresses were thrown immediately into a role of tactical defense and utilized for missions better suited to dive-bombers.

The only positive news from the Pacific was that all three aircraft carriers assigned to the United States Pacific Fleet had, by pure chance, escaped destruction. It would take time to realize that there was some other good news in Hawaii. As men sifted through the wreckage on Oahu, their commanders would come to appreciate that Japan had failed to cripple Pearl Harbor as an operational naval station. With functional facilities, the Hawaiian base could act as a launch platform for a regarrisoning of the Pacific. In fact, most of the ships the Japanese naval aviators had so proudly claimed as "sunk" would be resurrected from their shallow, watery graves. Of course, the bastions of the Far East would fall long before Pearl Harbor's ghosts emerged to seek their vengeance.

Japan's sweeping success on that first infamous day of the air campaign in the Far East ensured its air superiority for at least the first few months of the Pacific War. General Brereton and Air Vice Marshal Pulford would be in a state of denial for several more days, but the facts were undeniable. Building a new supply line to replenish initial aircraft losses would not be easy. Ships already at sea carrying fighter, dive-bomber, and other short-range aircraft had been immediately diverted to lengthy southern routes across the Pacific as soon as news of the Pearl Harbor attack had been received. Other shipping being readied for transit would be delayed, awaiting availability of suitable escorts. Given the high rate of naval casualties in Hawaii, it would be some time before enough warships could be gathered to accompany the merchantmen. Until new bases in the South Pacific were completed, the flow of heavy bombers beyond Hawaii was curtailed. President Roosevelt himself would become involved in an ambitious new effort to supply bombers for duty in the Far East, but those aircraft would have to be sent on an untried and challenging route, circling the globe from west to east. They would not arrive in time to play a part in the defense of the Philippines or Malaya.

All this disruption of Allied defenses came at a surprisingly modest price for Japan. Only seven Zeros failed to return to Formosa from the Philippines. No Japanese bombers had been damaged over U.S. territory, though two were claimed by mechanical failures: one bomber and its crew had been lost when a tire blew on takeoff from Tainan; a second was wrecked in an emergency landing during the return flight over Formosa. The small unproductive raids on Davao City and USS *Preston* cost the Japanese navy proportionately more, but still not much: one fighter and one bomber had been forced down, and two fighters were damaged, in exchange for sinking just two PBY flying boats. In Malaya, the British had done very little to stem the tide of the Japanese air offensive; Mother Nature proved a greater threat. Just three Japanese fighters were downed by air action, while five were lost in weather-related crashes; as many as eighteen more were written off in landing accidents on the rain-slicked grass of Singora and Duong Dong airfields. Seven bombers either ditched or crashed during storm-battered return flights to Indochina. So-called friendly fire from overexcited Japanese antiaircraft gunners accounted for the destruction of one additional bomber. No losses had been recorded during the successful bombing of Wake Island.

ADMIRAL TSUKAHARA DID NOT WAIT LONG to follow up with another strike at air facilities on Luzon. He was eager to keep the U.S. leadership off balance. Just after midnight, Lieutenant Yoshiro Kaneko led nine G3M bombers of the *1st Kokutai* off their field at Tainan. His flight had been conducting nightly reconnaissance missions over the Philippines since December 2 and had become familiar with finding its designated targets in darkness. Kaneko's was the only unit from the 11th

Air Fleet on Formosa that did not participate in the daylight attacks on December 8. Consequently, his crews were especially anxious to get into battle after nearly a week of playing hide-and-seek with FEAF interceptors. They were given the honor of leading the first attack of December 9, while the rest of the IJN bomber force prepared for another massive assault later in the morning.

Anticipating that the next Japanese attack would probably focus on Nichols Field, Colonel George and Major Grover reassigned the 17th and 21st Pursuit Squadrons to Clark Field. This was done despite Clark's poor condition, because it was assumed that the enemy would not be back there until they hit other key installations. Nichols, on the other hand, would certainly be high on Japan's list of priority targets. The 21st Pursuit was redeployed to Clark, as planned, during the late afternoon of December 8. The 17th Pursuit was unable to get to the cratered field before dark. Lieutenant Wagner, worried about the runway conditions for a night landing, brought his planes into Del Carmen instead. The fighters would be safe enough there. That small dirt runway surrounded by sugarcane fields would have been almost impossible for the Japanese to find at night.

Remnants of the dislocated 3rd Pursuit had been scattered all across central Luzon after the midday battle. In light of the unplanned evacuation of Iba, it would take a few days to reorganize the squadron. Most of the men from the ground echelon were hiking away from the base, traveling on foot along a difficult mountain trail over the Zambales Mountains toward Clark. Small numbers of Hank Thorne's serviceable planes clustered at Nichols Field or the small auxiliary airstrip at Rosales. It would take at least a day to round up the pilots and their fighters.

Most American aviators were badly in need of rest, but the 24th Pursuit Group remained on alert. FEAF Headquarters wondered whether the Japanese were capable of mounting an effective night raid. Intruding was one thing, but precision bombing in the darkness was another. Then again, hardly anyone had been of the opinion the previous morning that the Japanese were capable of bombing accurately in daylight. Although the record had certainly been set straight on that account, some AAF officers remained confident of their safety under the shield of diminished visibility. Many were less certain. Either way, few among them would get a good night's sleep.

Deprived of its radar, the FEAF AWS was forced to depend on the telephone-linked spotter network and army ground units for enemy aircraft detection. This was a giant step backward. In the early, dark hours of December 9, no sighting reports were received. It was not until the drone of Lieutenant Kaneko's aircraft could be heard from Clark Field itself that an alert was finally issued.

Major Grover quickly radioed the 17th Pursuit at Del Carmen to send off six of its P-40s to attempt an interception. At about 0200, Willie Feallock roared down the dirt strip toward a single light at the other end of the Del Carmen runway. As Feallock's plane rose into the night, his wingman, 2nd Lieutenant Jim Rowland, and second element leader, 1st Lieutenant Walt Coss, followed suit. In the fourth plane, 2nd Lieutenant Lawrence Lodin—apparently confused in the darkness and roiling dust clouds—veered left during his takeoff run with disastrous results. Lodin's P-40 tore through the wingtip of the third element leader, 1st Lieutenant William "Red" Sheppard, cartwheeled into the waiting P-40E of 2nd Lieutenant Maurice Hughett, and burst into flames. Squadron-mates rushed to the burning wreck but couldn't get close enough to extract Lodin from the fighter. Hughett and Sheppard were shaken, but uninjured.

Airborne in the dark skies, Feallock, Rowland, and Coss left the fiery mess behind but found themselves incapable of joining together in formation. Separately chasing after the Japanese bombers, none of them was able to find the enemy.

Kaneko's planes had already passed well to the south of Del Carmen by the time the Americans got off the ground. Only seven G3Ms remained in the formation: two of the aging bombers aborted the mission before reaching the Philippines, forced to turn back because of mechanical problems. Some minutes after 0300, the Mitsubishis rumbled overhead at Nichols Field. Their 132-pound bombs whistled toward the ground, causing a great stir, but relatively little damage. Of all the aircraft on the ground at Nichols, just one B-18 and a Curtiss O-52 observation plane were disabled by the blasts. Hangar Four received a couple of direct hits from the small bombs. One corner of the large building was heavily damaged, but the structure was still usable.[1] Operations at the airstrip were hardly disrupted at all: two P-40s scrambled into the night less than half an hour after the attack in a belated attempt to intercept the raiders. None of the pursuit activity was noted by the Japanese. However, the mission was not without cost: one of the returning G3Ms crashed on landing at Tainan, killing all on board.[2]

The psychological effect of this night raid was much more important than any physical damage to Nichols Field. Another bigoted opinion was invalidated: the perception that "chronically nearsighted" Japanese aviators could not fight in aircraft at night was proven quite wrong. The first twenty-four hours of war actually shattered most long-nurtured illusions about the presumed superiority of U.S. aviation and the relative ineffectiveness of Japanese air forces as thoroughly as if they had been crystal glasses dropped on a stone floor.

The next Japanese attack wave was expected at first light. Major Grover was determined to have his interceptors in the air before dawn to greet the enemy. This was another decision he likely regretted. At about 0500, with Ed Dyess in the lead, the P-40s of the 21st Pursuit began to churn through the fading darkness along the small auxiliary strip at Clark. Dyess instructed his pilots to take off at specific intervals. Ideally, this would minimize the disorienting effect of dust and ash stirred up from the burnt-out field. In a horrible repetition of the events that happened earlier at Del Carmen, the pilot of the fourth plane lost his bearings while accelerating down the runway. Circling above, Lieutenant Dyess saw the fighter stray off course. Frantically, he screamed a warning into the microphone of his radio. It was to no avail. Second Lieutenant Robert Clark continued to speed ahead until his fighter fatally collided with Lieutenant Colonel Eubank's parked Flying Fortress. Both planes were destroyed in a massive explosion. The blazing pyre, visible for miles around, was a sobering spectacle for the other pilots. Cautiously, in the eerie glow of the flames, the next few P-40s crept into the air. On his turn, 2nd Lieutenant Lloyd Coleman drifted slightly off the narrow surface and caught one wheel in a bomb crater. With a landing strut ripped from its wing, the Warhawk nosed forward and spun into the dirt. Coleman survived, but his new P-40E was a total wreck. Another rattled pilot, taking off after Coleman, destroyed a third fighter in a high-speed collision with an unlit field light.[3]

Once airborne, the squadron's brand-new P-40Es generated plenty of their own problems. Johnny McCown was in for a truly terrifying experience. McCown's engine seized up just after his speeding fighter lifted off the ground. Crashing blindly back to earth through a stand of trees at the end of the runway, he miraculously escaped the clutches of death, emerging essentially unhurt from the mangled remains of his airplane. Up above, Sam Grashio thought his fighter was destined for a similar fall from the sky when its Allison engine began acting up. As Grashio descended back to the field outside the normal approach pattern, trying desperately to save the valuable aircraft, he drew the unwelcome attention of almost every antiaircraft battery around the base. Amazingly, he was able to coax his balking plane through the firestorm and back to the ground without taking any flak damage.

By the time the sun's first rays shimmered over the eastern coast of Luzon, it had already been a costly day for the Far East Air Force: two pilots were dead, six new P-40s and one reparable Flying Fortress had been destroyed, and another P-40 was damaged. At that rate, the 24th Pursuit Group would be wiped out before the end of the week. Some of the men began to question whether the air force could provide any protection at all for its Philippine bases.

Conscious that offensive operations against Japanese airfields might still yield the best defense for the Philippines, FEAF Headquarters fervently hoped to launch at least one bombing strike on Formosa. Toward that purpose, General Brereton had ordered the Flying Fortresses of the 14th and 93rd Bomb Squadrons to fly back up from Mindanao during the evening of December 8. He anticipated their arrival that night for an early-morning staging at Clark Field.

Radio communications with Del Monte suffered some difficulties after the Japanese attacks. Orders from Manila to the 19th Bomb Group on Mindanao had been sent in plain language, without proper authentication. For that reason, Major O'Donnell was understandably suspicious about their origin. By the time correctly coded messages were received at Del Monte, it was too late to send the bombers north. Though he chose not to inform Eubank or Brereton of his modified departure schedule, Rosie O'Donnell had no intention of letting his aircraft land on Clark's cratered airstrip at night. The major independently decided to send the Fortresses up to Luzon in time for a late-afternoon landing. This would allow the FEAF to orchestrate the proposed raid at dawn on December 10. Strong-willed, as always, he failed to see any logic in having the B-17s arrive at Clark in the morning or midday—the time when the airfields were most likely to be attacked by the Japanese.

For the morning of December 9, Major O'Donnell was content to focus his thoughts on local reconnaissance around Mindanao. If the Japanese aircraft that hit Davao—definitely from carrier-based air forces—returned for more strikes, O'Donnell could keep his bombers busy enough around the large southern island. Perhaps his men could even bag an aircraft carrier. At first light, he sent Captain Elmer Parsel out to fly over the Davao Gulf. If he saw nothing of interest at Davao

City or the waters of the gulf, Parsel was to circle the rest of the island looking for shipping that might indicate an enemy move against Mindanao. The other fourteen operational B-17s at Del Monte would remain on the ground, preparing for the upcoming flight to Luzon or an opportunity to fight back against the Japanese navy.

Throughout the archipelago, the early daylight hours brought numerous reports of suspicious activity. It was impossible to sort out fact from fiction in a timely manner. The most intriguing of these reports alleged that an enemy aircraft carrier had been spotted off Catanduanes Island, some three hundred miles east of Manila. This "sighting" fulfilled the prophecy that Japanese fighters supporting action in the Philippines must have been flown from carriers. The presence of Zeros over Luzon and the attack on Davao left the FEAF staff with a distinct impression that Japan's flattops lurked somewhere nearby. Major O'Donnell would continue the search around eastern Mindanao, but the radio waves brought new orders to Del Monte. Major Cecil Combs—commanding officer of the 93rd Squadron—was assigned to take six Fortresses north from Mindanao to investigate the area around Catanduanes. If possible, these B-17s would locate and attack the ship and then land at Clark Field. Each bomber had been loaded with twenty 100-pound bombs. Such small explosives were capable of producing a dense bombing pattern but could hardly inflict much damage on a capital ship. Without any particular worries about this limitation, Combs resolutely led the others off the grass and dirt strip at about 0730 to go hunting.[4]

Meanwhile, Colonel Eubank sent Lieutenant Carpenter's crew north from Clark to Formosa in another attempt to snoop on the Japanese air bases. Eubank also ordered Lieutenant Wheless to take his B-17 up the west side of the Babuyan Islands—between Formosa and Luzon—on a parallel course. Wheless would pursue confirmation for sightings of a large southbound enemy naval formation. The Japanese were already known to have seized Batan Island at the northernmost reach of the Philippine Archipelago. Possibly the forces participating in that invasion were heading south. A third Fortress rose from the embers at Clark Field at 0800. This bomber was by no means mission ready. It had been cobbled together during the night by enterprising mechanics. First Lieutenant Jack Adams had been assigned to get it off the field and south to the safe haven at Del Monte.[5]

Later that morning, Lieutenant Colonel Eubank tasked Lieutenant Frank Kurtz—who had lost his Fortress and all but one member of its crew during the bombing—to run the control tower at Clark. The structure was a mess, full of bullet and shrapnel holes and deprived of regular communications equipment. Eubank had personally given Kurtz very restrictive direction regarding landing authorization policy: "the Colonel wasn't taking any chances losing any more on the ground. He said when any Fortresses came back, to keep them in the air, circling the field, until he changed the order."[6]

Because only three Fortresses at a time could be serviced within the protective revetments, just three would be allowed on the ground at Clark during daylight hours. Even those lucky revetment holders were to leave the field, if possible, whenever an air-raid alert was posted. As one can imagine, nearly constant—mostly false—alarms would send the bombers rushing away at the slightest provocation. Incompletely serviced Flying Fortresses scrambled off to hide in the clouds instead of continuing preparations for missions. Under these conditions, Clark Field became virtually useless as a staging base.

Although the weather cooperated with the Americans on December 9, Lieutenants Carpenter and Wheless were not able to reach their designated patrol locations. Both B-17s were plagued with mechanical problems: Carpenter's generator went out again, and Wheless's plane suffered intermittent losses of electrical power. Running critical systems on battery power, both pilots headed back for their base. Still, the reconnaissance missions were not a total loss. Wheless was able to spot a large formation of Japanese ships on the horizon, apparently headed for the west coast of Luzon. On their return to Clark Field, both aircraft were denied landing permission by Lieutenant Kurtz. Carpenter decided he would stay near Clark until someone allowed him to land. He was prepared to land against orders as soon as his electrical or fuel situations became critical. Wheless, with a less urgent requirement for service, opted not to wait. He proceeded south toward Mindanao, where his crew would spend a more peaceful night at Del Monte than they had at Clark.

Japan's air forces fully intended to be back over Luzon by sunrise. Again, the bombers had been grounded by storms covering most of southern Formosa. This time, an entire day would pass without Japanese attacks on the Philippines. For the Americans, this quiet day would be analogous to resting in the eye of a hurricane.

THE FURIOUS STORM OF WAR did not spare Malaya on December 9, 1941. A new day in Singapore brought little consolation to weigh against Air Chief Marshal Brooke-Popham's knowledge that the most important air station in northern Malaya had been conceded to the enemy after only twenty-four hours of ground battle, that the key forward-area fighter base had been effectively destroyed in two uncontested bombardments, and that a third airstrip was in the process of being abandoned as the sun rose.

For personnel assigned to the underdeveloped Kuantan station, it must have seemed that their position was consigned to a similar fate. Morale deteriorated quickly as stories of the Japanese invasion of Kota Bharu spread from No. 1 Squadron fliers. If Kota Bharu was the strongest British position north of Singapore, Kuantan was probably the weakest. Everyone present was well aware of that fact. With no army troops, and no weapon more formidable than a .303-caliber machine gun, the base was defenseless. Virtually any Japanese landing party could overrun the position in a matter of minutes. The only opportunity for salvation at Kuantan appeared to be a timely intervention on the part of the Royal Navy. Some of the officers were undoubtedly aware that *Prince of Wales* and *Repulse*, with a screen of four destroyers, had gone north from Singapore the previous evening. Of course, they had no idea where their potential saviors were heading.

Admiral Sir Phillips intended to move in and hit the smaller Japanese ships of the Singora invasion fleet with his heavy long-range guns. Although his "Force Z" formation was small, its two battlewagons were certainly capable of manhandling the IJN cruisers and mauling the transports without much risk of retaliation. However, with only four destroyers to hunt for submarines, he would be hard-pressed to detect and counter undersea threats. To compound that problem, *Prince of Wales*'s surface radar was out of commission, nullifying Phillips's principal advantage should he happen to engage any Japanese battleships. The small flotilla was also handicapped in dealing with enemy attacks from above the seas. Without escorting cruisers, his antiaircraft umbrella would be limited. Vulnerable to Japanese submarines and aircraft, electronically blind, and unable to request assistance because Phillips elected to maintain strict radio silence, "Force Z" planned to go it alone—an extremely risky proposition.

At Kuantan, rain had poured in buckets all night long. With a total blackout in effect, it had proved all but impossible to service the many aircraft on the field. It was a challenge for fueling crews just to find some of the bombers during the pitch-black deluge.

Very early in the morning of December 9, Air Headquarters instructed Wing Commander R. B. Councell—the Kuantan station commanding officer—to return RAF 60 Squadron's Blenheims and two target-towing Swordfish biplanes to Singapore. The Australian Hudsons, torpedo-toting Vildebeests of RAF 100 Squadron, and one disabled Blenheim were to remain at Kuantan. On hearing of this order, Squadron Leader Henderson, the senior officer representing both Australian squadrons, urgently requested that Air Headquarters also allow the Hudsons to fly back to Sembawang. It did not seem wise to keep the valuable Lockheeds on a base subject to surprise air attacks when no antiaircraft weapons or fighter protection was available. Additionally, some of his planes required repairs that could not be rendered with the limited resources at Kuantan.

Henderson knew it would be some time before he could expect a response, so he dutifully dispatched three No. 8 Squadron Hudsons to search for Japanese shipping that might indicate enemy movement south from Kota Bharu. Such a discovery would only bolster the case for withdrawal of his unit to a safer location.

The weather was still fairly miserable as No. 8 Squadron's three Lockheeds flew on parallel tracks along the coastline toward Singora. Somehow, through the mist and rain, Flight Lieutenant Robert Arnold eventually managed to spot a naval formation heading east, past Kota Bharu. This Japanese task force reportedly consisted of two cruisers, seven destroyers, and three transports.[7] It was exactly the kind of ship grouping that would be perceived as a direct threat to Kuantan. Upon receiving the sighting information radioed from Arnold's plane, six Vildebeests were sent out to attack with torpedoes.

THE JAPANESE HAD BEEN HAVING their own difficulties with the weather. Although most JAAF heavy bombers had taken off from western Indochina at first light, and the army fighter umbrella over Malaya was substantial, JAAF operations on December 9 would prove largely ineffective.

A huge formation of seventy-nine Ki-21s from the 60th and 98th Sentai flew toward the British airfield at Victoria Point in Burma. Heavy cloud cover in the western reaches of the Gulf of Siam prevented these bombers from approaching Burma or making a rendezvous with their escort. Frustrated, the bomber crews set a course back to Krakor. It was a long flight without much opportunity to break the monotony.

A sizable wave of Ki-27 fighters from the 11th Sentai at Singora eventually attacked Victoria Point that day. In spite of the importance of the location, there was no equipment on the field for them to strafe. The fighter sweep provided some recreation for the pilots, but their 7.7-mm guns could hardly do much damage to the buildings.

Ten Ki-21s of the 62nd Sentai were tasked with a final bombing of Kota Bharu—also a wasted effort since no British troops remained in the area. The futility of the mission was compounded by the loss of one Ki-21, which crash-landed when it experienced severe engine problems on its way to the target.[8]

A half-hour after the needless raid on Kota Bharu, thirty-nine Ki-48s from the 75th and 90th Sentai at Kompong Trach, escorted by six Ki-43s from the 59th Sentai, flew over the coast toward Machang. Eighteen of the bombers mistakenly released their weapons on Kota Bharu, which had just been occupied by Japanese soldiers. The rest bombed Machang in another pointless strike. Within the hour, the wooden decoy aircraft at Machang were splintered by another group of Ki-48s from the 82nd Chutai.[9]

Pilots of the seventeen wayward Ki-43 fighters that failed to find their flock for the aborted mission to Victoria Point decided to land at Singora for fuel. Before heading back to their base at Duong Dong—perhaps to add a little excitement to their day—seven of the 64th Sentai fighters staged a strafing run on Bayan Lebas airfield, across the Malayan Peninsula on Penang Island. This impromptu activity was actually more productive than the planned JAAF raids of that morning: a handful of trainers from the local flying club were shot to pieces. The strafers expended the balance of their ammunition on a thorough bullet-hole ventilation of the empty corrugated-steel hangar.[10]

BRITISH AND AUSTRALIAN SQUADRONS expended most of their effort on December 9 attempting to recover from the disaster of the previous day.

Across the channel from Penang Island, the air station at Butterworth had been in a general state of confusion, with planes taking off and landing all morning. As each could be made ready, flyable Blenheims from RAF 34 Squadron departed for Tengah. Their places were soon taken by bomb-damaged 62 Squadron Blenheims limping in from Alor Star. Mechanics gave priority to the one 27 Squadron Blenheim "fighter" and four damaged Buffaloes of RAAF No. 21 Squadron that had been flown down from Sungei Patani the previous evening. By about 1000, two of the Buffaloes were restored to operational status.

At 1040 Flying Officers Daryl Sproule and Geoffrey Sheppard took off for a much-needed reconnaissance of the road between Alor Star and Singora. After a short flight along that highway, the two Australians picked out a concentration of more than a dozen tanks near Ban Sadao for their first strafing run. Surprisingly, no antiaircraft fire met their approach. In fact, one Japanese soldier stood in the middle of the road and waved at them with a signal flag. Undoubtedly, the troops thought the diving planes were JAAF fighters, at least until .50-caliber gunfire raked along the column of vehicles. Though they might have gotten away with another pass, the two Buffalo pilots prudently headed back south without inflicting noticeable damage. Near Jitra, another column of vehicles was spotted at what appeared to be the spearhead of the Japanese ground offensive. This time, Sproule and Sheppard left four trucks in flames before returning to Butterworth.[11]

Back at Kuantan, Squadron Leader Henderson was still lamenting the fact that he had not heard from Air Headquarters. All but three of his Hudsons were still on the ground. A few minutes after 1100, as the last Singapore-bound Swordfish was lifting off the airstrip, nine unidentified twin-engine planes roared out of the offshore cloudbank. Led by Lieutenant Shigeji Makino, this chutai of G3M bombers from the *Genzan Kokutai* raced over the field at an altitude of five thousand feet, dropping half its bomb load in passing. Men on the ground were completely unprepared. For most, the first warning of the raid was the blast of exploding bombs. Flying out of sight beyond the airfield, the bombers quickly turned and then released their remaining bombs as they flew back in the opposite direction. Once out to sea, the G3Ms again turned, descending down to the deck for a treetop-level machine-gunning pass along the runway.

Seeing low-flying Japanese aircraft over Kuantan as he returned from his reconnaissance mission, Flight Lieutenant Ron Widmer swung his Hudson into Makino's attack with guns blazing. From the ground, Flight Lieutenant Herb Plenty thought he saw parachutes falling from one of the enemy planes, which also seemed to be smoking. While it appeared to Plenty that Widmer may have downed a bomber, in reality, all of the *Genzan* planes headed safely back toward Saigon.[12] The illusion of a victory was perpetuated when eight *Mihoro Kokutai* G3Ms from Lieutenant Yoshimi Shirai's chutai appeared for another double bomb run over the smoking airfield. Of course, neither Widmer nor Plenty had any way of knowing they had viewed two separate groups of bombers.

By the time the last IJN attackers left the scene, three Hudsons, two Vildebeests, and a Blenheim were in flames. Two more Hudsons and the previously disabled Blenheim sustained serious shrapnel and gunfire damage. In addition, the armory, workshop, main storeroom, and a fuel truck had been destroyed. Despite this, a certain amount of good fortune prevailed; none of the personnel on the base had been killed.[13]

As men around the station shakily emerged from their shelters to survey the destruction, Squadron Leader Henderson finally received from Air Headquarters a curt denial of his request for evacuation of the bombers: "Tell Squadron Leader Henderson to stay where he is. The bombing of Kuantan is not in the scheme of things."[14] It was not recorded, but one can imagine Henderson's probable commentary on the wisdom of that forecast.

A report of the raid and its disastrous results was promptly telephoned to the decision makers in Singapore. This time, the officers sitting in the safety of their conference rooms decided it might actually be a good idea to withdraw all remaining combat aircraft from Kuantan. Relocation would begin as soon as surviving planes from Australian squadrons and 100 Squadron could be checked out and refueled.

SQUADRON LEADER HENDERSON was not the only officer irritated by the poor judgment of others that day. A few choice comments may have been heard at Vice Admiral Jisaburo Ozawa's invasion fleet headquarters on board the cruiser *Chokai*. Shortly before 1400, the Japanese submarine *I-65* stumbled upon "Force Z." When the sub could safely surface, its captain sent a contact report indicating that *Prince of Wales* and *Repulse* were headed north, past Kuantan. This was startling news for the Japanese admiral. The crew of a mid-morning IJN reconnaissance flight over Seletar air station and the Singapore naval base had reported that both British capital ships were still in port. After a review of their photographs, it was evident that the fliers had misidentified two large tankers as the warships. Vice Admiral Nobutake Kondo, overall commander of the Japanese Southern Fleet, ordered his cruisers to launch their floatplanes for an immediate search of the area. In Saigon, all available IJN bombers were hastily mustered in an effort to find the British ships and sink them.

AT TENGAH, THE REMNANTS of RAF 34 and 60 Squadrons had been merged into one flying organization. Some of the planes were still being serviced after their morning exodus from Malaya, but at 1245 six readied Blenheims were sent on a bombing raid to Singora. Although no fighters escorted them, they arrived over the Japanese landing zone unscathed. One of the bombers targeted unloading transports. Others dropped bombs on Singora airfield, causing some damage to parked aircraft before 1st Sentai fighters intervened. The price for this small strike was heavy in proportion to the results attained: two of the Blenheims were shot down over Singora; a third crashed along the southeastern coast of Malaya as a result of battle damage. Two RAF crewmen were killed and four were captured. The three surviving planes struggled to reach Butterworth.[15]

At Butterworth, resourceful technicians returned two more Buffaloes to duty and serviced most of the 62 Squadron Blenheims by mid-afternoon. The air force command decided that three of those Blenheims should linger to regroup with the three 34/60 Squadron bombers just returned from Singora. Together, they could execute a late-afternoon raid on enemy landing forces. With any luck, they would catch Japanese air units on the ground. Even if the plan failed in that regard, the Blenheims would finally have an escort: four No. 21 Squadron Buffaloes were available to accompany them.

Unfortunately, the mission did not start out as planned. By 1530 the fighters had taken off from Butterworth but were forced to circle around the area waiting for the Blenheims to join them. After biding their time for almost an hour, Flight Lieutenant Williams and his wingman, Flying Officer Clifford McKenny, decided to go back to the airstrip to refuel and find out what had happened to the bombers. As the two Buffaloes approached from the north, the reason for the missed rendezvous became clear. The Australians were surprised to find more than twenty Ki-27s milling around near Butterworth. The Japanese fighters were escorting a number of Ki-21 bombers in a heavy attack on the British base.

Only two Blenheims managed to get off the ground before the raid: one turned back to the field after being fired on by fighters; the other, flown by Squadron Leader Arthur Scarf of 62 Squadron, continued on alone toward Singora without being spotted by either the Japanese raiders or the Buffalo pilots.

A dismal scene greeted Fred Williams and Clifford McKenny after they dived safely through the Japanese formation and landed at the smoking airfield. Yet again, Japanese bombardiers had been successful:

two Blenheims had been completely destroyed, and all but two others heavily damaged. Buildings were on fire, casting a pall of smoke over the scene, but, miraculously, the mobile fuel tanker was still intact. However, when the two Australians taxied over to it, they found the pump padlocked. Of course, none of the shell-shocked ground crew would come out to unlock it or service the planes.[16]

Spotting more enemy aircraft above, the daring duo gunned their engines and roared back into the sky. This time they headed straight for the bombers. Before they got much chance to inflict damage, they were swarmed by the little Ki-27s. McKenny's fuel tank was hit in the first moments of combat and caught fire right away. Severely burned before he bailed out over the channel, he was fortunate enough to splash down near a fish trap that kept him afloat until he could be rescued. Flight Lieutenant Williams took effective evasive action but found his guns inoperative thereafter. As he headed back toward the runway, his Brewster's engine started missing and then stopped altogether. Williams made a dead-stick landing and scrambled away from his plane just in time. Three pursuing Ki-27s buzzed overhead, their gunfire stitching the Buffalo with holes from one end to the other. Some of the bullets apparently found the fuel tank, for the fighter was soon in flames.

Up above, the other two Buffaloes fared no better. Flying Officer Harold Montefiore was floating earthward after having bailed out of his Buffalo during another swirling dogfight. From his chute, Montefiore had seen McKenny and Williams go down, but at least he felt that he had exacted some repayment for the loss of their aircraft. Though no one was present to confirm the claim, Montefiore was certain he had shot down one of the enemy planes before being shot down himself.[17] Caught up in the same battle, Flight Lieutenant Alan White was also overwhelmed by the sprightly Japanese fighters. Escaping in a steep dive, White successfully belly-landed his thoroughly shot-up Buffalo on Penang Island near the runway at Bayan Lebas.

While the Japanese fighter pilots were distracted by the exchange with the Buffaloes, Squadron Leader Scarf snuck off to the north. He managed to reach Singora, dropping all of his bombs on the airfield. Turning back to the south, he met with heavy fighter opposition and was grievously wounded. Heroically, Scarf was able to get himself and the severely damaged bomber back to Alor Star, where his wife was a nurse at the base hospital. He executed a well-controlled crash landing near the hospital building and was rushed to its operating room. Sadly, with his wife by his side, he died during preparation for surgery. Though valiant sacrifice did not result in much harm to the enemy, he did bring his crew back safely to fight another day. For this action, he was later given a posthumous award of Britain's highest honor, the Victoria Cross. Scarf would be the only pilot to receive such decoration during the entire campaign over Malaya and Singapore.

Because no fighters were left in Malaya, and the bomber squadrons had been eviscerated, a decision was made to evacuate all aircraft from the Butterworth station before sundown. Two undamaged Blenheims were flown to an auxiliary field at Taiping, just northwest of Ipoh. Damaged, flyable planes were sent off to Singapore for completion of repairs. Only a skeleton crew would remain at Butterworth to provide fuel service and conduct salvage operations. For the second time in two days, ground crews from No. 21 Squadron and RAF 27 Squadron packed up to migrate southward.

At about the same time that the evacuation of Butterworth began, seven Vildebeests and ten Hudsons left the field at Kuantan, each of the latter carrying as many men as could be stuffed inside its cabin. More resourceful than other fellow pilots who had been left behind, Herb Plenty and Flying Officer Dave Dey scouted out damaged aircraft around the field and were able to find two that they could mend well enough to make the trip to Singapore. After helping each other with repairs, Dey took off in a 100 Squadron Vildebeest, while Plenty managed to get a jury-rigged No. 1 Squadron Hudson back into the air. Both made their flights to Sembawang without difficulty.

Although Air Headquarters had definitely not decided to evacuate the Kuantan station itself, the aircraft relocation order was poorly communicated to men around the base. Once the bombers were away, panic gripped jumpy ground personnel and a number of airmen who could not be carried in the planes. Many simply wandered off down the road toward Jerantut. Some temporarily lost their senses, stealing any form of transportation available. One desperate lieutenant went so far as to hijack the local postal truck at gunpoint. The general disorder of this evacuation and related acts of misconduct resulted in Wing Commander Councell having to stand before a formal Board of Inquiry. Whether it was Councell's fault or not, it was indeed a very poor showing, as later described by Flying Officer Roy Bulcock of the station staff:

> In half an hour that little flame of panic had spread like wild-fire. I looked out on a deserted station. . . . There were only four of us left—the C.O., the Adjutant, the Armament Officer and myself . . .

myself still too numb to appreciate the sarcasm of the other men's conversation. Then I realised they were talking of Australians, that I was an Australian, and that many curious glances were being cast in my direction. . . . For the first and last time I felt ashamed of being an Australian.[18]

THE REST OF THE DAY WAS considerably less traumatic in the Philippines. Around 1430 Major Combs's flight of six Fortresses came into Clark Field after several hours of fruitless searching around Catanduanes Island on the wild goose chase for an enemy carrier. As the weary men from Mindanao stepped down from the cabin doors of their Fortresses onto the charred grass of Clark's runway, the devastation around them came as quite a shock. They would have time to reflect on the situation while they flew their bombers in wide circles above the Lingayen plain. In keeping with Colonel Eubank's precautionary measure, the 93rd Squadron B-17s were allowed to land, but Combs and his men had been asked to depart again as soon as they could be refueled; they would remain in the air until dusk.

When the 93rd Squadron could finally land for the evening, Combs orbited the airstrip to watch his other B-17s set down in the gathering darkness. Major O'Donnell's seven 14th Squadron Fortresses just coming in from Del Monte joined him in the approach pattern. One last Boeing appeared shortly thereafter: Captain Parsel was concluding his grueling, ten-hour-long reconnaissance mission. To disperse the bombers for the night, Eubank decided that the 14th Squadron, along with Parsel, should continue west to the new field under construction at San Marcelino. The Flying Fortresses were to be joined there by the 34th Pursuit Squadron's last fourteen P-35As, which had just taken off from Del Carmen on dispersal orders from Colonel George.[19] Unfortunately, no one had informed the Filipino guard troops of these movements, so the aircraft approaching San Marcelino were welcomed with a dangerous fireworks show of light machine-gun tracers. Adding to this confusion, the 34th Pursuit personnel were unaware of the bomber relocation. Arriving at the same time as O'Donnell's planes, some of the fighter pilots began to shoot at the B-17s, which, in turn, responded with their own gunfire. Before everyone came to their senses, Captain Parsel's plane had an oil line punctured by a stray bullet, and Lieutenant Frankie Bryant collapsed the landing gear of his Seversky in a rough landing under fire.

Across Luzon, it would be another long, sleepless night for the tired men of the FEAF, especially those stuck at San Marcelino, which had no facilities of any kind—neither shelter nor food nor water supply.

SCOUTED OUT AND TRAILED by Japanese floatplanes during the last hours of the afternoon, Admiral Sir Phillips decided that loss of the element of surprise could doom his small formation to a concentrated air attack the next morning if it continued on toward Singora. Without air cover, the risk to his ships was too great.

At 2040 Phillips prudently abandoned his attempt to strike back at the Japanese landing forces lying off the southern coast of Siam. Turning about-face for Singapore, "Force Z" steadfastly maintained radio silence but continued to monitor regular signals from the communication network. Shortly before midnight, Admiral Sir Phillips received a status message from Rear Admiral Arthur Palliser, his chief of staff in Singapore. The report included a summary of the day's air force losses and noted the evacuation of aircraft and personnel from Kuantan.[20] Undoubtedly, this information left Phillips with the impression that it would be pointless to request fighter protection for his return trip. He was aware that any planes assigned to that task would have had to use Kuantan as a refueling base. A short time later, Phillips received a report that Japanese troops were executing a landing assault near Kuantan. Acting on this report, the admiral ordered "Force Z" to change course to Kuantan. He expected to arrive offshore in the very early morning, before any Japanese air raids might be scheduled. Perhaps he would have a chance to inflict serious damage on the Japanese invasion fleet after all.

CHAPTER 8

Lightning Strikes Twice

December 10, 1941

THE IJN MOVED QUICKLY to land troops from General Masaharu Homma's 14th Army onto Luzon. The plan called for two relatively small landings of two thousand men each: one at Vigan, on the western coast, north of Lingayen Gulf; the other near Aparri, at the mouth of the Cagayan River valley, near the eastern tip of the north coast. In addition, the force that seized Batan Island on December 8 would also invade Camiguin Island, just north of Luzon. The objective at each of these locations was a small civilian airstrip capable of supporting army fighter operations, or emergency refueling for other planes.

Contrary to General Douglas MacArthur's often-touted plan for aggressive defense at invasion points, there were few U.S. or Filipino army forces near Vigan or Aparri to oppose enemy landings. Major General Jonathan Wainwright did not want to overextend his lines into the rugged territory of northern Luzon to meet the Japanese.

MacArthur and his staff correctly expected that the largest Japanese landings would eventually be made at Lingayen Gulf. To counter that anticipated attack, the majority of army units would be held in reserve. USAFFE did not have the infantry resources to counter Japan's challenge in any location outside central Luzon. Only the air forces were capable of engaging enemy armies at the extremities of the island of Luzon. Of course, the most efficient way to disable the invaders would be to catch them during their unloading process, before solid beachheads could be established.

Sinking Japanese transports is precisely the operation for which the fifty-two dive-bombers of the 27th Bombardment Group were most needed, but they were in crates on board the US Army Transport *Meigs*, some 4,500 miles away from Manila, near the Phoenix Islands. The probability of getting them to the Philippines seemed low. In the meantime, General Brereton would do whatever he could to strike at enemy shipping.

Obtaining accurate information about Japanese landing sites was the first priority. At 0210 on December 10, a single P-40E flew away from Nichols Field under specific orders from Colonel George. The handpicked pilot, 1st Lieutenant Grant Mahony, was one of a very few FEAF fliers who was thoroughly familiar with Philippine geography. Though posted to a ground-based staff job as base operations officer for Nichols, the former "3rd Pursuiter" was anxious to get into action. Unlike most of his peers, the combative Mahony had actually requested assignment to the Philippines, recognizing that this would likely be the first U.S. battlefront. To prepare for defending that territory, he had taken advantage of every opportunity to fly cross-country since arriving in Manila. The experience paid off; Mahony easily navigated through the darkness to his reconnaissance objective near Vigan. Once there, he spotted the Japanese landing fleet just offshore. While weaving around the scattered clouds, Mahony recorded that the force consisted of six transports, escorted by a cruiser and about ten destroyers.[1] His observations were remarkably accurate. Admiral Nishimura's fleet was composed of six "marus," covered by the light cruiser *Naka*; the destroyers *Murasame, Yudachi, Harusame, Samidare, Asagumo, Minegumo,* and *Natsugumo*; and six minesweepers.[2]

Lieutenant Mahony's trip back to Nichols was uneventful until the last few minutes of his flight. During the final approach to the airstrip, little balls of fire reached up toward the P-40, striking it from nose to tail. Like a flaming meteor in the night sky, Mahony's plane streaked past the field. Beneath it, the shadowy form of its pilot fell toward the earth. Tracers continued to arc through the blackness where the silvery canopy of Mahony's parachute billowed in the slipstream. Fearing an attack by enemy paratroopers, the antiaircraft gunners thought nothing of targeting the falling man. Fortunately, they missed. The guns were silenced when a screaming 1st Lieutenant Bob Hanson—Mahony's roommate—ran toward the soldiers and ordered them to cease firing. He knew the sound of an Allison engine and was certain the "invader" was actually his close friend. Armed with a rifle, Hanson was prepared to shoot the gun crew had they failed to comply with his order.[3] Justifiably annoyed, but otherwise unscathed, Mahony was able to telephone his vital information directly to Colonel Francis Brady at FEAF Headquarters.

No similar effort to reconnoiter Aparri was undertaken that night. For a P-40E equipped with an auxiliary fuel tank, such a mission would have represented a maximum-range sortie with dangerously little margin for navigational error. Even a pilot with Mahony's experience would have been hard-pressed to find his way over the mountain ranges and across the cloudy Cagayan valley to Aparri. To take stock of the landing fleet and then fly back to Nichols in darkness, without running out of gas, would have been a miracle. In any case, the quantity of 52-gallon droppable fuel tanks was very limited; they would be reserved for use only when absolutely necessary.

From a strategic point of view, knowledge of Japanese fleet activity near Vigan was of greater significance. It was also vital for USAFFE to know whether any enemy ships were heading farther south, past Vigan, toward the Lingayen Gulf. The situation at Aparri would have to be assessed by a B-17 reconnaissance flight during daylight hours.

A graying dawn brought the departure of four other important reconnaissance flights. Three of these missions were intended to cover likely approaches for Japanese invasion forces that might try to sail south, farther offshore. The search began at 0500 when a trio of PatWing-10 PBYs lifted off the waters near Cavite for long-range coverage of the South China Sea. A short time later, 1st Lieutenant James "Jim" Connally pulled his 93rd Squadron B-17C off the charred grass at Clark. Connally's plane had been equipped for a photo survey of Japanese air bases on Formosa in preparation for the long-awaited retaliatory strike by the 19th Bomb Group.

Also in the air at dawn were the B-17Ds of Major O'Donnell and Captain Parsel. The two experienced bomber pilots successfully accomplished risky low-light takeoffs from San Marcelino. Neither had orders from 19th Group Headquarters, but both were anxious to get to Clark Field as early as possible. Parsel wanted to have his punctured oil line properly replaced, a repair that could not be done with the limited equipment on hand at San Marcelino. O'Donnell—never one to leave things to chance—intended to find out the day's mission plans personally from Colonel Eubank. For good reason, the 14th Squadron commander did not have complete faith in the radio "station" at San Marcelino. That radio set was actually the unit on board a well-camouflaged 27th Group B-18 parked in the trees alongside the field and rigged with an external antenna.[4]

Lieutenant Mahony's report was disseminated in time for Lieutenant Colonel Eubank to launch a dawn attack on the Japanese fleet near Vigan. The vortices of twenty propellers churned dust into billowing clouds at Clark Field as five 93rd Squadron Flying Fortresses took off at 0600. In the lead, Major Combs climbed through a thick overcast. He flew north over the Lingayen Plain, eventually reaching an altitude of twelve thousand feet. At this height, his formation cruised just above the puffy cloud layer on a direct path toward Vigan.

Colonel George also planned to send several sections of 24th Pursuit Group fighters to Vigan. They were not assigned as escorts for the 19th Group bombers. Instead, their pilots were instructed to strafe enemy transports and landing craft. This first U.S. fighter sweep of the Pacific War did not begin smoothly. The 17th Pursuit Squadron P-40Es had been scheduled to leave Clark in two flights of six aircraft each, about half an hour after the bombers departed. However, while waiting for his planes to form up, 1st Lieutenant Brownewell tested his guns and found all of them inoperative. Reluctantly, he circled back to make a landing, leaving the formation in the care of his second-section leader, 2nd Lieutenant Jack Dale.

Brownewell's plight would become distressingly familiar to the P-40E pilots in the Philippines. Due to severe .50-caliber ammunition shortages, none of the guns in the planes had been test-fired prior to combat operations. The new guns—probably not completely cleared of the antioxidation coating used to protect the metal during shipment—were prone to cartridge jams. The situation was unwittingly exacerbated by implementation of a September 1941 AAF Technical Order that required temporary disconnection of the hydraulic in-flight gun chargers until newly released parts could be distributed. Pilots with failing guns had no choice but to land and manually clear their guns. It was a regular occurrence that frustrated several pilots of the 3rd Pursuit on December 8, and would haunt the 24th Pursuit Group for most of its brief existence.

NAVY MEN ON BOARD the three PatWing-10 Catalinas that headed west from Luzon had no idea what they might encounter during their offshore patrols. Slowly flying across the middle search sector, almost halfway between the northwest coast of Luzon and the southeast coast of China, Lieutenant Clarence "Nick" Keller hit the jackpot. At 0645, through a broken layer of clouds, the PBY crew spotted the wakes of what appeared to be two battleships, a cruiser, and four destroyers. In a rather odd extrapolation of the known intelligence information—perhaps because the warships were headed north and the disposition was similar—Keller assumed they were the British "Force Z" and continued on past to the northwest. His radioman, Ed Bedford, duly logged the contact with patrol wing headquarters. Captain Wagner could hardly believe that Keller had flown past the ships; he had no doubt the task force was Japanese. Wagner immediately instructed Bedford to have Keller relocate the warships, maintain contact, and transmit a homing signal. Once Keller could confirm his previous report, a strike force of PBYs would be sent out to attack.[5]

THE FIVE 93RD SQUADRON B-17S reached Vigan about fifteen minutes ahead of the P-40s. Heading due west, Cecil Combs led the bombers across the beach and over six transports that wallowed offshore in heavy surf. Forty 100-pound bombs were dropped among the ships without scoring any hits. One Fortress—flown by 1st Lieutenant Elliott Vandevanter Jr.—experienced a failure of its bomb-release mechanism. Attributing this to the cooler temperatures at twelve thousand feet, Vandevanter descended into warmer air to "unfreeze" the jamming parts. Bounced around by the concussion of flak bursts from the naval guns, all five Boeings turned around for a reversing bomb run back to the east. Making a second pass at seven thousand feet, Vandevanter found that his bomb rack functioned properly, and he released the entire load. By sacrificing its altitude, the low-flying bomber presented a better target for the shipboard gunners. Before the B-17 could clear the area, shrapnel from a flak burst hit its wing. Sixty bombs carpeted the Japanese ships, but only a few appeared to have hit anywhere near the stationary transports. Although one of the ships—*Oigawa Maru*—may have been damaged below its waterline, this was not a very promising combat debut for the United States' legendary Flying Fortresses.[6]

Appearing as the bombers sped back over the hills, the fighters of the 17th Pursuit arrived over Vigan in a piecemeal fashion. Many of the pilots had been separated from their flights while nervously feeling their way through the clouds right after they left Clark. Available records do not account for the actions of all members of both flights, but apparently most of the fighters focused their strafing on suppression of antiaircraft fire from the Japanese warships. This would not prove to be a good use of ammunition. Pilots who made reports about the mission described ineffectual attacks on "cruisers and destroyers." Bullets seen bouncing around the decks, superstructures, and gun mounts may have caused sailors to run around in frenzy but inflicted only slight damage. Difficulties with the .50-calibers in the Curtiss fighters were numerous. Many P-40s experienced gun failures while diving into the attack. Second Lieutenant William "Bill" Hennon had to turn back for Clark Field when all of his weapons refused to fire. Several other planes had one or more guns jam while making repetitive passes at the ships. Concentrated machine-gun fire destroyed some equipment on the invasion force flagship, the light cruiser *Naka*, but that was the extent of the squadron's success.[7]

The preponderance of gun problems would not be the sole controversy surrounding this particular action. For "leading the attack in the face of severe anti aircraft fire," Lieutenant Dale subsequently received the Distinguished Flying Cross. This would be the first of a number of questionable citations that General MacArthur would issue during the Philippine campaign.

While the first raids on Vigan were under way, Major O'Donnell had his own B-17 loaded with eight six-hundred-pound bombs. After conferring with Colonel Eubank, O'Donnell radioed back to San Marcelino to have the rest of the 14th Squadron planes sent over to Clark. He wanted the Fortresses serviced for a mission to Vigan as soon as possible. Surprisingly, but not out of character, the impatient O'Donnell decided not to wait for the other planes. As soon as the crew was ready, he flew away on a solo sortie to the enemy landing site.

Responding to O'Donnell's instructions, Captain Kelly Jr. led the other six 14th Squadron bombers from San Marcelino to Clark Field. They arrived just after 0730. Lieutenant Kurtz, still manning the Clark tower, continued to follow the standing order that only three B-17s should be landed at one time. Only Kelly and 1st Lieutenants Guilford Montgomery and George Schaetzel were allowed to bring their bombers in for servicing. Lieutenants Henry Godman, Teats, and Donald Keiser were obliged to stay airborne, circling around Mount Arayat and listening to their radios for new orders.

NO OPERATIONAL COMBAT AIRCRAFT were left in Malaya on the morning of December 10. Air activity above the peninsula was limited to observation of the situation near Kuantan by Singapore-based aircraft. RAAF No. 8 Squadron Hudsons flying out of Sembawang had been patrolling the area since about 0400, without noting any activity. RAAF No. 453 Squadron, on alert at Sembawang, was belatedly detailed to provide fighter cover for *Prince of Wales* and *Repulse* but received no instructions to rendezvous with the ships. Admiral Sir Phillips—still observing strict radio silence—had not told Singapore of his last-minute decision to cover Kuantan, so Air Headquarters had absolutely no idea where "Force Z" was located. The Buffaloes stayed on the ground.

The only aircraft readily available to Phillips were a handful of Walrus seaplanes carried on board the two capital ships. One of these was launched at 0715 from *Prince of Wales* to reconnoiter the Kuantan air station and the coast northward to Beserah, where the enemy landings had been reported. After a half-hour search, with nothing observed but a few apparently abandoned and drifting boats, the Walrus passed back alongside its mother ship, flashing a report via signal lamp.[8] The small, empty boats were probably landing craft cast aside during the Kota Bharu invasion. Prevailing strong currents would have carried them southeast along the coast. Scouts operating along the shoreline must have spotted these boats as they cast their shadows on the moonlit waters and suspected the worst. After receiving acknowledgment for receipt of his message, Lieutenant C. R. Bateman banked away to the south, bound for Seletar. He had been instructed before his departure to land at Singapore. Phillips did not want to hamper his task force operations by slowing down for the recovery of any seaplanes.

Deciding that the report of a Japanese landing was erroneous, Admiral Sir Phillips ordered a course change back to Singapore at 0800. Shortly thereafter, another Walrus was catapulted out for anti-submarine patrol. This aircraft, one from *Repulse*, was flown by Petty Officer W. J. T. Crozer. Actually, the lurking submarines had been left far behind. By the time Phillips was heading away from Kuantan, it was the Japanese naval air service that posed the greatest threat. All available IJN bombers in Indochina had been tasked to seek out and destroy "Force Z." At the point position of this ninety-four-plane assault wave, a chutai of nine fully fueled G3Ms fanned out across the South China Sea between Singapore and Singora to hunt down the British task force.

ON THE OTHER SIDE OF THE SOUTH CHINA SEA, the radio at PatWing-10 Headquarters crackled at 0800 with another message from Nick Keller's PBY: "1 KUMA CLASS CL 4 DDS 2 KONGO CLASS BBS POSITION 6-40 X 8-10 COURSE 180 SPEED 10."[9] The group of zigzagging ships had been relocated. By this time, they were heading due south. As he dived across the wakes of the Japanese ships, Keller turned his Catalina through a steady barrage of antiaircraft fire into some low-hanging clouds. There, the PBY could safely shadow the fleet while his radioman continued to transmit a homing signal.

The observation of the enemy fleet composition was accurate in count, if not exact description. In the open seas beneath Keller's plane, the heavy cruisers *Ashigara* and *Maya*, the light cruiser *Kuma*, the destroyers *Asakaze* and *Matsukaze*, and the seaplane tenders *Sanyo Maru* and *Sanuki Maru* sailed as a distant covering force for the landings at Vigan.[10] The men on board the PBY could easily be forgiven for mistaking the two cruisers for battleships; their overall length was only about sixty feet shy of the *Kongo's* measurement—but longer than most U.S. battleships—and the deck layouts would have appeared quite similar to *Kongo's* as viewed from the air while under fire. These were just the targets Captain Wagner wanted to hit. Almost instantly, a dispatch was sent to Lieutenant Commander J. V. Peterson, in charge of the PBY strike group moored at Los Baños, on the southern shoreline of Laguna de Bay. Peterson's five Catalinas were already armed with four 500-pound bombs each, but someone made a last-minute decision to rearm the planes with torpedoes. Presumably, these would have a better chance of inflicting damage on the heavily armored capital ships. However, just minutes after the torpedoes had been fitted, a new order was given to remove them and reload with bombs. Perhaps it was felt that the additional drag of torpedoes would impede the long-range mission. In any case, it wasn't until after 0900 that the bomb-laden flying boats splashed across the still waters of the lake and headed northwest toward Keller's PBY.

AT VIGAN, MAJOR O'DONNELL ARRIVED over the Japanese invasion force after the fighters from the 17th Pursuit had departed. He came over the target at twenty-five thousand feet. The bombardier, Master Sergeant J. F. Carter, hunched over his Norden sight in the clear nose of the Fortress and tried to release the bombs. O'Donnell waited for the sudden rise of his aircraft that he expected to occur when the load dropped free of the bomb bay. Nothing happened. Apparently O'Donnell's bomb racks were suffering the same malady Lieutenant Vandevanter had experienced. Correcting the problem in the same way, O'Donnell traded the safety of additional altitude for the proper functioning of his bomb-release mechanism. Determined to hit a ship, the major kept his lone B-17D over the target area for almost forty-five minutes, dodging a constant barrage of antiaircraft fire while

Carter dropped one or two bombs at a time. Frustrated at scoring no hits after making five passes at the warships, the Fortress crew finally headed back to Clark at about 0900. Hitting those "pickle barrels" was definitely a lot harder when they were in motion, and shooting back.

Even at this early hour, the staging process for FEAF missions to Vigan was not working well. Originally, the P-35As of the 34th Pursuit were to have joined with the P-40s of the 17th Pursuit in the first fighter sweep. This did not happen. The 34th Squadron planes were unable to depart from San Marcelino in the dark and still had to be serviced back at Del Carmen; they needed fuel and ammunition. Thirteen of the stubby little fighters flew over to Del Carmen at dawn, but only twelve could be made ready for a sortie by 0830.[11] The tired engine in 2nd Lieutenant Claude Paulger's plane could not be restarted. During the forty-minute flight to Vigan, four more P-35s suffered engine troubles, causing their pilots to abort the mission. In fact, just as the rest arrived over the target, 2nd Lieutenant Ed Houseman's engine seized without warning, forcing the pilot to bail out above the Abra River valley. The Severskys were all in need of overhaul after more than nine months of continuous training service. However, there were no spare engines and no facilities to properly rebuild the worn ones. Combat operations from extremely dusty airstrips like Del Carmen and San Marcelino would only increase the incidence of mechanical problems.

Squadron commander Sam Marett dove into the attack with the four other planes still left in his flight. When no enemy aircraft were seen, the top-cover flight—by this time numbering only two planes—followed. Marett led his men in at wave-top height, attempting to stay beneath the heavy antiaircraft bursts. Concentrating on the transports, the squadron believed they started fires on several. The strafers wounded a number of officers and men on the bridge of *Oigawa Maru*. Lieutenant Marett also shot up the deck of the minesweeper *W-10*. This turned out to be a fatal mistake. As Marett's P-35 passed by the stern of the small ship, a depth charge exploded. Apparently detonated by gunfire, the blast sheared the wing off the Seversky, cartwheeling the little fighter into the sea. The 230-foot-long warship did not fare much better: the after section of its hull was blown completely apart. *W-10* disappeared beneath the waves in a matter of minutes, carrying seventy-nine of its crew to the bottom of the sea.[12]

While the 34th Pursuit was busy attacking the Japanese landing force at Vigan, returning P-40Es of the 17th Pursuit straggled into Clark. The last of these touched down at about 0845. When the pilots and planes of the 17th and 20th Squadrons had been pooled together the previous evening, Buzz Wagner and Joe Moore created a squadron-level duty rotation based on alternating missions. They felt it was better to keep the pilots from each squadron flying together as a unit. The practice was analogous to the rotations Moore usually employed with his "1st and 2nd Sections." Wagner's 17th Squadron had won the coin toss to take the morning's first flight to Vigan, but as soon as the fighters could be refueled and rearmed, pilots of the 20th Pursuit were ready to take them out for another run at the Japanese.

Lieutenant Moore and his wingman, Randy Keator, roared off the strip at Clark into the low-hanging clouds at around 0915. Ed Gilmore tried to follow their path through the dust. An unnoticed bomb crater caught one of his wheels, wringing the P-40E around and slamming its propeller into the ground. Gilmore would be left behind this time, but he was unhurt and the fighter could be repaired. The rest of the 20th Squadron pilots assigned to the mission made it off the field without incident but became separated in the clouds over northern Luzon.

One unidentified member of the 20th Squadron flight gained a welcome wingman when Red Sheppard of the 17th Squadron joined with him on the way to Vigan. Sheppard had taken off alone from Del Carmen in his freshly repaired P-40 just before Moore's group departed from Clark. While most of the 20th Squadron pilots flew strafing runs against the transports and landing craft, Sheppard and his new companion noticed three pale-green twin-engine bombers heading north, a few miles inland from the beachhead. They had to be Japanese, and the setup was perfect. Racing in from astern, at the same altitude as the bombers, Sheppard passed through them with guns blazing. Only two of his weapons were working, but he observed pieces falling off the enemy planes as he streaked by. Though he lost track of his partner during the first pass, he returned alone for a second and third shot at the fleeing bombers. Two of them were streaming smoke, and one of those appeared to have an engine out by the time Sheppard realized the needle on his own coolant temperature gauge was pegged. Turning abruptly inland and following the Abra River toward Bangued, he gently urged his fighter as far as possible from the Vigan area. Inevitably, the Allison caught fire, and Sheppard bailed out.

The planes Sheppard attacked were Ki-48s from the third chutai of the JAAF 8th Sentai. Unescorted, that air group had just bombed the area outside the Vigan beachhead. A small formation of Ki-27 fighters from the 24th Sentai had been assigned to cover the 8th Sentai raiders and the Vigan landing zone. Their rendezvous with the bombers had failed. One of the Ki-48s was indeed shot down, and apparently Sheppard, or his mystery wingman, also hit some of the other bombers. JAAF records reflect that P-40s damaged six other Ki-48s.[13]

Back at Clark, Lieutenant Schaetzel had just taken off on the first mission to Aparri. His B-17D had been fully serviced and loaded with eight 600-pound bombs. Captain Parsel's Fortress had also been "bombed up" with seven 300-pound bombs but was still being worked over by the mechanics. Replacing the severed oil line took a bit longer than refueling or loading bombs. Parsel would head for Vigan as soon as he could. Captain Kelly and Lieutenant Montgomery were still supervising the winching of bombs into their aircraft when the red air-raid warning flag was hoisted shortly before 1000. The warning network had sighted incoming bombers. Following Eubank's directive, the B-17s would leave before they were ready. Kelly, like Schaetzel, had orders to bomb the landing zone at Aparri. However, he had also been asked to investigate reports of a possible carrier sighting off the north coast of Luzon. Montgomery had no orders. His crew took some extra time preparing for takeoff but planned to head directly for Vigan on Montgomery's own initiative.

The anticipated raid on Clark failed to materialize. Most likely, the reported bombers were actually inbound B-17s from the 93rd Squadron. Within a few minutes of the warning, Major Combs returned from Vigan with his Fortresses. This time, despite Colonel Eubank's standing order, all five planes were allowed to land at Clark. Almost before the propellers stopped spinning, Major Combs was out of his plane, demanding more bombs. The field officers refused that request, ordering that the planes top off with fuel and take off as soon as possible. The enemy raid was still expected at any moment. Combs, along with Lieutenants Ford and Vandevanter, got back in the air shortly thereafter, without the requested ordnance. Lieutenant Morris Shedd's plane experienced mechanical difficulties and had no choice but to stay on the ground for repairs. Shedd himself was not feeling well. Lieutenant Young of the 30th Squadron, who had taken command of Lieutenant William "Bill" Bohnaker's B-17 that morning when Bohnaker suddenly became ill, also remained on the field, as did Bohnaker's bomber.

THINGS SEEMED MUCH QUIETER along the east coast of Malaya. About an hour after their launch from the deck of *Repulse*, the crew of Petty

Officer Crozer's Walrus spotted a coastal steamer towing four smaller boats away to the north. Still bound by orders to maintain radio silence and obliged to report all contacts by signal lamp, Crozer turned his aircraft back toward "Force Z."

Well above the low-flying seaplane, a single Japanese bomber passed by on its way home after an uneventful search for the British fleet. Gazing down at the calm sea, its pilot, Ensign Masane Hoashi, glimpsed the movement of the gray Walrus. Noting that it appeared to be a small floatplane, Hoashi decided to lose altitude and trail behind it. He had no bombs, but he had plenty of fuel. Within fifteen minutes of shadowing Crozer's Walrus, Hoashi spotted "Force Z" beneath the broken cloud layer. At 1015 his radio operator excitedly flashed the news back to 22nd Air Flotilla headquarters in Saigon and to all other Japanese planes in the air.

Prince of Wales's air-search radar operators had picked up several "blips"—including that of Hoashi's G3M—but weren't sure what to make of them. After all, Crozer was just flying alongside to make his report and he had been very near two of the bogeys, so it seemed hard to believe any of them could be hostile. Several Australian Hudsons were presumed to be on patrol in the area, but the naval personnel had no information about their flight plans.

In fact, Flight Lieutenant Plenty was flying his Hudson just offshore from Kuantan on a parallel course. Plenty spotted Crozer's Walrus and "Force Z" but missed Hoashi's higher-flying G3M. In accordance with standard identification procedure, Plenty turned toward the ships to flash his recognition code to *Prince of Wales*. Within minutes, radar plotters were overwhelmed with signals. In dangerously close proximity to the battleship, both Crozer and Plenty were startled when heavy anti-aircraft weapons erupted along its decks. Low on fuel, and not anxious to be caught in the middle of an air battle in his almost defenseless seaplane, Crozer decided to head straight for Singapore. Thinking his Hudson an equal to any Japanese aircraft he might encounter, Herb Plenty was unafraid of the raiders. Still, he turned west to watch the fireworks at a safer distance from the shipboard guns.

The commotion had been caused by the arrival of Lieutenant Shirai with his 1st Chutai of the *Mihoro Kokutai*. His eight G3Ms were the nearest Japanese strike units to "Force Z." At 1115 eight well-aimed 250-kilogram bombs bracketed *Repulse*. One struck squarely on the seaplane deck, knocking the second Walrus off its catapult track. Aviation gasoline spilled all over the aircraft service area.[14]

The first attack on Repulse as viewed from the G3Ms of Lieutenant Shirai's 1st Chutai from the Mihoro Kokutai on December 10, 1941. One of these eight bombs impacted amidships, as evidenced by the smoke plume. Prince of Wales *is seen at the top of the photo, just before it was hit by two torpedoes.* (Courtesy of Naval Historical Center)

Although it did not prevent the enemy from damaging *Repulse*, antiaircraft fire from Phillips's ships had been accurate; five of Shirai's G3Ms were damaged. Two of the bombers were badly hit and had to jettison their remaining bombs in the sea as they turned away and limped back toward Indochina.[15]

While Shirai regrouped his flight off to the side of the action, Lieutenant Kauro Ishihara brought nine torpedo-armed G3Ms from the 1st Chutai of the *Genzan Kokutai* in low against *Prince of Wales*. Gunners on the flagship bought down one of the Mitsubishis, but eight torpedoes were already in the water. Two of the torpedoes impacted near the stern of the British flagship, causing considerable damage and flooding in the engineering spaces and a loss of rudder control. Immediately, a number of electrical generators went off-line, disrupting power to most of the long-range antiaircraft guns.[16]

As damage control parties worked feverishly to restore electricity on the stricken battleship, another flight of eight *Genzan* G3Ms approached across the wave-tops. Lieutenant Sadao Takai opted to make his run against *Repulse*, which appeared undamaged. Takai's 2nd Chutai, wary of interception but undaunted by flak, bored in on the battle cruiser: "It was standard practice among us for the 1st Chutai to attack the largest ship, and the 2nd Chutai the next largest. All crew members searched the sky vigilantly for the enemy fighters which we expected would be diving in to attack us at any moment. Much to our surprise, not a single enemy plane was in sight. This was all the more amazing since the scene of the battle was well within the fighting range of the British fighters."[17]

Four bombers in Takai's flight were riddled by antiaircraft fire, but none was downed. Takai himself made a second pass at the warship once he realized that his torpedo had not released during the first run. The 2nd Chutai attack was completely unsuccessful: *Repulse* was able to "comb" all eight torpedoes without harm.

It was not until this time, at 1158, that Admiral Sir Phillips's radio silence was finally broken. Captain W. G. Tennant of *Repulse* ordered transmission of news of the attack to headquarters. That signal was the first information anyone in Singapore had on the location of "Force Z." In shock, Air Headquarters ordered the urgent dispatch of a ready flight of two RAF 243 Squadron Buffaloes to the scene. Ten RAAF No. 453 Squadron Buffaloes already assigned to Royal Navy air-cover duty were also scrambled.

There was barely time for a sigh of relief on the bridge of *Repulse*. As soon as Takai's planes departed, six of Shirai's bombers returned overhead along with nine more G3M torpedo bombers. This time, Shirai's bombs fell short as the battle cruiser maneuvered violently to thwart a wave-top attack by Lieutenant Katsusaki Takahashi's 4th Chutai of the *Mihoro Kokutai*. Amazingly—no doubt because of expert seamanship on the part of Captain Tennant and his crew—none of the torpedoes hit their target.

For a short time, it may have seemed that the worst was over. Damage was heavy on *Prince of Wales*, but the ship was not in danger of sinking. For nearly twenty minutes, calm descended over the area. The only aircraft in the vicinity were Flight Lieutenant Plenty's Lockheed and, somewhat farther north, Ensign Hoashi's Mitsubishi. The more formidable torpedo-armed G4Ms of the *Kanoya Kokutai* were well to the south, and a heavy cloud formation stood between them and "Force Z." It did not appear that they would find the British ships, in spite of receiving Hoashi's location report.

One may say that lightning never strikes the same place twice, but just as the twenty-six G4Ms were turning away toward Saigon, one of Lieutenant Commander Shichizo Miyauchi's observers caught sight of a seaplane flying in a southward direction, low over the water. It was the second time a Japanese airman had spotted Petty Officer Crozer's Walrus. Miyauchi correctly deduced that the aircraft must be flying on a direct course from the British task force to Singapore. Quickly, he ordered his formation to dive through the clouds on a reciprocal heading to that being followed by the British plane. As the Japanese pilots emerged beneath the clouds, they saw the ships of the Royal Navy dead ahead in the distance.

Without the ability to maneuver or to fire any heavy antiaircraft weapons, *Prince of Wales* was a sitting duck. The G4Ms raced to close the distance with their target. Six bombers from the 1st and 2nd Chutai hurtled across their already hobbled quarry. Four torpedoes found their mark, sealing the fate of the once proud battleship.

The twenty remaining G4Ms did not need to bother with the British flagship. Instead, they concentrated for a massive attack on *Repulse* from all points of the compass. Nine torpedo launches by the 1st and 2nd Chutai gained one strike amidships, which was still not enough to slow down the battle cruiser. The major blow came from Lieutenant Haruki Iki's 3rd Chutai, which braved an intense storm of antiaircraft fire to deliver four torpedoes against the hull of the veteran warship. Iki and his two wingmen held fast at deck level up to a distance of six hundred yards from the speeding ship before dropping their "fish." As the three torpedoes entered the water, the flanking bombers exploded in balls of flame. Iki's own G4M—looking more like a sieve than an airplane—barely cleared the afterdeck of its target when three explosions geysered water over almost the entire length of the ship. Coming in from the opposite direction in a perfect "anvil attack," Iki's other six G4Ms dropped their weapons at nearly the same moment. One of these struck in a boiler room, dooming the ship when the power plant was destroyed by an internal explosion.[18]

Captain Tennant suddenly realized that *Repulse* might likely rest on the bottom of the South China Sea even before *Prince of Wales* went under. At 1230 Tennant gave the order to abandon ship. In less than three minutes, *Repulse* disappeared beneath the surface, taking 513 officers and men with her.[19]

Prince of Wales was still afloat when the last seventeen Japanese bombers approached at 1245. These G3Ms of the *Mihoro Kokutai* carried single 500-kilogram bombs. Lieutenant Yoshiro Ohhira's 3rd Chutai prematurely dropped its bombs well away from the ship; Ohhira had accidentally released his bomb while lining up the target. His wingmen, in line with standard bombing practice, dropped their own bombs when they saw his fall. Lieutenant Hachiro Takeda managed a better showing. One of eight bombs from his 2nd Chutai got a direct hit between the funnels of the battleship. This probably did not change the fate of *Prince of Wales*, but it may have speeded up the abandonment process. After this bombing, Captain J. C. Leach finally gave the order to evacuate the crew of the thirty-five-thousand-ton pride of the British Far Eastern Fleet. The destroyer *Express* pulled alongside to take off survivors at 1300. There was not much time. Within ten minutes, the ship began to settle and list, forcing the destroyer to cast away. *Prince of Wales* capsized and gradually sank lower until its screws finally vanished at 1320. Captain Leach, Admiral Sir Phillips, and 325 other officers and sailors disappeared with her.[20] It was the worst blow the Royal Navy had taken since going to war in 1939.

THE JAPANESE NAVY WAS JUBILANT as news about its airborne victory over the British battleships quickly propagated across communication channels. In spite of all the excitement, Admiral Takahashi, in command of the Philippine Operation, could personally identify with

Phillips's experience by the time he heard the reports. At nearly the exact moment that the *Kanoya Kokutai* was launching torpedoes at Phillips, Takahashi himself had come under attack.

Following Lieutenant Keller's homing signal, Commander Peterson's five VP-101 Catalinas arrived in their target area at high noon. A rapidly steaming fleet—consisting of what appeared to be two battleships, a light cruiser, and four large destroyers—lay exposed some fifteen thousand feet below. Eight floatplanes were seen milling around the ships, but it would be some time before they could reach the altitude of the PBYs. Lining up to come in from the sun, Peterson led his small formation toward the "largest enemy battleship in the center of the disposition." In unison, twenty five-hundred pound bombs fell toward Takahashi's flagship, the heavy cruiser *Ashigara*.[21] As the sea erupted across the stern of the ship, the sky exploded in a pattern of black puffs.

Free of their loads, and rocking from the concussion of antiaircraft fire, PatWing-10's PBYs broke formation and dived for some low-lying clouds. Peterson let his Catalina down in a gentler arc than the rest so he could observe the bomb impacts. He noted that three of the bombs near-missed close astern to the target. The warship immediately slowed, coasting around a complete circle in the port-side direction. Like a herd ignoring the fall of one of its number to a feared predator, the other ships left their large companion behind. It was clear that some damage had been done. There was no smoke evident, so the wounds must have been slight, or contained below the waterline.

At 1230 Peterson's radio operator signaled ComPatWing-10 that the bombing had been completed. Captain Wagner responded by ordering two planes from the attack group to relieve Lieutenant Keller on shadow duty while the rest returned to Manila. Wagner planned to send another strike from Cavite as soon as possible to attack the wounded "battleship."

LIEUTENANT SCHAETZEL TURNED HIS B-17 west toward Aparri from its long trek up the east coast of Luzon. Until entering the Babuyan Channel at about noon, he had detected no enemy presence. Between Gonzaga and Aparri, the Fortress crew found plenty of targets. A row of ships anchored along the shore attracted Schaetzel's attention. From his altitude of twenty-five thousand feet, he guided the plane parallel to the beach, along the line of transports. The bombardier, Sergeant E. T. Oliver, released half of the bombs in this first run. Some light cloud cover partially obscured the view of any results, but smoke rising along the beach suggested that at least one of the heavy bombs had struck a ship.[22] As Schaetzel turned for a second run, flak bursts rocked the plane.

Leaving the smoke behind, the Fortress turned inland down the Cagayan valley. Schaetzel's crew did not have much time to fret about what they might have hit. Within a few minutes, the men were frantically trying to save their B-17D from destruction by a flight of four fighters. Their aggressive pursuers were probably 50th Sentai Ki-27s led by 2nd Lieutenant Teizo Kanamaru.[23] The Fortress gunners projected a solid stream of fire at the fighters, to no avail. The big bomber's tail surfaces were peppered with holes, one engine had been hit, and a holed oil tank seeped a sticky, dark stream from one wing. With his gunners nearly out of ammunition, Schaetzel dived at an almost 45-degree angle toward a large bank of clouds built up in the direction of Tuguegarao. Holding the descent for almost eighteen thousand feet, and hitting a top speed in excess of 350 miles per hour, he outran the fighters. Safely in the clouds, Lieutenant Schaetzel leveled off and headed south.

Captain Kelly Jr. initially headed in over Aparri, probably some minutes earlier than Schaetzel. Kelly was coming from the opposite direction. Also tasked to find an enemy aircraft carrier, he had flown his B-17C along the west coast of Luzon. As Kelly passed above Vigan at twenty thousand feet, the Japanese landing forces were working busily to put troops ashore. He observed no aircraft or supporting carriers, so he continued flying northward. Approaching Aparri from the west, the Fortress crew noted ships along the beach, screened by six "cruisers" further offshore and a single "battleship" that was leisurely shelling the shoreline. Captain Kelly did nothing at this time. He still wanted to find a carrier, so he turned north toward Formosa.

The observations of Kelly's crew were essentially correct, though overstated in terms of warship type. The Aparri invasion force actually consisted of six transports escorted by the light cruiser *Natori*; the destroyers *Fumitsuki, Satsuki, Nagatsuki, Minatsuki, Harukaze*, and *Hatakazi*; and three minesweepers.[24] To the inexperienced army fliers, the large destroyers must have seemed like cruisers when compared to the small, destroyer-like minesweepers.

FOR PILOTS OF THE 20TH SQUADRON, their recently completed mission to Vigan had been an exciting way to get their "check rides" in the

P-40E. Before that morning, none of the men had even sat in the cockpit of an "E" model. Fortunately, no P-40s were lost on this trip to Vigan, but one of the last to return to Clark crashed. Shortly after 1130, 2nd Lieutenant Morgan McCowan, not adjusting well to the heavier plane, sank too fast in his landing approach. Hitting the ground hard, the fighter wobbled out of control and headed off the runway at a sharp angle. It tore into the trees where a number of pilots and line crew were watching incoming planes. When the P-40 slammed against a large tree, McCowan's head banged against his unpadded gunsight. The resulting skull fracture killed him instantly. Two others also perished: a sergeant, forced to dive beneath the plane, was hit in the head by the whirling propeller; and 1st Lieutenant Glen Alder—a senior 20th Squadron pilot—was also hit on the head when a broken tree branch dropped on top of him.[25]

At 1228 an air-raid scramble was ordered. When the red flag went up, more than one hundred Japanese planes were inbound. They were almost over the field. Around the airstrip, it looked like an exact repetition of the December 8 fiasco. Pilots began running toward parked fighters, desperately trying to get them started and off the ground. This time there were many more pilots than P-40s. The men nearly pushed one another off the wings deciding who would take each plane. In a boiling dust cloud, fighters began moving across the field in all directions. It was a minor miracle that only one of the scrambling fighters crashed. Just as he lifted off the ground, almost blinded by swirling dust, 2nd Lieutenant Bob Newman saw the ghostly specter of Lieutenant Carpenter's parked Flying Fortress, dead ahead. Collision was unavoidable. Newman's fighter sliced through the left wing of the bomber just outboard of the engines and crashed through the top of the B-17, between the radio compartment and the waist-gun positions. The fuselage of the bomber broke in half. With a screech of tearing aluminum, the P-40 came to rest on the other side. Both aircraft were completely destroyed. Because neither aircraft caught fire, an incredibly lucky Lieutenant Newman was able to walk away from the wreck.

Complete chaos certainly would have been complemented by an equal amount of devastation had the Japanese bombers not been headed farther south. The 24th Pursuit Group could easily have taken enormous losses on the ground if bombs had fallen during the scramble at Clark. As it was, most pilots found their airplanes incompletely prepared for battle. A number of planes from the 17/20th Squadron had not been serviced after their return from Vigan. Many of the fighters had little fuel in their tanks and no ammunition for their guns. Several flights from the 21st Squadron had just landed after a patrol near Rosales. Pilots scrambling in those aircraft found themselves in a similar quandary. Some planes simply ran out of fuel before they could get airborne. A bad situation was rapidly made worse when radio channels became overloaded with requests for fighter cover at numerous locations. Pilots who had taken off in combat-ready planes would have to decide on their own where to engage in battle. Others with low fuel, or no ammunition, would have to flee to emergency landing fields, hoping that Japanese escort fighters did not spot them.

Twenty-seven *Takao Kokutai* G4Ms, led by Lieutenant Commander Taro Nonaka, found their target at Del Carmen Field blanketed by low clouds. Eighteen *Tainan Kokutai* Zeros escorting the *Takao* bombers broke away from the formation to dive under the shrouding weather and strafe Del Carmen. Unable to sight the field from their altitude, the G4Ms continued south toward Manila Bay, where they were authorized to bomb targets of opportunity. Another twenty-seven *Takao Kokutai* G4Ms planned to hit Nichols Field, while twenty-six G3Ms of the *1st Kokutai* would bomb Cavite Naval Yard. Once the high-flying bombers reached the Manila area, they would be covered by thirty-four A6Ms of the *3rd Kokutai*.[26]

At least five P-40 pilots responded to urgent distress calls from Del Carmen, where the Zeros were thoroughly shooting up the 34th Squadron's P-35As and service vehicles. Ed Gilmore joined with 1st Lieutenant Al Strauss shortly after taking off from Clark. Second Lieutenant Henry Rancke took a wing position with squadron-mate 2nd Lieutenant Carl Gies. In a very loose formation they headed south. Jack Dale closed in on Del Carmen alone. Dale had tested his guns on the way over. When he dove on the Zeros, the guns failed. Frustrated, but glad the Japanese had not spotted him, he turned in the direction of Nichols Field.

Gilmore and Strauss reached Del Carmen just as two Zeros popped up through the overcast after a strafing run. The two Americans split up, chasing both enemy fighters back down through the clouds. Gilmore got in only one burst before his guns jammed. It was not enough to bring down the A6M, although the plane began streaming black smoke. Unaware that his hydraulic gun chargers were disconnected, Gilmore closed in stubbornly, pulling the recharge handle as he gained on the Zero. Of course, nothing happened. Furious that his guns would not recharge while he had a target in his sights, Gilmore pulled back above the cloud layer. Al Strauss was nowhere to be found, so Gilmore headed back to Clark Field.

Carl Gies had better luck with his attack. Diving toward the airfield, he latched onto the tail of one Zero. A long burst from all six machine guns sent the fighter in a smoking glide to the ground, just past the Del Carmen runway. The tables were turned, however, when a shotai of A6Ms swung around on Gies and his wingman, Rancke. In a head-on pass, Gies damaged one more Zero, but his P-40 took a number of hits from the Japanese planes.[27] As his opponents broke up for another run, Gies decided to retreat back toward Clark.

In spite of the interceptions, the *Tainan Kokutai* strafers destroyed seven P-35s, seriously damaged five more, and blew up the mobile fuel tanker. When the Zeros left Del Carmen, the 34th Pursuit had no flyable planes remaining.[28]

Not too far away, sixteen other Zeros from the *Tainan Kokutai* had been circling over Clark Field, looking for signs of activity. Not finding anything of interest, Lieutenant Hideki Shingo turned his formation northeast to head for Aparri.

Many of the P-40s that took off from Clark honored requests for fighter support over Manila Bay. Ed Dyess—who very nearly collided with Buzz Wagner during their takeoff in the dust—had climbed to the height of the Japanese bombers by the time he got near Manila. The bombers were almost in range when he tested his guns and found them inoperative. Dyess had no choice but to pick a landing field nearby where he could set down to recharge the guns. It was probably just as well that he disengaged; he had forgotten to bring along a parachute during his scramble from Clark.

Two 20th Pursuit Squadron pilots found an immediate need for parachutes when they were bounced by Zeros on the way to Manila. Second Lieutenant Milton Woodside had no idea that enemy planes were on the tail of his P-40 until its instrument panel exploded in a shower of broken glass and torn aluminum. Discovering that his plane had no ammunition, Woodside elected to bail out. Similarly, 2nd Lieutenant Kiefer White did not realize Zeros were on his tail until bullets and cannon shells began thumping against the fuselage and wings of his plane. The Allison engine caught fire almost immediately, forcing White to hit the silk. Neither pilot was injured, but two more P-40s were gone.

Although he did not have to jump from his plane, 2nd Lieutenant John Posten—a "17th Pursuiter" on temporary duty with the

21st Squadron—ran into a flock of Zeros between Clark and Manila. In the brief encounter, Posten got off a few shots but quickly learned that a P-40 could not dogfight with a Zero. After his P-40 received numerous hits in the wings and tail section, Posten dived for the deck. Using cloud cover to his advantage, he eluded two pursuing A6Ms. His fighter, which was streaming fuel from a punctured main tank, barely made it back to Clark.

The situation around Manila was a complete disaster. Just before 1300, the first bombs began to fall on the wharves of Manila, the Cavite Naval Yard, and Nichols Field. Again, weather over Formosa had delayed the Japanese strike, and again, as on December 8, the U.S. pursuit aircraft were caught in the worst possible position.

Lieutenant Mahony was just leading a flight of seven P-40s off the ground at Nichols for a standing patrol around the bay. None of his fighters had reached an altitude of more than two thousand feet by the time the Japanese struck. Lieutenant Feallock's formation of eight fighters was slowly circling overhead, at a medium altitude of less than ten thousand feet. It was covering the departure of Mahony's flight before landing at Nichols to refuel. Feallock had been on patrol for more than two hours; all of his planes had less than fifteen minutes of gas left. In fact, most of them were already lowering their landing gear in preparation for the return. Just then, Feallock heard a distress call from the navy radio station at Cavite, announcing that enemy bombers were overhead. Neither flight would be able to gain sufficient altitude to intercept the bombers. To make matters worse, Zeros of the *3rd Kokutai* were perched above the low-flying Americans like hawks above a field of mice. Feallock desperately called the air controller at Nichols for instructions. The tower signaled back that he should use his own discretion in making the decision to engage or withdraw.

A true fighter pilot, Willie Feallock pulled up his wheels and banked around to pursue the enemy. He did not have far to look to find a target. Three A6Ms were swooping down on the PAAC base at Zablan Field a few miles northeast of Manila. This time, surprise would be on his side. He charged in from behind the Zeros and pressed his trigger. Nothing happened. He clicked the button a few more times before the Japanese pilots noticed his approaching P-40. Still, nothing happened. Feallock watched in stunned disbelief as the nimble fighters practically flipped over on their tails to meet his attack. After several attempts to turn away from the Zeros, he decided to see if his Curtiss could outrun them.

View from the first Japanese bombers above Nichols Field on December 10, 1941, shows bombs falling toward hangars of the Philippine Air Depot. At the bottom of the photo, one can see the eastern shoreline of Manila Bay. At the top, the northwestern shore of Laguna de Bay is visible. (IJN Photo Courtesy of O. Tagaya)

Heading back in the direction of Nichols Field, Feallock brought the fighter down on the deck, not more than fifty feet off the ground. Advancing the throttle to full emergency power, he raced across the landscape at more than three hundred miles per hour, dodging houses and trees as he went. The tenacious Japanese were still behind him. Almost every time he turned, gunfire thudded across the tail of his P-40. When smoke began to fill his cockpit, Feallock knew it was time to get out. Using what was left of the shredded elevators, he pulled straight up to about six hundred feet. As the plane began to stall, he pushed himself out of the cockpit. With barely enough height to open his parachute, Feallock hit the ground hard enough to sprain both ankles. He had been lucky: lucky the armor plate behind his seat absorbed so many bullets, lucky he got out of the burning aircraft safely, and luckier still that his abandoned airplane did not fall on him or explode—it crashed a mere sixty feet away.

Other members of Feallock's flight faced a similar predicament. Andy Krieger found himself in a ground-level chase with two A6Ms. He got off a few shots at one of them before he had to flee for his life. Krieger flew so low at one point that his plane actually skimmed off the surface of a small creek. Clipping treetops and bushes with the tips of his wings, he desperately tried to shake off the Japanese planes. Finally, his engine quit. As with Feallock, the chase ended with a dramatic pullout, in which Krieger jumped from the plane as it went into a vertical stall.

Krieger's 3rd Pursuit squadron-mate, Gordon Benson, had two A6Ms latch onto his tail near Nichols. As he fled back across the airfield, his P-40 caught fire. With nowhere to land a flaming plane safely, Benson ditched his fighter in Manila Bay.

Second Lieutenant Bill Rowe of the 17th Pursuit was leading the second section of Feallock's flight. Rowe was providing top cover and, therefore, commenced battle with the highest altitude. Even so, A6Ms swarmed around him at the outset. Deciding he did not have enough fuel to fight, he dived immediately. Heading almost straight down, he lost some, but not all, of his pursuers. With a slight speed advantage, he was able to outdistance the rest as he headed toward Clark Field.

Gus Williams of the 21st Pursuit felt he had no choice but to land at Nichols in spite of the attack. He had no fuel to go anywhere else and did not want to lose his plane in a crash. Japanese bombers had already been over the base, dropping full loads neatly across the airfield in one pass. Their aim was as precise as it had been two days earlier. The main hangars and the Philippine Air Depot were smoking ruins. Some army observation planes had been destroyed. A Sikorsky amphibious flying boat belonging to Philippine Air Lines was on fire. The Philippine Air Lines terminal itself took some damage.[29] As Lieutenant Williams landed, he saw Japanese planes making strafing passes at the other end of the field. He knew that if he left his fighter in the open, it would almost certainly be destroyed. While the strafers were busy working over a disabled B-18 bomber assigned to the 27th Bomb Group, Williams made a quick turn off the runway, parking his P-40E in the trees alongside the golf course.

Above the devastated field, Ray Gehrig had just discovered that his guns were not working when Zeros fired on him. A cannon shell exploded against his canopy, blasting it to shards. With a bloodied face, shattered instruments, and his hydraulic system shot out, he was thankful to find some clouds north of the city to shield his escape. Lieutenant Gehrig headed for Del Carmen but found that the field was still being strafed. Staying away from the Japanese fighters, he used the emergency hand pump to get his gear down. While attempting to land on a small grass airstrip at Plaridel, Gehrig ran into bigger trouble. Before he made it to the runway, his engine shut down from fuel starvation. The P-40 was close to the ground, but not clear of the woods. As it slammed into a large mango tree, the lieutenant's head struck the gunsight. Fortunately, the wreck did not burn, and Gehrig's injuries were not fatal.

Second Lieutenant John Burns also headed north when the fighting began at Nichols. He made it about sixty miles to the Philippine army auxiliary airfield at Maniquis. The runway was covered with obstacles that Filipino troops rushed to clear away while Burns circled. Not having enough fuel to make a third pass at the field, Burns came in before it was completely cleared. The P-40 struck some oil drums and was wiped out, but its pilot walked away uninjured.

The last pilot in Feallock's flight, 2nd Lieutenant Earl Stone of the 17th Pursuit, went south when he was jumped by the Zeros. It was a good decision. The Zeros, already at their maximum endurance, did not follow him. He landed safely at the PAAC base at Batangas with just a few minutes of fuel to spare.

Lieutenant Mahony's flight ran into trouble from the beginning. The last plane off the runway, piloted by 2nd Lieutenant Forrest Hobrecht of the 17th Pursuit, was hit by strafing Zeros before it ever left the perimeter of Nichols Field. The P-40 caught fire and plumed smoke almost immediately. Hobrecht rolled his canopy back and attempted to jump clear, but apparently he struck the tail surfaces of his own aircraft. This either killed him outright or knocked him unconscious. His body was found a few miles away at Navarro—near the downed fighter—with an unopened parachute. Hobrecht's flying school pal and squadron-mate, 2nd Lieutenant A. W. "Dub" Balfanz, accompanied Hanson and Mahony in a race away from Nichols. All three were able to evade the marauding fighters without taking any hits.

Second Lieutenant Wilson Glover, another pilot on loan from the 17th Pursuit, suffered engine damage from A6M gunfire. He was able to get away to the north, but the bullet-holed Allison quit near San Fernando. Glover bailed out unharmed, but one more P-40 was gone.

Don Steele had just retracted his landing gear when he noticed two A6Ms closing in on his tail. Before he could do anything about it, his P-40 was taking their fire. Pulling up into a cloud, then turning a bit to the left while inside it, Steele was able to slip behind one of the Zeros. When Steele and the Japanese plane emerged into clear air, Lieutenant Steele had a perfect shot:

> When I came out, the Zero was just ahead and below me, to the right. He was rocking his wings frantically and trying to find me, looking below him all the time, and flying fairly straight.
>
> I skidded over on to his tail and gave him one burst, and he completely disintegrated. The air was filled with flying wheels, cowling, and scraps of airplane. He rolled over half on his back and crashed into the shore of Laguna de Bay, just east of Nichols Field.[30]

Returning back toward the disaster at Nichols, Steele decided there was nothing more he could do to help. Clearly, it would not be safe to land there, so he headed south to Batangas.

Another pilot from Mahony's flight, 2nd Lieutenant James "Jim" Phillips, chose to head toward the naval yard at Cavite. There, he saw some Zeros strafing a handful of PBYs that were struggling to get airborne. Phillips's plan to protect the flying boats was a noble one, but a Zero pilot spotted his P-40 and maneuvered onto its tail. Realizing that he could not shake the A6M, Phillips decided to lead it over the gun positions at Sangley Point, hoping Marine gunners might shoot it down, or at least scare it away. Unfortunately, the Marines missed the Zero and shot down Phillips. After taking a direct hit from one of their 3-inch shells, Phillips guided his doomed P-40 out over the bay, where he bailed out.

The four Catalinas on the water were the second PatWing-10 strike force being marshaled for a follow-up attack on *Ashigara*. Lieutenant Commander Clayton Marcy and the other pilots were completing pre-flight checks or just turning over their engines when the first bombs struck Cavite. Geysering water from the first bomb bursts added a sense of urgency to their flight preparations. By the time *3rd Kokutai* A6Ms began strafing, three of the PBYs were rushing across the bay. Marcy led the way. Lieutenant (j.g.) William Robinson was left floating behind them due to difficulty in starting one of his engines. Fortunately for Robinson, the Zero pilots were more eager to chase down the moving planes. With each Catalina carrying a torpedo and two 500-pound bombs, it was more difficult than usual to get off the water.

Ensign Earl McConnell had just gotten his PBY into the air by the time cannon fire and machine-gun bullets raked the plane from tail to nose. In one pass, Zeros crippled the large flying boat. One engine was shot to pieces, oil and fuel were spraying out dozens of perforations in the wing, and there were holes all over the hull. Somehow, McConnell managed to bank the plane in the direction of Manila so he could glide to a landing on Laguna de Bay. None of his crew had been injured, but they quickly abandoned their sinking plane.

Lieutenant Harmon Utter's PBY had barely broken free from the water when one of the gunners yelled that three Zeros were attacking the plane. Ensign Richard Roberts, the copilot, started to bank to the right, into the onrushing fighters. Manning the nose gun, their third pilot, Chief Petty Officer Payne, fired steadily at one of the A6Ms. Neither the screaming engines of the other two Zeros passing over-head, nor bullets thudding into the PBY, distracted him. Payne held the gun on target. Behind him, Roberts watched as tracers struck the enemy's cowling and cockpit canopy. In the blink of an eye, the low-flying Mitsubishi tipped over and exploded in shower of water and flame as it went into the bay.[31] Almost as quickly as its wreckage sank, one of its companions turned for a second pass, heading straight at the bow of the Catalina. This time the Japanese pilot was on target. The right engine of the PBY was shot out in the first burst of gunfire. In a quick reaction, Utter and Roberts slammed the flying boat into the water with a large splash. Believing the flying boat was downed, the A6M pilot flew away. Utter's crew was shaken, but unhurt. Their PBY would be repaired to fly again.

The crew of Ensign Robert Snyder's PBY was not as fortunate. Snyder was returning to Laguna de Bay from his morning patrol.

Flying low over the water, his Catalina was an easy target for some A6Ms that approached from astern. The men on the flying boat probably never knew what hit them. Cannon fire struck the vulnerable fuel tanks, igniting the vapor in a violent explosion that literally disintegrated Snyder's plane. There were no survivors.

Although the major air combat between U.S. and Japanese fighters took place around Del Carmen Field and near Manila, returning *3rd Kokutai* Zeros passed near Clark Field to shoot at targets of opportunity. Bill Rowe, having avoided combat after his narrow escape at Nichols Field, was surprised when tracers started flying past his canopy on the final approach into Clark. Determined to get his plane on the ground before the enemy could shoot it to pieces, Rowe made an abrupt turn from the landing path and dived for the airstrip. In doing so, he very nearly collided with an inbound B-17, but both planes made it safely onto the runway.

The Fortress encountered by Rowe was probably Lieutenant Gil Montgomery's, which returned to Clark shortly after 1300. Montgomery, after his earlier scramble, decided the best use of his time would be dropping his plane's single six-hundred pound bomb. He had carried it to Vigan, aimed at one of the ships near shore, and missed. His crew was anxious to get some more bombs to try again. Although Major Combs had been ordered to leave Clark without bombs, and Major O'Donnell had been sent directly back to Del Monte during the air-raid alert, Montgomery's request was granted. Ordnance men rearmed his Fortress with twenty one-hundred pound bombs. Lieutenant Bohnaker's B-17 had been similarly armed but remained on the ground because its pilot was still too ill to fly.

Captain Parsel had bombed the Vigan invasion force at approximately the same time as had Lieutenant Montgomery. Parsel's bombardier, 2nd Lieutenant Cecil Gregg , also missed the first target, a moving warship. However, a second salvo of three 300-pound bombs straddled one of the stationary transports. The ship he attacked, *Takao Maru*, was last seen belching smoke and flame. Damage forced the skipper to beach the leaking transport to prevent a complete loss of its cargo.[32] Instead of returning to Clark after completing that second run, Parsel turned southwest toward San Marcelino.

WHILE THE JAPANESE COMPLETED THEIR RAID on Nichols and Cavite, Captain Kelly and his crew were heading back south toward Aparri after their fruitless search for an enemy carrier. They had gone almost as far as Formosa before turning around. A great deal of Japanese shipping had been seen around the islands of the Luzon Strait, but the large warship they had noticed shelling Aparri seemed the ripest target. As Kelly's Fortress closed in, the ship was still slowly moving, all by itself, along the coast.

Flying serenely above at twenty thousand feet, Kelly approached the "battleship"—actually the light cruiser *Natori*. The nearest of the six large destroyers sailing between *Natori* and the transports circled back to put up a barrage of antiaircraft fire. Most of the flak bursts were much too low to worry Corporal Meyer Levin as he hovered over his Norden bombsight. Looking down from the nose, Levin and 2nd Lieutenant Joe Bean, the navigator, noticed a floatplane catapulting from the target as their B-17C lined up for the drop. As the three bombs fell toward the sea, Bean noticed six fighters far below, headed in their direction. The planes appeared to have come from the Aparri airfield. He did not give them much thought because he was engrossed in watching the bomb strikes.

To the Fortress crew, it appeared that one bomb hit the water on either side of the ship and the other struck nearly amidships on one of the after turrets. Bean noted a large number of splashes on both sides of the "battleship." It seemed to the young lieutenant that hundreds of sailors were jumping overboard. Also, what appeared to be an oil slick was trailing where the bombs hit. Elated with his apparent success, Kelly turned the bomber due south on a course back to Clark Field. With the bomb load gone and minimal fuel remaining in its tanks, the B-17 gained speed as Kelly trimmed it for a subtle descent.

Captain Kelly's crew did not notice that seven A6Ms were trailing behind them. These fighters from the *Tainan Kokutai* were part of a formation that had patrolled near Vigan and then passed over an empty Clark Field. On their way home to Formosa, they flew over Aparri. Some of the pilots glimpsed blast circles radiating on the sea near *Natori*.[33] Looking anxiously around for marauding U.S. bombers, they were shocked to find only one, far above them.

Even with throttles to the firewall, the Zeros had a difficult time trying to climb fast enough to catch the speeding Fortress. The performance of the B-17 at altitude was genuinely surprising to the Japanese pilots. In fact, they chased the bomber for more than a hundred miles before they could get close enough to fire on it. Just as the *Tainan* A6Ms lined up to shoot, three more Zeros approached from the opposite direction and then cut in front of the *Tainan* flight to make the first shots. Petty Officer Saburo Sakai, leading the second shotai of the *Tainan* fighters, observed:

> Approximately fifty miles north of Clark Field we maneuvered to make our firing runs. Abruptly three Zeros appeared—it seemed from out of thin air—and sliced across the B-17's course. Evidently they were from the Kaohsiung Wing [*3rd Kokutai*] which had strafed Nichols Field earlier in the day.
>
> We were still out of gun range when the three Kaohsiung fighters peeled off and made their firing passes from above on the big plane. The bomber continued serenely on, almost as if the Zeros were no more bothersome than gnats.[34]

The Fortress gunners were only awakened when bullets from these first Zeros hit their plane. The cockpit and nose of their bomber took the first damage. Joe Bean had just stepped down from the observation dome when it shattered above his head. Immediately in front of him, an exploding cannon shell destroyed the pilot's instrument panel. On the other side of the bomb bay, at the left waist-gun position, the direct hit of another cannon shell gruesomely decapitated the radio operator, Staff Sergeant William Delehanty. Kelly and his copilot, 2nd Lieutenant Donald Robins, began to fish-tail the plane so the remaining gunners could get a better field of fire on the enemy. The next four Zeros made their passes, gaining hits in the left wing, fuel tanks, and engines. Privates Robert Altman and Willard Money hammered away with their .50-calibers, striking at least two of the A6Ms. Kelly's Fortress was already done for, but the coup de grâce may have been a final pass made by Sakai and his two wingmen.[35] They rushed in line-abreast, directly on the Fortress's tail. In this run, the right wing and the bomb bay took severe damage. The elevator cables were shot away, sending the smoking B-17 into a fatal plunge with its engines still pulling at full power.

As Sakai followed the bomber toward low-lying clouds near Mount Arayat, he noticed fierce flames raging in the bomb bay and radio compartment. Severed fuel and oxygen lines combined their flow to feed a blast jet of fire throughout the tail section. Just before the stricken plane entered the clouds, three men jumped from its tail: Altman, Money, and Sergeant James Halkyard, the flight engineer. Captain Kelly did his best to hold the plane level so the rest of the crew could bail out. Levin and Bean were having trouble with a corroded pin in the lower hatch beneath the cockpit, and Robins had difficulty knocking out the damaged overhead escape panel with its splintered astrodome. Levin finally got the bottom exit open, tumbling out with Bean right behind him. Robins successfully freed the upper exit just moments before the aircraft exploded. Halfway through the opening, he was blown clear of the plane. Singed black from head to toe, Robins somehow found his ripcord, which deployed a charred but still useful parachute canopy. Captain Kelly, at the controls to the end, never had a chance. The fiery disintegration of Kelly's B-17 happened within a few miles of Clark, in full view of those on the ground. The sight of one of the seemingly invincible Fortresses being shot out of its realm by Japanese fighters—right above the home field, no less—was very demoralizing.

Although not documented as such, the downing of Captain Kelly's plane apparently was an important catalyst in Lieutenant Colonel Eubank's decision to order all remaining B-17s to Del Monte. Major Combs and Lieutenant Ford had been flying in close proximity to Clark and quickly headed south together when they received this order over their radios. Elliott Vandevanter proceeded toward Del Monte by himself. Captain Parsel and Lieutenants Teats and Keiser, all at San Marcelino, had been busily loading up some five-hundred pound bombs that had been trucked over from Del Carmen. Disappointed at not getting a chance to use them, the Fortress pilots reluctantly prepared to leave for Del Monte. Their three B-17s departed from San Marcelino by 1530. Also grounded at that remote airstrip, Lieutenants Godman and Schaetzel labored to make temporary repairs to their planes for the trip south.

A final raid on Aparri was under way and did not get recalled. It was out of radio range. Only two Flying Fortresses participated: Lieutenant Gil Montgomery's, which departed from Clark at 1400; and Bohnaker's, with 2nd Lieutenant Harl Pease at the controls, trailing a short distance behind. The B-17s arrived over Aparri independently. Montgomery dropped all twenty of his small bombs in train across the transports. His run was apparently successful, leaving one transport burning and taking on water.[36] Pease, whose plane carried nineteen 100-pound bombs, made two passes: the first on a "cruiser," the second on a transport. His crew claimed no hits, although several bombs were logged as near misses.

Neither Fortress encountered fighter opposition; both headed directly back to Clark Field. On his return, Gil Montgomery was ordered to continue on to Del Monte without landing. Despite his request to take on more fuel before heading south, Montgomery was refused permission to land. Dutifully, he continued toward Mindanao. With seeming inconsistency, Harl Pease was allowed to land at Clark when he returned from Aparri a short time later. This sudden reversal in policy may be explained by the fact that both Lieutenants Connally and Kurtz both relentlessly pleaded with Lieutenant Colonel Eubank to change his standing order and let the B-17s come in whenever they needed fuel. Connally's personal dilemma that afternoon added the necessary weight to their argument. Very nearly out of fuel, Connally had landed at about 1500—against the signals from the tower—as described by Lieutenant Kurtz:

> [F]ollowing orders, I was still giving the Fortresses the red light to stay in the air, and I began to worry about this. Maybe orders had been issued to bring them in, but someone had failed to notify me. Some of them would circle for a while, and then would head on back for Del Monte, more than six hundred miles away, while they still had enough gas to get there.
>
> Finally old Jim Connally said the hell with it, and came on in without my giving him any light at all. He needed more gas to get back to Mindanao and couldn't perch up there all day, and a little after this the Colonel said I could give the others the green light to come in and gas up, although any hour, any minute, we were expecting the Japs back. He wanted to save those remaining Forts at any cost.[37]

Kurtz was justified in his worries about the Fortress flights to Mindanao. There was bad weather to the south that evening, with thunderheads built up all over the central islands of the Philippines. Captain Parsel, accompanied by Teats and Keiser, managed to skirt around most of the turbulence to land at Del Monte just after dark. Combs, Ford, and Vandevanter ran into the worst of the weather after the storm front closed in from behind them. Combs and Ford, too short on fuel to return to Luzon, landed on a civilian airfield at San Jose, on the island of Mindoro. Vandevanter persisted longer, eventually making a landing at a Pan American Airlines emergency airstrip at Tacloban, on Leyte. His tanks were completely dry. Lieutenant Montgomery's navigator got disoriented in the storm and thought he had lost his bearings on Del Monte. Figuring they were far to the east of their intended course, Montgomery turned west. In fact, his navigator had been dead-on the original mark. In darkness, the Fortress flew over Mindanao almost on top of Del Monte before its pilot changed course. The bomber was soon too far west to make it back to the field with the remaining fuel. Finally getting a definitive bearing on Zamboanga, at the western tip of Mindanao, Montgomery turned around. He was bringing the B-17 in toward a small airfield on the coast at Zamboanga when its engines sputtered. Still four miles offshore, the big plane came down on the sea at around 2230. Fortunately, none of the crew was seriously injured, and all of the men were sturdy enough swimmers to make landfall on the beach within four hours.

Lieutenant "Harl" Pease also attempted to fly to Mindanao that evening. He took on a full load of fuel in Bohnaker's plane and left Clark Field at 1830. Once he was back in the air, he had difficulty flying toward Del Monte. The storm front was impenetrable. He gave up on the weather after a few hours, returning to Clark to spend the rest of the night.

The last planes taking flight over Luzon on December 10 were the barely serviceable B-17s of Lieutenants Godman and Schaetzel. They lifted off together from San Marcelino at 2300. Schaetzel soon received a radio report stating that Del Monte had been overrun by enemy forces, so he set his Fortress down on the island of Cebu to wait for better flying conditions and confirmation of the report. Godman had not heard the radio transmission but flew around in the weather all night, finally landing at Del Monte after sunrise. Old Glory and the United States Army were still firmly rooted on the remote pineapple plantation.

CHAPTER 9

Reckoning

December 11–14, 1941

THE FIRST THREE DAYS OF WAR in the Pacific had been an unqualified disaster for the defenders of Malaya and the Philippines. Sinking *Prince of Wales* and *Repulse* had earned the IJN incontestable control of the South China Sea. The only battleships still roaming the Pacific Ocean sailed under the flag of the rising sun. If Allied naval units remaining in the Far East were compelled to engage in surface battle, they would have to do so at a nearly suicidal disadvantage. By December 11, it was evident that the Allies had lost control of the skies as well as the seas. At the command level, it could be seen that the Allied forces already present in the Far East were insufficient to stem the tide of Japanese conquest. There were enough bombers to sting the enemy, but not to repel invasion forces. Fighter aircraft to protect the bombers and their bases—in short supply before the war—had been reduced to pitifully low quantities.

Although the Asiatic Fleet possessed a relatively strong submarine force, with twenty-six boats immediately available, the IJN had taken most of the wind out of its sails. Destruction of the base at Cavite was actually worse than at Pearl Harbor. The torpedo depot and 230 of its deadly weapons had gone up in smoke. After the raid, the only supply of torpedoes was the load that each boat already carried, supplemented by limited stocks previously stored on the tenders *Canopus*, *Holland*, and *Otus*.[1]

Admiral Hart had witnessed the conflagration of the naval yard while steadfastly standing on the roof of his office in the Marsman Building in downtown Manila. It was painfully obvious to him that the

AAF was incapable of protecting his fleet. Without air cover, his meager surface forces had little choice; they would have to retire south to safer harbors, as soon as possible. Continuing to base U.S. warships in Manila Bay, within range of Japanese bombers, would be irresponsible. On December 11, Hart gave the order to move his main fleet units to Java, where they could be operated in cooperation with the Dutch navy. Together, these warships might provide at least some deterrent to Japanese southward expansion into the oil-rich Netherlands East Indies. The submariners, along with a handful of PT boats from Motor Torpedo Boat Squadron 3, and the planes of PatWing-10 would linger in the Philippines as long as support was available for refueling and provisioning. Their presence would allow the navy to "show the flag" around the Philippines without too much risk to its assets.

The Japanese bombings around Manila Bay had more of an impact on the submarine force than on PatWing-10. Even though the Cavite Naval Yard had been razed, the seaplane base at nearby Sangley Point was virtually untouched. Several PBYs had been "shot down" on December 10, but only one of those was a complete loss. Still, Frank Wagner knew that his small compound would not remain a sanctuary. He immediately ordered all operable PBYs away from the Manila area. A detachment of seven VP-102 planes under the control of Commander Marcy was sent north to the Olongapo station in Subic Bay. The rest of the Luzon-based Catalinas were dispersed along the southern shore of Laguna de Bay, near Los Baños.

Of course, flying boats were safe on the water only when well camouflaged. In the absence of army fighter protection, freely roaming enemy planes could strike at any time. Ensign Butch Swenson and Ensign John Ogle discovered this the hard way. Their PBY was shot up by a Japanese army twin-engine bomber while taxiing across Laguna de Bay toward the Los Baños anchorage on the morning of the relocation.

The AAF was, by this point, completely unable to intervene against such incursions. Losses in 24th Pursuit Group aircraft had reached a critical point. In fact, the FEAF's morning assessment of fighter resources recorded only twenty-two P-40s remaining in operational condition, not enough to fully equip even one squadron. Twelve of these were assigned to the merged 17/20th Squadron at Clark Field. Ten remained at Nichols Field, where the 3rd Pursuit was finally joined with the 21st. Maintenance personnel assessed that a dozen more fighters could be resurrected from wrecked or battle-damaged aircraft with some intensive effort and a week's time.[2] Just one more disastrous day of scrambling to meet the Japanese could wipe out the entire lot, leaving the Philippines both defenseless and blind.

The situation forced General Brereton to issue an unpopular order for the 24th Pursuit Group to immediately cease all interception activity. Because the raid on Nichols finished off the remnants of the 2nd Observation Squadron, pursuit aircraft would have to be conserved for use in monitoring enemy ground movements and spotting new landing operations. Completely contrary to their natural instincts to be aggressive, the disgruntled fighter pilots were instructed to engage Japanese planes only if fired on. Until new planes arrived from the United States, Japanese air forces were to be granted unchallenged command of the air above the Philippines. If not for the abiding faith that their country was sending help in this hour of need, the American fliers might have felt their battle was already lost.

In northern Luzon, General Wainwright anxiously watched as the Japanese army expanded from its landing zones. Without air support from the air force or naval interdiction by the Asiatic Fleet, there was no means to engage the enemy at Vigan. Geography prevented any flanking of that invasion site on the ground. Near Aparri, the situation was even worse. Japanese troops were moving quickly up the Cagayan valley, evidently intending to occupy the more desirable airfield at Tuguegarao. The JAAF had already flown thirty-five Ki-27s of the 50th Sentai into the small airfield at Aparri to cover the ground forces' advance.[3] By the afternoon of December 11, eighteen of those fighters migrated southwest to the airfield at Vigan. With complete air superiority, Japan could bring as much materiel ashore on Luzon as shipping capacity allowed. Japan's navy was essentially free to land wherever it wanted in the Philippines, disgorging as many soldiers as it could carry, whenever it was convenient. This was a bitter pill for MacArthur's command to swallow. As General Wainwright's stated, "[T]hat was the day I realized, for all time, the futility of trying to fight a war without an Air Force."[4]

At FEAF Headquarters, the staff belatedly concluded that running bomber operations out of Clark Field without fighter cover was impossible. All Flying Fortresses would have to be based on Mindanao, out of range of the Japanese aircraft. Because the B-17s at Del Monte Field required intensive maintenance after three days of round-the-clock operations under combat conditions, the 19th Group did not undertake any bombing missions on December 11. Fortress crews that had not been able to return their planes to Del Monte on December 10 spent the next day flying to Mindanao.

Lieutenant Schaetzel—who discovered one aileron control cable literally hanging by a thread—remained at Cebu. Major Combs and Lieutenant Ford flew their Fortresses south from San Jose, on Mindoro. Lieutenant Vandevanter and his crew finally got their plane into the air from Tacloban, on Leyte, after a laborious refueling by hand pump. In a difficult departure from the tiny airstrip, their B-17 failed to clear a fence at the end of the runway. Vandevanter managed to keep the plane airborne, but, on arrival at Del Monte, the bomber was taken out of commission for extended repairs to the bottom of a severely dented tailplane. Lieutenant Bohnaker recovered enough from his illness to retake command of his aircraft at Clark Field and fly it to Del Monte. Also making flights to Mindanao were Lieutenant Connally and Lieutenant John Chiles. Chiles—a 30th Squadron pilot who lost his plane on December 8—piloted Lieutenant Shedd's B-17 on the trip south as Shedd reported for sick call at Fort Stotsenberg Hospital.

THE SITUATION IN THE SKIES OVER MALAYA was much the same as that in the Philippines. Air Headquarters decreed that aircraft would be used only for reconnaissance purposes or the direct protection of Singapore Island. Fighters would be retained at Singapore to provide an interception umbrella over the city. Catalinas from RAF 205 Squadron, and those Australian Hudsons not under repair, reverted to maritime patrols over the South China Sea and the northern coast of Borneo.

General Percival's ground forces were left to fend for themselves as they rapidly retreated down the Malayan Peninsula. Continual harassment by Japanese aircraft made an orderly withdrawal of British and Commonwealth army units from Alor Star to the Penang area extremely difficult. The JAAF transferred several dozen Mitsubishi Ki-51 "Sonia" attack aircraft from the 27th Sentai and the 71st and 73rd Independent Chutais to Singora on December 11 to increase pressure on Percival's command. Pinpoint bombardment of British and Indian strongpoints using these planes caused constant confusion and disruption of transportation services, complicating an already disorganized retirement from the north.

Carrying up to 200 kilograms (440 pounds) of bombs, and equipped with two forward-firing 7.7-mm machine guns and a single rear-facing, flexibly mounted 7.7-mm gun in the aft cockpit, the Ki-51 dive-bombers were designed to work in close cooperation with Japanese infantry units. From a distance, the two-place, fixed-gear plane resembled the smaller Nakajima Ki-27. More important, once the bombs were away, the maneuverability and speed of the Ki-51 nearly matched that of the fighter. This unexpected aerial combat capability would surprise and embarrass Allied pilots who carelessly pursued it as an "easy kill."

THE IJN HAD BOMBED LONELY WAKE ISLAND each day, on a very regular schedule. As the Mitsubishi bombers arrived for their predictable noon-time run on December 9 and 10, Major Putnam's F4Fs had counterat-tacked the bombing force. The interceptions had been ineffective. Although the Marine pilots had made three aerial victory claims, only one of the *Chitose Kokutai* G3Ms had actually been brought down. Returning Japanese crews attributed that loss to antiaircraft fire.[5] More than a dozen raiders had been damaged on those two days, either by Wildcats or the 3-inch antiaircraft artillery operated by Marine gunners and civilian volunteers. Despite that, casualties among the Japanese flight crews had been much lighter than IJN commanders expected, and maintenance personnel at the Roi airfield were able to repair most bombers within a few days.

Commander Cunningham and his Marine security force leader, Major James Devereux, had been expecting a Japanese invasion force ever since the first air raid of December 8. In the early hours of December 11, sentries pacing the outer beach on Wilkes Island noticed shadows moving on the ocean. Clouds drifting over water at night can play tricks on the most sensitive vision, so the Marines carefully observed the motions until they were certain the images they saw were enemy ships plying the seas outside the reef. At about 0300, Major Devereux's command post received confirmation of the sight-ings. Realizing that shelling would begin shortly, the major instructed all of his officers to withhold return fire from shore batteries until he gave explicit orders to commence shooting.

Devereux knew that his 5-inch guns could cause significant dam-age if the enemy ships drew near enough to the shore. He also knew that the range of the 6-inch or 8-inch guns of Japanese cruisers likely to accompany an invasion fleet was much greater than that of his own guns. The garrison's only chance of success lay in drawing the enemy in as close as possible. With surf battering the reef heavily that night, Devereux figured the Japanese would want to come as far toward the beach as possible before stopping to launch their landing barges. If the Japanese commanders thought their air strikes had neutralized the

U.S. weapons, they would come well within range of Marine guns. If they sensed resistance, their ships could remain distant while bombarding Wake's defenses into submission. Like patient spiders in a web, the disciplined Marines would wait for Devereux's signal.

The presence of aircraft would have the same effect as premature counterbattery fire. At the same time, Devereux did not want to risk losing the last few Grummans to Japanese guns. He instructed Paul Putnam to muster his available fighters as soon as the shelling began. If the gunnery exchange had not commenced by 0500 Major Putnam was to send the planes up then. The F4Fs were not to attack the enemy until Wake's guns answered the Japanese naval bombardment. Putnam would lead the mission himself and agreed with Devereux to circle the Grummans north of the atoll until dawn.

At the designated time, Major Putnam and the other three fliers turned over their engines. One after another, they lined up on the narrow runway and roared into the dark gray skies. Armed with two 100-pound bombs each, the Wildcats could do damage to the invaders only if they scored direct hits on sensitive parts of the ships. They would need daylight to strike with that kind of accuracy.

Admiral Sadamichi Kajioka unintentionally cooperated fully with Devereux's plan. His warships took up a position eight thousand yards offshore to sail in a line from east to west, parallel to the southern coast of Wilkes and Wake. They would hold this distance for the duration of their first bombardment run. At 0530 Kajioka's flagship, the light cruiser *Yubari*, commenced firing. A chorus of blasts followed from the light cruisers *Tenryu* and *Tatsuta* and the screening destroyers *Mutsuki, Hayate, Kisaragi, Oite, Yayoi,* and *Mochizuki*. When Kajioka noted no response from the islands by the end of that first run, he turned toward Wilkes Island and sailed in the opposite direction—two thousand yards closer to shore.[6]

In the distance, from an altitude of twenty thousand feet, Major Putnam, Captain Elrod, Captain Frank Tharin, and Captain Herb Freuler could spot the red-orange muzzle flashes from the long line of Japanese ships. The view seemed almost surreal. Over thrumming engine noise and the whistling of air rushing past their cockpit canopies, the pilots could not hear the hollow booms of gunfire, the shrieking descent of projectiles, or the echoing blast of shells bursting on impact.

Nearly deafened after the first explosions, men sheltering on Wake could feel, more than hear, each successive detonation. With incredible fortitude, Marine gunners held fast while the enemy ships passed across the horizon a second time. As the Japanese turned again to close another thousand yards toward the island, Major Devereux finally gave the order to fire. At 0610 *Yubari* received the first hits— much to Admiral Kajioka's surprise. Destroyers rushed to lay a smoke screen between the islands and the cruisers, but it was too late. Marine batteries on Wake and Wilkes fired rapidly into the line of ships. *Yubari*, several of the destroyers, the light cruiser *Tenryu*, and one landing ship took hits. The destroyer *Hayate*, closest to Wilkes Island, was struck in its powder magazine and blown completely in half. It sank with all hands on board in less than a minute.[7] Around the batteries, Marines stood up and cheered wildly.

Major Devereux's wily plan had wounded and turned back the Japanese invasion force. While the rest of Admiral Kajioka's ships turned tail and ran after *Yubari*, Putnam's Wildcats plummeted down from the direction of the rising sun. Captain Frueler and Major Putnam missed their targets with bombs but sprayed the bridges of several ships, including *Yubari*, with heavy machine-gun fire. Kajioka himself barely escaped serious injury by bullets from the strafing F4Fs. Tharin landed a bomb on *Tenryu* that damaged the cruiser's torpedo launcher. Farther out to sea, Captain Elrod chased the destroyer *Kisaragi*. Practically oblivious to intense antiaircraft fire, "Hammering Hank" screamed in with his own guns firing. As he pulled out of the shallow dive, he dropped his bombs. One managed to explode through the destroyer's deck into a storage compartment, which caught fire. The fire burned out of control, gradually approaching the powder magazine. A half-hour later, and more than thirty miles south of Wake, an explosion rocked the ship. *Kisaragi* rolled over and sank immediately, taking 150 Japanese sailors to their deaths.[8]

Putnam, Frueler, and Tharin each returned to the airstrip with minor damage, but Hank Elrod's F4F trailed smoke as it left the blazing *Kisaragi* behind. Before he could get back to Wake, his engine seized. Elrod skillfully glided to a belly-landing on the beach in an attempt to save the plane, but the combat damage was too great to repair. The three serviceable Wildcats were rearmed and sent out again two more times. During the final sortie, Captain Freuler's F4F absorbed a bullet in its engine while strafing a troop transport. Despite losing one cylinder head, Freuler was able to coax the tough Grumman in for an emergency landing. With the aid of parts stripped from other grounded planes, Lieutenant Kinney would get it flying again in two days.

Intending to provide close air support for a Japanese beachhead, seventeen *Chitose Kokutai* G3Ms approached the island three hours earlier than their usual high-noon appearance. As this bomber formation separated into two flights, Lieutenants Kinney and Davidson intercepted it. The two F4Fs split up to follow both enemy groups. After repeated passes at the bombers, each pilot managed to score one kill before exhausting his ammunition.[9]

The Marine victory over Admiral Kajioka's invasion force on December 11, 1941, would become one of the most celebrated U.S. actions of the Pacific War. It was the first good news the American public received from the Pacific. It would be the only good news until April 1942, when "Doolittle's Raiders" bombed Japan.

WITH CLARK FIELD NO LONGER CONSIDERED a safe staging point, Fortress crews were required to fly fatiguing round-trip sorties from Del Monte Field to their targets around Luzon. Conducting operations from Mindanao would be tough on both the men and the planes. If the B-17s required any significant service, their crews would have to fly to Batchelor Field in Australia. Major airframe work would mean an even longer trip to RAAF Headquarters on the southern coast of Australia at Melbourne, because the repair depots at Townsville were not yet completed. In an attempt to alleviate the problem of long missions, Colonel George and his energetic engineer, Captain Eads, focused their efforts on creation of new bomber fields in southern Luzon, Mindoro, and Cebu. Of course, this activity would compete for the same construction resources required for similarly urgent efforts to develop camouflaged fighter strips on, or near, the Bataan Peninsula.

Regardless of any expansion in the number of available airfields on Luzon, resources at Clark Field would have to be evacuated from the island. To accomplish this, the 19th Bomb Group planned to move as many men and as much support equipment to Mindanao as could be flown out. Displaced bomber crews, experienced fliers from the 27th Bomb Group, and the occasional pursuit pilot would take on the duty of flying a nightly shuttle service between Clark and Del Monte. There were enough spare pilots to handle the flight schedules, but capable aircraft were in short supply. All airworthy B-18 bombers and several C-39 cargo planes that survived the Japanese attacks were immediately assigned to this operation. Even the B-17s were used as transports whenever possible. For courier and VIP transport service, General Brereton commandeered three twin-engine Beechcraft Model

18s from Philippine Air Lines (PAL). Along with the planes came four highly experienced and very resourceful civilian fliers: Paul Gunn, Dan Stickle, Harold "Buzz" Slingsby, and Louis Connelly. Gunn, who had been PAL's director of operations, was sworn into the AAF as a captain. The other three former airline pilots were spot-commissioned as first lieutenants.

This was more than a little ironic for the forty-one-year-old Gunn, who had retired from the navy as a chief petty officer and naval aviation pilot four years earlier. During twenty years in the navy, he had amassed more flying experience and aircraft maintenance knowledge than any other man serving in the FEAF. Paul Gunn would eventually emerge as one of the most colorful characters to fight in the Pacific War. His first "official" operation—relocating the Beech transports from Nielson Field to a safer field—was typical of the unorthodox manner in which Captain Gunn ran his "business." Seeking to exploit superstition, he decided that Manila's Grace Park Cemetery would be the most secure, convenient place to base his planes. Presumably, shooting up a graveyard would be taboo for even the most battle-hardened Japanese pilot.

Gunn's plan was not quite as far-fetched as it sounds. The original airfield servicing Manila had actually been located at Grace Park some twenty years earlier, before the grounds of the cemetery had been expanded. After Nielson Field was opened, the Grace Park runway had simply been incorporated into the graveyard as a long driveway. To make the new base usable, some large tombs close to the road suffered the indignity of having their spires or crosses knocked over to allow for wingtip clearance. Gunn resolved to atone for such sins later, after the Japanese had been defeated. Until then, no task that would serve to ensure his unit's survival or aid in the United States' victory over Japan would be beyond his imagination or consideration.

December 12

In the predawn hours of December 12, it appeared that the big Japanese push against the Philippines was about to be felt. Filipino coast-watchers reported that five battleships and an aircraft carrier, screened by five destroyers, were heading south past Santa Cruz Point. Said to be moving at high speed, the task force seemed to be heading for either Subic Bay or Manila Bay. Based on the type of

Japanese warships noted and their position and estimated course, it was plausible that this formation included the "battleships" PatWing-10 had bombed on December 10.

Lieutenant Clayton Marcy wasted no time in preparing his detachment of PBYs for an immediate attack on the suspected enemy battle group. He figured his seven flying boats could achieve complete surprise by intercepting the ships at dawn, just north of the entrance to Subic Bay. In spite of the darkness, Marcy had the Catalinas fitted as quickly as possible with four five-hundred-pound bombs each. By 0500 engine noise echoed off the hills surrounding the bay. Still waters were churned into a pattern of frothy wakes fanning out from the base at Olongapo. Inside the aircraft, the men surged with adrenaline, eagerly anticipating their chance to avenge U.S. naval losses at Pearl Harbor and Cavite.

Aerial view of the naval station at Olongapo during the summer of 1941. PBYs of Patrol Wing 10, painted with an uncharacteristic brown and green upper surface camouflage, can be seen near the buildings. At the left, USS Langley *rests in the floating drydock,* Dewey. *The ship in the foreground is the aircraft tender Preston, a former "four-piper" destroyer. Astern of Preston, is the seaplane ramp. Seven VP-102 Catalinas were destroyed by strafing Zeros along this waterfront on December 12.* (Courstey of the Naval Historical Center)

AS THE OVERCAST BEGAN TO GLOW under the sun's first rays, a single Allison engine wheezed and snorted to life at Clark Field. Strapped into his belly-tank-equipped Warhawk, Lieutenant Boyd Wagner prepared himself for a four-hour mission to reconnoiter the Japanese landing zone at Aparri. Wagner was away from the airstrip within a few minutes, climbing up above the overcast on a course directly toward the north coast. Fastening on his oxygen mask at sixteen thousand feet, the young squadron commander gazed around. He had the skies completely to himself as the pink of dawn yielded to the sunrise. Beneath him, the ground was still shrouded in shadow gray. If not for the war, it would have been a beautiful morning to soar along above the cottony puffs of the cloudbank, lazily curving around the occasional pillar formed by taller plumes of moisture and watching the changes in color along the eastward horizon that one can observe only from high above the land.

FAR TO THE SOUTH, AT DEL MONTE FIELD, the pineapple-spiked hilltop awakened to the roar of twenty-four Cyclone engines as six Flying Fortresses warmed up for a departure at 0730. Rosie O'Donnell—in the absence of any clear orders for the use of his planes—planned to take five available 14th Squadron B-17s and the repaired 30th Squadron bomber of Lieutenant Adams on his own mission to Vigan.[10]

Jack Adams's Boeing—a survivor of the bombing at Clark Field—may have sustained some hidden damage on December 8. Something had been overlooked during the repair process. When the big plane made its full-power takeoff run down the airstrip, both engines on one side faltered; the resultant change in thrust twisted the plane abruptly off the runway toward an arroyo that ran along one side of the field. Its brakes were not operational, so the best Adams could do to steer the Fortress away from the small canyon was to ground-loop it in the other direction. Fast footwork on the rudder pedals kept the plane on the field but did not prevent it from careening into Lieutenant Tash's bomber—still under repair from its brush with the Zeros on December 8. In a sideways skid on the damp grass, Adams's plane knocked the nose section off the parked aircraft while fracturing its own fuselage, aft of the wing. Fortunately, the mechanics scurried away from Tash's stationary B-17 before impact, and none of the aircrew on board Adams's Fortress was injured. Still, it was a very costly accident: both bombers were damaged beyond any hope of repairing them for a flight to Australia.

Major Combs already had his crew and their aircraft prepared for a reconnaissance of Mindanao. Abandoning that mission, he rushed to follow O'Donnell's planes to Vigan in place of Lieutenant Adams. A sure chance to strike at the enemy seemed more meaningful than a long patrol.

The other bombers at Del Monte Field were either undergoing maintenance or taking their turn at the single spray gun for a quick application of camouflaging paint.[11] According to those who viewed the product of that painting effort firsthand, the outcome was poor, at best. Most of the shiny silver bombers disappeared under a messy, thin, gloss coat of mottled green and dark brown. No flat-toned paint was available, so the Fortresses still reflected the bright sunlight when parked in the open—despite their hideous appearance. The pilots and crews had a difficult time judging whether any benefit was gained for all the effort.

THE NAVY FLIERS OF PATWING-10 experienced less success in finding the reported Japanese battle force. Three hours of pointless searching along the west coast of Luzon failed to produce a single ship sighting. Commander Marcy decided there was no value in chasing phantoms. Shortly after 0800, his seven Catalinas banked around and headed back toward Olongapo. Marcy was greatly annoyed. He suspected the Filipino coast-watchers of providing a deliberately misinforming report and was anxious to reprimand someone for wasting his squadron's time.

The coast-watcher report that spurred PatWing-10 to action that morning had indeed been a false one. However, the large Japanese fleet off another coast of Luzon was not a figment of some observer's imagination. Unfortunately, that task force was nowhere near any anticipated location. Three hundred miles to the southeast of Olongapo, seven transports lurked off the eastern shore of Luzon. They were escorted by three heavy cruisers, two light cruisers, twelve destroyers, the seaplane carriers *Chitose* and *Mizuho*, and the aircraft carrier *Ryujo*.[12]

Delivered by this group of ships, a Japanese infantry regiment had come ashore near Legaspi at 0145 on December 12. It was not until 0640 that USAFFE Headquarters was informed of the new landing operation by Philippine army units in the area.[13] General MacArthur had a serious new problem to address, a major security threat that posed even greater challenges than the two previous enemy incursions. The new invasion site would allow Japan to move its ground units toward Manila from both directions, forcing MacArthur into defending a second front. Worse yet, Legaspi had a better airstrip for heavy aircraft than Vigan or Aparri; Japanese bombers located there could easily strike as far south as Mindanao. There would be no more safe havens for Americans in the Philippines.

BOYD WAGNER'S NAVIGATION was nearly as good as his piloting skill. When he finally descended through the clouds, Wagner emerged just a mile or two offshore from the mouth of the Cagayan River. Directly beneath him were two Japanese destroyers that began blasting away at his plane with all of their antiaircraft weapons. To avoid the deadly bursts, Lieutenant Wagner dived straight for the water. Pulling out just above the waves, he stayed beneath the depression limit of the most dangerous shipboard flak weapons while he banked toward the shoreline. As he made landfall, Wagner noticed tracers arcing at him from above. Instinctively, he rolled his plane to the left and pulled up toward the sun. When he reached the peak of this chandelle, he looked over his shoulder. Two "low-wing, fixed landing gear single seaters" were climbing behind him, firing wildly. Three more flew overhead. The fighters above him had not yet seen the P-40; the two behind had lost him in the sun.

Taking a chance that the higher-flying planes would not pursue him, Wagner rolled downward, neatly falling in behind the pair of Ki-27s that had fired on him. In a quick pass from close astern, he pulled the trigger. The volume of bullets from his .50-caliber wing guns was enough to strike both of the small fighters in one burst. His quarry split and dived, engines smoking as they dropped. Watching their descent, Lieutenant Wagner noticed that he was directly above the Japanese-held airfield. Twelve more fighters were neatly lined up along the runway. Even though he was under orders not to attack, the target was too tempting to leave untouched. He sped along the airstrip with guns blazing and then pulled into a tight turn for another strafing run. Looking up after this second pass, Wagner realized that the other three Japanese pilots had finally seen him. As those Ki-27s dived in to strike back at the audacious American, he decided it was time to save his plane. After dropping his belly tank, Wagner rammed the Warhawk's throttle to the firewall. The Ki-27s gave up the chase as the faster P-40 quickly pulled away, heading south up the Cagayan valley. Buzz Wagner was ecstatic; he believed he had shot down two

Japanese fighters and destroyed five more on the ground.[14] The 24th Pursuit Group finally had something to celebrate.

AT AROUND 0900, Commander Marcy's PBYs began splashing down into the waters of Subic Bay. Each flying boat anchored or took up a position at a vacant mooring buoy near the Olongapo seaplane ramp. Within an hour, all the Catalinas had been refueled and their crews were back on board. Anxiously, their pilots awaited orders to attack a real target. None of the men in the PBYs were comfortable floating around like ducks on a pond during the daylight hours. When a small formation of single-engine planes flew overhead at 1010, the Catalina crews grew even more nervous. At least this group was heading northward, probably back toward Aparri, Vigan, or Formosa. In a few minutes, the aircraft passed from view and tensions eased.

It came as a complete surprise when the droning sound of engines returned from the direction of the mouth of Subic Bay. In horror, navy aircrews watched as a flight of Zeros flashed in just above the glassy calm. Little blinks of light from their noses and wings were followed momentarily by small splashes on the still water, and then the sounds of dull thuds, punctuated by sledgehammer bangs, as bullets and 20-mm cannon shells ripped through the floating PBYs. Waist gunners in several of the flying boats returned fire, but it was too late. Men jumped frantically into the water as three of the fully fueled, bomb-laden aircraft caught fire. Pilots in the other planes rushed to man their nose guns. Side hatches belched puffs of smoke as gunners continued shooting at the marauding Zeros.

Undeterred, the Japanese pilots turned for another pass at the helpless PBYs. The second strafing run left two more Catalinas on fire and the rest taking on water through holes in their hulls. Burning gasoline rapidly spread across the mooring area. As the flames rose, more crewmen dived off their planes and swam through ponds of fire and choking fumes toward the shore. After a third and final run along the line of flying boats, the Zeros flew away from the area as quickly as they had appeared, leaving the last two Catalinas to sink beneath a burning sea.

Though the PBY gunners thought they might have shot down two or three of the fighters, all nine *Tainan Kokutai* A6Ms got away from Olongapo with hardly a scratch. In part, this may have been due to the fact that many of the PBY guns had been accidentally loaded with low-power practice ammunition. Lieutenant Masuzo Seto's

chutai had been thorough; VP-102's entire detachment of flying boats
was completely destroyed. Clayton Marcy had been fortunate that
only two crewmen died during the attack.[15] The death toll could have
been much higher if the Catalinas and their bombs had exploded in
the manner that many of the men feared.

OVER VIGAN, MAJOR O'DONNELL and his five B-17s had no luck at all
dropping their bombs on the Japanese fleet from high altitude. They
did not even register a near miss. No interceptors reached the
bombers—which was a relief—but Rosie O'Donnell was still taking no
chances in setting his planes down at Clark Field during the midday
hours. The Flying Fortresses headed directly back to Del Monte without stopping for fuel. It was a wise choice. Clark was bombed again
during the late morning by G3Ms from the *1st Kokutai*. If O'Donnell's
planes had landed at the base, they probably would have been
destroyed on the ground.

Following about half an hour behind O'Donnell's formation, Cecil
Combs's lone B-17 also passed over the invaders at Vigan. From the
high altitude of twenty-five thousand feet, Combs did not record any
hits on the ships during his first bombing run. After half his bombs had
fallen clear, one of the solenoids controlling the electromechanical
release mechanism jammed and caught fire. The bombardier manually
jettisoned the rest of the bombs, and the flight engineer was able to
extinguish the flames without much difficulty. However, the radio
operator was found unconscious on the floor of his compartment.
Apparently, he had gotten a kink in his breathing tube at the start of the
run and passed out from lack of oxygen. Combs made a rapid descent to
twelve thousand feet, where the fallen crewman could get enough air
to regain consciousness. With no way of knowing that O'Donnell
intended to return immediately to Mindanao, Major Combs headed for
Clark Field. When he arrived, he was surprised to find the base nearly
deserted. Combs managed to meet with Colonel Eubank, who
informed him of the new enemy landing at Legaspi.

There were several other new developments. FEAF Headquarters
had decided to bring Eubank down to its refuge at Fort McKinley. He
had been asked to step aside from command of the 19th Group to
devote his time and leadership to creating the 5th Bomber Command.
General Brereton felt this was important duty in light of the need to
prepare for the expected bomber reinforcements. Major Gibbs—
commander of the decimated 30th Squadron—was to be placed in

charge of the 19th Group. Major O'Donnell would remain in charge of the 14th Squadron, and Combs would continue to lead the 93rd. Gibbs was ordered to relocate 19th Group Headquarters to Del Monte Field so that operations from Mindanao could be closely controlled without the need to issue orders remotely from Clark Field.

Eubank instructed Combs to take the newly appointed group commander with him on his return to Del Monte. Major Gibbs declined, preferring to go out that evening on one of the B-18 shuttle flights. Instead, Major Combs agreed to take a planeless Fortress crew as passengers on the flight south. When they parted company, Eubank made it absolutely clear that he wanted Combs and O'Donnell to organize their planes for a raid on the Japanese landing at Legaspi as soon as possible. This time, coast-watchers were certain the Japanese navy had one of its aircraft carriers on station near the landing zone.

Until the 19th Group could launch an attack, the only resource available to combat Japanese invasion forces was the 24th Pursuit Group. In theory, its P-40Es could have been a formidable force against enemy ships if each could be equipped with the five-hundred-pound bomb it was capable of carrying. Unfortunately, the Philippine Air Depot had never received any of the required bomb racks. In fact, the squadrons possessed only a handful of fittings needed to attach smaller bombs to the wings. With those, the P-40s could carry a maximum load of six thirty-pound antipersonnel bombs. That type of fragmentation bomb would have little effect on a warship or transport. But because most early-production P-40Es were not modified to accept wing racks, very few 24th Group Warhawks could carry bombs of any type.[16]

In an uncharacteristically bold move, Major Grover quietly authorized an "armed reconnaissance" of the Legaspi railhead and airfield by two aircraft from the pool at Nichols Field. This was done despite General Brereton's new orders prohibiting strafing attacks. One of these P-40Es, flown by Grant Mahony, was fitted with a load of thirty-pound bombs to use in case the Japanese had landed any aircraft on the airstrip or congregated any troops around the Legaspi train station. The other plane, piloted by Bob Hanson, could not carry any bombs but would be available to cover Mahony should he decide to attack. Given his combative personality, it was a foregone conclusion that Mahony would attack.

It turned out that there were no planes on the Legaspi airfield, so Mahony bombed and strafed the railway facilities until his ammunition was exhausted. Pulling up, he planned to return to Nichols and make his report. Hanson was not content to let his roommate "have all the fun." He radioed for Mahony to wait while he did some strafing of his own. After shooting at enemy troops and equipment along the runway, Hanson strafed and buzzed a number of landing barges, forcing their occupants to jump over the sides. Moving farther away from shore, toward the transports, he spotted a four-engine flying boat that was just getting airborne. Pouncing on this, he fired until it splashed back down into the water.[17] Hanson roared back across the wave-tops toward the beach, shooting at a destroyer until his guns ran out of bullets. He successfully skirted heavy antiaircraft fire from other warships to join with Mahony on the flight back to Manila. For his single-handed disruption of so many enemy landing activities while under fire, Lieutenant Hanson was awarded the Distinguished Flying Cross.

December 13

The rain clouds that had been drenching the central Philippine islands for several days finally drifted over northern Mindanao. Cecil Combs made his return flight from Clark Field through the worst of this weather and had difficulty finding the Del Monte airstrip in the night-time downpour. After circling the area a few times, he finally spotted the dimly lit marker signals and landed safely on the soggy field.

Major Combs immediately ventured over to Major O'Donnell's tent to relay the latest information and instructions from Colonel Eubank. He was enthusiastic in his presentation of Eubank's plan to hit the Japanese carrier task force at Legaspi. O'Donnell was skeptical. After all, no previous carrier sightings had materialized into tangible targets. He was not anxious to chase apparitions, and he was tired of trying to bomb moving ships. Besides, most of the B-17s at Del Monte were in poor mechanical shape. In fact, while Combs was still flying back from Luzon, O'Donnell requested that FEAF Headquarters allow him to take all the bombers back to Australia for servicing. As the two majors debated the course of action—while watching mechanics struggling to work by lantern and flashlight in a pelting rain—Emmett O'Donnell became even more convinced that Del Monte was no place to house the Flying Fortresses. In deference to the fact that Major Gibbs had been designated as 19th Group commander, O'Donnell decided to await Gibbs's arrival rather than concluding his disagreement with Combs.

Anxious to take on his new command at Del Monte, David Gibbs departed from Clark Field at 1800 on the evening of December 12 in a B-18 fully loaded with men and parts. A number of fellow officers at the base tried to dissuade him from taking off, knowing that the old plane would run into severe storms before it got even halfway to Mindanao. The young major was an expert pilot, not intimidated by the weather; he would head south anyway.

Major Gibbs would have done well to wait for better flying conditions. By midnight, when the plane had not reached Del Monte—but would have exhausted its fuel supply—David Gibbs and his passengers were officially posted as "missing." The fate of his crew would remain unknown for some time, but wreckage of the B-18 was eventually found near a high mountain peak on the island of Negros; there were no survivors.[18]

Blackout conditions were nearly as hazardous on the ground. During his drive to join General Brereton at Fort McKinley, Colonel Eubank was injured in a car accident. With a broken wrist and two sprained ankles, he found himself laid up at Sternberg Hospital in Manila.[19]

The two unrelated twists of fate left Emmett O'Donnell as the senior Bomber Command officer. Much to O'Donnell's dismay, General Brereton decided to recall him to Luzon immediately to work with the FEAF staff and to supervise the evacuation of equipment and personnel from Clark. Major Walsh would be sent to Del Monte to take charge of flight operations and mission planning for the Mindanao-based Fortresses.

When it was apparent that the missing Major Gibbs would not reach Del Monte anytime soon, Major O'Donnell decided on a compromise with Major Combs: two planes—one from each squadron—would be sent to survey the Legaspi area. If they found a worthy target, a maximum-effort bombing strike would be launched from Mindanao. At 0545 Lieutenant Bill Bohnaker and Lieutenant Weldon Smith took off from Del Monte and headed north. The mission was to be strictly one of reconnaissance; the Fortresses carried no bombs and were specifically instructed not to attack any ships they might find.

OBSERVING THE 24TH PURSUIT GROUP'S newly instituted daily reconnaissance routine, three P-40s left their fields on Luzon at dawn to conduct single-plane scouting missions. One of these fighters flew southeast from Nichols Field to the invasion site at Legaspi. The other two departed from Clark and headed separately toward the enemy landing zones in the north.

In an uneventful mission, 1st Lieutenant Marshall Anderson scanned the coast from Vigan south, as far as Iba. He noted only two transports, both very near shore at Vigan.[20] The rest of the enemy fleet had already departed to prepare for its next mission. Japan's military leaders were on a tight schedule and wasting no time.

The pilot of the P-40 detailed to survey the Legaspi landing zone reported spotting a cruiser, several destroyers, and seven other ships of an unknown type. In addition, he confirmed the coast-watcher's sighting of an aircraft carrier.[21] The prime target had finally appeared, but no planes were available to attack it. The news must have been very frustrating to Brereton. Officers at FEAF Headquarters did not know that O'Donnell had dispatched a pair of B-17s to investigate— which would have pleased them until they found out that the two Fortresses carried no bombs.

Walt Coss did not get the opportunity to report what he had seen on his mission. Coss traveled alone above the clouds until he was certain he had overflown Aparri, and then turned south and descended through the opaque layer. He finally emerged a few thousand feet above the sea. Staying close underneath the cloudbank—dodging in and out of its cover every few minutes—Lieutenant Coss made his way toward the shore and across the enemy-occupied airfield. After heading up the Cagayan River for about ten miles, he fatefully dropped out of the covering moisture directly in front of two Japanese fighters. At nearly point-blank range, one of the Ki-27 pilots fired reflexively. Though Coss had already started to dive away, the engine in his P-40 was mortally wounded by a lucky shot. The Allison ran roughly for a few minutes before quitting altogether. With his canopy open and seatbelt unfastened, Walt Coss rolled the stricken fighter onto its back and pushed himself out of the cockpit. He fell freely for a few moments and then pulled the ripcord. By the time his parachute canopy billowed, the young pilot barely had a chance to catch a breath before he plunged into the middle of the river.

The Japanese army pilots had no intention of letting the downed American get away. In contrast to the chivalry typically demonstrated by IJN fliers, JAAF airmen often did their best to actually kill their opponents. It was an ingrained lesson of the Nomonhan fighting that elimination of experienced enemy pilots had greater impact on the outcome of an air campaign than did destruction of aircraft. The two fighters made several passes to strafe the area around the floating parachute. Coss was able to free himself from the dragging harness to dive under the water during each pass—a move that saved his life. Eventually, the Japanese gave up and turned north toward Aparri. Wet and angry, but relieved to be unhurt, Lieutenant Coss swam toward the riverbank. It would take him more than a week of difficult travel to make it back to Clark Field.

The two surviving P-40s cautiously made their way home as Lieutenant Bohnaker's B-17 neared Legaspi. Bohnaker continued his descent down to about two thousand feet. The clouds suddenly faded away to reveal an aircraft carrier directly below the Flying Fortress. The excited army airmen got an unexpectedly close-up view of numerous single-engine planes lining the deck. Caught completely by surprise, dozens of terrified Japanese crewmen rushed to take cover. For Bohnaker, this must have been the ultimate disappointment— being unable to attack while confronted with the proverbial chance-of-a-lifetime target. Churning with an emotional mixture of elation at the discovery of such a significant warship, disgust at not being able to inflict damage on it, and fear of interception by an angry hornet's nest of fighters, the American bomber crew circled around once and headed back toward Mindanao at full speed. Knowing their mission was successfully accomplished, or even suspecting that they had scared the daylights out of the enemy sailors, could hardly equal the satisfaction the crew would have felt if they had dropped even one bomb on the crowded flight deck of Ryujo.

WHILE THE ARMY BOMBER CREW had its adventure above the sea, the U.S. Navy flight crews rested with their camouflage-covered flying boats, nestled alongside the southern shore of Laguna de Bay near Los Baños. By this time, the men who had lost their planes at Olongapo had been trucked down to join their squadron-mates. Two crews from Olongapo had been detached from the motor convoy to pick up a pair of PBYs from the Sangley Point service hangar. Before long, word spread that Admiral Hart had ordered Captain Wagner to immediately evacuate PatWing-10 to Java. Hart was sending all four seaplane tenders—*Langley, Childs, Preston,* and *Heron*—south to Soerabaja.

THE BRITISH WERE HAVING DIFFICULTY deciding how best to use the remnants of their squadrons in Singapore. The JAAF had been bombing in the vicinity of Georgetown, on Penang Island, and the adjoining peninsula city of Butterworth for two days without interference. As the tempo of these raids increased, Air Chief Marshal Brooke-Popham conceded that some fighter support should be provided for the protection of Penang, because that was where General Percival expected to anchor his ground defense. In particular, it was important to keep Japanese tactical aircraft from causing critical damage to British ground units while they were in the process of setting up their positions. The Air Headquarters decision of December 11 that removed all combat aircraft from Malayan bases was abruptly reversed on December 13. This time the bombers would remain at airfields in Singapore, but the Australian Buffalo squadrons would be sent north.

RAAF No. 453 Squadron was instructed to send sixteen Buffaloes up to Malaya as soon as possible. Because the airfields at Penang and Butterworth were considered far too vulnerable to enemy air action, it was decided that the fighters should be based at Ipoh. There, they could be serviced by the ground staff of RAAF No. 21 Squadron, without the distraction of nearly constant alerts. The two forward bases would still be used for rearmament, refueling, and emergency landings.

The first flight of three Buffaloes dispatched from Sembawang arrived at Butterworth shortly after 0800. Although they had orders to refuel and fly a reconnaissance over southern Siam, Flight Lieutenant Richard "Doug" Vanderfield and his wingmen, Sergeants Vivian "Wild Bill" Collyer and Malcolm "Mac" Read, were barely able to top off their tanks before being sent up to intercept an enemy bomber formation. The Georgetown port facilities on nearby Penang Island were under attack by a mixed group of 75th Sentai Ki-48s and 71st Chutai Ki-51s.

As soon as he left the runway, Lieutenant Vanderfield discovered his landing gear would not retract. The intrepid Australian charged his Buffalo directly at a flight of three Ki-48s anyway. After a short stream of fire from his four heavy machine guns, the lead bomber exploded in a cascading splash of burning fuel and debris. Responding to this, six Ki-51s jettisoned their bombs and dived to challenge the Buffaloes. A swirling dogfight ensued as Collyer and Read broke away to defend their flight leader from the nimble dive-bombers. Working together, the two sergeants dropped one Ki-51 as it was lining up on Vanderfield's tail. They also shot up a second plane, which they last saw streaming black smoke as it headed toward the coast. By this time, Mac Read's plane had been thoroughly filled with holes, so the pair descended for a landing and quick inspection at Butterworth. Their intervention provided enough distraction to allow Vanderfield to continue his chase after the fleeing twin-engine bombers without further harassment from the Ki-51s. One of the two Ki-48s fell to his guns; though it did not disintegrate in a spectacular fireball like the first victim, it trailed a smoky path all the way down into the jungle below.[22] Unable to catch any other bombers, Vanderfield turned around and headed to Ipoh for repairs.

The second flight of Buffaloes traveling to Malaya that day ran into heavy weather within half an hour of its departure from Sembawang. Those three planes, led by RAF Wing Commander Leonard Neale, had been unable to climb over the towering clouds and continued flying west in an attempt to skirt around them. Neale, a senior officer and former flight instructor, was on his way to take command of the air station at Ipoh. Despite extensive flying experience, he could not manage to penetrate the storm before his wingmen's fuel tanks began to run dry.

Pilot Officer Thomas "Tom" Livesey finally decided to drop out of formation to make a landing in a large field. The other two pilots circled to follow their comrade. From altitude, the area appeared flat and dry. Livesey realized he was landing in a rice paddy only when spray from his lowered wheels showered the fighter with water just before its landing gear settled into the mud. By then, it was too late to take action. He could only cut the power and hope for the best. The wheels stuck fast, abruptly tipping the Buffalo over onto its back. Tom Livesey was hurt, but conscious.

Wincing with the pain caused by several fractured ribs, he crawled out from under his fighter just in time to see Neale and Pilot Officer David Brown—of the Royal New Zealand Air Force—approaching to land in the same field. Livesey was in no condition to wave them off. Both Buffaloes came in with their wheels up after the pilots saw what happened when Livesey attempted to land. However, neither man expected that their belly-landing fighters could skim so far across the surface of the paddy. Like stones skipping across a pond, both planes skidded and bounced into the adjoining forest. The results were fatal. Neale's Buffalo caught its wingtip on a large tree trunk and flipped over. It was destroyed in a sudden, flaming blast before the pilot could even think of getting out. Brown's aircraft did not strike any trees, but it did catch fire. So entangled in jungle undergrowth that egress from the cockpit was impossible, the Buffalo became a smoldering coffin.

Traumatized, Pilot Officer Livesey wandered away from the scene. Eventually, he encountered some natives who escorted him to a local police official. The policeman promptly arrested the mud-covered, wounded Australian and held him until a district officer finally arrived to intercede. The young flier was hardly expecting to be liberated by a Dutchman. Apparently, Neale had gotten so disoriented in making repetitive turns to avoid the storm that his flight had landed near Pakan Baroe on the island of Sumatra—a course nearly 90 degrees off its intended heading.

The third flight, consisting of five Buffaloes squired by Flight Lieutenant Vigors, arrived at Ipoh shortly before 1100. As soon as the fighters refueled, they took off in company with Flight Lieutenant Vanderfield. Vanderfield's undercarriage again refused to retract. This time, he turned back to Ipoh for additional repairs while Tim Vigors led the rest of the planes on toward the Penang area, landing at Butterworth around noon.

The four Australians and their British flight leader did not have to wait long for action. Vigors and Sergeant Matthew "Matt" O'Mara had barely topped off their tanks before the red-alert flag was hoisted. As Vigors and O'Mara ran for their Buffaloes, Vigors yelled for the other three pilots to take off as soon as the ground crews had finished refueling. The Battle of Britain veteran quickly hopped into the cockpit of his Brewster, racing it down the runway with O'Mara following close behind.

Once airborne, Tim Vigors spotted a swarm of about thirty enemy fighters over Penang Island. He radioed for O'Mara to cover his tail and then lanced into the center of the hornet's nest. The sudden move had the intended effect; the Japanese diverted their attention from the assigned target in order to chase down the two Buffaloes. Ki-27s buzzed around furiously as the two Australian fighters twisted and turned to stay out of a hail of Japanese bullets. Vigors thought he had shot up at least two of the nimble enemy fighters.[23]

Pleased with that success, the former Spitfire pilot realized—too late—that he had seriously underestimated the Japanese planes' ability to outmaneuver his heavier, U.S.-built fighter. One of the Nakajimas turned inside the path of Vigors's sharpest bank and sent a single burst of gunfire into the most vulnerable part of the Buffalo, its fuel tank. Located in the wing structure just below the pilot's feet, the punctured container exploded in flames, seriously burning Vigors before he could jump free of the falling aircraft. In considerable pain from his burns, he managed to survive several strafing passes by JAAF fighters as he floated earthward in his parachute toward a rough landing on the mountainous western side of Penang Island. Ignoring his injuries as much as possible, he hiked for several days across the island, caught a ferry to Butterworth, and hitched a ride to Singapore, where he could receive proper medical care.

Matt O'Mara may not have been successful in protecting his flight leader, but he managed to save his own aircraft by weaving through the clouds until his pursuers gave up the chase. The Buffalo had taken heavy damage, so sergeant O'Mara elected to force-land it on an emergency field at Kuala Kangsar, some ten miles northwest of Ipoh.

Flight Lieutenant Bert Grace, the third pilot to take off from Butterworth, encountered angry Japanese fighters before he had even climbed a thousand feet. Just seconds after leaving the ground, Grace banked his Buffalo into a hard turn and shot at one of the Ki-27s, claiming a probable victory.[24] He had not had time to notice another Japanese fighter sliding onto his tail. In moments, the Japanese plane shot up the Buffalo. Bullets struck all around the cockpit, narrowly missing the startled Australian. Convinced that he did not stand a chance of surviving if he stuck around Butterworth, Grace dived for the deck and raced south toward Ipoh.

Pilot Officer Geoff Angus and Sergeant Ron Oelrich had barely gotten off the ground when they were bounced by several flights of Ki-27s that descended to chase Flight Lieutenant Grace. Angus was hit by one three-plane element, and then another, in rapid succession. His shot-up Buffalo belly-landed in a nearby rice paddy. Angus had been wounded by a bullet in one ankle, had banged his head on the gunsight, but still managed to get out of the aircraft fast enough to avoid several follow-up strafing runs by the victorious Japanese. As Angus watched their bullets ripping apart his downed Brewster, he observed his wingman frantically flying back and forth across the airfield, seemingly disoriented. Trapped between a swarm of enemy fighters and the friendly fire arcing up from Butterworth's antiaircraft defenses, Ron Oelrich eventually fell victim to the hailstorm of bullets and crashed into the jungle. Although the wreckage of his Buffalo was only a short distance from the base, the sergeant's body could not be extricated from the cockpit until the following day.

By the time the last five Buffaloes of RAAF No. 453 Squadron arrived at Ipoh, it was mid-afternoon and Japanese raids in the Penang area were finished for the day.

THE BEECHCRAFT MODEL 18 WAS never intended for service in a combat zone. It had been designed as a speedy, twin-engine, six-passenger

executive transport. In that role it excelled; many are still in use for that
purpose today. Usually, one would not expect such a plane to fare well
under a concerted attack by cannon-armed fighters. Then again, there
was nothing usual about the pilot flying this particular Beechcraft on its
journey from Del Monte Field to Manila. Paul Gunn had chosen the
timing of his return flight carefully. He wanted to leave early enough to
avoid evening storms over the central islands of the Philippines but did
not want to be near Legaspi during daylight hours. Of course, he could
not have guessed that the Japanese navy would select this afternoon to
dispatch its first fighter reconnaissance to Cebu City.

As Captain Gunn approached the southern coast of the island of
Cebu, three Zeros dived on his prized Beechcraft, peppering it with
holes in their first pass. If the Japanese pilots figured they had an easy
kill, they must have been surprised when their quarry skidded smartly
away from the line of fire and screamed down to the floor of the jungle
valley below. The men flying the A6Ms had a great deal of difficulty
trying to follow the Beechcraft's zigzagging, 250-mile-per-hour pace
through the rough terrain. Flying like a stunt pilot at "grass level"
within the canyon, Gunn was able to keep the Zeros from lining up
for any other effective shots at his plane. As their fuel ran low, the
Japanese fighters eventually gave up the pursuit and pulled up into the
darkening skies.

For Captain Gunn the war with Japan was now a personal matter.
Fuming at the damage his aircraft had taken, he stayed on the deck
until he reached the northwest coast of Cebu; he then headed north
across the Visayan Sea. His troubles were hardly over. While making
a landing approach toward the improvised Grace Park Cemetery
airstrip, he inadvertently passed over the PAAC base at Zablan Field.
Unable to flash proper recognition signals because its landing lights
had been shot out, the Beechcraft attracted the full attention of
Filipino antiaircraft gunners. In darkness, they had little choice but to
assume the twin-engine aircraft was an enemy bomber. After all,
most of the planes flying over Luzon at that point bore Japanese
markings. Unfortunately, one gun crew's aim was true; a short burst
of tracer fire reached up for the low-flying aircraft, ripping into it from
nose to tail. Paul Gunn's Beech 18 was mortally wounded this time,
but somehow the master pilot managed to nurse it along just far
enough to execute an emergency wheels-up landing at the edge of
Nichols Field. Gunn chose this airfield because any sort of crash at
Grace Park would have taken his tiny personal base out of action.

December 14

It was still dark as runners began to stumble along the southern shoreline of Laguna de Bay searching for the locations of nine heavily camouflaged PBYs. Captain Wagner was anxious to get his flying boats on their way south before the Japanese bombing campaign resumed at dawn. Pulled up alongside the water's edge, covered with tree branches and netting, the planes were as difficult to spot from the ground as from the air. Consequently, messengers managed to deliver movement orders to only six of the flight crews. By 0430 pilots who actually received instructions were cranking up their engines. They were to fly to Dansalan, on the shore of Lake Lanao, high in the mountains of Mindanao, to the west of Del Monte. Each PBY would carry a maximum load: twelve-hundred gallons of fuel, four five-hundred-pound bombs, and nine men with all of their personal gear. The planes and crews were not expected to return to Luzon anytime soon.

Most of the navy airmen were relieved to be heading for Mindanao. As the pace of enemy air attacks continued to escalate, Catalina crews were increasingly aware of their vulnerability on Luzon. Amazingly, they harbored no fear of attacking Japanese warships using their plodding flying boats, but servicing their craft under a constant threat of attack was demoralizing. None of the aviators wanted any repetition of the Olongapo disaster.

Five PBYs got off the water without difficulty, but Lieutenant John Hyland and his copilot, Ensign Hawk Barrett, were unable to coax theirs into the air. For some reason, the left engine was not developing full power. After a two-mile run, the pair tried to pull the plane up. They only succeeded in having it smack back down into the water. The shock of that rough landing dislocated a cowl flap, which delayed their next takeoff attempt while a mechanic was forced to climb onto the wing to remove the dangling piece of aluminum. Hyland and Barrett only separated the heavy plane from the surface of the lake by dropping one of the unarmed bombs during their takeoff run. It was a scary experience to be sure—certainly a procedure they had never practiced—but the sudden removal of weight was enough to spur the reluctant Catalina to flight. With a sigh of relief, they cleared the tree line at the shore and climbed southward, slowly leaving Luzon behind.

GRANT MAHONY LEFT NICHOLS FIELD AT DAWN. Pointing the nose of his P-40 south, he settled in for a long, lonely courier flight to Mindanao.

At the least, this solo trip to Del Monte would give Mahony some desperately needed time for reflection. That morning he was trying to adjust to the loss of his good friend Bob Hanson, who had been killed the previous afternoon when Japanese navy bombers had carpeted Nichols with fragmentation bombs. From this day forward, like many other men in the Philippines, Mahony would pursue the battle with Japan as if it were his own personal vendetta.

ABOVE MALAYA, five Buffaloes roared northward across the emerald canopy of jungle, quickly closing the distance between Ipoh and Alor Star. Dense cloud cover and turbulence in the vicinity between Butterworth and Sungei Patani caused the formation to spread apart. Flying Officer Montefiore and Sergeant Stanley Scrimgeour elected to return to Ipoh. Flight Lieutenant White was able to lead Sergeants Greg Board and Geoffrey Seagoe to a point south of Alor Star where a large enemy motor convoy was spotted.

The three Australians immediately swooped in to attack, strafing up and down the column until they saw other planes approaching. Swinging north to intercept, Alan White led the charge toward what the trio thought was a formation of fighters. Latching onto the tail of one of those Japanese planes, he pulled his Buffalo in close, to fire with maximum effect. The enemy aircraft were actually Ki-51 dive-bombers of the 27th Sentai. A gunner in the rear cockpit of the target fired back, hitting the Buffalo squarely and apparently killing the young Australian. White and his fighter plummeted into the jungle below. In separate combats, Greg Board claimed destruction of one "fighter," while Geoff Seagoe was sure he had damaged another.[25] Having chased all the other Japanese planes from the area, this duo expended the rest of their ammunition in another strafing run. In that, they lingered too long; antiaircraft fire finally hit the mark. An exploding shell struck Seagoe's Buffalo and tore a gash in his shoulder. Despite this wound, Seagoe was able to follow Board in safe return to Ipoh.

AT DEL MONTE FIELD, the morning of December 14 was a busy one, filled with preparations for a six-plane raid on the Legaspi invasion fleet. The bomber crews were excited to think that a Japanese aircraft carrier could be their prize. This time they would be heading out with 600-pound bombs that could do some real damage if they hit a ship. The mission plan called for the Fortresses to fly in formation to a rendezvous twenty-five thousand feet above Catanduanes Island, where they would split into two flights of three planes each before making a final thirty-five-mile run to the target area. These flights would converge on Legaspi from opposite directions, at the same time, in order to throw off enemy gunners and any fighters that might intercept them.

At 1000 Lieutenant Jim Connally lined up his B-17C on the runway and advanced the throttles to takeoff power. Halfway down the strip a tire blew, dropping one wingtip into the dirt. Clearing Lieutenant Connally's aircraft out of the way delayed departure of the others by nearly an hour. Even with that extra time, no additional B-17s could be readied to take its place. Only five would proceed to Legaspi, with Lieutenant "Shorty" Wheless leading the way.

Fate was not on their side. About one hundred miles into the flight, the small formation entered a severe storm front gathered above and between the islands of Cebu and Leyte. In this heavy weather, one of Lieutenant Wheless's engines quit. Unable to continue his climb, he dropped out of sight as he tried desperately to restart the failing Cyclone. Before the others made it past the turbulent cloudbanks, Lieutenants Walter Ford and Lee Coats also experienced engine problems; their two Fortresses turned directly back to Mindanao. Unknown to Lieutenants Vandevanter and Adams, who continued toward the target together, Wheless eventually regained use of his engine and continued on toward Legaspi at a somewhat lower altitude.

As planned—and not much was going as planned those days—when Elliot Vandevanter and Jack Adams passed Catanduanes Island, they separated and began their descents toward Legaspi. While passing through the eighteen-thousand-foot mark, Lieutenant Adams's bombardier spotted the fleet. No aircraft carrier was in sight, so Adams and his copilot, 2nd Lieutenant Bill Railing, lined up on a row of transports. They did not have time to observe any results. In less than a minute, five Zeros were approaching from dead astern.[26] Adams guided his large bomber in a powered dive to the southwest, in the direction of a friendly cloudbank. The A6Ms, climbing at full throttle from their patrol position over the Legaspi airstrip, won the race. In a single pass, the two leading Mitsubishis shot out both engines on the left side of the Fortress and wounded the navigator, 2nd Lieutenant Harry Schreiber, and one gunner, radio operator Sergeant Anthony Jumia Jr.

The crippled bomber, chased down to an altitude of about four thousand feet, continued due south across the Sibuyan Sea toward the island of Masbate with one persistent A6M in tow.[27] Adams intended to set the Boeing down on a beach but found the coastline too rocky.

Turning inland, he spotted a rice paddy surrounded by a tall stand of trees. Skillfully, he clipped the top of the tree line just as he shut off the two remaining engines. Pulling the control wheel all the way back, Adams was able to stall the large plane just above the surface of the paddy. With a great thud, his bomber flopped on its belly and stopped before crashing into any of the trees at the other end of the small field. Lieutenants Schreiber and Adams climbed quickly out of the top hatch of the cockpit, hitting the ground just as the shadowing A6M made its parting shot. Approaching parallel to the wing of the B-17, the Japanese plane strafed the downed bomber. Bill Railing, stunned from the hard landing, remained in the cockpit but was not hit by any of the bullets that raked across the plane. As the Zero pulled up and disappeared, the other men exited from the tail section through the cabin door. They stumbled out of the bomber just in time to face a welcoming party of angry Filipino farmers swinging large bolo knives. As the Masbate natives came to understand that the downed airmen were American, they helped make a stretcher for the wounded Sergeant Jumia and eagerly escorted the crew to a local doctor. Despite receiving help from many people, Adams and his crew would take almost a month to get back to the Del Monte airstrip on Mindanao.

Lieutenant Vandevanter was able to take advantage of the distraction afforded by Adams's attack. Bombing from twenty-one thousand feet, his crew made several unmolested passes over the transports unloading at Legaspi.

Lieutenant Wheless flew straight in toward Legaspi at about 9,500 feet. Coming in more than fifteen minutes after Vandevanter and Adams, his low-flying B-17 drew the attention of the four Zeros that elected not to follow Adams. Wheless dropped all eight of his 600-pound bombs in train across the half-dozen transports but did not bother to check for results. The A6Ms were already firing at his plane, with bullets and cannon ripping holes through every surface. Private 1st Class William Killin, the radio operator manning the "bathtub" gun position beneath the fuselage, was struck in the head and killed instantly. The other three gunners—Staff Sergeant John Gootee, Sergeant Russell Brown, and Corporal Willy Williams—were also hit. Williams had taken a 20-mm cannon round in his thigh and was in serious trouble. Gootee and Brown had each taken small bullets in their right wrists. The bombardier and navigator, Sergeant Robert Schlotte and 2nd Lieutenant William Meenaugh, hurried aft to relieve the wounded men. Meenaugh pulled Killin's decapitated corpse from the belly position but found the twin .50-calibers inoperative; the firing mechanism was apparently jammed by the explosion of the cannon shell. Gootee and Schlotte fired the waist guns as the four Japanese fighters made repeated passes at the damaged Fortress.

Each time the fighters bored in from astern to point-blank range, they would pull up nearly beside the B-17, bank on one wing, roll inverted, and dive away smoking. The men were certain they had shot down at least seven of the Zeros before their waist guns finally jammed from excessive use. The smoke, however, was no indicator of damage; the same four A6Ms pursued Wheless for nearly seventy-five miles before their ammunition ran out. It is possible some of the Japanese planes were damaged, but none were lost, and no enemy pilots were injured.[28]

Lieutenant Wheless was hardly home free. In the half-hour battle, his left engine had been shot out, all of his fuel tanks had been holed, seven of eleven control cables were severed, the radio had taken a cannon hit, all the oxygen tanks had been blown up, both main tires were cut to ribbons, and the tail wheel had been completely shot away. Somehow, streaming fuel and oil all the way, Shorty Wheless managed to keep the plane in the air for another two hours—long enough to bring it back to the north shore of Mindanao. He knew it would never climb to the altitude necessary for a landing at Del Monte, but he figured a controlled crash on the short, barricaded airstrip at Cagayan del Oro would be good enough. With the gear down, but only shredded rubber on its wheels, the big Boeing gouged two furrows down the runway until the metal hubs locked. The B-17 rocked forward—straight up on its nose—crushing the empty compartment in front of the cockpit. Despite this rough landing, none of the men received further injury. With more than a thousand bullet holes scarring virtually every surface inside and out, the Fortress had proved to Wheless and his men that it could take everything the Japanese could throw at it and still come home.

Sadly, the only result noted for this pitifully small raid on the Japanese fleet was a probable near miss. Although the mission was essentially a failure, Lieutenant Vandevanter received a Distinguished Flying Cross for his effort. General MacArthur awarded Lieutenants Adams and Wheless the even more prestigious Distinguished Service Cross. The Flying Fortress earned the undying admiration of all the airmen from the 19th Bombardment Group for its ability to absorb punishment and protect its crews. The amazing performance of the

B-17 was immortalized in an evening speech by President Franklin Roosevelt, who told the country a sensational story of U.S. servicemen doing their duty and taking destruction to the enemy. That the three Japanese transports claimed sunk in this speech were never even damaged, or that the more than a dozen enemy fighters alleged to have been shot down did not fall, in no way diminishes this tale of aircrew bravery—which was very real indeed.

HEADING IN THE OPPOSITE DIRECTION of Lieutenant Wheless, Grant Mahony was returning to Luzon in his P-40E. He independently decided to take a small detour over Legaspi, arriving at about 1630. Coming in at around thirteen thousand feet, he dived to strafe the radio station. As Japanese troops in the vicinity scattered wildly, Mahony noticed antiaircraft fire arcing up at him from the airfield. Deciding to investigate, he noted a number of bombers, a transport, and a handful of fighters lining the runway. Above him, four Zeros were heading straight down in his direction. Mahony figured he had time for just one pass. He would make it an effective one; his six heavy guns hammered a path through the standing aircraft, seriously damaging two *Tainan Kokutai* A6Ms and five *Takao Kokutai* G4M bombers.[29] Before he could finish, the diving Zeros were on his tail. Lieutenant Mahony tried every maneuver he knew in an effort to elude his pursuers. As experienced as he was, all his aerobatics failed to shake them. Realizing his plane was completely outmatched, he headed for nearby Mount Mayon at full speed.

The Japanese planes split up; two chased him, and two headed around the eight-thousand-foot volcano in the opposite direction. As Mahony banked around the other side, all five planes met in a frenzy of tracers. He aimed straight for his onrushing adversaries in a dangerous game of "chicken." The Japanese pilots were not sure whether they were firing at the American or at each other. Even this ploy failed to shake Mahony's pursuers, but he grasped an opportunity to escape. Making one more revolution around the mountain, he took advantage of the momentary confusion caused by the closing Zeros to dive away to treetop level. With just enough of a head start, his P-40 raced away toward Nichols Field.

IN WESTERN MALAYA, the afternoon of December 14 had been fairly uneventful. Though Japanese air raids on the British forward positions continued, no air-to-air combat occurred. Flying Officer

Montefiore of RAAF No. 21 Squadron led a three-plane attack on Japanese transportation convoys but had to abort this mission due to mechanical trouble with his Buffalo's engine. His wingmen, Flying Officer Fred Leigh-Bowes and Sergeant Jim Austin from No. 453 Squadron, continued on, making several successful runs against trucks and armored vehicles before returning to Ipoh. At the end of the day, the Australian fighter pilots received a welcome present when three more Buffaloes landed at the airfield. It was a testament to the mechanical aptitude of the service personnel at Butterworth that these formerly unserviceable fighters had been restored to duty. Despite air raids and other distractions, the intrepid mechanics had patched the Brewsters together. The arrival of these planes was unexpected; they were flown south by pilot volunteers from RAF 62 Squadron—none of whom had ever been in the cockpit of a Buffalo before this flight.

CHAPTER 10

Exodus

December 15–21, 1941

One week of hard fighting against the Japanese air forces had decimated U.S., British, and Australian air units in the Far East. More than 60 percent of all Allied combat aircraft had been completely destroyed.[1] Most remaining planes had been damaged in some way. The best mechanics in the world—with appropriate tools, adequate facilities, and access to spare parts—would have had trouble keeping pace with such losses. As it was, spare parts were almost nonexistent, and many of the tools and mechanics had been spread across hundreds of miles of territory during hasty evacuations. Replacements were desperately needed, but deploying the required quantities of airplanes halfway around the world was a logistics challenge of the greatest magnitude.

Deliveries of additional P-40s from the United States to the Philippines had been suspended upon the outbreak of hostilities, although nearly a hundred Curtiss fighters were already crated for shipment to the Far East. The delay meant that very few fighters could be sent to Australia before the end of the year. Sailing merchant ships to the Philippines was out of the question. With Japan in solid control of the skies, there was no place ships could safely unload without fear of an attack by Japanese air forces. The convoy carrying the fifty-two dive-bombers for the 27th Bomb Group, and eighteen P-40s for the 35th Pursuit Group, was ordered to alter course for Brisbane, Australia, instead of the Philippines. It would be another week before the ships arrived there. After they were unloaded, the planes—all crated—would have to be assembled in Australia and then flown for several thousand miles to bases in the Philippines. Because the A-24s and P-40s were capable of only short-range flights, many stops would have to be made along the way; each landing at an underdeveloped field increasing the risk of aircraft loss or damage. If the dive-bombers and fighters made it to their destination in one piece, they would immediately require maintenance service before they could be used in combat. It was a project that would have been difficult under the best of conditions. Under wartime conditions—with the clock running out of time for any defense of the Philippines—it was an impossible task. Still, there was no choice but to attempt it.

On December 15, General MacArthur forwarded to the War Department an urgent request for an additional ten pursuit squadrons, two hundred replacement pursuit aircraft for existing units, and fifty additional dive-bombers—which he hoped could be delivered by navy aircraft carriers. Although President Roosevelt personally directed that every effort should be made to honor these requests, the only commitment was for a delivery of sixty-five Boeing B-17Es and fifteen Consolidated LB-30 Liberators to Brereton's FEAF as soon as possible—which did not mean right away.[2] The plan for moving these eighty bombers to the Philippines was officially referred to as Project X and was shrouded in strictest secrecy.

Less mystery was attached to British plans to supply aircraft to Singapore. Delivering equipment there by sea was still a possibility, but finding aircraft to ship to the Far East was a problem. Aircraft production in Great Britain was still unable to meet requirements for the European theater. It was fairly clear that any fighters to replace the lost Buffaloes could only come from aircraft previously allocated to the defense of the Middle East. Two wings of Hawker Hurricanes already in transit to Egypt would be redirected on an emergency priority basis to the Far East. It was assumed that this force of more than a hundred fighters and their RAF pilots would be enough to protect the bastion at Singapore from the Japanese. After all, the Hurricane was considered the most maneuverable of all European fighter planes, and its top speed of 335 miles per hour was thought to match that of a Mitsubishi Zero. The greatest concern seemed to be how and when these planes could be delivered to the other side of the globe.

Crated Hurricanes would have to sail all the way through the South Atlantic, around the cape of South Africa, and across the Indian Ocean—a voyage that would require nearly a month to complete. To provide additional bombers for Commonwealth forces in the Far East, several sources would be tapped. A prewar Australian order for fifty-two Lockheed Hudsons was on the seas at the outbreak of hostilities. In several different shipments, these planes would arrive at Melbourne throughout the month of December. Because they needed some assembly in order to be combat ready, it was unlikely that any new Hudsons could be transferred to Singapore before January. To fill in the gap, RAF leadership decided to strip a couple of Blenheim squadrons from the Middle East. Their operational crews would ferry those planes to Singapore via India. Another fifty-two RAF Coastal Command Hudsons could be reassigned from Lend-Lease inventory and flown to the Far East from England, but that process would take even more time. And time was running out quickly.

IN MALAYA, EARLY-MORNING ACTIVITIES on December 15 would highlight the cost of sending fighters from the rear area to the front line. At dawn Squadron Leader Allshorn took off from Sembawang in a new Buffalo. Six members of his RAAF No. 21 Squadron trailed behind as he left Singapore Island and headed north across the Malayan Peninsula toward Ipoh. As had been the case with previous flights, stormy weather blocked the way. Allshorn and Flight Lieutenant Kinninmont skirted around the rough air, to the west, swinging out over the coast into the Strait of Malacca. Flying Officer Hooper and four other pilots headed back to Sembawang. Hooper became separated from the rest of the flight and eventually decided to set down in a nice, flat field. He had fallen for the optical illusion presented by a rice paddy. As Hooper settled in for the landing, the wheels of his Buffalo caught in the underlying morass, quickly transforming the fighter into a tangled wreck. Luckily, he emerged with only minor scratches.

Even secondary airfields could be tricky landing spots. Running low on fuel, William Allshorn and Jack Kinninmont managed to find the small airstrip at Port Swettenham, despite the cloud cover. When the pair of Buffaloes came in to land, Kinninmont's plane hit a mushy spot in the turf on its landing roll. Predictably, the tires bogged down, and the fighter tipped up on its nose, heavily damaging the propeller, engine, and forward fuselage structure. No. 21 Squadron had just suffered a 28-percent aircraft loss for the ferrying operation, and none of the planes even reached their designated forward base. This incident and a spate of disagreements with the RAF staff in Singapore earned Allshorn some time in the "penalty box." RAAF No. 21 Squadron was slated for reorganization, and Allshorn was relegated to a ground position on the Sembawang air station staff. No. 453 Squadron and its British commanding officer, Squadron Leader William Harper, were given the responsibility of leading the air battle for Malaya—a single fighter squadron pitted against the JAAF. It would hardly be a fair fight.

PROBLEMS WITH WEATHER in the Far East were not always constrained to aircraft in flight. The winds had blown fiercely over Lake Lanao during the night of December 14. The surface of the lake was still choppy in the morning, and John Hyland's PBY suffered two incidents of damage as a result. First, his mechanic—working on top of the wing—had thrown an oil can overboard, misjudged the wind, and damaged the aileron fabric when the can failed to clear the wingtip. As the crew was trying to figure out how to repair that, a motor launch from the dock approached too closely from astern and got caught under the Catalina's rocking tail. This accident bent the lower frames of the rudder. Lieutenant Hyland was beginning to feel cursed, but, fortunately, no other mishaps occurred on Lake Lanao that day. Two more PBYs flew in from Manila, while the others were being serviced for a trip south from Mindanao to the Netherlands East Indies. The winds died down as the day progressed, so at least some of the navy aircrews got to spend a relaxing evening at the Dansalan Inn—one of those rare moments in which servicemen would enjoy some freedom from the strain of wartime duties.

GENERAL BRERETON'S COMMAND had reached a critical juncture. After personally surveying the condition of the B-17s on Mindanao and the base's maintenance capabilities, Major Walsh reiterated Emmett O'Donnell's previous request for a temporary relocation to Australia. General Brereton concurred. General MacArthur finally conceded that Flying Fortresses in various states of disrepair could not do much to deter a Japanese invasion.

Very careful not to imply that this constituted any sort of retreat of the AAF, MacArthur ordered Brereton to send all of the B-17s south to Darwin for "maintenance purposes."[3] On the way south, the bombers would evacuate as many aircrews, mechanics, and service items as possible. Before they could leave the Philippines, however, B-17s—at a rate of three per evening—would have to return to Clark Field for installation of bomb-bay fuel tanks. At least one tank per plane would be needed for the long, nonstop flights to northern Australia.

The army fighter planes would never be evacuated, but they had to keep a low profile during daylight hours. Japanese bombers roamed freely—usually accompanied by heavy fighter escort—bombing U.S. air installations around Luzon at will. Aircraft not out on reconnaissance missions were kept under camouflage in the wooded areas near the airfields. The only time they were reasonably safe in the open was at night. Essentially, the FEAF had been driven underground.

Service work would still have to be performed at Clark and Nichols, but dispersal of Warhawks away from those fields became a primary concern of the beleaguered 24th Pursuit Group. If any replacement fighters were going to be delivered to the Philippines and used to defend Luzon, they would have to be based at fields not known to the Japanese. Colonel George and Captain Eads made so much progress in recruiting Filipino labor and annexing useful properties during the first week of war that two secret airstrips were already under construction by December 15. One was a fighter field at Lubao, southeast of Del Carmen, near the road to Bataan. The other was at Tanauan, forty miles south of Manila, on the route between Laguna de Bay and Batangas. Tanauan was large enough to house small numbers of B-17s. These two specially camouflaged bases had covered revetments and disguised runways. They were impossible to spot from the air, and even difficult to see from the ground.

To speed the projects along, officers with strong managerial skills were assigned to take surplus pilots and ground crews to assist base engineering and construction personnel in completing the necessary tasks. Lieutenant Dyess and many of the men from the 21st Pursuit Squadron were sent to Lubao to manage work there, while Hank Thorne and most of his displaced 3rd Pursuit contingent left Nichols to finish the field at Tanauan.

THE BRITISH AIRMEN IN MALAYA did not have to worry about the additional distraction of air station construction while they were trying to fight against the Japanese, but they could commiserate about continual harassment by enemy bombers.

In the middle of the day on December 15, nineteen Ki-48s of the 90th Sentai executed an unescorted raid in the Butterworth area. A flight of three No. 453 Squadron Buffaloes led by Flight Lieutenant Vanderfield intercepted them. As Dong closed in for the kill, he discovered that all four of his machine guns were jammed. He stayed with his wingmen, guiding the flight in for the attack. Sergeants

Board and O'Mara fired away at the speeding bombers, though each pilot had two guns malfunctioning. The combined firepower was still enough to down one of the Ki-48s in a spectacular rolling ball of flame.[4] The three Australians might have been able to do even more damage, but Vanderfield prudently decided to return his flight to Ipoh rather than risk another pass at the enemy formation with failing guns.

The Ipoh airfield itself was hardly secure. Most of the fliers stationed there expected the Japanese to begin a bombing campaign against Ipoh shortly. Later in the day, after Vanderfield's flight had been serviced, personnel working around that base heard the normally unwelcome sound of many engines coming in toward their location. Much to their surprise, as the men anxiously scanned the skies for signs of the enemy, they saw ten Buffaloes approaching from the south. It was the largest flight of friendly fighters anyone had seen since the war began. Without any of the weather problems that had plagued Squadron Leader Allshorn's flight, Squadron Leader Harper managed to lead six of his own No. 453 Squadron aircraft and four No. 21 Squadron planes—those that had returned to Sembawang from the aborted morning flight—safely to Ipoh. With a victory to celebrate, and a full complement of fighters to challenge the Japanese, morale among the Australians rose considerably that evening.

December 16

Orrin Grover was increasingly fond of the idea of conducting fighter sweeps against planes on the ground at enemy-held airfields. The successful impromptu "strafing missions" executed by Buzz Wagner and Grant Mahony inspired Grover to plan dawn raids on Vigan and Aparri for the morning of December 16. The strength of Japanese air units around Aparri was largely unknown at this time. None of the pilots had visited since Walt Coss was lost, but General Wainwright's ground forces reported enemy troops closing in on the larger landing field at Tuguegarao. The result of the December 15 aerial reconnaissance over Vigan was much clearer: 1st Lieutenant Russel "Russ" Church had seen nearly thirty Japanese fighter planes on the airstrip there. Major Grover independently decided to launch the strikes even though they represented a probable violation of FEAF Headquarters' order not to engage in combat except in self-defense.

Against the rules or not, the young fighter pilots were extremely
enthusiastic about the mission. Lieutenants Boyd Wagner and Joe
Moore engaged in the usual coin toss competition to determine which
of their squadrons would lead the raid on Vigan. Once again, Lieutenant Wagner emerged victorious for the 17th Pursuit. He chose Russ
Church to be his wingman—a good candidate given that Church was
the pilot who profiled the target. Both P-40Es would be equipped
with six 30-pound fragmentation bombs in wing racks. Al Strauss,
whose plane had no bomb racks, would fly with Wagner and Church
to provide some top cover. As a consolation prize, Lieutenant Moore
would lead Marshall Anderson on a mission to Aparri. This pair also
flew some of those rare Warhawks that had been fitted with wing
racks and antipersonnel bombs. Just before daybreak, at 0550, all five
fighters took to the air and roared away from Clark Field.

Approaching Vigan at sunrise, from an altitude of fifteen thousand
feet, Buzz Wagner descended westward into the shadows of the tall
mountains that lined both sides of the Abra River. Beneath him in the
gray morning mist, the small airfield occupied by the JAAF was lined
with nearly two dozen single-engine planes and one twin-engine
transport. Eighteen Ki-27s of the 24th Sentai and a handful of fighters
from the 50th Sentai sat motionless in the dim light.[5] Wagner tilted
the nose of his olive-drab P-40 toward the runway, gaining speed rapidly as he dropped down to twenty-five hundred feet. Lieutenant
Church followed in trail, holding position about half a mile behind
his squadron commander. The airstrip was narrow, and Church had
to be sure to avoid the blast of any secondary explosions that might
be triggered by Wagner's bombs. The scream of diving planes sent
Japanese gunners scurrying for their weapon pits. Buzz Wagner's
plane was over the field, dropping bombs before the men on the
ground could react.

The sharp "pop-pop" sound of antiaircraft guns was quickly
drowned out by the explosions of several fueled and armed Ki-27s. By
the time Church came across the base, the defenders were fully awake.
Wagner was just pulling up in a chandelle at the far end of the runway
when his wingman started firing at the parked aircraft. Flames had
already started streaming back from the cowling of Church's P-40 as he
sped along the airstrip; the Japanese gunners had fatally struck the U.S.
plane—and possibly its pilot. Wagner screamed over his radio for
Church to abort the run and bail out. The call was to no avail. Church
elected to stay the course, releasing his bombs carefully before his

fighter rolled out of control and plummeted to earth in a long splash of flaming gasoline and charred wreckage.

Angry at the loss of his wingman and friend, Lieutenant Wagner furiously attacked the base with his guns. Lieutenant Strauss dropped down to join him. Together, they made several more strafing runs. As the two P-40s temporarily turned away from the smoking field between passes, a single Ki-27 struggled to get airborne. Wagner spotted the small plane speeding down the runway. In a daring maneuver, Buzz rolled his P-40 onto its back, slowing the fighter appreciably as he sat upside down tracking his prey through the canopy. He continued to fly inverted until the Japanese plane gained enough airspeed to get off the ground and climb in front of him. Wagner snap-rolled back to an upright position directly behind the enemy aircraft and pressed his trigger. A devastating fusillade of bullets sent the Ki-27 back to the ground.

In debriefings after the mission, Wagner and Strauss would claim that the three-plane raid had cost the enemy at least ten aircraft destroyed, including Wagner's single victory claim.[6] The JAAF record does not directly acknowledge those losses, but the overall tally of aircraft destroyed on the ground at Luzon in that time frame seems to endorse the claims. Apportioning this number could only be a guess, but options are limited; few American pilots had any opportunity to attack the Japanese airfields. The raid must have been damaging, given that the JAAF command immediately stepped up its air base protection patrols and relocated a number of surviving fighters fifty miles up the coast to a safer, though less desirable, location at Laoag. Uncharacteristically, the Japanese army also announced in a radio address that its forces at Vigan had buried the American lieutenant with full military honors. Such recognition would prove to be an extremely rare occurrence during the Pacific War. For that matter, it was not often that Japan's own troops were publicly lauded in death. Details beyond what was reported by Wagner have not surfaced, but Church's determined "suicide dive" apparently impressed the enemy soldiers around the airfield.

The outcome of Lieutenant Moore's raid on Aparri was anticlimactic: the mission was scrubbed before he and Anderson reached their target. Moore had traveled approximately half the distance to Aparri when he discovered that his compass was severely malfunctioning. The two disappointed pursuit pilots returned to Clark Field without firing a shot.

However effective the Vigan raid may have been, and however impressed the Japanese may have seemed, FEAF Headquarters was decidedly unimpressed. Wagner and Church would both receive Distinguished Service Crosses on General MacArthur's recommendation, but General Brereton unofficially reprimanded Major Grover. He issued an edict to Interceptor Command that the 24th Pursuit Group could no longer initiate any missions on its own accord. Grover would be allowed to dispatch planes and pilots only when specifically directed to do so by Brereton's office via Interceptor Command Headquarters.

IN AN ODD COINCIDENCE, Squadron Leader Harper found himself subject to similar constraints from Air Headquarters in Singapore. The Buffaloes were to be conserved for flying local patrols around the vicinity of Ipoh rather than risking their loss during ineffective interdiction strikes on Japanese motor convoys—not that any losses had occurred.

Pressure was building on the front lines between Sungei Patani and Butterworth. The original plan had been for ground forces to hold Penang Island and a security zone on the mainland surrounding Butterworth. General Percival decided to change that strategy in favor of a defense centered on Taiping—a crossroads where the highways from Singora and Patani finally converge. Troops falling back from both Sungei Patani and Kroh could meet at Taiping and hold the line without much risk of being outflanked—at least on the ground. Despite long-standing intentions for its last-ditch defense, Penang was hastily abandoned on December 16. As had been the case at Kota Bharu and Alor Star, key items of military value would fall into Japanese hands intact. Evacuating British troops failed to scuttle or destroy a large number of coastal freighters, ferries, and fishing boats that were left in the harbors. As the Malayan campaign progressed, these small vessels would prove invaluable as landing craft for the advancing Japanese army. In several significant actions, the boats acquired at Penang would enable Japan to skirt British lines of defense.

IN A MORE ELABORATELY PLANNED encirclement policy, the Japanese were moving quickly to hang a noose around the Philippines. Even if their major objective was still destruction of the U.S. forces on Luzon, Japanese planners realized that cutting off southern routes of supply from Java and Australia would accelerate that process. Because most of the military base locations on Borneo were also oil production centers, a rapid advance southward would serve a dual purpose for Japan.

The Japanese first landed on Borneo on December 16, when troops rushed ashore at Baram Point on the north shore of the island, near the towns of Lutang and Miri in Sarawak. There was no resistance. British troops had already abandoned the area, destroying as many facilities as they could. They had also set demolition charges on the airfield at Miri in an attempt to deny its use to the enemy for at least a few weeks. When the invaders occupied the air station, they found the runway heavily cratered.

With very little knowledge of these enemy activities—or the British responses—PatWing-10 and the 19th Bombardment Group continued preparations for their exodus from the Philippines. Borneo would be a critical waypoint in the travels of both air groups. The tenders *Langley* and *Preston* were already speeding south to Balikpapan, a large Dutch oil port on the eastern coast of Borneo. The smaller *Heron* proceeded more slowly in that direction; it had to stop periodically to refuel its four short-range Vought OS2U Kingfisher floatplanes. Captain Frank Wagner was aboard USS *Childs*, headed for Menado, on the northeastern tip of the island of Celebes (Sulawesi). He intended to have a dozen PBYs and two Grumman J2F Ducks fly from Lake Lanao to the Dutch seaplane base at Lake Tondano—near Menado—when the *Childs* arrived. Once all of his planes were refueled from the tender, Wagner would send them on to Balikpapan for their next service stop. *Langley* would steam ahead to Makassar, on the southwestern edge of Celebes. The smaller planes would be flown there for one last refueling and maintenance stop before heading to Soerabaja.

A few of PatWing-10's PBYs were to be retained at Los Baños for use in evacuating high-ranking personnel from Luzon. Several other PBYs in the vicinity of Manila might be repaired before the Japanese completed an invasion of that city and could be used for evacuation of other key officers, aircrews, and aircraft mechanics.

Ensign John Sloatman was grateful when he got a call to fly his Catalina from Los Baños over to Manila at dawn on December 16. Because so much of the Asiatic Fleet had already been sent south, Admiral Hart decided to establish a headquarters office at Soerabaja. To lead this effort, Admiral William Purnell and six senior staff officers would need one of the flying boats to take them to Java. The urgent nature of this VIP flight meant that Sloatman and his crew should have been the first men from PatWing-10 to reach Java. Unfortunately, during wartime, things have a way of not going according to plan. As the young aviator raced his plane across the open waters of Laguna de Bay in the faint predawn light, he failed to notice a native fish trap obstructing his path. With a large thump, the bamboo frame

posts of the enclosure tore a jagged hole in the thin aluminum hull of
the PBY. Sloatman and his copilot, Ensign Jack Grayson, knew they
were in trouble as their plane sank lower into the water. Kicking the
rudder hard, and cross-throttling the engines, Sloatman and Grayson
executed an abrupt turn toward the shoreline. They tried desperately
to beach the craft, but it was too late. The chagrined flying boat skipper had to cut his engines and give the order to abandon ship before
the PBY could reach shallow water. Wet and cold, the men scrambled
into rubber rafts while they watched their ticket out of the Philippines
disappear beneath the dark surface of the lake.

To further illustrate that operational loss could occur under any
conditions, regardless of enemy involvement, another incident
occurred that morning, far away on Lake Lanao. Ensign Dennis Szabo
slowly taxied his Catalina along the shore of the mountain lake toward
a new mooring location. The sickening sound of tearing metal momentarily drowned out the noise of his chugging engines. A submerged
pinnacle of rock had gashed the fragile hull of the PBY. Like Ensign
Sloatman, Ensign Szabo rammed his throttles forward and turned hard
in the direction of the beach. Again, luck had run out. Szabo's Catalina
took on water quickly, sinking before it could reach solid ground.

With two PBYs sunk in accidents, and an impatient admiral waiting in Manila, Lieutenant Commander Marcy elected to fly the
scheduled evacuation mission himself. Late in the afternoon of
December 16, Marcy took off from Lake Lanao and headed north
toward Luzon. He would land in the evening—after the threat of
Japanese air raids subsided—and fly Admiral Purnell and his party
south during the night.[7]

SERVICEMEN AROUND MANILA may have been worried about their
future—for good reason—but the situation facing the U.S. Marine
aviators on Wake Island seemed hopeless. If a Japanese rope was just
being hung around the Allies' necks in the Philippines, it was already
cinched snugly around Wake Island. Major Putnam's squadron was
down to its last two Wildcats after one week of enemy bombing raids
and the attempted invasion. Undoubtedly, the Japanese would soon
be back to try another landing operation. Certainly Japan would
employ a much stronger naval and air force presence the second time
around. Without assistance from the Pacific Fleet, the Marines were
sure to succumb. The stubborn defenders of the sandy atoll did
not know it, but Admiral Kimmel was sending a relief expedition

out from Pearl Harbor. On December 16—still December 15 in Hawaii—the ships charged with that mission departed from Oahu. Fourteen Brewster F2A-2 Buffaloes of VMF-221 were included in the list of resources to be delivered. Getting the task forces to Wake before the Japanese returned was a race against time, but it would have to be a careful one; the navy could ill afford to lose any of the three aircraft carriers assigned to the operation.

December 17

At 0200 on December 17, Major Combs led six worn Flying Fortresses off the dark runway at Del Monte and headed south in the direction of Australia.[8] It would be a long nine-hour flight to Darwin—covering some seventeen hundred miles—but the crews were glad to be getting a break from their grueling routine in the Philippines. Difficult, unproductive tactical missions in dangerous skies were a problem, but the inability to care for the planes or themselves was quite another. Conditions at Clark Field were abysmal. By this time, almost every facility of value had been gutted by enemy bombers. During the day, the base was a ghostly landscape of rubble and charred wreckage. At least the aircrews mostly visited that base at night, when the Japanese typically halted bombing operations. San Marcelino had no morbid reminders of Japan's domination of the air, but it had nothing else either. Though enemy planes had not appeared over Mindanao since December 8, none of the men doubted that the Japanese would be back to attack Del Monte. Therefore, it did not matter to the 19th Group crews that Darwin itself was practically a ghost town, or that their actual destination—the blisteringly hot, dusty, fly-infested Batchelor Field—was nearly forty miles farther south. What mattered was that they would be a long way away from the Japanese. With a little luck, maybe the tired men might finally get a full night of sleep— their first since the war began.

Conditions for the naval aviators of PatWing-10 had been much better. On December 16, the patrol plane crews had enjoyed another night of resortlike conditions at the Dansalan Inn on the edge of Lake Lanao. They had not yet suffered the hardships of their fellow servicemen in the army, and most had limited involvement with the devastation at Cavite. Their journey south was about to begin, and they felt relieved that their time as sitting ducks might be over. It would mean arduous flights, but the men had managed plenty of those on their daily patrols. Travels through Borneo, Celebes, and Java seemed like a great adventure. If war rendered these exotic locales something short of paradise, at least each stop was picturesque and pleasant, a new and exciting experience.

Lieutenant Commander J.V. Peterson received word from Captain Wagner early in the morning of December 17 that all the planes on Lake Lanao were to head immediately for Menado. They would refuel from *Childs* in Menado Bay during the late afternoon and then relocate to Lake Tondano for the evening. The pair of J2Fs was in for a more difficult journey; they did not possess the range to make a direct flight to Menado. They would have to land at sea to refuel from a stash of five-gallon cans carried in the cramped observer compartments beneath their cockpits. Regardless of the additional risk involved, the J2F pilots, Ensign Al Seaman and Lieutenant Commander J. C. Renard, were relieved to be on the move. By 0900 the Ducks were away, and ten Catalinas were taxiing into takeoff position.[9] As they bid farewell to Lake Lanao and Dennis Szabo's half-submerged PBY, none of the PatWing-10 personnel who gazed at the scenery of Mindanao felt that the large island would provide a refuge from Japanese planes for much longer.

No crew was happier to be leaving than the one on John Hyland's plane. In peacetime, their PBY would have been grounded as being unsafe. Hyland had only just managed to persuade Peterson not to scuttle the plane. With makeshift repairs to its aileron, rudder, and engine cowling, and one weak engine, the PBY barely escaped the waters of the mountain lake. At the controls, Hyland and Barrett were crossing their fingers that their Catalina would make it all the way to Celebes. If they could make it to the rendezvous with *Childs*, maintenance men from the ship could easily make better repairs and install a fresh engine.

About two hours after the planes of PatWing-10 left Lake Lanao behind, they received an urgent radio message from Captain Frank Wagner on board *Childs*. The support ship had reached Menado but had been bombed by a Japanese four-engine flying boat shortly after its arrival. Fearing additional attacks later in the day, by more capable bombers or strafers, Wagner ordered the formation of vulnerable Catalinas to change course and fly directly to Balikpapan. It was impossible for the J2Fs to comply; they did not have enough fuel. John Hyland was pretty sure his limping PBY could not make the full distance either; its ailing engine would need a transfusion of oil before long. Hyland, Seaman, and Renard would have to continue on toward Menado, regardless of any risk of enemy intervention. Hyland and his crew would soon find themselves alone—the Ducks had already fallen behind to make their pit stop. With a wistful look, Hyland and Barrett watched through their windscreen as the other nine PBYs banked away to the west, gradually disappearing from sight.

THE JAPANESE READILY EXPLOITED the latest British retreat in Malaya. As British forces withdrew toward Taiping, the IJA launched an invasion of Penang Island and seized both Sungei Patani and Butterworth on the Malayan Peninsula. These key locations were taken with virtually no casualties. The careless manner of the British evacuations emboldened the Japanese army to push forward even harder.

If the Australians at Ipoh thought that the change in combat policy prohibiting active attacks was going to make life boring, they were wrong.

Three Buffaloes flying the morning patrol above the airfield were surprised to see a like number of Ki-43 fighters from the 59th Sentai conducting an armed reconnaissance. For once, the men flying the Brewsters had the benefit of altitude as they dived to pursue the low-flying enemy. It afforded them no advantage. In a wild melee, the six fighters screamed around the skies in a low-altitude dogfight, giving troops on the ground quite a show.

Though he may have taken the first shots at his opponent, "Wild Bill" Collyer had the tables turned on him. Before he knew what happened, the Ki-43 handily outmaneuvered his comparatively clumsy Buffalo and quickly latched onto its tail. In a frighteningly fast chase through the nearby valleys, Collyer was able to outrace the Japanese plane but ended up miles away from Ipoh. His wingmen, Sergeants Alfred Clare and James Summerton, stayed in the vicinity of their base and fought the other two Ki-43s to a draw. All six planes came away with bullet holes, but neither side lost any aircraft in this evenly matched first engagement between the Hayabusas and Buffaloes.

In the middle of the day, reports of incoming aircraft reached the operations room at Ipoh. Eight Brewsters were scrambled to protect the base. The Australian pilots were glad to be off the ground—finally in numbers great enough to challenge their enemy. It was hard to say whether they were excited to be flying into combat or just relieved not to be sweltering in the nearly unbearable heat and humidity on the ground. The Australian flight had been ordered to climb to an altitude of twenty thousand feet, but before it could get anywhere near that height, the leader spotted ten single-engine aircraft heading toward him. Surprisingly, those approaching Japanese planes turned around and headed north at high speed. The Australians pushed their throttles wide open, slowly closing the distance in pursuit. Evenly matched with the speed of the Brewsters at the altitude of this encounter, the JAAF Ki-43s had too great a head start. Only Sergeant Stanley Scrimgeour managed to get close to the enemy, and his over-stressed engine started throwing oil before he could fire his guns. As the brown fluid seeped out of the joints in the cowling panels and streamed back over his windscreen, Scrimgeour gave up.

However frustrated they were at not being able to take any shots at the enemy, the Australian pilots' spirits were raised in knowing that they had chased the Japanese fighters away for the first time. The illusion did not last long. As the returning flight of Buffaloes approached Ipoh, the pilots noticed more than half a dozen plumes of black smoke rising from their airfield. The Japanese had lured them away from the base in order to allow a formation of bombers to attack at low altitude, without the risk of interception. The ruse worked well: two of three Buffaloes on the service line had been completely destroyed, and the third heavily damaged. Several buildings around the base were also on fire.[10]

The Japanese were relentless. As the eight incoming Brewsters landed, only a few had taxied off the runway before another group of enemy bombers materialized overhead. Again, the bombing was highly accurate. One rolling Buffalo had a bomb strike directly beneath it. The explosion lifted the craft up to one side, completely shearing off a wing as the plane slid along the runway. Nearby, Flying Officer Bob Kirkman tried to avoid a similar fate. Giving an overly sharp kick to the rudder, he lost control of his plane and skidded into a deep drainage ditch with equally damaging results.

December 17 had been costly and embarrassing for the RAAF at Ipoh. Fortuitously, none of the pilots had been killed or seriously injured, but the squadrons lost four more fighters without a single enemy plane being downed by the air patrol. This poor showing during the first day of serious enemy activity above the new airfield crushed morale, especially among the ground crews of No. 21 Squadron. To those men—who had already experienced traumatic moves from Sungei Patani and Butterworth—it seemed a foregone conclusion that Ipoh would be caught in the tide of the Japanese advance.

ON THE AFTERNOON OF DECEMBER 17, Major John "Big Jim" Davies finally got the news he had been waiting so long to hear: the USAT *Meigs* with his "missing" A-24 Banshees was scheduled to arrive at Brisbane on December 22. General Brereton wanted the 27th Group commander to take twenty pilots to Australia to supervise the unloading and preparation of the dive-bombers for a flight back to the Philippines. Davies and his men were charged with pioneering the proposed replenishment route through the Australian Outback and the Netherlands East Indies. The group was allocated two B-18s and a C-39 cargo plane as transportation but would also have to take some AAF maintenance officers and fighter pilots to Darwin. Those men would help ready the P-40s for a similar venture. The assigned aircraft would be used for the trip south only as far as Batchelor Field. The planes would then be used to carry vital supplies of .50-caliber ammunition from Darwin back to Del Monte Field. The passengers would receive local Australian air transportation to Brisbane on a priority basis.

"Big Jim"—who stood nearly a head taller than most of his audience—convened the chosen 27th Group men for a briefing at their makeshift group headquarters at Fort McKinley. Soft-spoken, but authoritative, the broad-shouldered, dark-haired major explained their mission. Excitement built with each word. They were finally going to have their planes, and a chance to strike back at the Japanese, but they would have to move quickly. Because it was no longer safe to travel in convoys on Manila roads during the day, they headed south to Nichols Field after dark. At Nichols, they met with the other AAF men who would join them for the trip south, including three Lieutenants—Grant Mahony, Al Strauss, and Gerry Keenan.

The two B-18s carrying Major Davies and most of his 27th Group personnel would fly directly to the Dutch airfield at Tarakan, Borneo. The Douglas transport did not have the range to make it that far and would have to stop at Del Monte to refuel. Because of recent Japanese activity around Mindanao and northern Borneo, Davies decided it was not a good idea for such a slow, unarmed aircraft to travel the route during the day. The versatile Grant Mahony—in command of that plane—would keep it hidden on the ground at Del Monte through the daylight hours and fly it to Tarakan the next night. Even though Mahony had plenty of hours' experience in piloting twin-engine planes, he would leave most of the flying to one of the maintenance group pilots, 1st Lieutenant Frederic "Fred" Hoffman.[11]

December 18

At 0200—just before the creaking airframes of the three planes under Major Davies's command groaned off the runway at Nichols Field— four Flying Fortresses roared down the strip at Del Monte into the pitch-black night. In the lead, Major Walsh guided Lieutenants Godman, Mueller, and Teats southwest toward Batchelor Field.[12] What the B-17s would do when they reached Australia was uncertain, but the men inside them were glad to be on their way.

By the time Lieutenant Mahony's C-39 arrived over Del Monte at dawn, only four operational B-17s remained on that airfield. Heavily camouflaged with truckloads of fronds and brush driven up from Cagayan del Oro, the aircraft around the pineapple plantation seemed reasonably well hidden—just not quite well enough to avoid the attention of a single Japanese navy flying boat that flew a photo reconnaissance over the area later in the day. It was the first time the enemy had been able to find the remote airstrip. The men on the ground had a sinking feeling when they heard the strange engine noise. They knew the Japanese would be back soon.

THE MORNING AT IPOH, MALAYA, started out in the same manner as the previous morning. Forward area spotters reported incoming enemy aircraft headed south. Six Brewsters sitting on alert were scrambled to fly north. This departure was a little more dramatic than usual: Sergeant Board, realizing he was on an intersecting course with two other Buffaloes, killed his engine and abruptly raised his landing gear. The craft dropped onto its belly. The young Australian pilot expected this would save his plane from a disastrous collision. As had been the case on several previous occasions, the mid-wing fighter slid too well on the slick turf. Not expecting this, Board quickly ran out of space around the narrow runway and hit a tree. The fuselage of his plane fractured in half just ahead of the cockpit but did not catch fire. Ground crewmen rushed to the scene and extracted Board from the broken plane. Fortunately, his injuries were minimal.

Once again, the Buffaloes that made it into the air gave chase to the Japanese. As on the previous day, the Australians were outdistanced in the chase and returned without firing a shot. For a second time, they were tricked. The Japanese demonstrated an almost psychic ability to guess when the Australians would return to the airfield. The landing process had scarcely begun when fifteen Ki-48 bombers of the 90th Sentai swooped across the runway dropping bombs. One of the taxiing Brewsters was destroyed. Wild Bill Collyer managed to escape by jumping out of its cockpit and flattening himself on the ground as bomb blasts walked up the field across his plane. No. 21 Squadron's equipment officer, Flight Lieutenant Francis Hordern, was less fortunate: the car he was driving on the field was shredded by shrapnel from a nearby explosion. Hordern was killed at the wheel.

After noon, as the Ipoh base air patrol was changing watches, three Ki-43s of the 59th Sentai rushed in over the treetops. Surprise was complete. Service personnel and fliers on the ground scattered for cover as enemy machine guns fired. When their heads were not pressed squarely to the earth, the men around Ipoh witnessed a superb display of aerobatics as the Japanese army fighters looped and turned to make several gunnery passes at the field. Three Buffaloes left out in the open were hit repeatedly, but none were destroyed. To the Australian pilots, this spectacle was quite intimidating. The new "Zeros"—as the Hayabusas were often erroneously identified—could outrun, outclimb, and effortlessly outturn the Buffaloes. As the Japanese planes zoomed back and forth overhead, the Australians cursed.

That the U.S.-built planes were suffering from gun failures, engine problems, and performance degradation due to poor maintenance and battle damage was only part of the problem. The Ki-43s were indeed superior fighters, piloted by seasoned veterans who possessed significantly better flying skills than most of the rookie pilots of the RAAF.

FOR JOHN HYLAND AND HAWK BARRETT, December 18 was an especially long day. The left engine in their PBY was burning prodigious amounts of oil and still overheating. After crossing the Makassar Strait, the powerplant reached its limit. Trailing thick black smoke, the Twin-Wasp eventually began to run roughly, backfiring and wheezing its objection at continuing the journey. Reluctantly, Hyland shut down the ailing engine and feathered its propeller; the spinning blades slowed and stopped, with the edges turned directly into the rushing air. The Catalina could fly on one engine for some distance, but it would continue to lose altitude. Running his right engine at the highest possible power output, Hyland headed down the eastern coast of Borneo. The flight engineer dumped unneeded fuel. The rest of the crew began tossing out unnecessary equipment in an effort to slow their descent. All of this did not seem to help much. The plane lost all but a thousand feet of altitude before it finally reached Balikpapan, but at least it got there. Hyland, Barrett, and the others had never been happier to rendezvous with their support ships. The bad engine would definitely have to be replaced before they could continue on toward Soerabaja. Of course, skilled maintenance men aboard the tenders could accomplish this in a day or two. The question would be whether the mechanics would have the time.

December 19

Engines roaring in the night had become such a regular sound on the remote mountain plain of the Del Monte plantation that probably no one noticed the departure of the Douglas C-39 carrying Grant Mahony and the other pilots headed for Australia. Their transport droned on through the dark skies. With the ground and seas covered in cloudy shadows, the crew could not positively locate their destination at Tarakan and worried that they may have overflown it. Some of the men thought they saw an enemy aircraft carrier in the seas below them. This caused a lot of extra anxiety on board the plane, but no Japanese were actually sailing in the Makassar Strait. The ship they spotted was probably USS *Childs* traveling along its course between Menado and Balikpapan. Mahony and the pilot, Fred Hoffman, decided there was enough fuel to try to continue on to Balikpapan. Doing so would get them farther away from the Japanese, and they would have gradually brightening skies to assist in finding the new destination.

At dawn, the pilots finally spotted the tank-covered hills above the large oil port; their navigation to Balikpapan had been good. One could say the men on that C-39 led a charmed life. They touched down on the airfield with just twenty-eight gallons of gasoline remaining— enough for only about fifteen minutes of flight.[13]

DAYBREAK AT IPOH WAS ushered in with a call for six pilots to fly Buffaloes back to Sembawang. The fighters would not be combat ready anytime soon, but the mechanical team of No. 21 Squadron had done a fantastic job of patching them back together enough for pilots to fly them down to Singapore. The departure of these planes left only seven operational Brewsters at Ipoh: five attached to No. 453 Squadron and two belonging to No. 21 Squadron.

The question of how the JAAF had been timing such effective bombing strikes while the Australian air cover was drawn away was resolved when Squadron Leader Harper was notified that retreating British troops had found a radio-equipped enemy observer on one of the hills overlooking the airfield.[14] The fact that the Japanese were not truly omniscient, and that their observer had been nabbed, was of some comfort to the men around Ipoh. Still, removal of the spotter did not stop enemy bombers from conducting another critical strike. Shortly after the first flight of evacuating Buffaloes headed south, three Ki-21s made a single pass over the Ipoh airstrip. Coming in at treetop height— approaching from behind one of the many hills—the speeding bombers yielded no advance warning of their attack. A rain of fragmentation bombs destroyed the last two Buffaloes assigned to No. 21 Squadron.[15]

After receiving the report of this raid, Air Headquarters ordered No. 453 Squadron to fly its five fighters down to the smaller airstrip at Kuala Lumpur. The squadron's maintenance staff would be sent north from Sembawang to join the fliers. Ipoh was to be abandoned. No. 21 Squadron and its tired mechanics were to entrain for Singapore. They would return to the rear area to be reformed under the temporary command of Flight Lieutenant Williams.

THE SOUND OF AIRCRAFT ENGINES near Sangley Point was distressingly common. Until December 19, Japanese aircraft regularly passed over-head as they traveled to other targets. On this date, bombs finally fell on the base, destroying the hangar and a PBY undergoing overhaul inside it, the radio station, most of the living facilities, and—in a spectacular cloud of smoke and flame—the fuel storage tanks.[16]

The end was near. All available Catalinas had been reserved for evacuating high-ranking naval officers and a handful of other officials. For the moment, the only visible PBY sat on the Pan American Airways service ramp, untouched by Japanese attackers. It was the barely flyable wreck of Ensign McConnell's plane, which had been salvaged from Laguna de Bay.

FROM THE OTHER SIDE OF MANILA, General Brereton announced several changes to the organization of his FEAF. Some were tactical responses to the situation on Luzon, others were further reaching, aimed at establishing FEAF presence outside the Philippines. Ironically, each effort to adjust to the new requirements would lead to an immediate and unnecessary loss of aircraft.

The most significant changes Brereton made involved reassignments in his own headquarters. Recognizing the need to staff a new air organization in Australia, he relieved General Clagett of his position in the Philippines. Shortly before the war began, Henry Clagett had taken ill and had been unable to manage a full duty schedule. Colonel George, who had effectively run the FEAF Interceptor Command on Clagett's behalf, became the official head of that organization. General Clagett was asked to start up a base and supply command in Australia to deal with arriving AAF personnel and materiel. He was an able organizer, and it was felt that his health would improve with the change in climate. A handful of staff officers would travel south to assist him.

Not observing the new convention of flying at night, General Clagett and his party left Nichols Field early in the afternoon of December 19 in three B-18s. The trio of worn-out planes touched down at Del Monte Field shortly before 1600. While line personnel serviced the aircraft, the evacuating staff officers milled about, mingling with other officers who had fled Luzon on the nightly shuttle missions. Above, the sound of engines preceded four planes that suddenly appeared high in the sky. As the formation broke apart, the unmistakable outlines of Japanese Zeros were exposed. Men yelled and ran for trenches, foxholes, ditches—any sort of shelter that might shield them from the strafers. Clagett himself opted for a ditch and rolled in on top of the recently promoted Del Monte base commander, Lieutenant Colonel Ray Elsmore.

Lieutenant Masuzo Seto of the *Tainan Kokutai* detachment at Legaspi was amazed at his good fortune. Beneath him were three green twin-engine planes in the open field, and a number of camouflaged larger aircraft—obvious if only because the huge piles of foliage were somewhat out of place on the mostly barren plain. Seto's attacking A6Ms were as efficient as ever, executing a near repetition of their wildly successful run against PatWing-10 at Olongapo. By the time the Japanese planes flew away, all three B-18s were in flames, and one of the brush-covered Flying Fortresses had also been destroyed. Two other B-17s were left smoking, but these were the wrecks of Lieutenant Adams's and Lieutenant Tash's bombers—both well along in the process of being stripped for useful parts. A few serviceable Fortresses emerged with fresh bullet holes.

With his transportation smoldering in the grass, General Clagett had to arrange a new departure plan. The 19th Bomb Group was preparing to fly its last few planes out of Del Monte early the next morning. Clagett and his aide, Major Eric Nichols, would leave the field at 2200 that evening on the first B-17 away from Mindanao, flown by

Lieutenant Weldon Smith.[17] The other members of Clagett's party would have to await a different opportunity to leave the Philippines.

FEAF aircraft losses on Luzon during December 19 were essentially self-inflicted. General Brereton had been greatly disappointed with the lack of dispersal for his fighters from the outset. By this point in the air campaign, only twenty-three P-40s were operable: twelve at Clark Field, the rest at Nichols. Industrious mechanics had resuscitated nine P-35As, but most of those were parked in the trees and brush around Clark. A few of these Severskys were hidden under camouflage netting at Nielsen Field for use in courier duty. They were well suited to that role. The baggage compartment behind the P-35A's cockpit was generously proportioned, had a Plexiglas window, and could even hold a passenger seated on its package shelf.

Given that Clark and Nichols were both subject to intense enemy scrutiny several times a day, General Brereton wanted some of his P-40s distributed to Del Carmen and San Marcelino. Lubao and Tanauan were not really ready to accept planes, and neither Colonel George nor his assistant, Captain Bud Sprague, wanted to compromise the security of those locations. Thus, Brereton's dispersal order resulted in the transfer of nine P-40s to San Marcelino. Because the movement was not carried out in daylight, pilots assigned to the mission experienced some difficulty—none of them had ever landed at San Marcelino before. It was almost amazing that seven of them made it safely to the unfamiliar airstrip in complete darkness. Predictably, there were crashes. Lieutenant Rowland came in too high on his approach and stalled onto the runway so hard that the landing gear fractured, critically damaging the Warhawk's wings. Lieutenant Jim Phillips never found the new field and returned to Clark. Realizing that his landing run was flawed, Lieutenant Phillips tried to pull out and turn away. It was too late; the plane mushed in the sudden maneuver, dropped a wing, and spun in. The P-40 was wiped out, but its lucky pilot survived, earning himself a trip to see the nurses at Fort Stotsenburg Hospital.

December 20

FEAF Headquarters was under pressure to provide some form of assistance to General Wainwright's forces holding the highway between Vigan and San Fernando. For once, it would have been an ideal task for 19th Group B-17s, but the only planes available were those of the 24th Pursuit Group.

General Brereton wanted to retain his P-40s in reserve to combat the anticipated enemy landing at Lingayen, which reconnaissance reports indicated would take place in the next few days. As a compromise on Wainwright's behalf, the staff settled on the idea of staging a raid on the Japanese forward command post south of Vigan. This operation would use all available P-35As. On the morning of December 20, six of the planes were gathered together at Clark Field and fitted with bomb racks. Each P-35 would carry six 30-pound fragmentation explosives. At dawn, the half-dozen dusty Severskys—their poorly applied olive-green paint peeling away as they zoomed along the west coast of Luzon—followed Highway 3 north toward Vigan. Arriving low and early, the flight completely surprised the Japanese infantry massing around their command post—an old schoolhouse just south of the town. In the first pass, the strafing fighters routed the enemy from the building.[18] As each Seversky passed over the Japanese position, fragmentation bombs fell from its wings. The thirty-six small explosives caused significant casualties among the sheltering troops. Following up with several strafing passes, the 24th Group pilots were elated to watch soldiers scattering and falling to their attack. Without taking any damage, the small formation happily returned to Clark. More important than any tactical support the raid provided to General Wainwright was the boosted morale of the airmen. For the first time since the war began, the Americans saw that they could actually cause harm to advancing Japanese armies.

Five of the returning planes were left in a makeshift service area under the trees at Clark. The sixth plane, flown by 2nd Lieutenant Steve Crosby, took off later in the day to return to Nielsen Field.[19] Crosby's sense of danger may have been diminished by excitement about the morning mission. On the way back to Manila, his aircraft was jumped by a pair of Ki-27s. He realized the enemy was approaching only when tracer fire passed over his cockpit. Startled, Crosby pulled the maneuverable Seversky into a tight loop, which placed him behind his adversary. The Japanese pilot had not expected this, so the young American almost succeeded in lining up the Nakajima in his sights. Unfortunately, Lieutenant Crosby failed to notice the trailing wingman until it was too late: machine-gun fire from that unseen pursuer ripped through the nose of the P-35, igniting fuel and oil in the engine area. Even though Crosby was at low altitude, he had no choice but to bail out. His parachute barely deployed before his body hit the ground. Knocked unconscious by the hard landing, he was lucky enough to avoid serious injury. His pride suffered greater wounds: much time would pass before Crosby stopped chastising himself for not being alert enough to avoid the loss of his airplane.

STEVE CROSBY WAS NOT the only American pilot to be humbled on December 20. Nine PBYs from PatWing-10 completed the long journey from Balikpapan to Java. Soerabaja harbor housed the largest seaplane base in the world, and the mass arrival of this relatively large formation of navy Catalinas was calculated to impress their Dutch hosts. Some of the naval aviators suffered a loss of face instead. The PatWing-10 aircrews had not been briefed on the landing and taxiing procedures necessary for the shallow waters of Soerabaja during low tide. All nine Catalinas made beautiful touchdowns, but five of them settled down from the step of their landing run directly on top of unseen mudflats. In those heavy PBYs stuck fast in the slime, embarrassed pilots could do nothing but wait several hours for the rising waters of a high tide to refloat them.

FAR AWAY FROM SOERABAJA, halfway across the Pacific Ocean, a lone Catalina landed to the sound of cheering. It was late afternoon when the blue-gray PBY touched down in the sparkling lagoon of the Wake atoll. It was the first aircraft from outside the islands to land at Wake since the war began. After making a few jokes about their disappointment at not being able to spend a night at the famous Pan American Airways Hotel, Ensign J. J. Murphy and his copilot, Ensign Howard Ady, found their way to the headquarters of Commander Cunningham. The message the two ensigns carried was of the utmost secrecy; in fact, it was the primary reason for their flight from Midway. Detailed information about the relief expedition was too important to transmit over the airwaves. The news was surprising and exciting for Cunningham, Devereux, and Putnam and a shot in the arm for those tired defenders of the isolated outpost.

What none of the men on Wake Island knew was that Admiral Chuichi Nagumo's Pearl Harbor strike force had detached Cruiser Division 8 and the ships of Carrier Division 2—*Hiryu* and *Soryu*—to support the second invasion attempt at their atoll. Naturally, Murphy and Ady had radioed ahead to Wake for clearance into the island airspace—it was never a good idea to arrive unannounced in a combat zone. Unfortunately, the transmission from their aircraft had been detected by enemy radio operators. Believing that the radio traffic from Murphy's Catalina signified the presence of a flying boat squadron on Wake, Admiral Nagumo was prompted to step up plans for air attacks against the U.S. outpost.

THE IJN WAS ALSO HARD AT WORK back in the Philippines. To complement a heavily supported invasion of Davao launched on the morning of December 20, that afternoon the JNAF staged a large bombing raid on the airfield at Del Monte. Flying from Palau, and escorted by six A6Ms of the *Tainan Kokutai*, fifty-four land-based attack bombers of the *Kanoya Kokutai* and eight flying boats of the *Toko Kokutai* plastered the AAF pineapple plantation refuge, but only two men were killed.[20] It was fortunate that the last of the 19th Group B-17s had left during the night; they would have certainly been destroyed had they still been at the airstrip.

By evening, the invaders had secured Davao and its small airport. This was no great surprise to Brigadier General William Sharp and his U.S. Army troops on Mindanao; the vast majority of the city's population was composed of Japanese expatriates or people of Japanese ancestry. However, Japan's possession of Davao meant that enemy fighter aircraft presence on Mindanao was only days away. The air force leadership knew that would severely limit Del Monte's usefulness as a bomber base. In effect, the Japanese invasion at Davao sounded the death knell for delivery of any aircraft reinforcements to the Philippines. Japan's encirclement of the archipelago was nearly complete.

December 21

Before the Japanese task force could muster its assault on Wake, Ensigns Murphy and Ady were taxiing across the lagoon for their departure. They carried with them a number of reports on the current situation at the island and a summary of events that had occurred there since the war began. In addition, the PBY was transporting a stack of letters written home by men around the islands, most of whom wished they could leave with their letters. Only one lucky passenger was added to the flight that morning: Major Walter Bayler from Marine Air Group Headquarters had been ordered to Midway to prepare electronics equipment for installation on that island. At 0700 the Catalina lifted off the still waters and banked around to the northeast. However wistfully the Marines may have gazed at that departing flying boat, they were relieved to know that their country had not completely abandoned them. With reinforcements on the way they stood a chance—as long as the Japanese did not strike before the additional men and weapons arrived.

Less than two hours later, forty-nine specks could be seen through the binoculars of lookouts around Wilkes Island. This time, the aircraft were descending from the northwest. When the outlines became clearer, depression set in on the men around the atoll. From information imparted by the PBY pilots, Marine officers knew that reinforcements were not due for at least another day. They realized they were in trouble. Single-engine planes could mean only one thing: aircraft carriers were nearby, and they were not friendly. Since Allied intelligence organizations still had no idea of the whereabouts of the enemy's Pearl Harbor attack fleet, Wake's defenders could only assume that these carrier planes indicated the presence of that entire naval force. Such attention devoted to Wake meant that another Japanese invasion operation was imminent, perhaps only a few hours away. Crestfallen, the Americans watched as the images of the aircraft grew larger and fanned out to approach Wake, Peale, and Wilkes islands from all directions.

With great precision, two Nakajima B5Ns, twenty-nine Aichi D3As, and sixteen escorting Zeros selected and attacked key positions around the atoll for nearly an hour.[21] Major Putnam had just driven onto the airfield when the raid began. He quickly abandoned his vehicle and tried valiantly to get to the sandbagged bunker where a single functional VMF-211 Wildcat sheltered. Attempting to take off with enemy planes roaring everywhere across the island would be suicidal; the F4F would be in flames before it ever turned onto the runway. Putnam had another objective in mind. When the raiders departed, he would follow them to their carrier in an effort to pinpoint the location of the Japanese task force. He finally eased his F4F off the airstrip at about 1030, but the Grumman's engine was not developing full power as he tried to climb after the retiring enemy aircraft. Unable to effectively chase the Japanese, the disappointed major returned to Wake. Now, only time would tell what the IJN would throw at the Marines. Even Major Devereux doubted he could repulse the landing parties a second time, though he would certainly try.

THE BRITISH RETREAT TOWARD SINGAPORE continued at a rapid pace; miles of territory in Malaya were being ceded to Japan every hour.

With each gain, the JAAF extended its fighter umbrella farther south. The airfield at Kuala Lumpur had been in use by RAAF No. 453 Squadron for less than one day when the sound of approaching Japanese aircraft engines was heard in the distance. It seemed like a repetition of the initial day at Ipoh. The morning patrol had just landed. Buffaloes were taxiing to the service area. A dozen Hayabusa fighters of the 59th Sentai and a split formation of Ki-48 and Ki-51 bombers appeared above the tree line. Disaster loomed once again.

Given the relative strength of the Japanese formation, surprisingly little damage was done to the base during this raid: a near miss at the Kuala Lumpur Flying Club broke most of the windows in that building, but no Buffaloes suffered serious damage. None of the men on the field were killed or injured. The closest the enemy came to inflicting a casualty occurred where Sergeant Alf "Sinbad" Clare had taken shelter near a grassy embankment. It collapsed on him after the explosion of a nearby bomb strike shook the rain-soaked earth. The large, balding aviator quickly dug himself out of the mudslide. Covered in red muck, Sinbad stood swearing vengeance and shaking his fists at the departing enemy.[22]

The Australians did not have long to wait for a second Japanese raid. Sergeants Keith "Ross" Leys and Eric Peterson were patrolling over Kuala Lumpur in the afternoon when another dozen Ki-51s, escorted by a similar quantity of 59th Sentai Ki-43s, appeared. In an effort to split up the attackers, Sergeant Leys chased the formation of fighters while Peterson turned on the dive-bombers. The tactic was reasonably effective. Peterson kept three of the bombers at bay, claiming one shot down with damage to the other two. Concentration on the part of pilots in the remaining bombers must have been shaken. For the second time that day, only slight damage was inflicted on the Kuala Lumpur airstrip.

Ross Leys had a very different experience; tangling with a dozen enemy fighters on his own was a dangerous game. The aggressive Australian was no match for that many experienced opponents. Sergeant Hiroshi Onozaki eventually shot up the Buffalo, forcing Leys to bail out. Without question, Sergeant Leys had flown his Brewster for all it was worth; the Japanese claimed four Buffaloes shot down in an engagement where they actually encountered only one aircraft.[23] No. 453 Squadron had done a much better job of protecting Kuala Lumpur against the destructive powers of the JAAF than they had at Ipoh. That was important, but how long could they continue to shield their new base?

CHAPTER 11

Collapse

December 22–24, 1941

Under cover of darkness, the Japanese assembled a large quantity of shipping in the Lingayen Gulf. Seventy-six transports were anchored in two rows along the wide, flat beach. On board these were some forty-three thousand soldiers of Japan's 14th Army. To protect the anchorage, the IJN had assigned two heavy cruisers (*Ashigara* and *Maya*); three light cruisers (*Kuma, Naka,* and *Natori*); sixteen destroyers; four seaplane tenders; and nearly three dozen minesweepers, subchasers, torpedo boats, and patrol craft.[1] It was an impressive armada. On a one-shot, one-kill basis, Admiral Hart's submarines did not have enough torpedoes to sink even half of these enemy ships. Of course, General Brereton's FEAF had no plane left in the Philippines that could put more than a dimple in the deck plating of any ship in the bay. The main thrust of the Japanese invasion was under way, and General MacArthur could no longer do anything about it.

On the morning of December 22, Colonel George only had a dozen P-40Es ready for battle in central Luzon. Four of those Warhawks were equipped with wing racks for the tiny fragmentation bombs.[2] The air force would get but one chance to strike at the invasion fleet that day. Because poor timing in any operation could result in the final destruction of the 24th Pursuit Group, great care was exercised in scheduling the mission. The dozen fighters would have to depart from Clark before dawn so they could return before the daily Japanese bombing raids began. Getting the Warhawks back on the ground and hidden before enemy planes came overhead was imperative.

Lieutenant Wagner led six planes of the 17th Pursuit away from Clark Field at 0545. He was followed closely by wingman Bill Hennon. It was almost a miracle that all of the pilots made it off the ground safely in the dark; visibility was miserable. The usual billowing dust was complemented by a low-hanging ground fog and thick overcast that rose as high as ten thousand feet. Wagner and Hennon circled for quite some time waiting for their flight to join in formation. None of the other pilots ever found the squadron leader and his wingman. The four missing pilots—Red Sheppard, Steve Crosby, Ed Kiser, and Walt Wilcox—proceeded toward Lingayen in a loose trail. They would arrive at the target ahead of Wagner and Hennon.

Lieutenant Moore had even worse luck rounding up his flight of six planes from the 20th Pursuit. Only Parker Gies and Kiefer White managed to follow their commanding officer to Lingayen. This pitifully small raid became even smaller when Percy Ramsey and Erwin Crellin returned to Clark because of the weather. Randy Keator, who circled above Clark for more than an hour looking for other P-40s, elected to head for a safer landing at Nichols Field. The giant Japanese fleet would be taken on by a grand total of nine P-40s.

Wagner and Hennon did not arrive over Lingayen until about 0715. Lieutenants Crosby, Kiser, and Wilcox could be seen making strafing runs on transports and landing barges along the shoreline. Bill Hennon split away from his leader to drop fragmentation bombs on a large group of troops wading ashore. From the corner of his eye, he noticed Wagner doing the same, farther down the beach. With all six bombs gone, Hennon circled to make another pass at the enemy soldiers, using the Warhawk's heavy machine guns. By the time he pulled up from this second pass along the beach, the area was crowded with Japanese fighters. Half a dozen of the small aircraft were behind him, so he quickly ascended to the clouds. When he dived back down, more planes were above him. Hennon turned and dropped to the deck for one last firing pass parallel to the sandy shore. Several Japanese fighters tried to latch onto his tail, but the faster P-40 was able to pull away in the direction of Clark.

Ki-27s of the 50th Sentai had already given squadron-mate Red Sheppard a difficult time. He made his initial strafing pass on the transports, setting a fire on one. A Japanese pilot immediately gave Sheppard's P-40 his undivided attention. The American tried every maneuver he could think of to shake his pursuer, but bullet after bullet struck his Warhawk. His fighter received more than two hundred holes before he executed a sloppy Immelmann, with which he finally eluded the persistent Ki-27. Looking around to get his bearings, Sheppard quickly turned his fighter in the direction of Clark Field. Only then did he allow his eyes to focus back in the cockpit. He gazed down at the instrument panel. Loss of coolant was causing Sheppard's Allison to overheat. The temperature needle was pegged. As he returned to Clark, the engine quit, forcing him to glide in for a dead-stick landing.

Buzz Wagner moved off the shoreline after his first pass, strafing a cruiser and a minesweeper as he swooped low across the bay. The heavy antiaircraft fire was inaccurate, but he soon found himself prey to several Ki-27s. With highly proficient marksmanship, the Japanese pilot nearest to Wagner's plane poured a bucketful of bullets into the nose and cockpit of the P-40.[3] Lieutenant Wagner was unable to retaliate, but somehow he managed to pull his smoking plane away from the enemy to avoid further damage. This in itself was quite a feat; Wagner had taken one round in his left shoulder, and the shattering windscreen filled his eyes and face with shards of glass and torn aluminum. Bill Hennon had already traveled too far away from Wagner to assist, but Lieutenants Kiser and Wilcox had seen the Japanese plane shooting up Wagner's P-40. Coming to the rescue, the duo guided the wounded Buzz Wagner back to Clark. Despite his injuries, the talented young pilot had no trouble landing, but he would spend most of his remaining time in the Philippines at the Fort Stotsenburg Hospital.

By the time the 20th Pursuit reached Lingayen, Lieutenant Gies trailed behind Moore and descended from the overcast farther out to sea than he intended. Coming down directly above a large cruiser— which he thought was a battleship—Gies received a furious barrage of flak. His plane was untouched as he pulled back into the protective layer of clouds. Heading toward shore, he descended again, this time above the transports. Gies made two strafing runs on the row of ships and gave up. Most of his guns had jammed, and enemy fighters were in the vicinity.

The actions of Moore and White are not clear. They expended their ordnance at the enemy beachhead, but it is doubtful that they obtained any useful results.

AT WAKE ISLAND, Lieutenant Kinney and his assistants had toiled all through the night. With this effort, VMF-211 had two Wildcats patched together for service when the sun rose on December 22. To preserve those fighters for combat operations, Major Putnam waited until about 1000 to send the pilots up on patrol. He thought his planes would be more likely to encounter the enemy at that hour. Captain Herb Freuler's Grumman required some last-minute engine adjustments and was delayed in taking off. Second Lieutenant Davidson departed on his own, heading out to scan the southern approaches.

Captain Freuler finally rose off the airstrip at 1030, banking away to the north and climbing quickly. He had time to ascend to his patrol altitude and comb his northern sector for more than an hour before he finally saw incoming aircraft on the northwest horizon. The formation was a strike force of thirty-three B5Ns escorted by six Zeros from *Hiryu*.[4] The Japanese planes evidently planned to strike Wake at high noon. Freuler pushed the throttle hard and roared toward the virtual cloud of enemy planes. Closing fast and wide, like a lasso-wielding cowboy approaching a herd of cattle, the Marine pilot lined up to slide behind the tail of his first target—one of the B5Ns. The four blazing "fifties" drew smoke from his quarry immediately. The Japanese bomber fell out of formation and curved away in a steep descent. Freuler sped ahead of the other enemy planes and then abruptly turned back into their formation. In a head-on pass, the F4F bucked again as Freuler's machine guns spat at another B5N. The daring Marine captain held the target in his sights as long as he dared, pulling up only at the last possible moment before a collision. He had come in a little too close. The Grumman was no more than forty feet away when the Nakajima blew up in a violent blast.[5] Turbulence from the explosion sent Freuler's Wildcat skidding and damaged its belly.

By this time, Carl Davidson must have noticed the commotion and flown back past Wake to engage in the air battle. When Herb Freuler recovered from his second pass at the enemy, he noticed the other blue-gray Grumman firing on a smoking Japanese plane in the distance. Freuler did not have much time to observe Davidson's other actions—an enemy fighter had already latched onto his own tail. As Freuler desperately tried to shake the Zero, his F4F was filled with holes. The armor plate behind its seat clanged loudly as Japanese bullets lodged in the steel. A few stray shots made it through the side of the cockpit, wounding the American pilot. Instinctively, Freuler nosed the F4F over in a full-power plunge toward the ocean. When he pulled out of this evasive maneuver, the Wildcat's engine was running roughly. He didn't have the time to manually crank down its landing gear and execute a proper approach to the runway. Reluctantly, he brought down the damaged Grumman in a belly-landing on the beach next to the airstrip. Men from the airfield rushed to pull Captain Freuler out of his cockpit. Their job was made difficult because the canopy had jammed in a partially open position. They finally extracted Freuler's limp body from the Wildcat and rushed him to the makeshift hospital.

The Americans never again saw Carl Davidson and his F4F after Herb Freuler had observed him engaging the B5Ns. The men on the sandy atoll had no way of knowing it, but the pilot of the Zero that shot up Freuler's aircraft—Petty Officer Isao Tahara—elected to engage Davidson's plane rather than chasing the diving Grumman that appeared mortally wounded. Tahara's A6M shot up the second F4F in a quick pass.[6] In a matter of minutes, the Marine plane was coasting toward the ocean, trailing black smoke. The air battle for Wake Island was over.

THE BRITISH RETREAT IN MALAYA made it difficult for men on the airfield at Kuala Lumpur to receive any advance warning of Japanese air raids. The forward observer network had not recovered from its withdrawal at Taiping. Notification about a large group of Japanese planes headed toward the new air base was received later than usual. At the vanguard of that enemy formation were eighteen green Hayabusas, carrying the distinctive red arrow of the 64th Sentai on their tails. These Ki-43s approached in two layers. To meet them, RAAF No. 453 Squadron dispatched the largest number of fighters the forces defending Malaya had seen in one action since the war began. At 1000 a dozen Buffaloes raced down the runway at Kuala Lumpur and clawed at the air to gain as much altitude as possible before the enemy arrived. Ordinarily, the squadron would have split into four "vics" of three planes each. In this urgent scramble, the flight organization was disrupted. Calling to pilots on his radio, Flight Lieutenant Vanderfield tried unsuccessfully to restore order as the Buffaloes behind him spread farther and farther apart.

Pilot Officer Livesey, who had just been returned to duty and still had a bandage wrapped around his ribs from the crash in Sumatra, was to have led one of the "vics." His aircraft may not have been developing full power. It failed to lift high enough to clear a sandbagged gun emplacement at the end of the runway. The wheels caught on this obstacle, and most of the Buffalo's undercarriage was torn away. Suffering from the extra drag of dangling metal, Livesey's plane quickly fell behind those of his squadron-mates. Seeing a lame duck, several Ki-43s quickly engaged Tom Livesey as he headed south from the airfield, away from the center of activity. Flying above him, Wild Bill Collyer spotted the handicapped Buffalo with a Japanese fighter on its tail. The enemy pilot was using a zoom-and-stall approach to shoot up Livesey's plane.

Sergeant Collyer tried to take advantage of this, diving in to set up his own shot as the Ki-43 reached its stalled position. He was surprised to see additional tracers flashing over his head and hitting the Japanese aircraft. As some of the fire struck his own plane, Collyer swiveled his head to spot his indiscriminate pursuer more clearly. He realized he was being chased by a second Japanese plane that had carelessly shot both the Buffalo and the leading Ki-43. One enemy bullet entered Collyer's cockpit and ricocheted off the fuel pump primer into his right foot. In pain, the Australian sergeant pulled up in a hard left turn, only to find himself engaged in a head-on pass at another Ki-43. He fired his guns until the two planes met. At the last moment before a crash, Collyer pushed the stick forward to slip underneath his opponent. Wounded, with a heavily damaged plane, he found himself outside the main area of battle. Reluctant to fight his way back in for a contested landing at Kuala Lumpur, Wild Bill Collyer decided to head for Sembawang. The medical care in Singapore would surely be better than whatever was available in Kuala Lumpur.

Sergeant Read challenged the leader of the lower flight of Ki-43s in a violent dogfight. Twisting and turning at treetop height, the combat was inconclusive until Read fatally rammed into his opponent. Whether the act was intentional is unknown. Both Mac Read's Buffalo and Lieutenant Takeo Takayama's Ki-43 fell into the jungle.[7]

Sergeant Harold "Griff" Griffiths managed to hold one vee of Buffaloes together, with Sergeants Clare and Board sticking to his wing up through about eight thousand feet. The small group did not remain in formation for long; Greg Board suddenly dived away. Griff Griffiths was surprised by Board's abrupt departure but quickly refocused on an enemy fighter that appeared in his sights. Pulling the trigger, he thought he saw his tracers hitting the plane as it dropped into a flat spin. Griffiths chose not to pursue that enemy. Instead, he rushed to the aid of another Buffalo pilot, Sergeant O'Mara.

The two Australians became engaged in a deadly game of tag with two Japanese fighters. Matt O'Mara was chased by one enemy, who was in turn trailed by Griffiths, with a second enemy behind him. Both Buffaloes ended up filled with holes. Some of those in O'Mara's plane may have actually come from Griffiths's guns. Griff thought he had shot the enemy off of O'Mara's tail, but it was hard to tell. In any case, he had his own problems to worry about when a third enemy fighter started firing on him in concert with the one already in tow. Hit in the fuel tank and covered with gasoline, the Australian tried every move he could think of to shake his pursuers. Nothing seemed to work. The Japanese fighters were too fast and too maneuverable. Like tigers, they chased Griffiths, taking turns at the attack until they ran out of ammunition. One of the enemy pilots arrogantly pulled alongside the Buffalo and then proceeded to execute a perfect barrel roll around it. Stunned by this display, Griffiths could only watch as the Japanese plane pulled back beside him, a little closer this time. The enemy pilot gave the Australian some sort of hand gesture, flicked his Ki-43 into a sharp, banking turn, and departed to the north.

Sergeant Griffiths returned to Kuala Lumpur and managed to land safely, just in time to witness Pilot Officer Bob Drury making a shallow, fast approach to the runway. Drury's aircraft came in too low, impacting on the embankment at the end of the airstrip. The fuselage of the Buffalo broke apart in the crash. Its engine, with the propeller still spinning, separated from its mounts and rolled out of the cowling. Drury had apparently been wounded during the action, impairing his ability to control the aircraft. His fighter's crash landing probably added further injuries. With help from Griffiths—who jumped from his own Buffalo and sprinted to the scene—men on the ground quickly secured medical assistance, but nothing could be done. Drury died on his way to the hospital.

When Griffiths engaged the fighters, Alf Clare had broken away into his own battle with a twin-engine Ki-48 and several dive-bombers. He sent the Ki-48 away smoking in a gentle glide and claimed one Ki-51 as a kill, with another as a probable.[8] Clare's own words neatly summarize the confusion in these events: "Everybody was shooting at everything, and there was no time to see your enemy aircraft crash if you wanted to stay alive."[9]

A low-flying Ki-48 bomber was the reason for Sergeant Board's unexplained dive away from Sergeants Griffiths and Clare. He had seen the plane sneaking toward the airfield and pounced on it. His aim was true: the target plumed fire and exploded in a shower of burning pieces.[10] As Board began to climb again, he was swarmed by Ki-43s. Handily outmaneuvered, the young sergeant was forced to hit the silk when his fuel tank burst into flame. He dived away, rolled the Brewster over on its back, and dropped free of the open cockpit: "It was a lovely feeling and I enjoyed it thoroughly. It was suddenly quiet after the terrific noise of combat and the scream of the engine. There was absolute silence, except for a lovely wind blowing by me. It was a relief and as I fell towards the trees, I pulled the ripcord."[11]

Sergeant Scrimgeour was directly over the airfield when he bailed out at high altitude. He had also been hit in the fuel tank. His experience, however, was considerably less pleasant than Board's. He was not able to get out of the plane before the exposed parts of his body were burned, and his descent was threatened by Japanese fighters firing on him as he hung helplessly in his parachute. Several times, Stanley Scrimgeour pulled hard on the shroud lines to spill air from the canopy so he could drift away from the line of fire. Eventually, the sergeant made it safely to the ground, his burnt hands raw and bloody from pulling on the cords.

From the ground, the battle had been an awesome spectacle—impossible to observe in its entirety. While Japanese and Australian fighters darted back and forth across the airfield, gunners from the Indian division pounded away with 40-mm Bofors cannon, and Australian ground crewmen ran for trenches or lay on their backs firing rifles into the sky. As combatants fell or disengaged, the most ferocious air combat that would take place over Malaya came to a close. For Japan, the event was a victory, but the young men from "Down Under" had flown their Buffaloes aggressively against the veteran sons of Nippon. In fact, in trying to outfly the Brewsters, a number of Major Kato's men had severely damaged their own aircraft in "high-g" maneuvers; mechanics found structural cracks in the wings of six of the Ki-43s that engaged the Australians.[12]

The great morning air battle over Kuala Lumpur convinced the men of No. 453 Squadron that operating from underdefended airfields in Malaya was unprofitably hazardous. The Australians had taken quite a blow. At 1530 a patrol muster was given, and Buffaloes again taxied out to the end of the runway. Over the treetops, four Ki-43s rushed in, guns firing. The pilots who had served at Butterworth stopped their aircraft and jumped out of their open cockpits, flattening themselves on the ground. Sergeant Peterson, without the benefit of that experience, continued his takeoff run and was shot out of the sky and killed before his Brewster had climbed even a thousand feet. The Hayabusas did not linger to taunt the men at Kuala Lumpur, but the very visible smoke plume from Eric Peterson's burning fighter was a grim reminder that the Japanese owned the Malayan skies.

IT HAD TAKEN more than twenty-four hours for news of the Japanese invasion of Davao to reach the 19th Bomb Group at Batchelor Field. In the absence of specific orders, Major Walsh decided to launch a raid on the enemy fleet in the harbor at Davao. The mission was unprecedented. Each Flying Fortress would carry four 500-pound bombs and one bomb-bay-mounted fuel tank; they would travel nearly two thousand miles in one direction to bomb Davao and arrive at Del Monte Field. The mission represented a leap of faith given that the men in Australia had no idea if the airfield would be in American hands when they got there. Some margin of fuel would remain that might allow the B-17s to divert to Tarakan if it was obvious that the enemy was occupying Del Monte. However, it would be difficult to determine the field status because the bombers were scheduled to reach Davao at dusk and Del Monte after dark. Despite the risk, the timing was deliberate. An evening strike would reduce the likelihood of interception by Japanese pursuit planes, and it would minimize the Fortress crews' chances of being caught on the ground by enemy bombers while they serviced their aircraft.

Walsh hoped the target would be worth all the effort. The 19th Group could not afford to do too many missions like this because the Boeings would wear out more quickly than they could be replaced. Maintenance requirements had already taken a toll.

Only nine of the fourteen B-17s in Australia could be readied for the operation. Major Combs led those planes off the runway at 1043, in a cloud of red Outback dust. After almost eight hours of flight, the formation arrived over Davao at an altitude of twenty thousand feet. As hoped, the Japanese navy was caught entirely by surprise. No anti-aircraft weapons retaliated, and no enemy aircraft were seen in the area. For the first time in the Pacific War, the B-17s dropped their bombs en masse. Thirty-three bombs fell in a single salvo. Three others in one of the planes jammed in the racks.[13] The men of the 19th Bomb Group claimed to have sunk a large tanker and heavily damaged the dock area. In reality, it appears no serious harm had been done: a few Japanese military personnel were killed along the wharf and on two destroyers hit by metal fragments. None of the ships were damaged, and the harbor facilities were still intact.[14] Turning west, into the Mindanao sunset, Major Combs led his planes toward Del Monte.

Landing in darkness, the airmen noticed the airfield was a bit rougher than they remembered. After two days of Japanese air raids, the once peaceful pineapple plantation at the top of the world was no longer serene. The tired crews climbing down from the bombers were relieved that the shadows running out to meet them were not enemy soldiers, but they were stunned to hear of the Japanese invasion at Lingayen. Men at the field were happy to see the bombers return. As long as planes kept coming back, there was a chance to get a ticket out of the Philippines.

December 23

A fortnight of battle in the Far East was complete. Overall, Japan suffered minimal casualties while inflicting maximum damage. With the exception of their first invasion attempt at Wake Island, the Japanese emerged victorious everywhere they attacked. It was the military equivalent of the Midas touch. Admiral Kajioka's tarnishing of this perfect record was about to be rubbed clean, and his humiliation at the hands of Wake's Marine garrison avenged. At about 0200 on December 23, the second Wake invasion operation commenced. It was clear almost immediately that the landing would be successful. The Pacific Fleet staff at Pearl Harbor followed the action at Wake as closely as possible through dispatches from Commander Winfield Cunningham. Not knowing that only a portion of Japan's carrier striking force lurked near the atoll, the officers in Hawaii concluded that the relief expedition could no longer approach Wake in reasonable safety. With that decision, the Americans on the three islands were doomed. There could be no retreat or evacuation. It would be up to Commander Cunningham and Major Devereux to decide whether the Marine garrison should fight to the last man or be taken prisoner. After a brief but vigorous struggle, the legendary defenders of the exposed outpost crumbled. To avoid further bloodshed, Commander Cunningham would surrender Wake that afternoon.

A less dramatic, though no less important, concession was made in Singapore during the morning of December 23. Air Headquarters elected to disband NORGROUP—the RAF operational organization for Malaya. Losses experienced by the Australian Buffalo squadrons could no longer be replaced. It would be necessary to retain as many fighters as possible for the direct air defense of Singapore itself until the shiploads of Hurricanes could reach the island. Reduced to a complement of just three serviceable Buffaloes, No. 453 Squadron was ordered to return immediately to Sembawang. The skies above Malaya were

Taken after the Japanese occupation of Wake, this photo shows at least seven wrecked Grumman F4F-3 Wildcats of VMF-211. Such sights were common at Allied fields throughout the Far East after the first fortnight of war. The plane in the foreground is the one Marine Captain "Hammering" Hank Elrod used to sink the destroyer Kisaragi. (Courtesy of the Naval Historical Center)

officially ceded from the realm of the British Empire and passed quietly to the realm of the Empire of Japan.

MOST OF THE HOURS since Cecil Combs's arrival at Del Monte had been filled with a constant downpour. The only real shelter around the airfield was inside the clubhouse, or the interiors of the aircraft, though none of the AAF men would have the luxury of worrying about staying dry that night. FEAF Headquarters had requested the 19th Group to undertake a bombing mission to Lingayen. Doing their best to ignore the heavy precipitation, the airmen and ground crews serviced the Flying Fortresses. A meal of tinned corned beef and coffee did nothing to lift their spirits. Those who would fly the B-17s knew they were in for a long and dangerous day. Those remaining on the ground would have eagerly volunteered to take the places of men in the bombers. At Del Monte, either the rain would continue or the Japanese would be back to drop bombs—neither prospect was pleasant. Even if it would not accomplish much, a chance to hurt the enemy was worth the personal risk.

Given equipment limitations at the field, only six of the B-17s could be prepared in time to execute a dawn raid. Half of the planes would carry ten 100-pound bombs, and the others up to seven 300-pound weapons. The number of bombs loaded in a Flying Fortress was limited by the need to retain one auxiliary fuel tank, which occupied half of the space in the bomb bay. The ordnance loaded on board the B-17s probably would not sink any large ships, but the cache at Del Monte did not contain heavier bombs.

At 0300 Major Combs was ready to lead his planes away from the drenched airstrip. The starters slowly turned his propellers, but the engines would not catch. After a short delay, Combs realized his Cyclones were not going to run without some help from the mechanics. Command of the mission was passed to Captain Parsel. Pelted by raindrops, Cecil Combs and his crew stood by their plane and watched as the other five B-17s trundled down the field and climbed away, position lights fading into the rainy darkness. If it was possible to get his bomber running, Combs would lead Lieutenants Connally, Walter Ford, and Godman on a second strike at Lingayen in the next few hours. After the episodes involving the lone B-17s of Colin Kelly, Jack Adams, and Shorty Wheless, Major Combs was adamant that his planes not fly alone into enemy-controlled airspace.

With Lieutenant Earl Tash on his wing, Parsel headed out to fly a circle over Macajalar Bay, while Lieutenant Lee Coats formed his own flight with Lieutenants Don Keiser and Ed Teats. All five pilots would attempt a rendezvous of their Boeings before heading north. It was worth expending some extra effort to have all the Flying Fortresses pass over the Lingayen beachhead together.

Gremlins whittled away at the Americans again. The initial trip across the Pacific, a month or more of hard use around Luzon, and the recent long journey from Australia were exacting their toll on the mission participants: Lieutenant Coats suddenly lost power on one engine and opted to retire to Batchelor Field while he still could. Lieutenant Keiser and Teats stayed in formation to complete the mission with Parsel and Tash. As the four B-17s droned northward across the darkened Mindanao Sea, Teats noticed an extra navigation light off to the right side of his plane, moving on a parallel course with Parsel's formation. Teats was almost certain the light did not belong to a friendly aircraft. Alerting his gunners over the interphones, he turned his bomber away from the other three Fortresses to investigate their mysterious companion. Each time Teats closed in, the other plane would slow and drop behind him: "It was maddening. He could fly much slower, and every time we turned or maneuvered, he . . . followed us. It was like trying to evade our own shadow. When I realized that we couldn't shake him and get in suitable firing position, I started to climb."[15]

The dodging aircraft remained unidentified, but it was probably a flying boat from the *Toko Kokutai* making a nightly patrol run between Davao and Legaspi. Lieutenant Teats decided to lure it away from the direction of his three companions. To throw his "shadow" off course, he headed due west and started to gain altitude. The plane followed him until the relentless climb of the B-17 left it behind. Once he was sure the enemy was far enough away from the others, and his own tail, Teats turned north again, increasing his speed in order to arrive over Lingayen at the same estimated time as the others.

Amazingly, Lieutenant Teats got to the target ahead of Captain Parsel and the other two B-17s. Coming in from the east, above the mountains, with the sun rising at his tail, he gazed upon the Japanese fleet in the shadowy waters of the gulf. The picture unfolding below must have been awe inspiring. The AAF men could never have imagined so many ships in one place. Even at Pearl Harbor and San Francisco they had not seen this quantity of cruisers, destroyers, minesweepers, patrol craft, transports, freighters, and landing craft. Like a kid in a candy store trying to decide where to spend two dollars, Teats had difficulty selecting where to drop his small load of bombs. His bombardier, Sergeant C. R. Payne, picked out two large transports. Flying at twenty thousand feet, tracking parallel with the shoreline, Payne released the bombs in a long trail. They fell across the bows of both ships but probably did a negligible amount of damage.

The original orders from FEAF Headquarters directed the 19th Group to land its bombers at San Marcelino after the raid on Lingayen. The B-17 commanders were reluctant to follow that plan after their previous stay at the remote airstrip. In the event that enemy aircraft pursued them from Lingayen, the bomber pilots would be foolish to attempt a landing at San Marcelino, or any other field on Luzon. A more reasonable stopover location would be at the previously unused field at Tanauan, which was outside the usual patrol area of the Japanese fighters. In fact, Lieutenant Thorne had been informed that B-17s might be ordered into that secret field sometime later in the day.[16] However, the bomber crews had little or no knowledge about Tanauan. Given that two-way communication necessary to inform the 19th Bomb Group of Tanauan's location and landing procedures was essentially impossible, that option could not be seriously considered—despite any notification Thorne may have received. When Teats and his crew spotted fighters rising to meet them after their bombing run, they decided to fly as far away from Luzon as they could. Because extra fuel had been burned in the early-morning encounter with the mystery plane, their B-17 could make it only as far as San Jose on the island of Mindoro. The Japanese chose not to pursue Teats as he headed south. Perhaps the pilots had seen the other three B-17s coming over the mountain toward the landing zone.

Captain Parsel and Lieutenant Tash flew across the wide shoreline together at twenty-one thousand feet. Lieutenant Keiser trailed a mile or two behind. Watching the numerous blasts of naval guns shooting at inland targets far below was almost mesmerizing for the aircrews. In contrast, it was disappointing to note the pathetically few muzzle flashes from U.S. and Filipino artillery positions that answered the Japanese fire. The FEAF bombardment was no less disappointing. Between the three planes, fewer than two dozen bombs fell on the Japanese fleet. No hits or secondary explosions were noted. Pursuit aircraft were spotted climbing from the vicinity of the small Lingayen airstrip—evidently already occupied by the enemy. Because the Fortresses flew away at more than 300 miles per hour after dropping their loads, the interceptors did not prove to be much of a threat.

To the men in the B-17s, this mission must have seemed a wasted effort, little more than a thorn in the side of the Japanese giant. They were thoroughly demoralized at seeing dozens of enemy ships at Davao and then spotting more than 150 vessels in the Lingayen Gulf. To survey tens of thousands of enemy troops disembarking from hundreds of landing craft along that beautiful, wide stretch of beach must have left the AAF crewmen with a knot in the pits of their stomachs. Captain Parsel did not even think twice about setting the B-17s down on Luzon. Turning south, he led his flight directly for the Dutch airfield at Laha on the island of Ambon. Having witnessed the overwhelming manpower and materiel support available to the enemy at Lingayen, every man on board the bombers could see that Japan would be able to wrest Luzon and the other islands of the Philippines from U.S. control in the very near future.

The situation may have seemed less dismal to the crews of the four bombers that lingered at Del Monte, but the news they received over their radios was uniformly bad. No actions in the Pacific were coming out in favor of the Allies. Personnel at the airfield were openly envious of the Fortress crews and their freedom to return to Australia. The men on board the B-17s were disappointed at their inability to take passengers back to Batchelor Field, but probably none of them would have traded places with their friends at Del Monte. Other planes would come, and some of those men would escape safely from Mindanao, but the end seemed very near.

Major Combs eventually got his engines started, lifting off from the airfield around 0430. A report from the previous day suggested that the Japanese might be launching another invasion at Cotabato on Illana Bay, along the southern coast of Mindanao. On December 21, Japanese aircraft had attacked the small airfield there. Cotabato was only about seventy miles away from Del Monte, so Major Combs decided to investigate the situation himself. Combs's reconnaissance over Cotabato was decidedly uneventful. He noted no enemy activity there, or around Illana Bay. Instead of returning to Del Monte, Combs kept heading south toward Darwin.

The other planes would take off and circle around Macajalar Bay as soon as they could be serviced and loaded with bombs. Lieutenant Connally would take the lead. He did not want them to remain on the ground any longer than necessary. If they could manage a rendezvous before dawn, they would head for Lingayen. If daybreak came with no contact, they were to head for Australia. Cecil Combs had been adamant: lone planes were not to attack any enemy-infested locations. When faint rays of sunlight shone on the horizon and none of the other B-17s had appeared to join him for the run at Lingayen, the normally independent Jim Connally eventually turned around and headed south.

Lieutenant Ford had become quite ill with a malarial fever. He was not completely capable of piloting his aircraft—just making the trip to Del Monte was a test of perseverance. Fortunately, several other command pilots had flown up from Australia as copilots on this trip. Lieutenant Bohnaker was able to take over for the ailing Walter Ford. Neither Bill Bohnaker nor Henry Godman completed the rendezvous with Lieutenant Jim Connally. Bohnaker opted out of any mission plans and headed straight for Darwin. Godman's B-17 was the last to take off from Del Monte on December 23, leaving at around 0600. The late departure gave his crew an opportunity to make an impromptu raid on Davao shortly after dawn.

Contrary to Major Combs's edict regarding lone bombers, Lieutenant Godman would fly a single-plane operation, but dropping the bombs would lighten his plane's load, adding a margin of safety to the long flight back to Australia. The Fortresses had not met with any resistance the previous evening, so Godman felt there was only a small chance of being intercepted by enemy fighters. In addition, during their time at Batchelor Field, his crewmen had removed their B-17's tail cone and rigged the opening with a single, belt-fed, fixed machine gun that could be fired by pulling a lanyard near the waist positions. Because the Zeros were now known to approach from the Fortress's unprotected tail, Godman's men figured they could dissuade any potential attackers with this new "stinger." The gunners were itching to test the device on an unsuspecting Japanese pilot.

Godman guessed correctly that an interception would not occur at this early hour, but faint light and low-lying clouds prevented his bombardier from obtaining any useful results from the release of their bombs over Davao. Like Coats, Godman had difficulty with an engine and limped back to Australia on three Cyclones.

December 24

In the early morning hours of Christmas Eve, the IJN launched another invasion of Luzon. This one was a critical threat aimed at the vulnerable backside of Manila. Another strong naval force with a large landing contingent of twenty-seven transports descended on the shores of Lamon Bay, between Mauban and Antimonan. Seven thousand Japanese soldiers waded ashore against light resistance.[17] Before long, these troops controlled the heads of the highways that curved around the south shore of Laguna de Bay. Manila was locked in a stranglehold. Brigadier General Al Jones's South Luzon Force—engaged with Japanese units in the Legaspi area—was threatened with the possibility of being cut off from its path of retreat.

A string of dominoes led directly to General MacArthur's doorstep. The USAFFE commander had no choice but to call for a rapid withdrawal to the Bataan Peninsula. MacArthur had never been enamored with the concept of a Philippine defense under the terms of War Plan Orange, but on the morning of December 24, he suddenly reverted to that strategy. All units were to leave immediately for Bataan. The lack of specificity in MacArthur's instruction was disastrous. To say that the confusion that followed was enormous is a gross understatement. Other than General Wainwright's forces holding the new Lingayen front at the Agno River, every military and civilian organization was thrown into absolute chaos. While they did not quite descend to the level of "every man for himself," many base evacuations somewhat resembled the process of rats trying to desert a sinking ship. In most cases, valuable equipment, ammunition, and food supplies were left behind or destroyed as junior and middle-level officers ordered their men to head for Bataan. Without this materiel, MacArthur's forces were plunged immediately into hardship once they arrived at the Bataan Peninsula. USAFFE fighting capability was thoughtlessly squandered.

From General Brereton's point of view, the specified retreat would deprive his FEAF of all functional airfields on Luzon. Within just a few more days, only the makeshift airstrip at Mariveles—little more than a widened section of roadway—would remain under FEAF control. Colonel George and Captain Eads would pull out the stops for a last-ditch effort to create additional airfields along the peninsula at Orani, Pilar, Cabcaben, and Lucanin (which became known as Bataan Field). None of these hastily cleared runways would support any aircraft larger than one of Captain Gunn's Beechcraft 18s.

Back in Australia, Major Walsh sent three more B-17s on the long, uncertain flight to Del Monte.[18] Walsh issued no mission plans this time. He simply instructed Lieutenants Weldon Smith, George Schaetzel, and Al Mueller to proceed north to Mindanao, with the assumption that they would receive targeting orders upon their arrival. Of course, Mike Walsh had no way of knowing that by the time his 19th Group bombers reached the Philippines, the FEAF command would already be dismantled.

Around noon on December 24, General Brereton received a summons from General MacArthur's office. Richard Sutherland—just promoted to the rank of major general—provided Brereton with these orders:

1. You will proceed to the south with your Headquarters, Far East Air Force. Your mission is to organize advanced operating bases from which, with the Far East Air Force, you can protect the lines of communications, secure bases in Mindanao, and support the defense of the Philippines by the U.S. Army Forces in the Far East. You will cooperate with the U.S. Navy and with the air and naval forces of Australia and the Netherlands Indies.

2. You will establish liaison with the Commanding General, U.S. Forces in Australia. [This referred to Lieutenant General George Brett, who was on his way to Australia by way of China.] He is charged with the organization of bases in Australia. You will

direct the operation of the Far East Air Force from those bases and the disposition of Air Corps troops in advance thereof in order to accomplish your assigned mission. You will make request upon the Commanding General, U.S. Forces in Australia, for such movement and disposition of the ground elements of your command as may be required in the execution of your mission.

3. The Commanding General, U.S. Army Forces in Australia, is being furnished with a copy of this directive.[19]

General MacArthur personally spent a few minutes with Brereton, sending the air commander on his way with the following words:

> You go on south. You can do me more good with the bombers you have left and those you should be receiving soon than you can here. Since communications over that distance are practically impossible now, I must depend to the greatest extent upon your own initiative to support our forces here.
>
> I hope that you will tell the people outside what we have done and protect my reputation as a fighter.[20]

One of the first tasks General Brereton undertook after the meeting with General MacArthur was a transfer of command for the remaining AAF personnel in the Philippines to Colonel George. It was an unusual break in the hierarchy of rank—there were other AAF officers senior to the young colonel—but Hal George was considered the best-qualified officer for the job, and General MacArthur enthusiastically supported the choice.

Colonel George was already buried by his workload when he was summoned to Brereton's office to receive the news. Airfield construction was frantically under way, reorganization of the evacuating pursuit squadrons still had to be accomplished, and an attack mission was just that moment heading toward the newest Japanese beachhead at Mauban. As usual, Hal George would take his new responsibilities in stride, moving forward, full speed ahead.

Reflecting the paucity of FEAF resources, the Mauban operation consisted of only two small flights of fighters. The first strike was made by four P-35As; the second by four P-40Es armed with fragmentation bombs.[21] All of the planes departed from Clark and planned to return there before relocation to Bataan. The risk for this mission was considered high. The pilots were all volunteers. Led by 1st Lieutenant Marshall Anderson, the Severskys arrived over the Japanese fleet at about the same time that General Brereton was concluding the meeting with General MacArthur. As Anderson led the planes down from the clouds into a strafing run along the beach, four Zeros from the *Tainan Kokutai* detachment at Legaspi pounced on them. A brief, swirling dogfight took place at low altitude. Amazingly, Anderson and his wingman, 2nd Lieutenant LaMar Gillett, managed to corner one of the Mitsubishis and shoot it down.[22] The Americans paid with heavy damage to both P-35s. Anderson's plane was shot up so badly that he was forced to crash-land and abandon it at Nichols Field. Gillett, escorted by 1st Lieutenant Hugh "Tex" Marble and 2nd Lieutenant Bill Carter, managed to make it all the way back to Clark. By the time these three fighters landed, the base had already become something of a ghost town; a steady stream of cars and trucks exiting through the gates was the primary sign of life.

About an hour after the P-35 raid, while General Brereton and the other evacuating FEAF staff officers were busy packing their bags, the Japanese at Lamon Bay were briefly disturbed, this time by the four P-40s. The Warhawks made several determined passes at transports and landing craft, but it was difficult to determine what, if any, results were achieved. Lieutenant Jim Rowland's plane was hit by antiaircraft fire. A large hole in its fuel tank streamed gasoline through the fuselage from behind Rowland's seat. There was no way the fighter could even make it the short distance to Nichols. To minimize the risk of explosion, Lieutenant Rowland elected a water landing in Laguna de Bay. He ditched the plane safely, making his way to shore with the help of some local fishermen.

MAJOR GENERAL LEWIS BRERETON officially closed FEAF Headquarters at 1600 on December 24. Sadly, most of the men under Brereton's command would be left behind, sacrificed to bolster the ranks of the infantry on Bataan. Those who did successfully escape would often take on incredible challenges to manage their personal journeys to freedom.

Brereton and a selected few officers expected to leave Manila using the small Beechcraft transports of Paul Gunn's "courier service." Other than Captain Gunn's few planes, no army transportation was readily available to the FEAF on Luzon. Because Gunn was in the middle of a run to Mindanao, it would be more than forty-eight hours before the evacuees could depart. If they waited that long, Brereton feared it would be exceedingly difficult to leave Manila while a wholesale retreat to Bataan was fully under way. Thomas Hart generously offered fellow Naval Academy alumnus Brereton space on one of the PatWing-10 PBYs tucked away at Los Baños. Admiral Hart planned to use several of them to evacuate himself and his own large staff to Java, but he could find room for the general and three other army officers. Brereton selected his chief of staff, Francis Brady; his senior aide, Captain Norman Llewellyn; and Lieutenant Colonel Gene Eubank to accompany him. They would join seventeen staff officers from the Asiatic Fleet, who would also be packed into the very crowded aircraft. They could each bring one bag.

On receiving orders from Admiral Hart's office, Lieutenants Harmon Utter and Tom Pollock prepared their Catalina for the short hop from Los Baños to Manila, while their crew removed the camouflage material from its wings and fuselage. As sundown shadows started to cast from the western shore of Laguna de Bay, Utter carefully taxied out from the lakeside and poured on the power. The PBY was off the waters of the lake within a few minutes. Taking advantage of the usual absence of Japanese aircraft in the evenings, the crew brought its flying boat in for a comfortable landing near the demolished air station at Sangley Point. As Brereton and his party loaded their bags on Utter's aircraft, a Japanese plane passed overhead. It was not quite dark yet, so the Catalina surely would have been visible from above. Expecting an attack, men on the ramp at the seaplane base held their breath. The enemy faded into the dusk. Apparently, its pilot had ignored the Catalina, or perhaps the craft was out of ammunition. Whatever the reason, the men standing by the PBY were greatly relieved.

At 2000, with darkness already descended, the PBY with all the officers crammed inside was finally released to begin its long journey south. Utter and Pollock started the engines and taxied out into the bay by the light of fires still burning in Manila and Cavite. They had not anticipated the dramatic increase in barge and boat traffic. Everything that could float was being sailed across Manila Bay to the harbor at Mariveles that night. Just as his Catalina began to lift from the water along the Manila shoreline, Utter spotted a boat dead ahead. Grabbing the throttles, he yanked them closed and pushed hard on his right rudder pedal. The heavily loaded plane swung around with a lurch as the extended left wingtip float slammed into the fifty-foot-long boat. The rest of the flying boat was fine, but with a damaged float it would never get off the water. Several disappointed crewmen climbed out on the right wing to balance the plane while the chagrined pilots taxied back to Sangley Point. Utter had saved Brereton and the other annoyed officers from an explosive death, but someone else would have to take them out of the Philippines if they were going to leave before Christmas.

Lieutenant Commander Edgar "Ed" Neale escorted the contingent of VIPs in a convoy to Los Baños under blackout conditions to commandeer one of the other Catalinas stashed along the shore of Laguna de Bay. It was not an easy drive heading in the opposite direction from withdrawing army troops. General Brereton must have wondered if the fates had it in for him when his car was sideswiped by a truck on the highway. The accident delayed the journey, but thankfully no one was injured. Difficulties continued after the group reached Los Baños. All of the men, laden with baggage and boxes, stumbled around in the dark on muddy trails trying to find the replacement Catalina. Gene Eubank, with his broken arm still in a sling and limping badly from leg injuries, had the most arduous hike. Not until midnight did an embarrassed and irritated Ed Neale finally find Ensign Andy Reid's PBY.

After Reid's plane was loaded with the unanticipated additional weight, its hull became mired in the mud of the lake bottom. Full power on the engines would not even budge the plane. In desperation, young Reid and his seasoned copilot, Chief Petty Officer Edgar Palm, ordered all the passengers to huddle as far forward as space permitted. The weight shift was just enough to do the trick. Roaring at dangerously high manifold pressures, the Twin-Wasps lugged the craft forward into the black waters. For a few minutes, power was reduced as Reid taxied into takeoff position. It was time for the most challenging part of the flight. Reid and Palm crossed their fingers as they pushed the throttles forward to their stops one more time. Significantly exceeding any capacity the Consolidated Aircraft Company ever envisioned, the PBY slogged along across the lake, slowly gaining speed. Running well out of their normal safe-takeoff zone, the pilots were scared they would hit a native fish trap or other dangerous obstruction before they became airborne. To a cheer worthy of Christmas celebration, the Catalina finally broke free of its viscous bond and took to the air. Reid circled the plane a few times to gain altitude and then headed southwest on the course to Soerabaja.[23]

CHAPTER 12

To Fight Another Day

WHILE GENERAL BRERETON WAS FLYING SOUTH in the navy PBY, the crews of the three B-17s that landed at Del Monte Field awaited orders from Manila. No messages had been sent from Luzon. No instructions came from Australia either. The radio channel remained silent. The men on Mindanao had not yet been told that FEAF Headquarters had closed, that Major O'Donnell was in the process of shutting down Clark Field, or that Colonel George was on his way to Bataan. In the absence of any higher directive, the three lieutenants decided to create their own mission plan. Loaded up with seven 300-pound bombs each, their B-17s would conduct a dawn raid on the airstrip at Davao and then return to Australia.

At 0430 Lieutenant Weldon Smith started to taxi his plane from the dispersal area to the runway. A loud banging sound echoed from under one wing, and the large aircraft suddenly tipped to that side. The wear of constant service finally destroyed the rubber shell of Smith's tire. Fortunately, this blowout occurred while the plane was maneuvering at low speed; otherwise the outboard propeller tips might have been bent when the wing suddenly dropped. If the plane had been on a takeoff or landing run, the rapid deflation could have been disastrous. As it was, fixing the problem would require some time and improvisation: there were no wing jacks left at the field, and a replacement wheel would have to be scavenged from one of the three wrecked Boeings. This also meant that Smith's bomber would be stranded in the open for a few hours while the sun was up.

Anxious to be away from the field before dawn, Lieutenants George Schaetzel and Al Mueller left Smith behind, taking off just a few minutes after their intended departure time. Flying close together at fifteen thousand feet, the two Fortresses arrived over Davao at first light. The target area was clearly visible below. As the pair of B-17s lined up to approach the airfield with the proper wind-drift compensation, black bursts of smoke puffed up beside them. Lieutenant Schaetzel had already experienced plenty of combat in his first fortnight of war but had never seen accurate antiaircraft fire before. The puffs came closer and closer, but there was not much sound to be heard from the blasts in the thin air outside the rumbling Fortress—which was traveling at three-hundred miles per hour by this time. Several dull thuds were the only indication that exploding shells had struck home. Schaetzel's B-17 was hit once; Lieutenant Mueller's twice. No serious damage was done before their belly doors opened and the bombs fell free.

The flak abruptly stopped, but not because the bombs had silenced any guns. From the "bathtub" positions underneath the Boeings, the gunners noticed fighters climbing rapidly toward them. A chutai of A6Ms from the *3rd Kokutai* had been transferred to Davao from Palau the previous afternoon. Mueller and Schaetzel pushed their throttles ahead and trimmed the planes to climb. The higher the Flying Fortress could get the better chance it stood against a Japanese fighter. Of course, to this point, Schaetzel's personal experience was limited to tangling with JAAF Ki-27s. To the B-17 crews, the Mitsubishis following them must have seemed to be incredible machines, climbing thousands of feet while gaining on the bombers at the same time.

In a few minutes, the black noses of the gray planes erupted in a shower of glowing, pebblelike flashes that arced in the direction of the two bombers. The Fortress gunners returned fire; their rattling .50-caliber machine guns sent rippling vibrations through the tails of both big bombers. Expended shell casings tinkled off the sides of the fuselage and accumulated in rolling piles on the floor. Oxygen masks kept the men from smelling the pungent odor of burnt gunpowder, but smoke wafted lazily through the aft cabin following each burst of their guns. In a few moments, the slipstream passing by the open side ports would clear the air. The gunners probably did not notice; they were too busy refitting their guns with new ammunition canisters during each break in the firing.

Schaetzel's Fortress took the brunt of the first pass. In a thoroughly professional manner, each Zero pilot approached from astern and blasted at the gun positions and the engines, and then swerved away before defensive fire could hit its mark. Staff Sergeant James Cannon in the gun tub was badly wounded but continued to man his position. One of the engines was shot out, forcing Schaetzel to feather its propeller. With its blades turned sideways into the air stream the prop would not "windmill" and destroy the engine or add drag, but the B-17's climb was topped out at twenty-eight thousand feet. In a short time, the big plane would actually lose altitude and airspeed, even with the other three engines pulling hard.

When Lieutenant Schaetzel's airspeed began to drop, Al Mueller slowed down his plane to stay between the other Fortress and the Zeros. Mueller's gunners would help fend off the attackers. Companionship meant a lot to the crew of the limping bomber, but Mueller's plane became the target of the next several passes. His old B-17C received so many bullet and cannon strikes that parts of it whistled in the rushing air. Most of the panels in its skin came to resemble the surface of a cheese grater. Two gunners in the plane, Corporal Frank Harvey and Private First Class Ed Olsen, were wounded. Somehow, none of the fuel or oil tanks had been punctured. The faithful craft held together with all four engines running smoothly; how that was possible, none of the men could guess.

The flight of Zeros finally dropped away and banked downward, toward the north. The two damaged B-17s settled into a gentle descent to the south. It would be a long trip to Darwin; it would be an even longer one for the men in Schaetzel's plane, who tried, but were not equipped, to save Sergeant Cannon from bleeding to death soon after the battle.

Back at Del Monte, Lieutenant Smith's crew worked feverishly to repair their bomber. With the help of mechanics and construction troops from Del Monte, a wooden stand was built to support the weight of the wing during the wheel change. Volunteers dug a pit under the flattened tire, clearing enough dirt away to remove the wheel assembly. After the replacement was fitted, a shallow earthen ramp was trenched in front of the new tire. In all, the process took almost five hours to complete.

Just when Weldon Smith was about to board his aircraft, he heard the sound of an engine in the distance. Hearts sank as a single-engine plane dropped out of the sky and sped across the field toward the big bomber. A machine gun clattered away. Bullets kicked up dust as they ripped across the ground and into the bomber, but only a few slugs hit the B-17. To everyone's relief, the enemy scout made only one pass above Del Monte before heading back toward Davao.

Inspection revealed a hole in the bomb-bay fuel tank. Mechanics worked quickly to patch the leaking container before more Japanese planes arrived. A few minutes before 1100, with a helpful push on the tail from some of the men on the field, Lieutenant Smith revved the Cyclones and eased the plane out of the small ditch. This time, the B-17 roared down the runway and took to the air before anything else could go wrong; its aircrew heaved a sigh of relief at being off the ground again. Their Flying Fortress would head for Australia, but first they intended to deliver a Christmas present to the invaders at Davao. Jogging his course to the east, Smith passed over Davao harbor at full speed and high altitude. As his bombs fell, A6Ms rose off the nearby airfield to chase the B-17. For once, the Americans were traveling too high and fast for the Zeros. The interceptors never caught up with Smith's plane. Dead tired, the men finally reached Batchelor Field at dusk. It was a hell of a way to spend a Christmas.

IN MANILA, THE NAVY WAS BUSY shuttering its headquarters in preparation for the final evacuation to Java. Admiral Hart's evacuation party planned to leave using two of the three PBYs at Los Baños; both had just been repaired. One was Lieutenant Utter's plane, on which the crew had spent the entire night repairing the wingtip float. The other Catalina was the one in which Ensigns Butch Swenson and John Ogle had been strafed on December 11. A brand-new engine had been installed under its bullet-riddled cowling. The third PBY was not ready to fly yet; it was the one Ensign John Sloatman had impaled on the bamboo fish trap on December 16. The plane had been pumped out, refloated, and patched up. There was still work to be done on its engines and electrical systems to rectify the water damage before it could be checked out as airworthy. All three of these flying boats had been moved away from the safety of their shoreline camouflage because the Los Baños base was to be abandoned the next day. Although the large planes were covered with green blankets and pieces of brush that might fool observers passing at altitude, any low-flying aircraft could spot them for what they were.

A short time after noon, navy personnel around the lakeshore heard the rhythmic thrumming of enemy bomber engines. One could always tell when twin-engine planes were Japanese; they lacked the engine synchronizer devices used on Allied aircraft to match the rotational speed of multiple propellers—a feature designed to minimize airframe vibration. The sound was louder than usual and approaching quickly. As heads turned toward the sky, two bombers flew over—low enough that individual crew members could easily be distinguished. The airplanes were flying too low to drop bombs, but the distinctive, high-speed chatter of several Japanese 7.7-mm machine guns overcame the drone of the engines. The Americans scrambled for cover as bullets struck the water and the shore. A line of small splashes worked its way toward one of the PBYs. Harmon Utter and his copilot, Tom Pollock, were on board the plane at the time. Their crew was ashore preparing for Christmas dinner. Lieutenant Utter and Lieutenant Pollock quickly jumped into the water through the open waist hatches. The pair swam for shore as the full fuel tanks of the Catalina erupted in a blazing liquid fire that quickly spread across the surface of the lake.

In Swenson's Catalina, Aircraft Machinist's Mate Robert Foster reached for a .50-caliber waist gun to return fire at the bombers. As the bombers made several strafing passes at the plane, Foster's heavy gun kept clanking away. Switching back and forth on the gun mounts, from one side of the plane to the other, the flight engineer was oblivious to anything but his targets. He managed to silence one of the enemy gunners, but water in the PBY hull rose up to his ankles before the Japanese bombers went away. Foster managed to escape without injury—a truly amazing feat given that his compartment was filled with holes.

Some distance from the other two PBYs, Sloatman's unoccupied flying boat had drawn equal attention from the raiders. When the enemy bombers finally faded into the northern horizon, that Catalina was also sinking quickly—for the second time in a week. This time, it would remain on the lake bottom, sharing a watery resting place with Lieutenant Utter's airplane.

Enterprising crews at Los Baños would manage to patch up Swenson's plane and fly it to Manila, but it would never leave the Philippines. In fact, only one last PBY would make a getaway from Luzon: the stripped aircraft being rebuilt by Lieutenant Joe Antonides on the Pan American seaplane ramp. That one would escape the next day, but it was not considered fit enough to risk transporting Admiral Hart. The commander of the Asiatic Fleet would have to depart from the Philippines on one of his submarines.

Most sailors and navy boats that could not make a journey to Java or Australia—including 154 men from PatWing-10—gathered at the Mariveles base to participate in the defense of Bataan.[1] All of these men would suffer great hardship. A few would eventually escape from the Philippines, but many were destined to die there.

FROM HIS NEW HEADQUARTERS in the Malinta Tunnel on the island of Corregidor, General MacArthur issued a proclamation that Manila should be considered an "open city," free of U.S. military presence. This political gesture was an attempt to save Manila from further destruction at the hands of the IJA, but the statement produced little effect other than a disruptive hastening of the already disorganized retreats to Bataan and Corregidor. The Japanese had no intention of honoring MacArthur's Christmas Day missive. Manila would suffer accordingly.

The USAFFE commander and his staff set about assessing their position under the newly imposed constraints of War Plan Orange. The situation was not promising. In part because MacArthur had chosen to ignore the retreat plan previously—as he focused on creating an organization to repel enemies at the beaches—many preparations that should have been completed on Bataan either were well behind schedule or had never been initiated. At half rations, Generals Wainwright and Parker figured they could hold Bataan for four to six months, maximum; after that, the men would starve—the peninsula offered little in the way of vegetation or wild game of nutritional value. Although General MacArthur did a fairly thorough job of hiding the truth from others at lower levels in his command, he knew that help was not on the way. In fact, one of the first messages he received at Corregidor provided confirmation to that effect: "In view of your message relative to future tactical operations on Luzon, it now appears that the plans for reaching you with pursuit planes are jeopardized, Stop. Your day to day situation and that of Borneo will determine what can be done at any moment but the War Department will press in every way for the development of a strong United States air power in the Far East based on Australia."[2]

Aerial resistance would continue from Bataan under Colonel George's leadership, but the incompletely equipped U.S. air forces in the Philippines—which had been so boldly positioned in the role of a strategic deterrent to Japanese aggression—had been totally defeated by the aggressors in barely more than a fortnight. With this failure, the collapse of the Philippines would come about just as War Department planners had predicted for so many years in their War Plan Orange scenarios. It would be a bitter pill for the American public to swallow, and much worse still—by a great measure—for the thousands of men stranded in a hopeless defense of Bataan. Those who were taken prisoner on Bataan or at Corregidor would discover that surrendering to the Japanese was even more perilous than fighting against them. Eclipsed in the spotlight by the focus on shortcomings of the commanders at Pearl Harbor, the plight of these gallant men, and women, in the Philippines—army, navy, and Marine; American and Filipino—was as desperate as any in uniform would suffer anywhere, during World War II. The United States' armed forces would experience no greater defeat in battle than they did on Luzon. The loss of the Philippines is the most infamous in the history of the U.S. military establishment, and a failed application of airpower was largely to blame.

FOR THE BRITISH, CHRISTMAS DAY BROUGHT the surrender of Hong Kong. With no air defense and very limited antiaircraft capabilities around that island, the Japanese air campaign was effective in breaking down strongholds on the ground. The long, exposed supply line to Hong Kong guaranteed that no reinforcements would have been forthcoming. Air Chief Marshal Sir Robert Brooke-Popham's last-minute prewar decision to increase garrison strength there had been a poor one.

After the first fortnight of battle, the Japanese were ready to shift their offensive into its next phase (and their primary objective): the seizure of the resource-rich Netherlands East Indies. Japan expanded the scale of its invasions during the Christian holiday to include Kuching (on the western side of Sarawak) and the island of Jolo (between Mindanao and northern Borneo). One could see an emerging parallel between the situations at Singapore and Hong Kong. As Japan swept through the islands south of Singapore, the "Gibraltar of the East" soon became just as isolated and nearly as vulnerable as Hong Kong had been at the start of the war.

The upcoming campaign would no longer be Air Chief Marshal Sir Brooke-Popham's concern. Conveniently, the term of his leadership agreed upon before he was sent to Malaya would expire on December 28. General Sir Henry Pownall was already on his way to relieve the British Commander in Chief, Far East. Because of this changing of the guard, there would be no serious inquiry regarding Brooke-Popham's performance in the defense of Malaya. He would be gone before Singapore fell. Nor would there be any investigation of Admiral Tom Phillips's role in the leadership of the campaign—he had already paid the ultimate price.

Brooke-Popham evidently came to understand some of the failings in the air campaign and had a few things to say about them. He issued a rather scathing confidential memorandum to Air Vice Marshal Pulford that remains one of the strongest appraisals of the RAF defense of Malaya—and, by proxy, Singapore:

> During the last fortnight it has been necessary to order the evacuation of several RAF aerodromes. It has come to my notice that in some cases the process has been badly carried out. This has been due largely to failure on the part of those responsible to organise in advance and set a proper example of leadership.
>
> There have been many cases of gallantry and devotion to duty on the part of individual officers and airmen, but there have also been instances where aerodromes appear to have been abandoned in a state approaching panic. Stores have been left behind, material that is urgently required has been abandoned and a general state of chaos has been evident.
>
> This is utterly opposed to all traditions of the Air Force over a period of 30 years. It is the duty of every commander, whatever may be his rank, to remember his first duty is towards the officers and men who are under his command; his second duty is to see that the aeroplanes or other material for which he is responsible is safeguarded, moved, or if no other course is possible, rendered useless to the enemy. After he is satisfied on all these points, then and only then is he at liberty to think of his own safety and comfort.
>
> In the majority of cases the bombing of aerodromes has been on a smaller scale than that suffered calmly by women and children in London and other towns in England, and aerodromes have usually been vacated whilst still well out of range of enemy land forces. Several of the moves back were carried out in a regular and orderly manner; there is no reason why they should not all have been.
>
> Let us hope that there will be no further need for withdrawal, but whether this be so or not, I look to everyone to play his part, not only in ensuring that there is no ground for criticism of RAF movements in future, but that we in Malaya add our full share to the high reputation being gained by the Air Forces of the Empire elsewhere.[3]

Pulford would bear this parting shot steadfastly and soldier on, leading the air units through the downfall of Singapore. A number of mid-level officers in charge of the Malayan air stations would be forced to stand before formal boards of inquiry at a later date. Pulford himself did not have to suffer the indignity of any official inquisition regarding his role in managing the air battle for Malaya. He died on a remote island between Singapore and Sumatra, when the Royal Navy patrol craft used for his evacuation came under attack and had to be abandoned. Seventeen of his companions, including Admiral Sir Phillips's successor, Rear Admiral E. J. Spooner, also perished. The others were eventually captured by the Japanese. Pulford's last words to General Percival at Singapore were "I suppose you and I will be held responsible for this, but God knows we did our best with what little we had been given."[4]

The British rout in Malaya had indeed been brought about by a failing in the employment of airpower. Even with an infusion of new fighter planes in January, the premature withdrawal from airfields in Malaya would come back to haunt the Far East Command. Too much valuable ground had been yielded, too soon. With Singapore Island air bases under constant attack by Japanese air forces, fighter dispersal and maintenance became a significant problem in January 1942. Without security in the skies above, the beleaguered defenders could not operate effectively, and the campaign was soon lost. Remarkably, very little blame for this was affixed to those in command at Singapore—despite evidence of some very poor decision making.

As General Sir Archibald Wavell—formerly Commander in Chief, India—took on overall responsibilities for Allied defense in the Far East, Prime Minister Winston Churchill implored Wavell to defend Singapore as aggressively as possible: "I want to make it absolutely clear that I expect every inch of ground to be defended, every scrap of material . . . to be blown to pieces to prevent capture by the enemy, and no question of surrender . . . until after protracted fighting among the ruins of Singapore city."[5]

Churchill's message rang in the same tone as Brooke-Popham's departing memorandum to Pulford. Wavell realized that the damage had already been done. By January 21, he acknowledged that the most important effort would be to build an air force presence in the Netherlands East Indies that was "capable of securing local air superiority and thereby checking the Japanese advance southwards." The general considered "naval and land efforts subordinate, for the time being, to the need for a really strong air force." Wavell's response to Churchill's plea was not encouraging: "I am anxious that you should not have a false impression of the defence of Singapore Island. I did not realize myself till lately how entirely the defences were planned against seaward attack only."[6]

The acknowledgment was important, if a little late. Under crushing pressure from Japanese airpower, Singapore would fall to an army of inferior numbers, three weeks later, on February 15, 1942.

On the U.S. side, only Admiral Thomas Hart and the leadership of his Asiatic Fleet emerge from history as being beyond reproach for their actions in the Philippines. In Manila, the navy faithfully followed its long-established prewar plans. If anything, Hart could receive criticism only for taking additional naval casualties by keeping too many people and resources on Luzon to assist the army.

Significant failings in the command of Douglas MacArthur's USAFFE were essentially overlooked. In large part, this oversight could be attributed to media focus on the situation closer to home, in Hawaii. Political agenda makers followed only a few steps behind the press. To whip up the American public into a war-winning frenzy, it seemed necessary to appeal to the United States' innate disdain for unfair treatment. Shining a spotlight on the event that represented a "sneak attack" was a useful way to accomplish this. Japan's "dastardly attack" had genuinely shocked the American people. Of course, the assertion that this spectacularly successful military operation could not have been accomplished solely on the merit of Japanese capabilities was patronizingly racist; someone in the U.S military leadership must have "fouled up" in allowing such an act to occur. In the court of public opinion, such a deed could not go unpunished for long. It would not. For this special situation, a full-blown witch hunt was in the offing. Within a week of the attack on Pearl Harbor, President Roosevelt established the Roberts Commission to carry out a full investigation of the military command in Hawaii. A joint congressional committee would eventually convene to provide additional judgment based on information available later in the war. Before the search for culpability was over, there would be no fewer than eight formal investigations into the incident—including one chaired by a recently retired Admiral Hart.[7]

It is beyond the scope of this work to delve into the details of the investigations about the leadership at Pearl Harbor. Suffice it to say, the two senior service commanders on the scene in Hawaii, Admiral Kimmel and General Walter Short, were given over to the pillory. Their otherwise untarnished careers—in the case of Husband Kimmel, one characterized by exemplary service—were ended in a very public humiliation.

Inquiry into the events at Pearl Harbor would officially continue until 1946. The last review by congressional committee would take some of the sting out of the previous findings of the Roberts Commission by stating that Kimmel and Short were guilty of "errors in judgment and not derelictions of duty." The findings are very interesting considering what might have surfaced, had anyone shown an interest in looking toward the Far East. The summary report blamed the two officers for failing

(a) To discharge their responsibilities in the light of the warnings received from Washington, other information possessed by them, and the principle of command by mutual cooperation.

(b) To integrate and coordinate their facilities for defense and to alert properly the Army and Navy establishments in Hawaii, particularly in the light of the warnings and intelligence available to them during the period November 27 to December 7, 1941.

(c) To effect liaison on a basis designed to acquaint each of them with the operations of the other . . . and to exchange fully all significant intelligence.

(d) To maintain a more effective reconnaissance within the limits of their equipment.

(e) To effect a statement of readiness throughout the Army and Navy establishments designed to meet all possible attacks.

(f) To employ the facilities, materiel, and personnel at their command . . . in repelling the Japanese raiders.

(g) To appreciate the significance of intelligence and other information available to them.[8]

While those findings constitute the official "last word" on Pearl Harbor, the verdict of history continues to receive play—occasionally spurred on by deathbed confessions of personnel involved. Sixty years after the fact, the United States has not quite put the topic to rest. Stockpiles of historical information regarding the attack compiled after the Pacific War lend credence to the validity of the preceding statements. However, were the failings cited really the reasons that the Japanese attack succeeded? Furthermore, how would such an investigative body have treated the role played by the two commanders had those officers known in advance that the Japanese were *definitely* going to attack? Would the success of enemy action under those circumstances have been judged a greater "dereliction of duty"? Looking at the debacle in the Far East, one wonders how MacArthur's actions in these categories—or those of Air Chief Marshal General Brooke-Popham—would have held up under similar scrutiny. These two commanders knew what was going to happen, and still failed to act appropriately—especially on the opening day.

Although Kimmel and Short could shift some blame for their surprise onto senior officers in Washington, D.C.—including some direct actions and inactions of the top military commanders, General George Marshall and Admiral Harold Stark—MacArthur and Brooke-Popham could never claim to have been surprised by the Japanese attacks on their areas of responsibility during December 8. It is, therefore, more than a little ironic that Admiral Kimmel, who had permanently lost only two aged battleships and slightly more than 2,500 men, and General Short, who had lost fewer than a hundred planes and less than a thousand men, would receive such negative scrutiny under the spotlight of historical study. To put those losses in perspective, Brooke-Popham's command eventually suffered more than 9,000 battle casualties, and nearly 130,000 British and Commonwealth soldiers would be interned in Japanese prison camps for the duration. This was Great Britain's worst military disaster—ever. The campaign in the Philippines was also the United States' most costly defeat. Combined U.S. and Filipino casualties totaled nearly 16,000 men dead or wounded, plus 84,000 troops captured after the fall of Bataan and Corregidor. Relative to the tragedy at Pearl Harbor, these were enormous losses.

As Air Vice Marshal Pulford so succinctly suggested—and the Pearl Harbor inquiries seem to have adroitly avoided—that first infamous fortnight of the Pacific War in the Far East reflected primarily a failing in the management and application of airpower. Inability to assimilate lessons of the air war in China was paramount. With few exceptions, the Allies did not understand the degree to which Japan would initially focus on activities by its air forces. Misunderstandings of Japanese strategic intent led Allied commanders to defend the wrong assets in several significant engagements, including those actions taking place on the first day of the war. As mentioned before, the Allies grossly underestimated Japan's technical capabilities with aircraft. Paying closer attention to Japanese air force activities over central China and

Nomonhon would have yielded the wisdom necessary to do a far better job of defending Malaya and the Philippines.

Of course, the general state of affairs in the Far East—as described in Chapters 1 through 3—was problematic. Apart from their lack of understanding of the enemy, Allied commanders were plagued by other serious issues. In addition to the qualitative and quantitative deficit of aircraft, many air units shipped to the Pacific and the Far East had arrived piecemeal, often without the necessary supplemental equipment or support organizations. By the time of the Japanese attack, Allied frontline squadrons were staffed largely with men just out of training, led by inexperienced junior officers who had not earned the trust and full confidence of recently arrived senior officers. U.S. organizations in place for any length of time had just rotated their most experienced personnel back home to form desperately needed cadres for newly recruited units entering training. Compounding these already serious command problems was an understandable lack of coordination between the multinational forces charged with defending the Far East. Despite detailed discussions such as the Argentia and Singapore conferences, little combined activity occurred prior to December 8, 1941. For fear of provoking Japan into conflict prematurely, U.S., British Commonwealth, and Dutch armed forces felt they could not visibly join in any firm alliance until hostilities with Japan actually commenced.

In the end, few questions were asked. General MacArthur emerged from the confines of the Malinta Tunnel to escape Corregidor in early 1942 as a national hero—a symbol of resistance to the powerful forces of the Empire of Japan.

Apart from some questionable command decisions, one glaring failure in MacArthur's relationship with his subordinates is evident: the fact that he rarely consulted directly with his air force commander, General Brereton, on whom he depended so completely. MacArthur seemed to prefer dealing with Brereton through the USAFFE chief of staff, Richard Sutherland. Until the very end, it appears that MacArthur could rarely find adequate time for discussions with Brereton. As captured in the narrative, this apparently inexcusable shortcoming in communication had a direct effect on the outcome of battle on December 8, 1941.

General Hap Arnold, commander of the AAF, stated after the war that he had never received adequate explanation for the FEAF's failures on December 8. Brereton's confidential, personal report to Arnold on this topic has yet to surface, but it apparently did little to satisfy Arnold's curiosity. After the war, Brereton rarely spoke of that first fortnight in the Philippines. His 1946 book, *The Brereton Diaries*, has been left to speak for him.

Lewis Brereton went on to lead the AAF in an equally difficult air campaign to defend the Dutch position in Java. After that episode, he would briefly organize and command the Tenth Air Force in the China–Burma–India theater. In preparation for the Allied counter-invasion of North Africa, Brereton was reassigned to the Middle East to take command of the Ninth Air Force. He would continue success-fully with this command into Europe, eventually earning the rank of lieutenant general.

As General Brereton summarized, airfield security was a major shortcoming in both the Philippines and Malaya. Reflecting on nearly four more years of wartime experience, General Brereton published the following assessment after the war:

> The ultimate collapse of resistance in the Philippines, which was due primarily to the loss of airpower, can best be explained by stating two basic principles of war, violation of which throughout history has invariably caused disaster. They are:
>
> (1) Failure to provide security.
> (2) Failure to provide mobility.
>
> Security was violated by not providing adequate defensive measures for protecting the air striking force; for the protection of the ground forces and maintenance crews; and for the protection of the installations essential to the air defense of Luzon. On 8 December we had only one radar set working on Luzon, and it was destroyed in the first air attack. Our communications and air warning service, totally inadequate at best, were unable to function in the critical first few days.
>
> Failure to provide mobility resulted from the early planning which had not foreseen heavy bombers in the organization of the Philippine Air Force. Thus, only two fields suitable for heavy bomber bases were available, at Clark Field and the one hastily constructed at Del Monte.[9]

In terms of security and mobility, the British, having been at war for two years, possessed the greatest knowledge. RAF Group Captain Robert Darvall from the Air Headquarters staff at Singapore made a tour of the AAF installations on Luzon during June 1941. His report, orally presented to General Clagett's Philippine Department Air Force at the conclusion of the visit, was officially presented at Singapore in August. It did not reach General Marshall's desk until November 10.[10] In the report, Darvall cited numerous deficiencies in Philippine air-field security. At the top of his list were inadequate dispersal capacity and an absence of camouflaged service areas. He also pointed out the lack of antiaircraft weaponry, along with more passive measures such as shelters for ground personnel to use during air raids. Overall, he was very concerned about the small number of airfields available to Clagett's air force. In particular, Darvall expressed distress about an almost exclusive dependence on Nichols Field for maintenance opera-tions. Because Nielson Field served as the commercial airport for Manila, it was nearly impossible to adequately secure it for military use prior to hostilities. Had Darvall known about the plan to move large numbers of heavy bombers to the Philippines, he probably would have been horrified; the focus of his evaluation was targeted primarily at establishing successful fighter operations.

Colonel Hal George and Lieutenant Colonel Lester Maitland—who was in charge of operations at Clark Field—evidently took the material to heart. Colonel George was relentless in his quest to identify and acquire new sites for airfields throughout the islands, but, as recorded in the narrative, the colonel was unable to secure additional properties until the war actually began and martial law was invoked. Once that happened, his preparation allowed him to move quickly; the creation of fields at San Marcelino, Lubao, Tanauan, near Del Monte, and around Bataan is ample evidence. That these fields materialized when they did is a tribute to Colonel George's initiative and energy, and the amazing capacity of his engineering officers: Captain Harold Eads and Lieutenant Colonel Ray Elsmore. Without the field develop-ments at Del Monte, the air battle for the Philippines might have been over in less than a week instead of a fortnight. In that scenario, proba-bly none of the personnel from the Far East Air Force would have been able to escape imprisonment by the Japanese. Critical knowledge of Japanese air strategy and tactics would have been lost.

Maitland—actually a celebrated aviation pioneer and Army Air Service veteran of the Great War—was only partially able to address the issue of ground shelters. In the fall of 1941, Maitland ordered a number of slit trenches dug around Clark Field. His network of ditches—humorously referred to as "Maitland's Folly" during the digging process—saved many lives on December 8 and thereafter. Other airfields in the FEAF command would not have such shelters until after Japan attacked. By then, it was too late, as discovered at Iba.

Aircraft dispersal, even at airfields with adequate real estate, was never really addressed. There was simply not enough usable area at Nichols, Iba, or the tiny airstrip at Nielsen Field to properly distribute airplanes to minimize damage from enemy air attacks. Yet, at Clark Field—which possessed more than enough area to create pursuit dispersals—only a few revetments were built before the war. Captain Allison Ind, General Clagett's intelligence officer, described the situation on the ground at Clark during the first Japanese bombardment—where an exact repetition of the situation General Brereton had personally witnessed on November 26 occurred—after the general insisted that it never should happen again:

> There had been some dispersion, unquestionably, but a photograph which fell into my possession for a few moments—a photograph made by one of our own pilots in flight over the stricken field—showed through a frame of sweeping smoke, four B-17s lined up neatly. Other photographs, taken on the ground, all told a nauseating story of half-measures. The dispersion conceivably might have been adequate for high-level bombing, but offered only some inconvenience to determined low-level strafers. This entire set of photographs was removed from my desk a few nights later. No one seemed to know what happened to them. Whether they were removed by order, I do not know—nor do I have any ideas as to whose order it might have been.[11]

Although there is no basis for any accusation, one can safely assume that a number of officers would have been very reluctant to have such photographic evidence available for General Brereton's, or General Arnold's, review. In Brereton's own words, citing a December 11 telephone conversation with Hap Arnold, Arnold was very unhappy with the air force's performance: "'How in hell could an experienced airman like you get caught with your planes on the ground?,' General Arnold asked. 'That's what we sent you there for, to avoid just what happened.'"[12]

As for the antiaircraft defenses, MacArthur's USAFFE command possessed no modern weapons, and no proper range finders for the artillery it did have. In addition, all the stockpiled 3-inch ammunition was of World War I vintage and therefore did not have adequate altitude or proximity fusing. Hitting aircraft at heights of twenty thousand feet or more was virtually impossible. Marine positions protecting Cavite and Sangley Point were better equipped, but their weapons were too few in number to make much difference. All the new antiaircraft equipment was on the ships of the "Pensacola Convoy," out in the middle of the Pacific during the first fortnight of the war. Japanese strafers would have succeeded in their destructive low-level attacks in any case; there were no intermediate antiaircraft weapons in the Philippines at all, and none in transit. Automatic cannon of the 20-mm Oerlikon and 40-mm Bofors types were virtually nonexistent in the U.S. Army inventory before the war. The only places one could find such weapons in U.S. hands during 1941 were on board newer, or recently refitted, naval ships. Shooting at speeding aircraft with manually aimed, canister-fed .30-caliber and .50-caliber machine guns was practically a waste of ammunition. Most gunners simply did not possess the skill or luck necessary to do much damage. In fact, there were more recorded cases of enemy aircraft being brought down by infantrymen using rifles.

Despite their additional combat experience, the British did not do a proper job of airfield security in Malaya. Unlike General Brereton's organization, Brooke-Popham's Far East Command possessed an adequate quantity of bases. However, most of those air stations— especially those south of the Penang area—were hastily constructed improvements of existing civilian landing fields. Even the purpose-built bases at Kota Bharu, Kuantan, and Sungei Patani were somewhat lacking in critical dispersal areas. A late start on these projects and prioritization of other activities prevented the dispersal task from being accomplished before the war began.

Apart from issues with assignment and capabilities of the fighters, the most significant factor affecting the defense of airfields in Malaya was the command decision to retain the vast majority of antiaircraft guns at Singapore, allegedly to appease the civilian population. As a direct result, no adequate weapons were put in place before the loss of the key northern air stations. By the time some Bofors cannon were deployed at Ipoh and Kuala Lumpur, the battle in the air was effectively over. As Air Chief Marshal Brooke-Popham highlighted in his dressing down of Air Vice Marshal Pulford, the unnecessarily hasty base evacuations caused the British war effort enormous setbacks. Indisputably, troops at the airfields and their commanders failed in some basic tasks. Still, the intense pressure of enemy bombing raids, combined with constant fighter harassment, quickly demoralized men who had no capacity to retaliate with the weapons they had on hand. That shortcoming in equipment was more the fault of the senior commanders than of the soldiers on the ground. The situation at Kuantan in particular—where large stockpiles of vital aviation supplies had been gathered with absolutely no means of protecting them—could hardly be forgiven.

Perhaps the primary reasons that proper thought had not been given to the air defenses were the poor understanding and incredible underestimation of Japanese aviation capabilities—misjudgments that affected both the Americans and the British equally. In the Philippines, the assumption that U.S. planes were vastly superior to those of Japan was a costly mistake. That viewpoint, complemented by a general lack of proper tactics for fighter aircraft deployment, caused an unnecessary loss of P-40s. Young, inexperienced AAF pilots were forced to learn by trial and error how to combat their skilled and well-equipped foes. Technical problems of machine-gun maintenance and inadequate oxygen supplies greatly compounded the difficulties caused by poor combat tactics. As much as the unfortunate loss of the radar set at Iba Field seriously handicapped the early warning system on Luzon, the edge afforded by radar technology would not have offset the numerous general errors in tactical deployment or pilots' disastrous predilection to engage in individual dogfights.

After two weeks of heavy combat with Japanese air forces, many surviving American fighter pilots became disillusioned with their aircraft. Some men developed an outright inferiority complex. Claire Chennault's "Flying Tigers" later proved that battle tactics better suited to the true capabilities of the Tomahawk and Warhawk could make a great difference in their success during air combat. The P-40 could bring down Zeros and Ki-43s effectively—when used properly. Curtiss fighters could never hope to prevail on equal terms with the Mitsubishi; no amount of skill could overcome the basic deficiencies of the design.

Apart from the initial missions flown by the RAF Blenheims over Malaya, the air campaign in the Far East was also basically a contest between U.S. and Japanese aircraft designs. The British did not hold the U.S. aircraft industry in very high regard prior to the war, and the Commonwealth employed U.S.-sourced planes out of desperation rather than desire. Of all U.S. aircraft types tested in England, the only one that had earned suitable respect by December 1941 was the

Lockheed Hudson. It rings with irony that U.S. air services never had a high opinion of that aircraft. Initial actions by the Australian squadrons in defending Kota Bharu added nicely to the Hudson's reputation in Great Britain. In comparison, the Bristol bomber, which was also well liked by the RAF, made a generally poor showing over Malaya and Thailand. The Blenheims were "easy meat" for IJA fighters.

Universally, the Brewster Buffalo earned the wrath of command- ers, pilots, and historians alike for its dismal performance above the Malayan jungle. There are some good reasons for that viewpoint— many resulting from Brewster's poor management practices rather than an inherently poor design. Without doubt, the Buffalo—especially the British 339E version—was underpowered. Brewster, observing ques- tionable ethics in attempting to meet production deadlines, fitted many of these Buffaloes with rebuilt airline engines. U.S. aircraft slated for export depended on their manufacturer for engine sourcing, and engine supplies were constrained at the time. The same airframes in U.S. livery usually had their engines supplied by the service purchasing the aircraft—as "Government Furnished Equipment." Test- ing in Singapore of a number of the "new" Buffalo engines revealed that the rated power was seldom achieved; in many cases, output was significantly below normal.[13] If that was not troubling enough, the fuel system employed substandard electric pumps that failed at altitude, requiring pilots to manually actuate a booster pump in the cockpit to maintain adequate fuel pressure. Fuel delivery was also inadequate when engaging in maneuvers that required full power. Both conditions had an adverse effect on the 339E's already inferior rate of climb. Today, the problems induced by the Brewster Aircraft Company would have surfaced in a major scandal and public outcry. At the time, the issues were lost in the shuffle.

There was also an inherent design weakness in the Buffalo's landing gear, which occasionally caused trouble. Australian pilots actually suffered less from this problem than their U.S. Navy and Marine coun- terparts. Soft turf fields in Malaya were more forgiving than a carrier deck or asphalt runway. The short-coupled nature of the Brewster's fore- aft balance took a greater toll; whenever the wheels dug in under hard landings, there was usually a propeller-destroying nose-over, or an even more dangerous turnover. At least the Brewster's structure was stout; most pilots who flipped their 339Es walked away with only minor injuries. Still, the majority of men who flew those planes would seldom remember Brewster's product fondly. The men who commanded them made certain that Brewster eventually went out of business—as soon as it was clear that other manufacturers could accommodate all future production volume requirements for fighters and dive-bombers. Other Brewster designs built after the start of the war would never be used in combat, and no Buffaloes would enter the fight after the Battle of Midway in June 1942. Interestingly, the Buffalo is the only World War II Allied fighter for which no examples of the plane exist any longer. By contrast, even a few of the much less produced Seversky P-35s can still be found in museums.

Some mechanical problems with British and Australian Buffaloes were not attributable to Brewster as a manufacturer. Most troubling was the frequent failure of the .50-caliber guns. As in the Philippines, the wet, tropical environment caused corrosion-related jams. Open ends of the gun barrels were exposed to moisture on the ground, extreme heat during firing, and extreme cold at altitude, not to mention the accumulation of dirt from dusty airfields and primitive maintenance environments. Most of these problems were compounded in Malaya because the aircraftmen servicing the Buffalo armaments were unfamiliar with the peculiarities in maintaining U.S. weapons.

The Buffalo was somewhat vindicated when the Hawker Hurricanes that were eventually acquired for the air campaigns over Singapore and Sumatra fared no better against the Japanese than had the Brewster— even with pilots of greater experience operating from better-defended bases, with much better air warning services. By that time, the damage to Brewster's already tarnished reputation was complete. Even historians have given no reprieve to the Buffalo in the years since the war. For the most part, the technical criticisms were fair. Squadron Leader W. J. Harper expressed many of these criticisms in his detailed summary report of RAAF No. 453 Squadron operations over Malaya.

The Buffalo's role as scapegoat for the loss of Malaya hides some failings better attributed to Air Vice Marshal Pulford's command in Singapore. For example, Harper, an English Battle of Britain veteran, was acutely aware of the inexperience of his very young Australian pilots. One could even go so far as to say that he was inordinately overcritical of their efforts. Harper was not alone. British RAF commanders did not hold Australian aviators in high esteem. The incident at Kuantan only reinforced that negative opinion. Unquestionably, Australian—and New Zealander—fighter pilots were the least trained of all Allied fliers to engage the Japanese at the outbreak of the war. On close observation of their record, however, there is little to suggest that they performed any less effectively than any other group of fighter pilots. Heavily outnumbered by the enemy, and with longer odds against their Buffaloes than most Allied pilots faced, the young Australians' record over Malaya actually appears quite admirable.

Overall, the British Far East Command in northern Malaya was deficient in its air warning system. Available radar sets had been reserved to provide air-raid warnings to Singapore. Thus, radar installations were located too far south for use in the early days of air combat over northern Malaya. In the first week of war, aircraft observer positions were only a few miles ahead of the forward airfields, not enough to give adequate notice of incoming enemy aircraft. By the second week of war, observer units were in full-blown retreat from the Japanese army. Observers could hardly be effective while on the run. A final contributing factor to the poor showing of the Buffalo over Malaya—peripherally mentioned in Australian summaries—was the nature of scramble operations conducted by invariably British air station commanders. Most of those officers were veterans of the air war in Europe. They were familiar with the response they could expect from fast-climbing Spitfires and Hurricanes but were quite slow to adjust to the need to have Buffaloes at altitude well before interception activities could take place. One memorandum near the end of the Malayan air campaign addressed expectations for station behavior in response to early warning reports for Singapore:

> Further to the decision that aircraft stay on the ground if aerodromes are attacked by the Japanese; reasons for this decision are:
>
> (a) Great confusion if rush take-off attempted.
> (b) Japanese fighters will probably either carry out attack alone or escort bombers; aircraft taking off would be easy meat.
> (c) If aircraft took off, aerodrome defences, including Bofors, could not fire.
> (d) Crews of aircraft can take cover in almost complete safety.
> (e) Good dispersal of aircraft and use of pens should keep aircraft losses down.
> (f) False alarms of attacks will not cause waste or damage.
> (g) Our aircraft floating about would greatly confuse A.A. defences.
> (h) This refers to air raids at any time of the day, not only at dawn.[14]

In contrast to the diminished capability of the British observer and warning systems, certain Japanese spotters were practically on top of

British airfields to constantly monitor activity. Japanese observations were somewhat limited by their lackluster implementation of radio technology. When one accounts for differences between U.S. and European equipment design and use philosophies and those of the Japanese, one realizes that much of Japan's weaponry was actually well suited to its purpose. Radio was the glaring exception: Japanese communications gear was seriously deficient. It was of shoddy enough quality that most fighter pilots had the radios removed from their planes to shed the extra weight. As a consequence of poor radio communications, Japan's forward observers may not really have had the full impact ascribed by the British.

One aspect of Japanese intelligence operations that did affect air battles was airborne reconnaissance capability. The JAAF was equipped with the extraordinary twin-engine Mitsubishi Ki-46 Type 100 Command Reconnaissance Plane (the "Dinah"). Capable of operating at altitudes of up to thirty-four thousand feet, and speeds of 375 miles per hour at altitudes above thirty thousand feet, the Ki-46 was untouchable by any Allied aircraft available in the Far East at the time. Allied pilots would have had a difficult time even spotting these planes. Intercepting them was out of the question. The Ki-46 had been employed to photograph Malayan and Philippine bases before the outbreak of war and was regularly used to monitor British and U.S. base activities after the battle began.

The intelligence these planes returned to the Japanese was invaluable. Comparatively speaking, Japan had an excellent reconnaissance-based grasp of Allied air situations, while the Americans and the British were virtually blind. As related previously, the long-range reconnaissance conducted by the Allied commands was limited to what could be accomplished by Catalina and Flying Fortress crews. General MacArthur's conservative directive regarding the use of the latter, even after receiving General Marshall's "war warning" message, prevented successful reconnaissance over Japanese air bases on Formosa. The Catalinas, especially the PBYs of PatWing-10, did an excellent job of patrolling the South China Sea and Japanese naval bases along the coasts of Formosa and Indochina, but their crews learned nothing useful about enemy air installations—which proved to be, by far, the more important consideration.

If there was any Allied aircraft that could have been considered deserving of praise, or exceeding expectations during the defense of the Far East, it would be the B-17. Although the big Boeing did not achieve any real measure of combat success in the manner in which it was employed, the design inspired reverence among its crews. The Flying Fortress more than lived up to its name during the battle over the Philippines. In all of the missions flown during that first fortnight, only four crewmen from the 19th Bomb Group had been killed in the aircraft. Just a handful of others were wounded.[15]

Under sustained and ferocious attack from cannon-armed Zeros, a number of the durable bombers had been shot to ribbons and still made it home to their bases; only two of the planes had actually been forced down—those flown by Captain Colin Kelly and Lieutenant Jack Adams. This was a tremendous testimony to the Fortress's survivability, something the crews would never forget. As those crews learned what could and could not be done with their planes, the Fortress would become one of the most valuable weapons in the "Arsenal of Democracy." Its reputation followed it from the Pacific to Europe. During the latter campaign, the B-17's durability would become legendary. Although the Consolidated B-24 Liberator would be produced in greater quantities—and would still be flying missions after the last Flying Fortress was retired—most aircrews preferred assignment to the beloved Boeing.

SADLY, IT WOULD TAKE MANY MONTHS for Allied military leadership to fully appreciate and apply all of the knowledge bitterly gained in this first fortnight of the air campaign in the Far East. Given the sacrifices and contributions made by this group of airmen in learning the lessons—which would change the way Allied airpower was applied in both the Pacific and Europe—it is distressing to see that history has largely ignored the story of these stalwart individuals who nobly fought against all odds—known and unknown—in the skies above Malaya and the Philippines. For men and women stranded at Bataan and Singapore, the suffering was just beginning. The "lucky few" who managed to flee the Philippines and Malaya would soldier on in an encore performance during the losing battle for the Netherlands East Indies. If they managed to escape from that fiasco, they were obligated to lead last-ditch efforts to defend New Guinea and Australia before they would have any chance of getting home.

While it is true that they may have been beaten by the enemy, that some of them may have complained vigorously about receiving a raw deal, one characteristic stands out: none of them ever gave up trying to take the battle back to the enemy. For that, succeeding generations can be thankful.

ACKNOWLEDGMENTS

FIRST AND FOREMOST, THIS BOOK IS DEDICATED TO the men who flew and fought under great hardship for the cause of freedom—especially to those for whom a wing and prayer were not enough to bring them safely home.

For many years, I have studied the battles in the Pacific War that took place between the United States and Japan, perhaps because I have spent my entire life on the doorstep of that vast ocean, perhaps because I have been acquainted with a number of participating veterans. Stories of this great conflict captured my imagination from a very young age. As a resident of Oahu during those formative years, I naturally had more than a passing interest in events at Pearl Harbor. Through succeeding decades, as I read each account of events taking place west of Hawaii, my quest for knowledge eventually took a turn down an unexpected path. I realized that a properly comprehensive story of the genesis of this war had yet to be written—one with the important facts, an impartial analysis reflecting the perspectives of both sides, and enough excitement to fully engage the audience. Up to this point, the only way to understand the whole story behind the U.S., British, and Australian military disasters was to read dozens of volumes.

It is, of course, my sincere desire that this book will provide serious students of the Pacific War with new insight about the early period of the campaign for control of the Far East. But, more important, I hope that other, more casual readers will find its material interesting enough that they too will be inspired to learn more about the contest for influence in Asia.

In the process of putting this story to paper, I have come to learn that creating a nonfiction book is quite a journey in many different respects, particularly for someone academically classified as neither a journalist nor a historian. Writing about events sixty years after the fact, I had to depend on the prior work of many others. I pored through hundreds, even thousands of pieces of information—accounts, reports, quotes, and photographs—in an attempt to reconstruct the scenes and personalities no longer accessible in their original form. As a researcher and writer, one must eventually rely on one's own judgment when laying down the final words. If, during that process, I have unfairly characterized any individual or organization, I alone accept responsibility and offer my sincerest apology.

It is impossible, within the space available, to acknowledge everyone who contributed to making this publication a reality, but I am duly grateful to all those who have provided assistance, advice, and motivation over a period of many years. There are, however, a few people I should thank directly for their support in my endeavor.

At the top of the list are some veteran writers who unselfishly invested their own scarce time to review various drafts and provide sage input: Henry Sakaida, Barrett Tillman, and Bill Bartsch have my unflagging gratitude, as does Colonel Dave Weisman, USAF (Ret.), for facilitating my dialogue with these gentlemen. I am also thankful that Colonel Weisman—a uniquely experienced fighter pilot who flew in combat from the desperate days of the Battle of Britain through the last day of war in the Pacific—was willing to share his own views on the topic.

My journey toward a manuscript would never have started without the influence and stories provided by two family friends and officers of the 19th Bomb Group who piloted bombers in the very first pioneering missions across the vast expanse of the Pacific: the late Brigadier General James Chapman, USAF (Ret.), and Colonel James Anderson, USAF (Ret.)—both of whom were first lieutenants in 1941.

Readers with knowledge of the Pacific War may be able to visualize the battle sequences, but most people need to rely on photographs to frame their image of the equipment and events described in this text. I am thankful, therefore, to the following individuals for their assistance in obtaining pictures for this book: photo collector Rod Larson of *Warbirdpix.com*; Jaques Trempe and the folks at *1000aircraftphotos.com*; Chris Widenbar, curator of the Aviation Heritage Museum in Western Australia; Laura Waayers, Historical Services Manager at the Naval Historical Foundation; Chris Marshall and Julie Lee from the Australian War Memorial; Sarah Parke at the National Museum of the U.S. Air Force; Lynn Gamma and Archie DiFante at the Air Force Historical Research Agency; Peter Dunn from *ozatwar.com*; Osamu Tagaya; Wilco Vermeer; Tina Coombe; and last—but not least—Mitch Williamson.

There are, as one might imagine, numerous other individuals—far too many to recognize by name—at various archives and museums around the world who, as a part of their daily routine, have cheerfully provided information in one form or another.

For having faith in this project and my ability to get the job done, I would like to salute Eric Mills, Chris Onrubia, Linda O'Doughda, Susan Artigiani, and the rest of the team from the Naval Institute Press. Special recognition is also in order for my copy editor, Linda MacLatchie at Stratford Publishing, and Stratford's project manager, Nick Maier.

A little closer to home, I owe a debt of gratitude to my friends Sharon Webb, Gary Pomeroy, Richard Schwartz, Jim Nybakken, Rich Miller, and Walt Furman for reading, and rereading, many chapters and providing valuable critique. And thanks to the many others not on this list who have reviewed various bits and pieces along the way. For reading more intently than most, while correcting many flaws, I must thank my mother—and talented grammarian—Marty Butler Furman. I must also give grateful credit to my son, Andrew Burton, for his excellent work in producing the maps included with this manuscript. Without doubt, the largest debt is owed to my wife and frequent proofreader, Wendy, and my children, Andrew, Sarah, and Michael, all of whom have graciously sacrificed copious amounts of their time, energy, patience, and bookshelf space—even their dining room table—to indulge me in this effort.

APPENDIX

U.S. and Australian
Combat Aircraft Losses

Since most Australian and U.S. aircraft were marked with a specific "tail number"—conveniently corresponding to the inventory serial number—it is frequently possible to trace the fate of a given RAAF or AAF aircraft to a particular date and crew assignment. The numbers are quite useful in correlating photographs with events. The U.S. Navy and Marine Corps assigned a Bureau Number to each aircraft—which served the same purpose but was not as obviously marked on the plane. Often, Bureau Numbers were painted in small black fonts under the tailplane—virtually indistinguishable from any distance, or in most photographs. During 1941, navy and Marine aircraft had their squadron and plane numbers painted prominently on the fuselage. In most cases, it would be a challenge to associate the plane number to a specific Bureau Number. As a result, the table refers to the squadron markings.

The greatest difficulty lies in positively identifying army pursuit aircraft shipped to the Philippines. FEAF P-40 and P-35 aircraft did not carry numerical markings with any sort of regularity. To make matters worse, aircraft maintenance cards with useful "tracking information" were lost during hasty base evacuations on Luzon. It is therefore nearly impossible to associate a given FEAF pursuit plane tail number with its actual AAF serial number. In the absence of squadron records, the problem of identifying fighters used on specific missions is compounded; those aircraft were generally assigned to pilots on an event-by-event basis. For defensive operations in the early stages of the Pacific War, pilots sometimes scrambled in whatever plane was available. When multiple aircraft were lost on a mission under such circumstances, one could not hope to determine a pilot-to-airplane relationship unless a wreck was recovered.

The following summaries are provided for those interested in a regular tabulation of daily U.S. and Australian combat aircraft losses across the entire Far East area. There is an entry for each aircraft lost in the air or ground—or a quantity of aircraft lost on the ground where no specific data are available—which includes the details of date of loss, aircraft type, serial number (if available), location, reason, unit affiliation, and pilot name (if manned). Losses are listed in approximate chronological order. Only aircraft "permanently lost" in the combat zone are considered. The list may contain inaccuracies. The author compiled it from information in a variety of sources, including (alphabetically): Army Air Forces Historical Study No. 29; Bartsch, *Doomed at the Start*; Cressman, "Magnificent Fight"; Cull, *Buffaloes over Singapore*; Hendrie, *Lockheed Hudson*; Messimer, *In the Hands of Fate*; Salecker, *Fortress Against the Sun*; and Shores, Cull, and Izawa, *Bloody Shambles*.

December 8, 1941

Aircraft Type	Aircraft Serial Number	Location of Loss	Reason for Loss	Unit	Pilot (Crew Disposition)
Hudson	A16-94	Offshore Kota Bharu	Antiaircraft	No. 1	Leighton-Jones (4 KIA)
Hudson	A16-19	Offshore Kota Bharu	Naval antiaircraft	No. 1	Ramshaw (3 MIA)
Hudson	A16-41	Kota Bharu	Shrapnel damage; crash	No. 8	Spurgeon
PBY-4	P-4	Malalag Bay	Strafing	VP-101	
PBY-4	P-7	Malalag Bay	Strafing	VP-101	
Hudson	A16-20	Kota Bharu	Strafing	No. 1	
Hudson	A16-24	Kota Bharu	Damage/strafing	No. 1	
Hudson	A16-52	Kota Bharu	Damage/strafing	No. 1	
Hudson	A16-53	Kota Bharu	Damage/strafing	No. 1	
Hudson	A16-70	Kota Bharu	Ground action	No. 1	
Hudson	A16-90	Kota Bharu	Ground action	No. 1	
Buffalo	W8222	Sungei Patani	Bombardment	No. 21	
Buffalo	NA	Sungei Patani	Bombardment	No. 21	
F4F-3	4024	Wake Island	Bombardment	VMF-211	
F4F-3	4027	Wake Island	Bombardment	VMF-211	
F4F-3	4028	Wake Island	Bombardment	VMF-211	
F4F-3	4030	Wake Island	Bombardment	VMF-211	
F4F-3	4032	Wake Island	Bombardment	VMF-211	
F4F-3	4037	Wake Island	Bombardment	VMF-211	
F4F-3	4049	Wake Island	Bombardment	VMF-211	
P-40E	NA	Iba Field	Bombardment; crash	3 PS	Woolery
P-40E	NA	Iba Field	Bombardment; crash	3 PS	Root (KIA)

December 8, 1941 *Continued*

Type	Serial	Location	Event	Unit	Name
P-40E	NA	Iba Field	Crash	3 PS	Roberts
P-40E	Qty. 5	Iba Field	Bombardment/strafing	3 PS	
P-40E	NA	Clark Field	Shot down	3 PS	Ireland (KIA)
P-40B	Qty. 20	Clark Field	Bombardment/strafing	20 PS	
P-40B	NA	Clark Field	Bombardment/strafing	24 PG HQ	
P-40E	NA	Nichols Field	Combat damage	21 PS	Grashio
P-35A	NA	Del Carmen Field	Forced landing	34 PS	Robb
P-40E	NA	Rosales Field	Combat damage	3 PS	Neri
P-40E	NA	Zambales Mountains	Shot down	3 PS	Ellstrom (KIA)
P-40E	NA	Clark Field	Shot down	3 PS	Ellis
P-40E	NA	Lingayen	Crash	3 PS	Powell
B-17C	40-2048	Clark Field	Bombardment/strafing	19 BG	
B-17C	40-2067	Clark Field	Bombardment/strafing	19 BG	
B-17C	40-2077	Clark Field	Bombardment/strafing	19 BG	
B-17D	40-3059	Clark Field	Bombardment/strafing	19 BG	
B-17D	40-3068	Clark Field	Bombardment/strafing	19 BG	
B-17D	40-3069	Clark Field	Bombardment/strafing	19 BG	
B-17D	40-3075	Clark Field	Bombardment/strafing	19 BG	
B-17D	40-3076	Clark Field	Bombardment/strafing	19 BG	
B-17D	40-3088	Clark Field	Bombardment/strafing	19 BG	
B-17D	40-3094	Clark Field	Bombardment/strafing	19 BG	
B-17D	40-3095	Clark Field	Bombardment/strafing	19 BG	
B-17D	40-3099	Clark Field	Bombardment/strafing	19 BG	

December 9, 1941

Type	Serial	Location	Cause	Unit	Pilot
P-40E	NA	Del Carmen Field	Crash	17 PS	Lodin (KIA)
P-40E	NA	Del Carmen Field	Struck by crashing plane	17 PS	Hughett
P-40E	NA	Clark Field	Crash	21 PS	Clark (KIA)
B-17D	40-3100	Clark Field	Struck by crashing plane	19 BG HQ	
P-40E	NA	Clark Field	Crash	21 PS	Coleman
P-40E	NA	Clark Field	Crash	21 PS	McCown
P-40E	NA	Clark Field	Crash	21 PS	unknown
Buffalo	W8224	Offshore Butterworth	Shot down	No. 21	McKenny
Buffalo	W8232	Butterworth Airfield	Forced landing; strafed	No. 21	Williams
Buffalo	W8236	North of Butterworth	Shot down	No. 21	Montefiore
Hudson	A16-92	Kuantan	Bombardment/strafing	No. 1	
Hudson	A16-4	Kuantan	Bombardment/strafing	No. 8	
Hudson	A16-15	Kuantan	Bombardment/strafing	No. 8	
Hudson	A16-43	Kuantan	Bombardment/strafing	No. 8	
Buffalo	AN188	Penang Island	Combat damage; crash	No. 21	White
Buffalo	W8151	Sembawang	Crash; engine failure	No. 453	Collyer
Buffalo	W8210	Sembawang	Ground accident	No. 453	Peterson

December 10, 1941

Type	Serial	Location	Cause	Unit	Pilot
P-40E	NA	Nichols Field	Shot down; own antiaircraft	3 PS	Mahony
Hudson	A16-69	Offshore Laha	Crash	No. 13	McDonald (4 KIA)
P-35A	NA	Vigan	Engine failure	34 PS	Houseman
P-35A	NA	Offshore Vigan	Crash; exploding target	34 PS	Marett (KIA)

December 10, 1941 *Continued*

P-40E	NA	Abra River	Shot down	17 PS	Sheppard
P-40E	NA	Clark Field	Crash	20 PS	McCowan
P-40E	NA	Clark Field	Crash	3 PS	Newman
B-17D	40-3063	Clark Field	Struck by crashing plane	19 BG	
P-35A	Qty. 7	Del Carmen Field	Strafing	34 PS	
P-40E	NA	North of Manila	Shot down	20 PS	Woodside
P-40E	NA	North of Manila	Shot down	20 PS	White
P-40E	NA	East of Manila	Shot down	17 PS	Feallock
P-40E	NA	North of Manila	Shot down	3 PS	Krieger
P-40E	NA	Manila Bay	Shot down	3 PS	Benson
P-40E	NA	Nichols Field	Shot down	17 PS	Hobrecht (KIA)
P-40E	NA	Manila Bay	Shot down; own antiaircraft	17 PS	Phillips
P-40E	NA	San Fernando	Shot down	17 PS	Glover
P-40E	NA	Maniquis	Crash; landing	21 PS	Burns
P-40E	NA	Plaridel	Crash; out of fuel	3 PS	Gehrig
PBY-4	P-12	Laguna de Bay	Shot down	VP-101	Snyder (8 KIA)
B-17C	0-2045	Clark Field	Shot down	14 BS	Kelly (2 KIA)
B-17D	0-3086	Offshore Zamboanga	Ditched; out of fuel	14 BS	Montgomery

December 11, 1941

F4F-3	4019	Wake Island	Crash; combat damage	VMF-211	Elrod

December 12, 1941

Type	Serial	Location	Cause	Unit	Pilot
B-17D	40-3098	Del Monte Field	Crash; engine failure	30 BS	Adams
B-17D	40-3087	Del Monte Field	Struck by crashing plane	93 BS	
PBY-4	P-16	Olongapo	Strafing	VP-102	
PBY-4	P-17	Olongapo	Strafing	VP-102	
PBY-4	P-18	Olongapo	Strafing	VP-102	
PBY-4	P-19	Olongapo	Strafing	VP-102	
PBY-4	P-20	Olongapo	Strafing	VP-102	
PBY-4	P-21	Olongapo	Strafing	VP-102	
PBY-4	P-27	Olongapo	Strafing	VP-102	

December 13, 1941

Type	Serial	Location	Cause	Unit	Pilot
P-40E	NA	Near Aparri	Shot down	17 PS	Coss
Buffalo	AN213	Penang Island	Shot down	No. 453	Vigors
Buffalo	W8192	Butterworth	Combat damage	No. 453	O'Mara
Buffalo	W8180	Sumatra	Crash	No. 453	Livesey
Buffalo	W8158	Sumatra	Crash	No. 453	Brown (KIA)
Buffalo	W8176	Sumatra	Crash	No. 453	Neale (KIA)
Buffalo	W8217	Ipoh, Malaya	Crash; landing	No. 453	Leigh-Bowes
Buffalo	W8152	Butterworth	Shot down	No. 453	Angus
Buffalo	W8225	Butterworth	Shot down	No. 453	Oelrich (KIA)

December 14, 1941

Buffalo	AN201	Butterworth	Shot down	No. 21	White (KIA)
F4F-3	4020	Wake Island	Crash; ground loop	VMF-211	Freuler
F4F-3	3980	Wake Island	Scrapped for parts	VMF-211	
B-17D	40-3073	Masbate	Shot down	19 BG	Adams (1 KIA)
B-17D	40-3096	Cagayan, Mindanao	Combat damage; crash	19 BG	Wheless

December 15, 1941

Buffalo	AN172	Port Swettenham	Crash; landing	No. 21	Kinninmont
P-40E	NA	Nielson Field	Crash; runway barrier	3 PS	Steele

December 16, 1941

PBY-4	P-24	Lake Lanao	Taxiing accident; sunk	P102	Szabo
P-40E	NA	Vigan	Shot down	17 PS	Church (KIA)

December 18, 1941

Buffalo	W8211	Ipoh	Crash; landing	No. 453	Collyer
Buffalo	W8216	Ipoh	Crash; aborted takeoff	No. 453	Board
Buffalo	Qty. 4	Ipoh	Bombardment/strafing	453/21	

December 19, 1941

B-17D	40-3093	Del Monte Field	Strafing	14 BS	
Buffalo	Qty. 2	Ipoh	Crash; landing in air raid	No. 21	Kirkman; unknown
PBY-4	P-14	Sangley Point	Bombardment	VP-101	
P-40E	NA	Clark Field	Crash; landing	20 PS	Phillips
P-40E	NA	San Marcelino	Crash; landing	20 PS	Rowland

December 20, 1941

| P-35A | NA | Near Manila | Shot down | 24 PG | Crosby |

December 21, 1941

| Buffalo | W8206 | Kuala Lumpur | Shot down | No. 453 | Leys |

December 22, 1941

P-40E	NA	Clark Field	Combat damage	17 PS	Wagner
P-40E	NA	Clark Field	Combat damage	17 PS	Sheppard
P-40E	NA	Nielson Field	Crash; runway barrier	17 PS	Hughett

December 22, 1941 *Continued*

F4F-3	4022	Wake Island	Combat damage; crash	VMF-211	Freuler
F4F-3	3988	Wake Island	Shot down	VMF-211	Davidson (MIA)
Buffalo	AN175	Kuala Lumpur	Collision with enemy	No. 453	Read (KIA)
Buffalo	AN204	Kuala Lumpur	Combat damage; crash	No. 453	Drury (KIA)
Buffalo	AN184	Kuala Lumpur	Combat damage; crash	No. 453	Livesey
Buffalo	W8160	Kuala Lumpur	Shot down	No. 453	Scrimgeour
Buffalo	W8170	Kuala Lumpur	Shot down	No. 453	Board
Buffalo	W8207	Kuala Lumpur	Shot down	No. 453	Peterson

December 23, 1941

P-40E	NA	Nielson Field	Crash; runway barrier	24 PG	Balfanz

December 24, 1941

P-35A	NA	Nichols Field	Combat damage; crash	24 PG	Anderson
P-40E	NA	Laguna de Bay	Antiaircraft damage; ditched	24 PG	Rowland
P-40E	NA	Nielson Field	Crash; aborted landing	24 PG	Fossey

December 25, 1941

| PBY-4 | P-5 | Los Baños | Strafing | VP-101 |
| PBY-4 | P-29 | Los Baños | Strafing | VP-102 |

December 26, 1941

| PBY-4 | P-2 | Manila | Demolition | VP-101 |

Legend for Unit Identification:

BG = Bombardment Group
BS = Bombardment Squadron
PG = Pursuit Group
PS = Pursuit Squadron
VMF = Marine Fighting Squadron
VP = Navy Patrol Squadron

NOTES

Introduction

1. Author estimate from aerial photographs. Sources vary considerably in description of usable runway width.
2. Cressman, "Magnificent Fight."
3. Dean, *Hundred-Thousand*, 473.
4. Cressman, "Magnificent Fight."
5. Ibid.
6. This F4F was 211-F-9, which Elrod had flown. Captain Frank Tharin was taxiing the craft at the time of the accident. Cressman, "Magnificent Fight"; O'Leary, *Naval Fighters*, 45.
7. Wukovits, *Alamo*, 58; Cressman, "Magnificent Fight."
8. Quote from Roosevelt address to Congress, December 8, 1941. Encarta Standard Encyclopedia (Redmond: Microsoft Corp., 2004).
9. Brereton, *Diaries*, 7.
10. Craven and Cate, *AAF in WWII*, 1:79.

Chapter 1

1. Chennault, *Way of a Fighter*, 89–95.
2. The P-26 could employ heavier mixed armament of one .30-caliber with one .50-caliber weapon, but none were deployed to the Far East in that configuration.
3. Diehl, *Front Page*, 119.
4. Sakaida, *JAAF Aces*, 11.
5. Hata and Izawa, *JNAF Aces*, 427.
6. Chennault, *Way of a Fighter*, 89–95.
7. Prange, *At Dawn We Slept*, 4.

Chapter 2

1. Miller, *War Plan Orange*, 53–64.
2. Craven and Cate, *AAF in WWII*, 1:104–5.
3. The PBYs were assigned the following aircraft numbers: 101-P-1 to 101-P-14, and 102-P-16 to 102-P-29. Messimer, *Hands of Fate*, xiv.
4. Craven and Cate, *AAF in WWII*, 1:176.
5. The Army Air Corps P-35A serial numbers delivered to the Philippine Air Depot were 41-17434 to 41-17473, and 41-17477 to 41-17493. Bartsch, *Doomed at the Start*, 433.

6. McDowell, *P-40*, 5–9.

7. Donald, *Encyclopedia of World Aircraft*, 352.

8. Quantity of B-17s delivered by the close of 1940 is from Davis, *B-17*, 9–11. The groups were the 2nd (Langley, Va.) and the 19th (March Field, Calif.). Maurer, *Air Force Combat Units*, 25–28, 65–68.

9. The medium groups were the 17th (Pendleton, Ore.) and the 22nd (Langley, Va.). The light groups were the 3rd (Savannah, Ga.) and the 27th (Hunter Field, Ga.). All four groups would serve in the Pacific. Maurer, *Air Force Combat Units*, 29–32, 61–63, 71–73, 78–79.

10. Persico, *Roosevelt's Secret War*, 60–62.

11. The AAC serial numbers were 41-18890 to 41-18899. Avery, *North American Aircraft*, 1:49.

12. Craven and Cate, *AAF in WWII*, 1:177.

13. Ibid., 1:105.

14. Ind, *Bataan*, 27.

15. The P-40Bs received at the Philippine Air Depot were 41-5258 to 41-5282, 41-5284, 41-5285, and 41-5287 to 41-5290. Bartsch, *Doomed at the Start*, 13, 433.

16. Dean, *Hundred-Thousand*, 233–34.

17. Bartsch, *Doomed at the Start*, 13–15.

18. Edmonds, *They Fought*, 33; Bartsch, *Doomed at the Start*, 13–15.

19. Layton, *And I Was There*, 131–35.

20. Spaatz, "Memo to Arnold, Sept. 1, 1939."

21. Army Air Forces Historical Study (AAFHS) No. 111, 8, 204; AAFHS No. 45, 18–20.

22. Spaatz, "Memo to Arnold, Sept. 1, 1939"; Stimson Secret File, "Nov. 4, 1941."

23. Bartsch, *December 8*, 118.

24. Ind, *Bataan*, 50–54; Edmonds, *They Fought*, 30–31; Bartsch, *December 8*, 119–20.

25. Freeman, *Flying Fortress*, as contained in *Great Book*, 101–56.

26. Dean, *Hundred-Thousand*, 233–34.

27. Craven and Cate, *AAF in WWII*, 1:178–79.

28. The pilots and B-17s that made this historic flight were Major Emmett O'Donnell (40-3061), Captain William Fisher (40-3093), Captain Colin Kelly Jr. (40-3095), Lieutenant Henry Godman (40-3097), Lieutenant Ed Teats (40-3078), Lieutenant Gil Montgomery (40-3086), Lieutenant George Schaetzel (40-3091), Lieutenant Donald Keiser (probably 40-3096), and Lieutenant Weldon Smith (40-3079). Salecker, *Fortress Against the Sun*, 395; author correction for Keiser plane number. Captain Fisher was the pilot of the damaged plane.

29. Brownstein, *Swoose*, 29, 33.

30. AAFHS No. 111, 23; Bartsch, *Doomed at the Start*, 23.

31. Phillips, *Beechcraft*, 20, 75; Kenney, *Pappy Gunn*, 30.

32. Ind, *Bataan*, 59; Edmonds, *They Fought*, 11.

33. Bartsch, *Doomed at the Start*, 30–32.

34. The most accurate tally of pursuit strength seems to be Bartsch, *Doomed at the Start*.

Chapter 3

1. Gillison, *Australia in the War, Air*, 1:11–12.
2. Ibid., 1:13.
3. Ibid., 1:16.
4. Ibid., 1:21.
5. Ibid., 1:143–46.
6. Dean, *Hundred-Thousand*, 436–39.
7. Ibid., 445. The RAF serial numbers of the 339Es delivered to the Far East were W8134 to W8250, and AN168 to AN217. Pearcy, *Lend-Lease Aircraft*, 114.
8. Derived from list in Cull, *Buffaloes over Singapore*, 230–34.
9. Gillison, *Australia in the War, Air*, 1:155–58.
10. Shores, Cull, and Izawa, *Bloody Shambles*, 1:50.
11. The Brereton Mission apparently flew in B-17 40-3067 rather than Eubank's normal aircraft, 40-3100. The reason is not clear, but "67" was one of very few Fortresses camouflage-painted by that date. Time and date of departure are accepted from Ind, *Bataan*, 70.
12. Ibid., 74.

Chapter 4

1. Ind, *Bataan*, 76–77.
2. Edmonds, *They Fought*, 56–57.
3. Ibid., 60.
4. Frank Kurtz recounted in White, *Queens Die Proudly*, 13–14. His B-17 was 40-3099.
5. Gillison, *Australia in the War, Air*, 1:195.
6. Edmonds, *They Fought*, 38–39.
7. Ind, *Bataan*, 91.
8. Prange, *At Dawn We Slept*, 445.
9. Messimer, *Hands of Fate*, 28.
10. Ibid., 28.
11. The pilots and Fortresses of the 14th Squadron at Del Monte were Major Emmett O'Donnell (40-3061), Captain Colin Kelly Jr. (40-2045), Lieutenant Henry Godman (40-3097), Lieutenant Ed Teats (40-3078), Lieutenant Gil Montgomery (40-3086), Lieutenant George Schaetzel (40-3091), Lieutenant Donald Keiser (40-3096), and Lieutenant Weldon Smith (40-3079). The 93rd Squadron had the following pilots and planes: Major Cecil Combs (40-3062), Lieutenant Jim Connally (40-2062), Lieutenant Bill Bohnaker (40-3073), Lieutenant Walter Ford (40-3064), Lieutenant Morris Shedd (probably 40-3072), Lieutenant Earl Tash (40-3087), and Lieutenant Elliott Vandevanter (probably 40-3066). Captain Elmer Parsel (40-3074) from the 19th Group HQ Squadron was sent to Del Monte as a replacement for Lieutenant John Carpenter and the ailing 40-3063. This list was based on the author's accounting of planes used in the campaign and their final dispositions indicated in AAFHS No. 29 and Salecker, *Fortress*

Against the Sun, 382–83. Most sources do not agree on planes assigned to Shedd and Vandevanter.

12. Bartsch, *Doomed at the Start*, 5.
13. Dyess, *Story*, 27–28.
14. Sighting data recorded in Gillison, *Australia in the War, Air*, 1:200.
15. Shores, Cull, and Izawa, 73–74; Gillison, *Australia in the War, Air*, 1:200.
16. Gillison, *Australia in the War, Air*, 1:200.
17. Shores, Cull, and Izawa, *Bloody Shambles*, 1:73–74.
18. Messimer, *Hands of Fate*, 29–30.
19. The Catalina was FV-Y. Shores, Cull, and Izawa, *Bloody Shambles*, 1:77.

Chapter 5

1. Gillison, *Australia in the War, Air*, 1:202.
2. Ibid.
3. Shores, Cull, and Izawa, *Bloody Shambles*, 1:80.
4. In 1941 Hawaiian time was a half-hour behind its current setting. Midnight, December 8, at Kota Bharu, Singapore, and Manila was 0100 Tokyo time and 0530 December 7 in Hawaii. Wheeler Field, Oahu, was attacked at 0735, and Pearl Harbor at 0755.
5. The Hudsons and their pilots were A16-21 (Lockwood), A16-19 (Ramshaw), A16-24 (Verco), A16-94 (Leighton-Jones), A16-92 (O'Brien), A16-51 (Emerton), and A16-52 (Diamond). Shores, Cull, and Izawa, *Bloody Shambles*, 1:80.
6. Ibid., 1:81.
7. The next three Hudsons engaged were A16-23 (Douglas), A16-53 (Smith), and A16-89 (White). Ibid.
8. Ibid., 1:82.
9. Ibid., 1:82–83.
10. Ibid., 1:86.
11. Ibid., 1:87.
12. Gillison, *Australia in the War, Air*, 1:221.
13. Ibid., 1:215.
14. Shores, Cull, and Izawa, *Bloody Shambles*, 1:89; Hata and Izawa, *JNAF Aces*, 143.
15. Hendrie, *Lockheed Hudson*, 93. Since Hitchcock's Hudson was hit only by small-caliber weapons, it is unlikely his pursuer was a Zero, though three A6Ms ditched on their way back to Saigon. Hata and Izawa, *JNAF Aces*, 143. It was probably a 64th Sentai Ki-43, and the pilot was likely recovered by ground forces, so the JAAF, per usual practice, did not explicitly record the combat loss.
16. Shores, Cull, and Izawa, *Bloody Shambles*, 1:91.
17. Ibid., 1:92; Sakaida, *JAAF Aces*, 35.
18. Gillison, *Australia in the War, Air*, 1:222.
19. Ibid., 1:223–24.
20. The 59th Sentai reported the loss of one fighter. Shores, Cull, and Izawa, *Bloody Shambles*, 1:92.

21. Ibid., 1:94.
22. Gillison, *Australia in the War, Air*, 1:222.
23. The evacuating Hudsons were A16-21 (Lockwood), A16-23 (Douglas), A16-51 (Emerton), A16-89 (possibly White), and A16-92 (probably O'Brien). Author compilation from lists in Hendrie, *Lockheed Hudson*, 169–72.

Chapter 6

1. Bartsch, *Doomed at the Start*, 52.
2. Prange, *At Dawn We Slept*, 517.
3. Morison, *Rising Sun*, 170–71.
4. Messimer, *Hands of Fate*, 37–38.
5. Brereton, *Diaries*, 38.
6. Ibid., 39.
7. Hata and Izawa, *JNAF Aces*, 31–32.
8. The pilot of 101-P-7, Ensign Robert Tills, was killed. RM 3rd Class Albert Layton was badly burned. Messimer, *Hands of Fate*, 40.
9. Hata and Izawa, *JNAF Aces*, 31.
10. Ibid., 32.
11. Shores, Cull, and Izawa, *Bloody Shambles*, 1:164.
12. White, *Queens Die Proudly*, 17.
13. Brereton, *Diaries*, 40.
14. Ibid.
15. Ibid.
16. Ibid.; Edmonds, *They Fought*, 82.
17. Edmonds, *They Fought*, 87.
18. Brereton reviewed the new plan with General Sutherland at 1156. Brereton, *Diaries*, 41.
19. Brereton's revised plan specified that he would bomb Formosan airfields, with or without reconnaissance information, in the late afternoon. If the 19th Group had waited for information from the photo operation, it would have had to delay its departure time until at least 1600 (by author calculation). Colonel George is on record as imploring the FEAF staff to "keep the bombers off the ground during daylight hours." Ind, *Bataan*, 94. Although it would have been possible for Lieutenant Colonel Eubank to send all eleven B-17s not under maintenance or engaged in reconnaissance operations into the air when the next alarm was raised at 1130, this was not done, nor does it appear that any additional attempt was made to disperse the planes on the ground. The three Fortresses slated for photo reconnaissance would have still been on the flight line preparing for their mission at the time of the Japanese attack in any case (author calculation based on the delivery time of equipment from Nichols Field).
20. Bartsch, *Doomed at the Start*, 444.
21. Ibid., 66.
22. Ibid., 69.
23. Ibid., 70; Ind, *Bataan*, 99.

24. Bartsch, *Doomed at the Start*, 81–82. Most likely the unidentified P-40s were those of the "missing" Powell and Roberts. Steele and Daniel were not over Clark at the same time as Woolery, and Grashio's flight had four planes.

25. Ibid., 76.

26. Ibid., 72.

27. Ibid.

28. Shores, Cull, and Izawa, *Bloody Shambles*, 1:166, 170–74; Bartsch, *Doomed at the Start*, 57.

29. Bartsch, *Doomed at the Start*, 91; Edmonds, *They Fought*, 96.

30. Several Zeros may have been damaged over Iba, but none were downed. Shores, Cull, and Izawa, *Bloody Shambles*, 1:170–74. No official claims were awarded. It is doubtful that any damage came from .30-caliber ground fire, so Krieger and Ellis share credit for any wounds inflicted.

31. Bartsch, *Doomed at the Start*, 80. Steele made no official victory claims during the campaign, but his diary information quoted in *Doomed at the Start*, suggests that he may have had several valid ones.

32. Dyess, *Story*, 30.

33. Sakai, *Samurai!*, 66. Sakai was not awarded credit for this kill, but Japanese victory credits were usually consolidated at the kokutai level. It was rare for an individual pilot to be singled out for a claim when multiple aircraft were engaged. If Sakai's recollection is correct—subject to debate—he could have possibly hit either Sam Grashio or Vern Ireland; there was no other time during the campaign that such an event could have taken place at altitude. The circumstances of Grashio's engagement, in quantity, positioning, and area of damage, do not fit well with Sakai's description. Additionally, Grashio states that he was chased in his descent. It seems more likely that the victim was Vern Ireland. As the "tail-end Charlie" of a flight of five P-40s, Ireland could have been picked off without anyone else noticing. The correlation of events is compelling, but only Ireland, Sakai, and Sakai's wingmen could have borne witness.

34. Edmonds, *They Fought*, 105. From the description and correlation of events, it seems likely that this plane was the falling P-40 of Vern Ireland. It was not in an area where any Japanese "pursuits" would have crashed. Only two P-40s were downed over Clark, both in the vicinity of Mount Arayat. The circumstances of Herb Ellis's bailout do not match at all with the account of Tash's crew. If Sakai's victim was indeed Ireland, the P-40 would have been descending out of the smoke at a steep angle, as in the incident witnessed by Tash.

35. Ibid., 106. Norgaard registered one claim. It seems impossible to judge its validity.

36. Brown's victory was witnessed by others who saw the Japanese fighter impact the ground. Because of the timing, and the assumption that the trailing plane was not that of a flight leader, it is likely that Brown shot down either Petty Officer 3rd Class Fumio Ito or Saburo Yoshii of the *3rd Kokutai*. Both Japanese pilots were part of a group that is known to

have engaged in the vicinity of Clark. Shores, Cull, and Izawa, *Bloody Shambles*, 1:170–74.

37. It is generally accepted that Keator's first claim was the A6M of Petty Officer 3rd Class Yoshio Hirose. Bartsch, *Doomed at the Start*, 448.

38. Keator claimed and was awarded a second victory. It is not possible to reconcile that claim, though four other *Tainan Kokutai* Zeros—any of which could have been in the area—failed to return to Formosa. Moore filed two claims and Gilmore filed one, all of which were awarded as official victories but cannot be reconciled.

39. Bartsch, *Doomed at the Start*, 103.

Chapter 7

1. Edmonds, *They Fought*, 114; Bartsch, *Doomed at the Start*, 130.
2. Shores, Cull, and Izawa, *Bloody Shambles*, 1:175.
3. Bartsch, *Doomed at the Start*, 131.
4. The 93rd Squadron B-17s and their pilots were Combs (40-3062), Connally (40-2062), Bohnaker (40-3073), Vandevanter (probably 40-3066), Ford (40-3064), and Shedd (probably 40-3072).
5. Adams's B-17 was 40-3098.
6. White, *Queens Die Proudly*, 40.
7. Gillison, *Australia in the War, Air*, 1:248.
8. Shores, Cull, and Izawa, *Bloody Shambles*, 1:100.
9. Ibid.
10. Ibid., 99.
11. Gillison, *Australia in the War, Air*, 1:244.
12. Ibid., 1:248; Shores, Cull, and Izawa, *Bloody Shambles*, 1:100–101.
13. Gillison, *Australia in the War, Air*, 1:248.
14. Shores, Cull, and Izawa, *Bloody Shambles*, 1:100.
15. Ibid., 103–4.
16. Cull, *Buffaloes*, 48.
17. Ibid., 49. There is no conclusive evidence of a Japanese loss in the engagement.
18. Gillison, *Australia in the War, Air*, 1:249.
19. P-35A quantity accepted from Bartsch, *Doomed at the Start*, 134–35. The Fortresses of the 14th squadron were O'Donnell (40-3061), Kelly (40-2045), Godman (40-3097), Keiser (probably 40-3096), Montgomery (40-3086), Schaetzel (40-3091), and Teats (40-3078). Lieutenant Smith and 40-3079 were left behind at Del Monte. Captain Parsel joined the squadron with 40-3074.
20. Gillison, *Australia in the War, Air*, 1:250–51.

Chapter 8

1. Bartsch, *Doomed at the Start*, 136.
2. Morison, *Rising Sun*, 162.

3. Bartsch, *Doomed at the Start*, 136.

4. Edmonds, *They Fought*, 125.

5. Messimer, *Hands of Fate*, 49.

6. *Oigawa Maru* was eventually beached. Damage and a small fire later caused by fighters were probably not enough to instigate that event. Edmonds, *They Fought*, 122; Morison, *Rising Sun*, 177.

7. Morison, *Rising Sun*, 176–77; Bartsch, *Doomed at the Start*, 137–39; Shores, Cull, and Izawa, *Bloody Shambles*, 1:177.

8. Shores, Cull, and Izawa, *Bloody Shambles*, 1:113.

9. Messimer, *Hands of Fate*, 49. The message refers to a location of latitude 16° 40', longitude 118° 10', more than two hundred miles west of Vigan.

10. Morison, *Rising Sun*, 161.

11. Quantity of aircraft from Bartsch, *Doomed at the Start*, 138.

12. Ibid., 450.

13. Shores, Cull, and Izawa, *Bloody Shambles*, 1:177. Sheppard was awarded credit for two bombers.

14. Ibid., 116–17.

15. Ibid., 118.

16. Ibid., 118–19; Tagaya, *Type 1 Rikko*, 25.

17. Quote from Lieutenant Sadao Takai. Shores, Cull, and Izawa, *Bloody Shambles*, 1:119.

18. Ibid., 121.

19. Ibid., 122.

20. Ibid., 123.

21. Messimer, *Hands of Fate*, 51–52; Morison, *Rising Sun*, 180; Shores, Cull, and Izawa, *Bloody Shambles*, 1:176.

22. Schaetzel appears to have struck and forced the beaching of minesweeper W-19. Morison, *Rising Sun*, 178; AAFHS No. 111, 63.

23. Kanamaru had to force-land on Colayan Island after taking hits from the B-17 gunners. Shores, Cull, and Izawa, *Bloody Shambles*, 1:182.

24. Morison, *Rising Sun*, 161.

25. Bartsch, *Doomed at the Start*, 141–42.

26. Shores, Cull, and Izawa, *Bloody Shambles*, 1:177–78.

27. Gies was officially credited with two Zeros. He definitely downed the plane of Sergeant 1st Class Masaharu Higa from the *Tainan Kokutai*, which was found nearby with its pilot still inside. Three other A6Ms were damaged. Shores, Cull, and Izawa, *Bloody Shambles*, 1:178; Hata and Izawa, *JNAF Aces*, 375.

28. Bartsch, *Doomed at the Start*, 144.

29. Kenney, *Pappy Gunn*, 31.

30. Bartsch, *Doomed at the Start*, 150. Petty Officer 1st Class Kiyoharu Tezuka of the *3rd Kokutai* disappeared under circumstances similar to those described by Steele, in the vicinity of Laguna de Bay. Although Steele did not pursue a credit, his story is convincing. Shores, Cull, and Izawa, *Bloody Shambles*, 1:178–79; Hata and Izawa, *JNAF Aces*, 375.

31. Chief Payne's victory was probably Petty Officer 2nd Class Tamotsu Kojima of the *3rd Kokutai*, who went "missing" while strafing flying boats at Cavite. Shores, Cull, and Izawa, *Bloody Shambles*, 1:178–79; Hata and Izawa, *JNAF Aces*, 375.

32. Parsel's target was undoubtedly the second transport beached at Vigan. Morison, *Rising Sun*, 177.

33. Sakai, *Samurai!*, 68. Sakai's description is a bit confusing in his reference to Vigan. His flight had been assigned to cover Vigan but was passing by Aparri on its way back to Formosa when it engaged Kelly's B-17. Shores, Cull, and Izawa, *Bloody Shambles*, 1:182. *Natori* did receive damage from aerial bombardment—on December 10, not December 12. Morison, *Rising Sun*, 174. Kelly's is the only U.S. plane that attacked a ship away from the beach at Aparri on any date.

34. Sakai, *Samurai!*, 69.

35. Ibid., 72. Sakai and his wingmen were not allotted any credit for destruction of the B-17, but they were recorded as participating in the attack. Shores, Cull, and Izawa, *Bloody Shambles*, 1:182. From Sakai's description, it appears that his companions had done the most damage.

36. Shores, Cull, and Izawa, *Bloody Shambles*, 1:182.

37. White, *Queens Die Proudly*, 48.

Chapter 9

1. Morison, *Rising Sun*, 158–59, 172.

2. Bartsch, *Doomed at the Start*, 153–54.

3. Shores, Cull, and Izawa, *Bloody Shambles*, 1:183.

4. Edmonds, *They Fought*, 164.

5. Cressman, "Magnificent Fight."

6. Morison, *Rising Sun*, 231–33. Cressman's correction substituting *Mochizuki* for *Asanagi*, with the benefit of more postwar files, is accepted here.

7. Ibid., 232.

8. Cressman, "Magnificent Fight."

9. Ibid.

10. The pilots and Fortresses that went to Vigan were O'Donnell (40-3061), Godman (40-3097), Keiser (probably 40-3096), Teats (40-3078), and Combs (40-3062). The additional B-17 was probably Captain Parsel's (40-3074). Schaetzel had not returned from Cebu, and Smith's plane was still under repair. The mission is not recorded in official AAF summaries.

11. Edmonds, *They Fought*, 151–52; Brownstein, *Swoose*, 33.

12. Morison, *Rising Sun*, 162.

13. Bartsch, *Doomed at the Start*, 159, 453.

14. Ibid., 157–58. 50th Sentai records definitely reflect one Ki-27 loss on the ground, perhaps a forced landing. Total JAAF losses for the week beginning December 8 give ample room to support Wagner's claim. Mysteriously, the "official" record doubled Wagner's total claim in an award of four air-to-air victories.

15. Messimer, *Hands of Fate*, 62. The two men killed were Ensign J. C. Watson and ACMM George Seeke.
16. McDowell, *P-40*, 16–21.
17. Hanson was awarded credit for a "seaplane," but, as noted regarding PatWing-10 planes, a flying boat downed in the water is not necessarily a "kill." The *Toko Kokutai* was the only Japanese unit in the area with four-engine aircraft, and no losses were recorded.
18. White, *Queens Die Proudly*, 52.
19. Brereton, *Diaries*, 64.
20. These were undoubtedly the beached *Oigawa Maru* and *Takao Maru*.
21. The identity of the pilot assigned to this mission is not recorded. Bartsch, *Doomed at the Start*, 164.
22. Vanderfield's two bomber claims are confirmed by the loss of two Ki-48s, including the plane of the formation leader, Captain Kunimi Hotta. The claims for two Ki-51s also appear to be valid. Shores, Cull, and Izawa, *Bloody Shambles*, 1:132.
23. No information is available to support Vigors's claim.
24. No information is available to support Grace's claim.
25. The validity of Board's claim is not clear.
26. Account of Adams's navigator, Harry Schreiber. White, *Queens Die Proudly*, 59. Most accounts indicate larger quantities of Zeros. Schreiber was correct. The A6Ms of the *Tainan Kokutai* were piloted by Petty Officer 1st Class Yoshimichi Saeki, Petty Officer 1st Class Toshio Kikuchi, Petty Officer 2nd Class Yoshiri Hidaka, Petty Officer 3rd Class Kosaku Minato, and Petty Officer 3rd Class Saburo Nozawa. Shores, Cull, and Izawa, *Bloody Shambles*, 1:189.
27. It was either Saeki or Hidaka who followed Adams to Masbate.
28. All five A6Ms returned to their new base at Legaspi. Only Lieutenant Masuzo Seto's 2nd Chutai had been transferred, and two of its planes had already been damaged in landing accidents on the rough field.
29. Bartsch, *Doomed at the Start*, 166–67, 453; Shores, Cull, and Izawa, *Bloody Shambles*, 1:190.

Chapter 10

1. By the author's calculation, recorded from data in the appendix, the unsalvageable loss rates among first-line combat aircraft in engaged units were 36 percent (PBY-4), 45 percent (P-35A), 59 percent (B-17), 64 percent (Hudson), 77 percent (339E Buffalo), and 83 percent (F4F-3).
2. Craven and Cate, *AAF in WWII*, 1:223, 332.
3. Brereton, *Diaries*, 55.
4. The 90th Sentai did lose one Ki-48. Shores, Cull, and Izawa, *Bloody Shambles*, 1:138.
5. Bartsch, *Doomed at the Start*, 454.
6. Wagner was awarded one official victory, which gave him a total of five victories, resulting in an award of ace status. Although it does not appear Wagner himself acted to inflate the score, he did accept his ace

status. The total to that date should have been just three victories, and only the last one over Vigan would have counted as a confirmed victory by the criteria established in 1942. One thing is certain regarding Wagner's skill: all who knew him considered him the best pilot they had ever seen—as good as any ever accorded ace status.

7. Marcy's PBY was 102-P-22.

8. The pilots and B-17s on the first flight to Australia were Combs (40-3062), Parsel (40-3074), Tash (40-3072), Ford (40-3064), Coats (40-3067), and Wheless (40-3070). Each plane carried two experienced mechanics in addition to the crews. AAFHS No. 29, 34. Tash was flying Shedd's plane. Wheless was flying his own plane, the same one he had flown across the Pacific.

9. The PBYs and pilots, where known, are believed to be 101-P-1 (Hastings), 101-P-3 (Campbell), 101-P-6 (Brown), 101-P-8 (unknown), 101-P-9 (Christman), 101-P-10 (unknown), 101-P-11 (Deede), 102-P-23 (Hyland), 102-P-25 (McCabe), and 102-P-26 (possibly Keller). One of the unknowns was probably flown by Lieutenant Commander Peterson. List created from data in Messimer, *Hands of Fate*.

10. Gillison, *Australia in the War, Air*, 1:277.

11. AAFHS No. 29, 36; Edmonds, *They Fought*, 174; Bartsch, *Doomed at the Start*, 171.

12. The flight of B-17s to Australia on December 18 was Walsh (40-3061), Mueller (40-2072), Godman (40-3097), and Teats (40-3078). AAFHS No. 29, 36.

13. Edmonds, *They Fought*, 175.

14. Gillison, *Australia in the War, Air*, 1:278.

15. Ibid., 278.

16. Messimer, *Hands of Fate*, 91.

17. This was Smith's regular plane, 40-3079. The other three B-17s left together: Connally (40-2062), Vandevanter (40-3066), and Schaetzel (40-3091). AAFHS No. 29, 40. Connally had Gil Montgomery as a passenger, and Vandevanter had Don Keiser as a passenger.

18. Bartsch, *Doomed at the Start*, 182.

19. Ibid.

20. Shores, Cull, and Izawa, *Bloody Shambles*, 1:192. The two casualties were Major Chauncey Whitney and Private 1st Class Allan Thibido. Edmonds, *They Fought*, 181.

21. Cressman, "Magnificent Fight."

22. Cull, *Buffaloes*, 76.

23. Ibid., 76–77. It is not clear if any of Peterson's claims can be validated. Shores, Cull, and Izawa, *Bloody Shambles*, 1:142; Sakaida, *JAAF Aces*, 29.

Chapter 11

1. Morison, *Rising Sun*, 160–63.

2. Bartsch, *Doomed at the Start*, 183.

3. Wagner's attacker was most likely nineteen-year-old Corporal Satoshi Anabuki of the 50th Sentai. Anabuki's first victory was recorded against a P-40E above Lingayen in a situation closely resembling that described by Wagner. Many accounts describe Wagner's plane as having taken a 20-mm cannon hit, but no Zeros were present. Shores, Cull, and Izawa, *Bloody Shambles*, 1:193; Sakaida, *JAAF Aces*, 34. Anabuki would go on to score more than fifty victories.
4. Cressman, "Magnificent Fight."
5. Ibid.
6. Ibid.; Hata and Izawa, *JNAF Aces*, 39.
7. Cull, *Buffaloes*, 80.
8. At least two Ki-51s fell in the air battle, but it is difficult to reconcile their loss to a given Australian claim. Cull, *Buffaloes*, 83.
9. Ibid.
10. Board's claim appears to be substantiated.
11. Cull, *Buffaloes*, 81.
12. Shores, Cull, and Izawa, *Bloody Shambles*, 1:145.
13. Edmonds, *They Fought*, 180. The pilots and planes on the mission were Combs (40-3062), Parsel (40-3074), Tash (40-3072), Ford (40-3064), Coats (40-3067), Connally (40-2062), Godman (40-3097), Vandevanter with Keiser as command pilot (40-3066), and Teats (40-3078). AAFHS No. 29, 44.
14. Morison, *Rising Sun*, 182.
15. Edmonds, *They Fought*, 182–83.
16. Bartsch, *Doomed at the Start*, 187.
17. Morison, *Rising Sun*, 162–63; Smurthwaite, *Pacific War Atlas*, 41–42.
18. The three pilots and planes were Smith (40-3079), Schaetzel flying Combs's plane (40-3062), and Mueller (40-2072).
19. Brereton, *Diaries*, 62–63.
20. Ibid., 62.
21. Bartsch, *Doomed at the Start*, 188–89.
22. The Tainan Kokutai lost an A6M piloted by Petty Officer 1st Class Toshio Kikuchi. Hata and Izawa, *JNAF Aces*, 376.
23. Reid and Palm's plane was 101-P-13, in this case "lucky" 13.

Chapter 12

1. Messimer, *Hands of Fate*, 112.
2. Radiogram 879, as quoted in Bartsch, *Doomed at the Start*, 203.
3. As quoted in Cull, *Buffaloes*, 86–87.
4. Gillison, *Australia in the War, Air*, 1:351.
5. Ibid., 340.
6. Ibid.
7. Prange, *Verdict of History*, 647–49.
8. Prange, *At Dawn We Slept*, 722–23.
9. Brereton, *Diaries*, 64–65.
10. Edmonds, *They Fought*, 28.

11. Ind, *Bataan*, 101.
12. Brereton, *Diaries*, 50.
13. Harper, "Secret Report, AIR 20/5578."
14. Gillison, *Australia in the War, Air*, 1:277–78.
15. The only B-17 airmen who died in their planes were, in chronological order, Staff Sergeant Delehanty, Captain Kelly, Private 1st Class Killin, and Staff Sergeant Cannon. It was quite unhealthy to be a radioman/"bathtub" gunner, given that three of these men, and the wounded Private 1st Class Jumia, occupied that position.

BIBLIOGRAPHY

Firsthand Accounts

Brereton, Lewis H. *The Brereton Diaries*. New York: William Morrow, 1946.
Chennault, Claire L. *Way of a Fighter*. New York: G. P. Putnam's Sons, 1949.
Dyess, William E. *The Dyess Story*. Toronto: Longmans, Green, 1944.
Ind, Allison B. *Bataan: The Judgment Seat*. New York: Macmillan, 1944.
Sakai Saburo, with Martin Caidin and Fred Saito. *Samurai!* Annapolis, Md.: Naval Institute Press, 1957.
White, W. L. *Queens Die Proudly*. New York: Harcourt, Brace, 1943.
———. *They Were Expendable*. New York: Harcourt, Brace, 1942.

Primary Documents

Harper, Squadron Leader W. J. "Report on No. 21 and No. 453 Squadrons," AIR 20/5578, Public Records Office, Kew, London.
Secretary of War Secret Papers File. "Memorandum for Secretary, General Staff: Air Offensive Against Japan," November 21, 1941, RG107, 381, Stimson Top Secret Papers, National Archives, Washington, D.C.
Spaatz, Lieutenant Colonel Carl A. "Memorandum for General Arnold: Strategically Offensive Operations in the Far East," September 1, 1939, RG18, 293B, Box 183, National Archives, Washington, D.C.

Official Histories

Army Air Forces Historical Study No. 29, "Summary of Air Action in the Philippines and Netherlands East Indies, 1941–1942," Air Force Historical Research Agency, 1945.
Army Air Forces Historical Study No. 33, "Administrative History of the Ferrying Command," AFHRA, 1945.
Army Air Forces Historical Study No. 34, "AAF in the War Against Japan, 1941–1942," AFHRA, 1945.
Army Air Forces Historical Study No. 45, "Development of the South Pacific Air Route," AFHRA, 1946.
Army Air Forces Historical Study No. 111, "Army Air Action in the Philippines and Netherland East Indies, 1941–1942," AFHRA, 1945.
Craven, Wesley F., and James L. Cate, eds. *The Army Air Forces in World War II*. Vol. 1, *Plans and Early Operations*. Washington, D.C.: Office of Air Force History, U.S. Government Printing Office, 1983.

"Diary of the 19th Bombardment Group, December 8, 1941–February 24, 1942." Office of Air Force History.

Gillison, Douglas. *Australia in the War of 1939–1945*, Series Three, *Air. Vol. 1, Royal Australian Air Force, 1939–1942*. Canberra: Australian War Memorial, 1962.

Maurer, Maurer. *Air Force Combat Units of World War II*. Washington, D.C.: Office of Air Force History, 1961.

Morison, Samuel E. *United States Naval Operations in World War II: The Rising Sun in the Pacific, 1931–April, 1942*. Edison, N.J.: Castle Books, 2001.

Books

Bartsch, William. *December 8, 1941: MacArthur's Pearl Harbor*. College Station: Texas A&M University Press, 2003.

———. *Doomed at the Start*. College Station: Texas A&M University Press, 1991.

Boot, Max. *The Savage Wars of Peace: Small Wars and the Rise of American Power*. New York: Basic Books, 2002.

Bowman, Martin. *B-17 Flying Fortress Units of the Pacific War*. London: Osprey Publishing, 2003.

Brownstein, Herbert S. *The Swoose*. Washington, D.C.: Smithsonian Institution Press, 1993.

Caidin, Martin. *The Ragged, Rugged Warriors*. New York: E. P. Dutton, 1966.

Cressman, Robert J., with Steve Ewing. *A Glorious Page in Our History: The Battle of Midway, 4–6 June, 1942*. Missoula, Mont.: Pictorial Histories Publishing Company, 1990.

Cull, Brian, with Paul Sortehaug and Mark Haselden. *Buffaloes over Singapore*. London: Grub Street, 2003.

Diehl, Digby. *Front Page: A Collection of Historical Headlines from the Los Angeles Times, 1881–1987*. New York: Harry N. Abrams, 1987.

Dorr, Robert F. *B-24 Liberator Units of the Pacific War*. London: Osprey Publishing, 1999.

Edmonds, Walter D. *They Fought with What They Had*. Washington, D.C.: Zenger, 1982Hata Ikuhiko and Izawa Yasuho. *Japanese Naval Aces and Fighter Units in World War II*. Translated by Don C. Gorham. Annapolis, Md.: Naval Institute Press, 1989.

Haugland, Vern. *The AAF Against Japan*. New York: Harper & Brothers, 1948.

Hess, William N. *Pacific Sweep: The 5th and 13th Fighter Commands in World War II*. New York: Doubleday, 1974.

Kenney, George C. *The Saga of Pappy Gunn*. New York: Duell, Sloan and Pearce, 1959.

Lambert, John W. *The Pineapple Air Force: Pearl Harbor to Tokyo*. St. Paul: Phalanx Publishing, 1990.

Layton, Edwin T. *"And I Was There": Pearl Harbor and Midway—Breaking the Secrets*. Old Saybrook, Conn.: Konecky & Konecky, 1985.

Lundstrom, John B. *The First Team: Pacific Naval Air Combat from Pearl Harbor to Midway*. Annapolis, Md.: Naval Institute Press, 1984.

McGovern, Terrance C., and Mark A. Berhow. *American Defenses of Corregidor and Manila Bay, 1898–1945*. London: Osprey Publishing, 2003.

Messimer, Dwight R. *In the Hands of Fate*. Annapolis, Md.: Naval Institute Press, 1985.

Miller, Edward S. *War Plan Orange: The U.S. Strategy to Defeat Japan, 1897–1945*. Annapolis, Md.: Naval Institute Press, 1991.

Morison, Samuel E. *The Two Ocean War*. New York: Little, Brown, 1963.

Nalty, Bernard C., ed. *War in the Pacific: Pearl Harbor to Tokyo Bay*. London: Salamander Books, 1991.

Pearcy, Arthur. *Lend-Lease Aircraft in World War II*. Osceola, Wi. : Motorbooks International, 1996.

Peattie, Mark R. *Sunburst: The Rise of Japanese Naval Air Power, 1909–1941*. Annapolis, Md.: Naval Institute Press, 2001.

Persico, Joseph E. *Roosevelt's Secret War: FDR and World War II Espionage*. New York: Random House, 2002.

Philbrick, Nathaniel. *Sea of Glory: America's Voyage of Discovery, the U.S. Exploring Expedition, 1838–1842*. New York: Viking Penguin, 2003.

Prange, Gordon W., in collaboration with Donald M. Goldstein and Katherine V. Dillon. *At Dawn We Slept*. New York: McGraw-Hill, 1981.

———. *Miracle at Midway*. New York: Penguin, 1983.

———. *The Verdict of History*. New York: McGraw-Hill, 1986.

Sakaida, Henry. *Japanese Army Air Force Aces, 1937–1945*. London: Osprey Publishing, 1997.

Salecker, Gene E. *Fortress Against the Sun*. Conshohocken, Pa.: Combined Publishing, 2001.

Shores, Christopher, Brian Cull, and Izawa Yasuho. *Bloody Shambles*. Vol. 1. London: Grub Street, 1992.

Tagaya, Osamu. *Mitsubishi Type 1, Rikko "Betty" Units of World War II*. London: Osprey Publishing, 2001.

Willmott, H. P., with Tohmatsu Haruo and W. Spencer Johnson. *Pearl Harbor*. London: Cassell, 2001.

Wukovits, John. *Pacific Alamo: The Battle for Wake Island*. New York: New American Library—Penguin, 2003.

Young, Peter, ed. *Great Battles of the World*. Northbrook, Ill.: Bison Books, 1978.

Technical References

Adcock, Al. *TBD Devastator in Action*. Carrollton, Tx.: Squadron-Signal Publications, 1989.

Army Air Forces. *Pilot's Manual for Curtiss P-40 Warhawk*. Reprint, Appleton, Wis.: Aviation Publications, 1988.

Breihan, John R., Stan Piet, and Roger S. Mason. *Martin Aircraft, 1909–1960*. Santa Ana, Calif.: Narkiewicz/Thompson, 1995.

Davis, Larry. *B-17 in Action*. Carrollton, Tx: Squadron-Signal Publications, 1984.

———. *B-24 in Action*. Carrollton, Tx. : Squadron-Signal Publications, 1984.

————. *C-47 Skytrain in Action*. Carrollton, Tx. : Squadron-Signal Publications, 1995.

————. *P-26 in Action*. Carrollton, Tx. : Squadron-Signal Publications, 1998.

————. *P-35 in Action*. Carrollton, Tx. : Squadron-Signal Publications, 1994.

Dean, Francis H. *America's Hundred-Thousand: U.S. Production Fighters of World War Two*. Atglen, Pa. : Schiffer Publishing, 1997.

Donald, David, ed. *American Warplanes of World War II: Combat Aircraft of the United States Army Air Forces, U.S. Navy, U.S. Marine Corps, 1941–1945*. London: Aerospace Publishing, 1995.

————. *The Complete Encyclopedia of World Aircraft*. London: Aerospace Publishing, 1997.

Freeman, Roger. *B-17 Flying Fortress*. New York: Zokeisha Publications, 1983.

Gunston, Bill. *Fighting Aircraft of World War II*. New York: Prentice Hall, 1988.

Hendrie, Andrew. *Lockheed Hudson in World War II*. London: Airlife, 1999.

Jane's Fighting Ships of World War II. New York: Military Press, 1989.

Linn, Don. *F4F Wildcat in Action*. Carrollton, : Tx. : Squadron-Signal Publications, 1988.

Lloyd, Alwyn T., and Terry D. Moore. *B-17 Flying Fortress: In Detail and Scale*. Blue Ridge Summit, Pa.: TAB Books, 1981.

Maas, Jim. *F2A Buffalo in Action*. Carrollton, Tx. : Squadron-Signal Publications, 1987.

McDowell, Ernest R. *Curtiss P-40 in Action*. Carrollton, Tx. : Squadron-Signal Publications, 1976.

Mikesh, Robert C. *Zero Fighter*. New York: Zokeisha Publications, 1983.

Nohara, Shigeru. *A6M Zero in Action*. Carrollton, Tx.: Squadron-Signal Publications, 1983.

O'Leary, Michael. *United States Naval Fighters of World War II in Action*. Poole, Dorset, U.K.: Blandford Press, 1980.

Olynyk, Frank J. *USAAF (Pacific Theater) Credits for the Destruction of Enemy Aircraft in Air-to-Air Combat, World War II*. Self-published, 1985.

Scarborough, W. E. *PBY Catalina in Action*. Carrollton, Tx.: Squadron-Signal Publications, 1983.

Smith, Herschel. *A History of Aircraft Piston Engines*. Manhattan, Kans.: Sunflower University Press, 1986.

Smith, Peter C. *T-6: A Pictorial Record of the Harvard, Texan, and Wirraway*. Osceola, Wi.: Motorbooks International, 1995.

Smurthwaite, David. *The Pacific War Atlas, 1941–1945*. New York: Facts on File, 1995.

Stern, Rob. *SBD Dauntless in Action*. Carrollton, Tx.: Squadron-Signal Publications, 1984.

Articles

Bartsch, William H. "Was MacArthur Ill-Served by His Air Force Commanders in the Philippines?" *Air Power History*, Summer 1997, 44–63.

Cressman, Robert J. "A Magnificent Fight: Marines in the Battle for Wake Island." Washington, D.C.: Marine Historical Center, 1992.

INDEX

Page numbers in *italics* indicate photos and illustrations. Aircraft are sorted by manufacturer name.

ABOUT THE AUTHOR

JOHN BURTON, a former naval systems engineer, and sales and operations executive at IBM for twenty years, has spent much of his life studying the aviation industry and aviation history. Now a marketing and business strategy consultant, he lives and writes in Irvine, California.

THE NAVAL INSTITUTE PRESS is the book-publishing arm of the U.S. Naval Institute, a private, nonprofit, membership society for sea service professionals and others who share an interest in naval and maritime affairs. Established in 1873 at the U.S. Naval Academy in Annapolis, Maryland, where its offices remain today, the Naval Institute has members worldwide.

Members of the Naval Institute support the education programs of the society and receive the influential monthly magazine *Proceedings* and discounts on fine nautical prints and on ship and aircraft photos. They also have access to the transcripts of the Institute's Oral History Program and get discounted admission to any of the Institute-sponsored seminars offered around the country. Discounts are also available to the colorful bimonthly magazine *Naval History*.

The Naval Institute's book-publishing program, begun in 1898 with basic guides to naval practices, has broadened its scope to include books of more general interest. Now the Naval Institute Press publishes about seventy titles each year, ranging from how-to books on boating and navigation to battle histories, biographies, ship and aircraft guides, and novels. Institute members receive significant discounts on the Press's more than eight hundred books in print.

Full-time students are eligible for special half-price membership rates. Life memberships are also available.

For a free catalog describing Naval Institute Press books currently available, and for further information about subscribing to *Naval History* magazine or about joining the U.S. Naval Institute, please write to:

Member Services
U.S. Naval Institute
291 Wood Road
Annapolis, MD 21402-5034
Telephone: (800) 233-8764
Fax: (410) 571-1703
Web address: *www.navalinstitute.org*